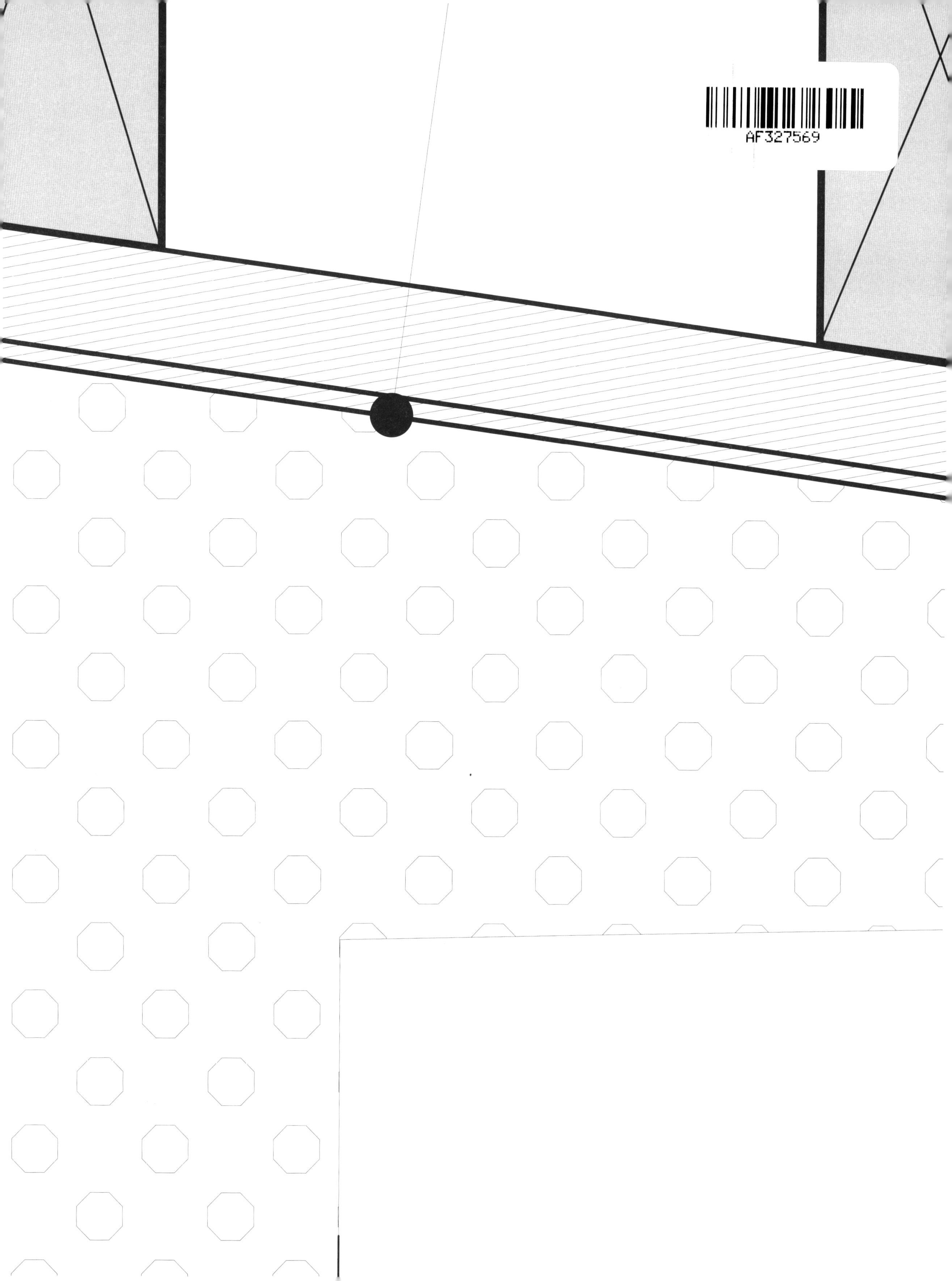

AF327569

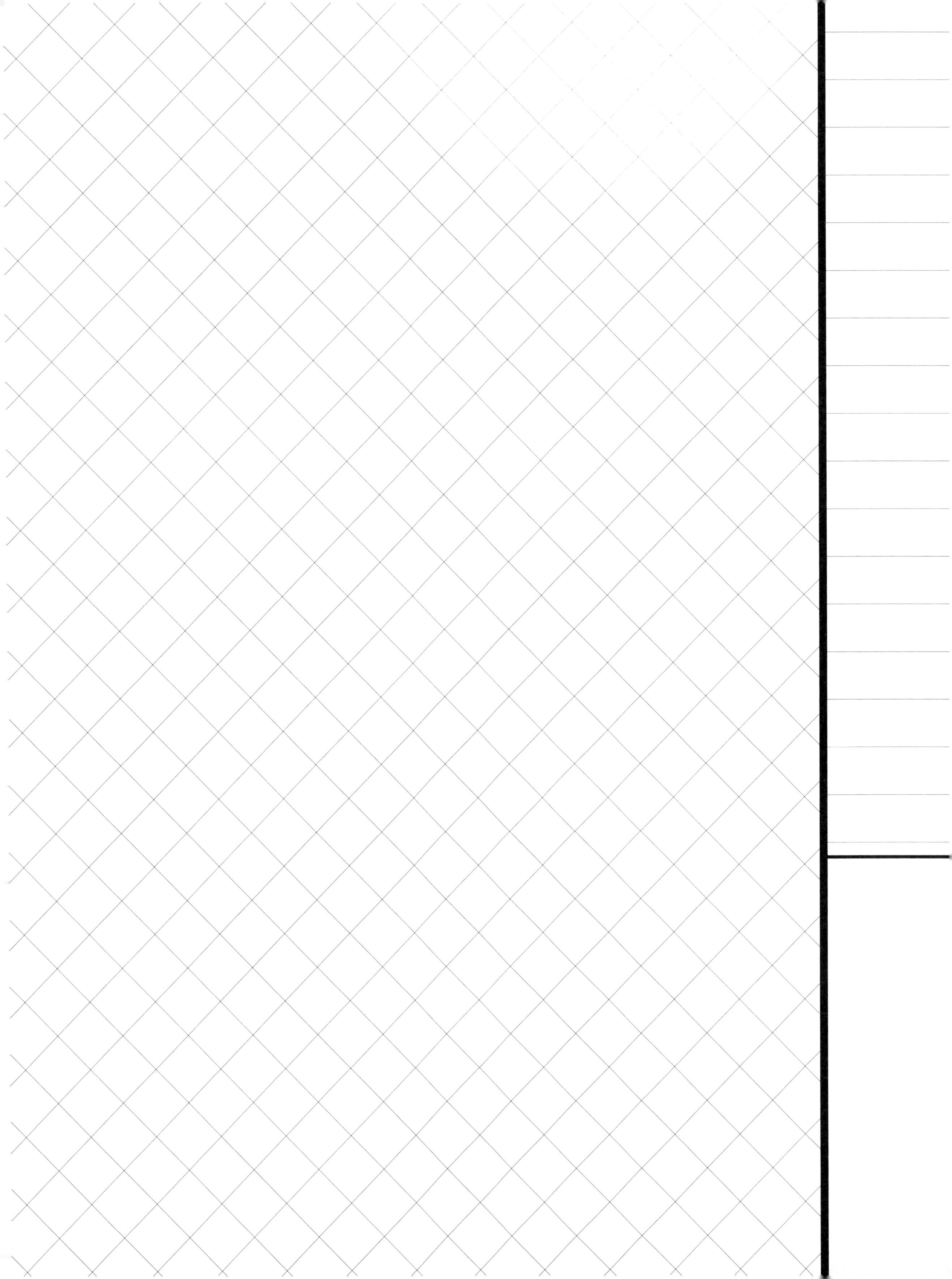

PHILIP JODIDIO

UNDER ONE ROOF
EPFL ARTLAB IN LAUSANNE
BY KENGO KUMA

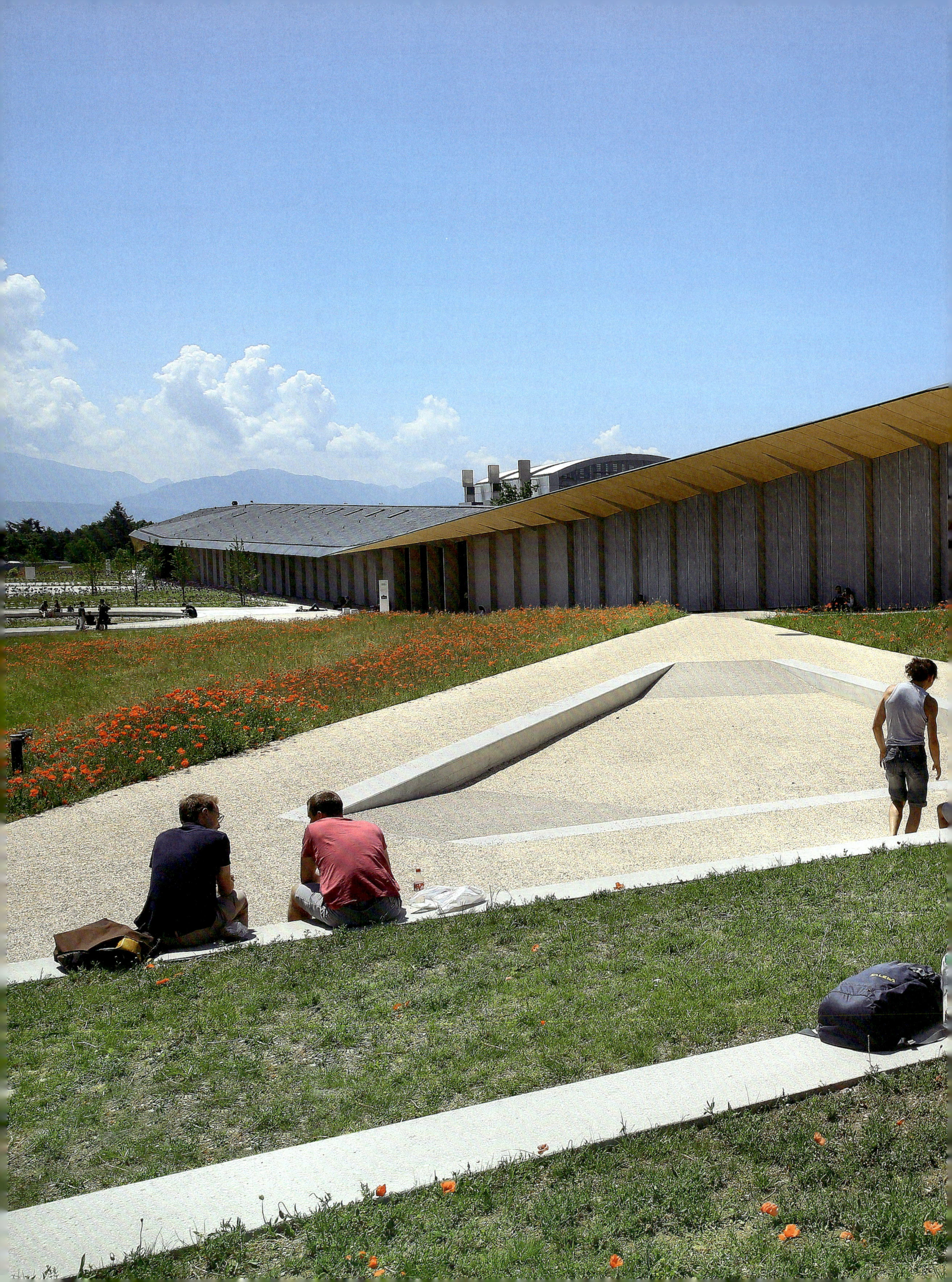

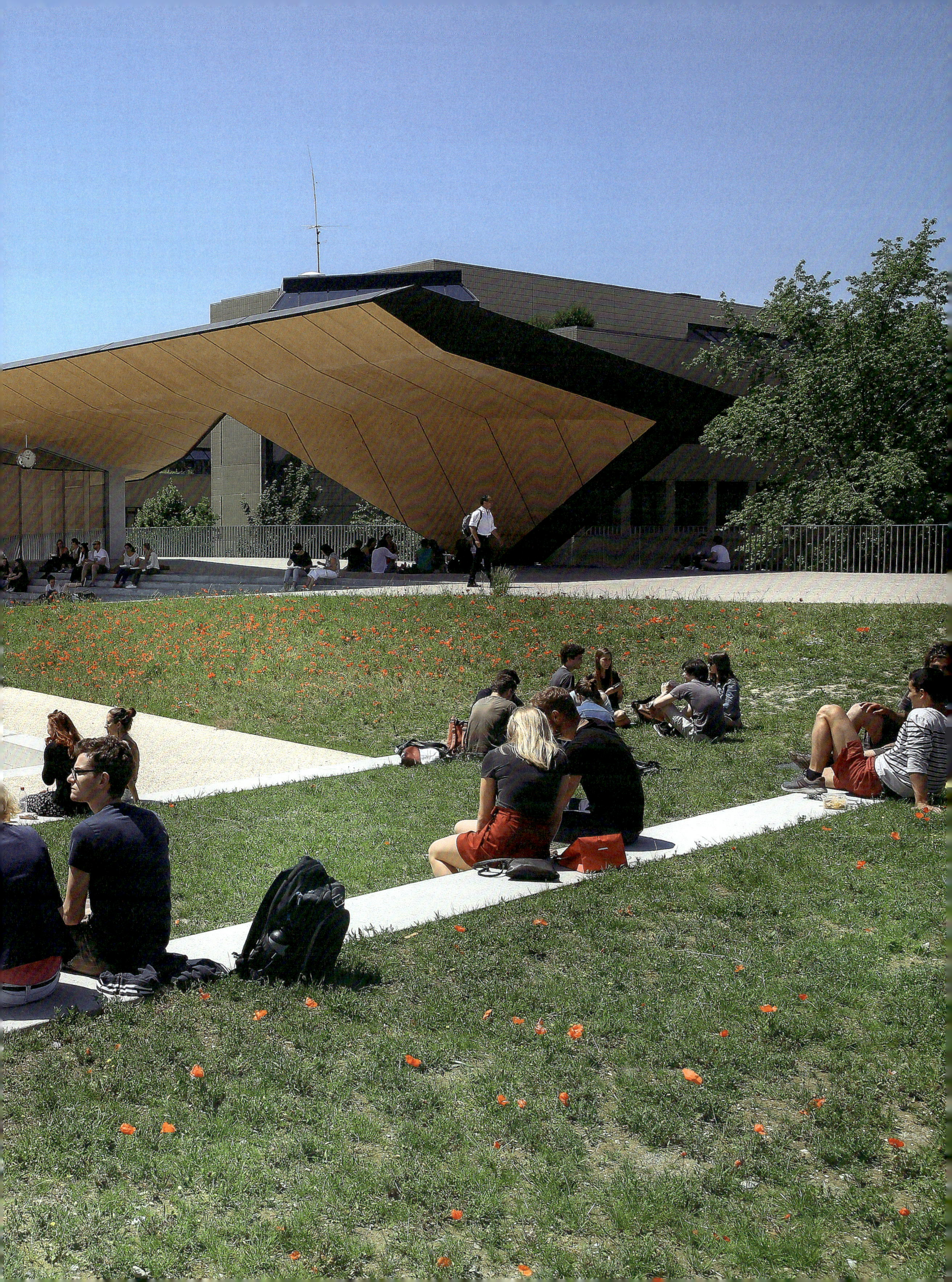

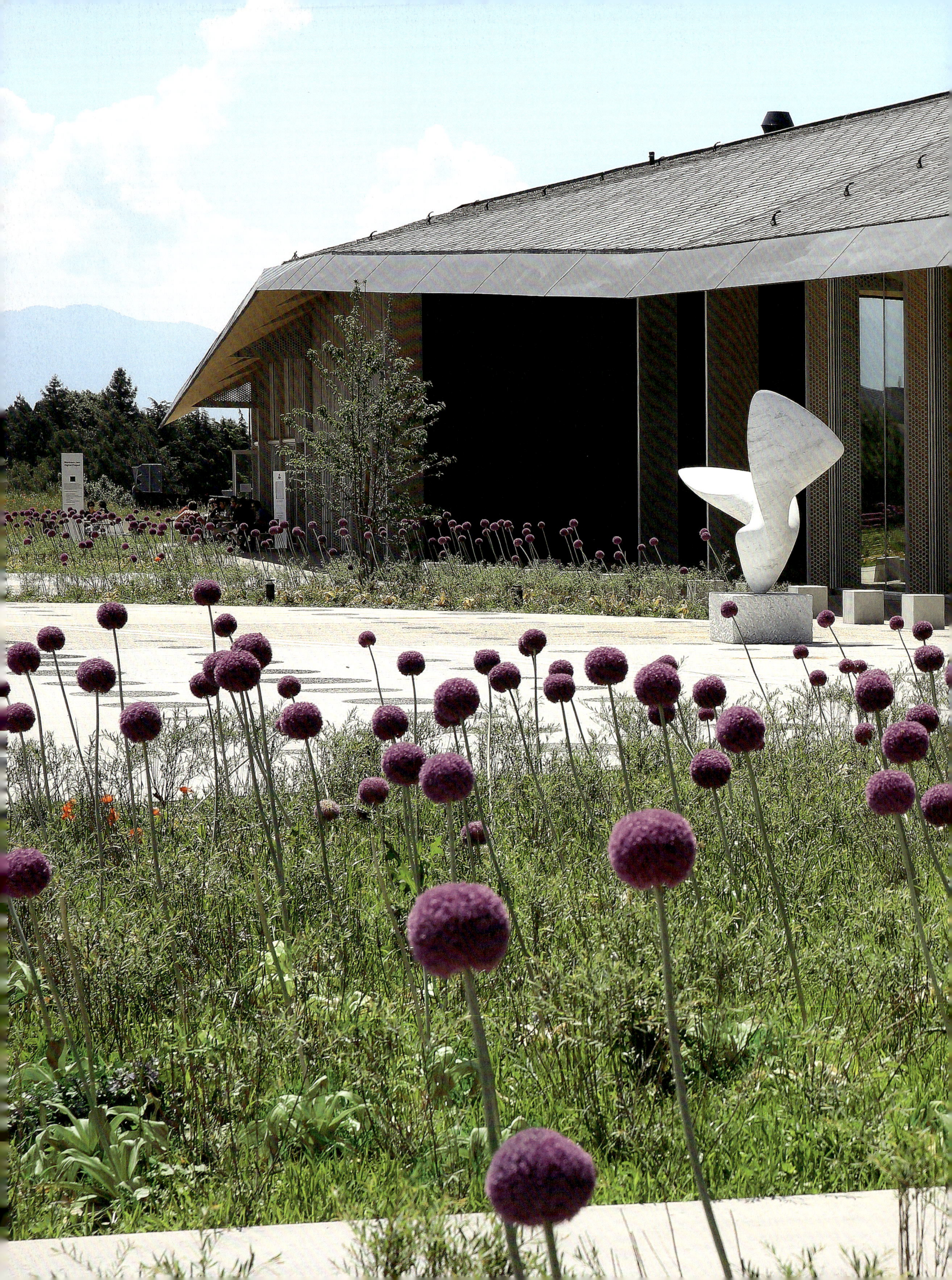

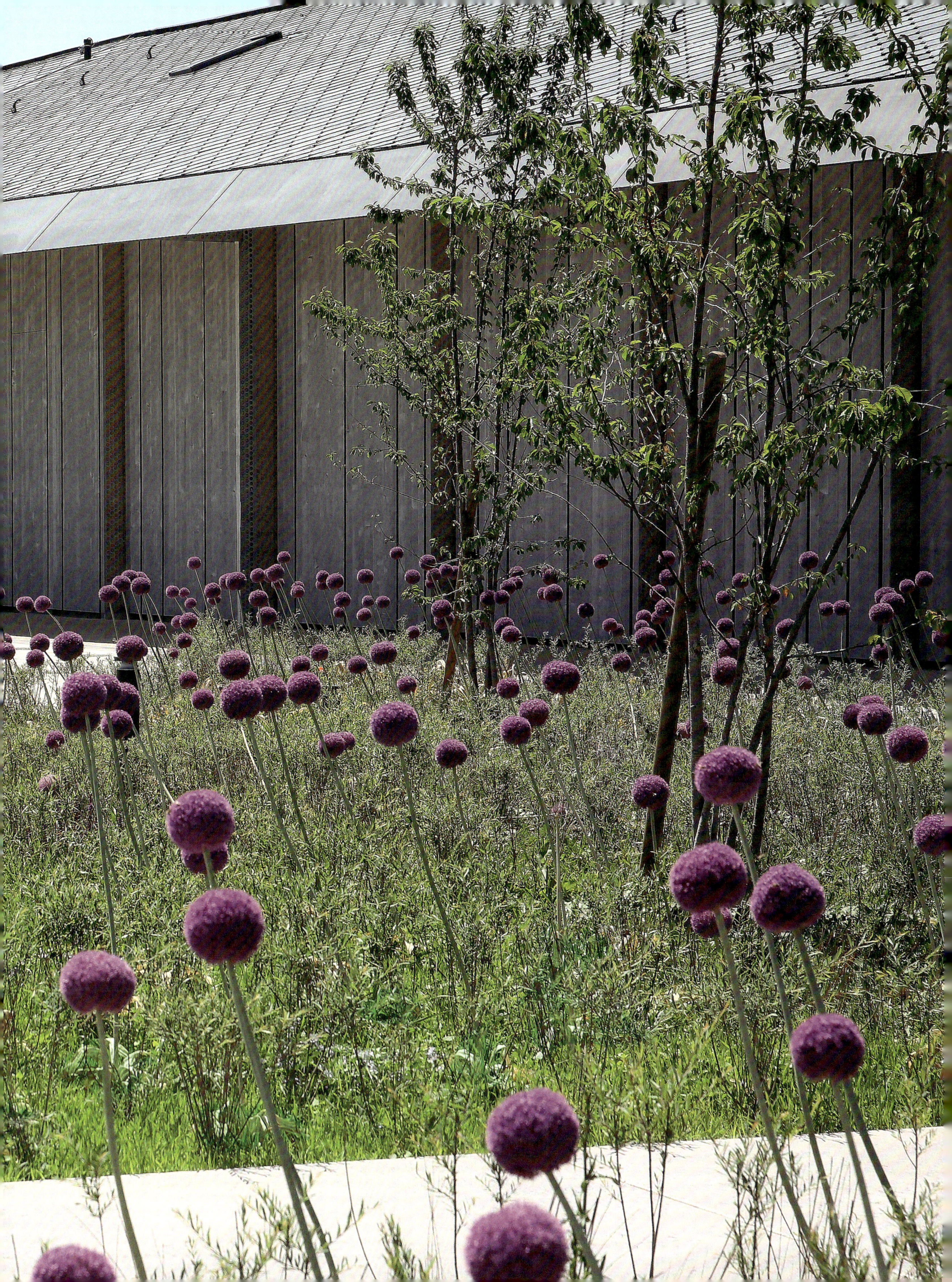

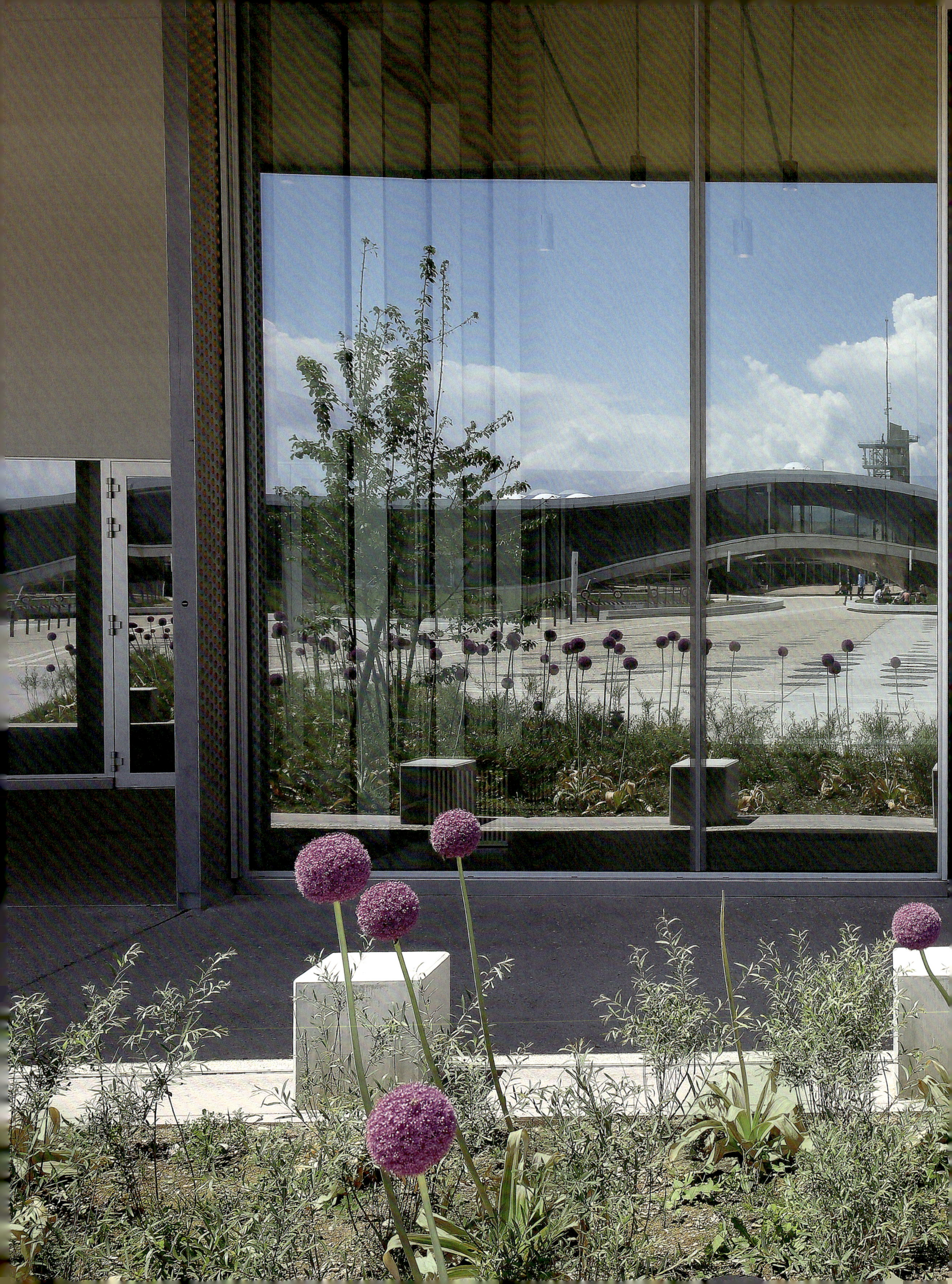

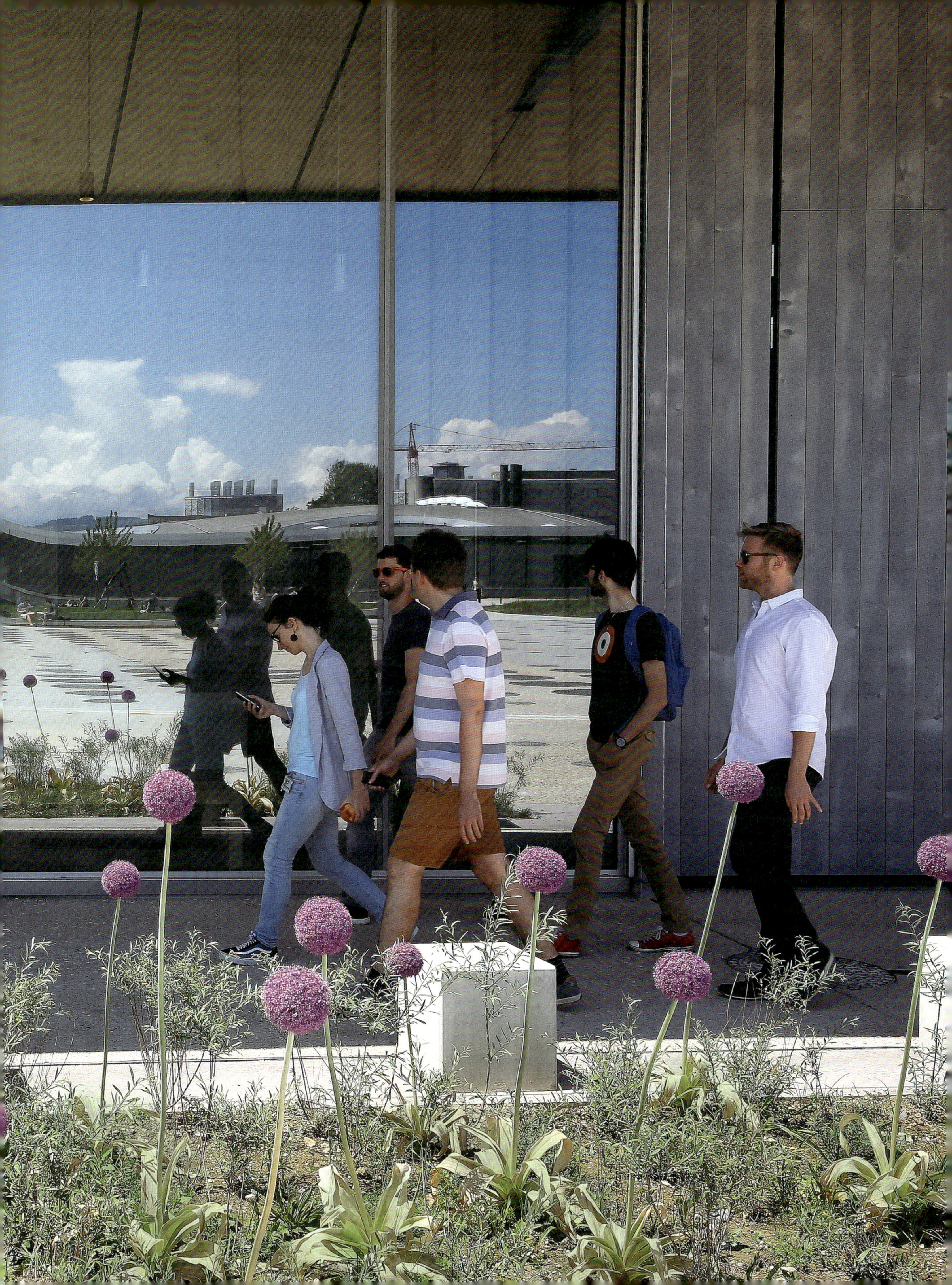

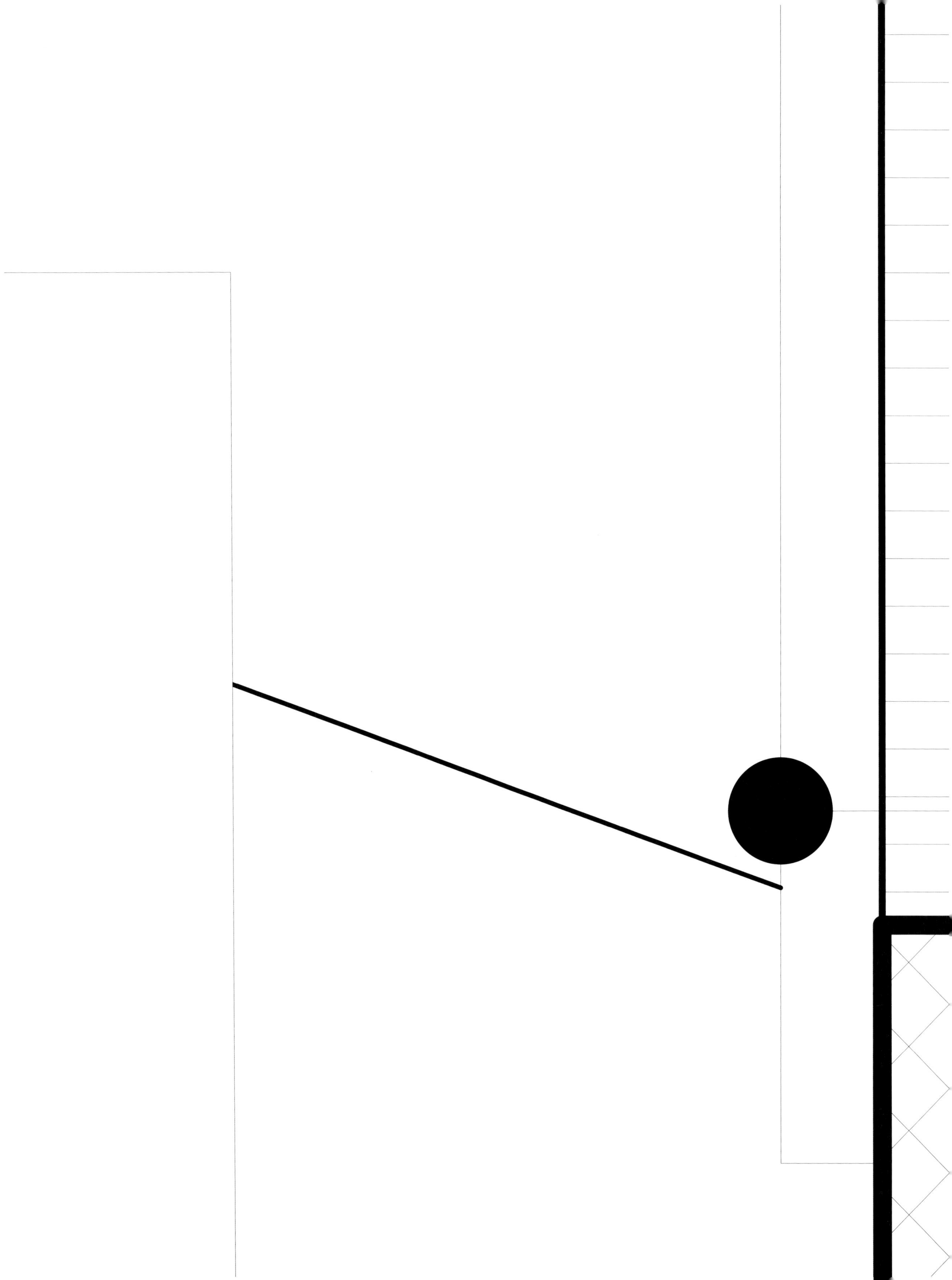

PHILIP JODIDIO

EPFL ARTLAB
IN LAUSANNE
BY KENGO KUMA

UNDER ONE ROOF

PRESTEL

MUNICH · LONDON · NEW YORK

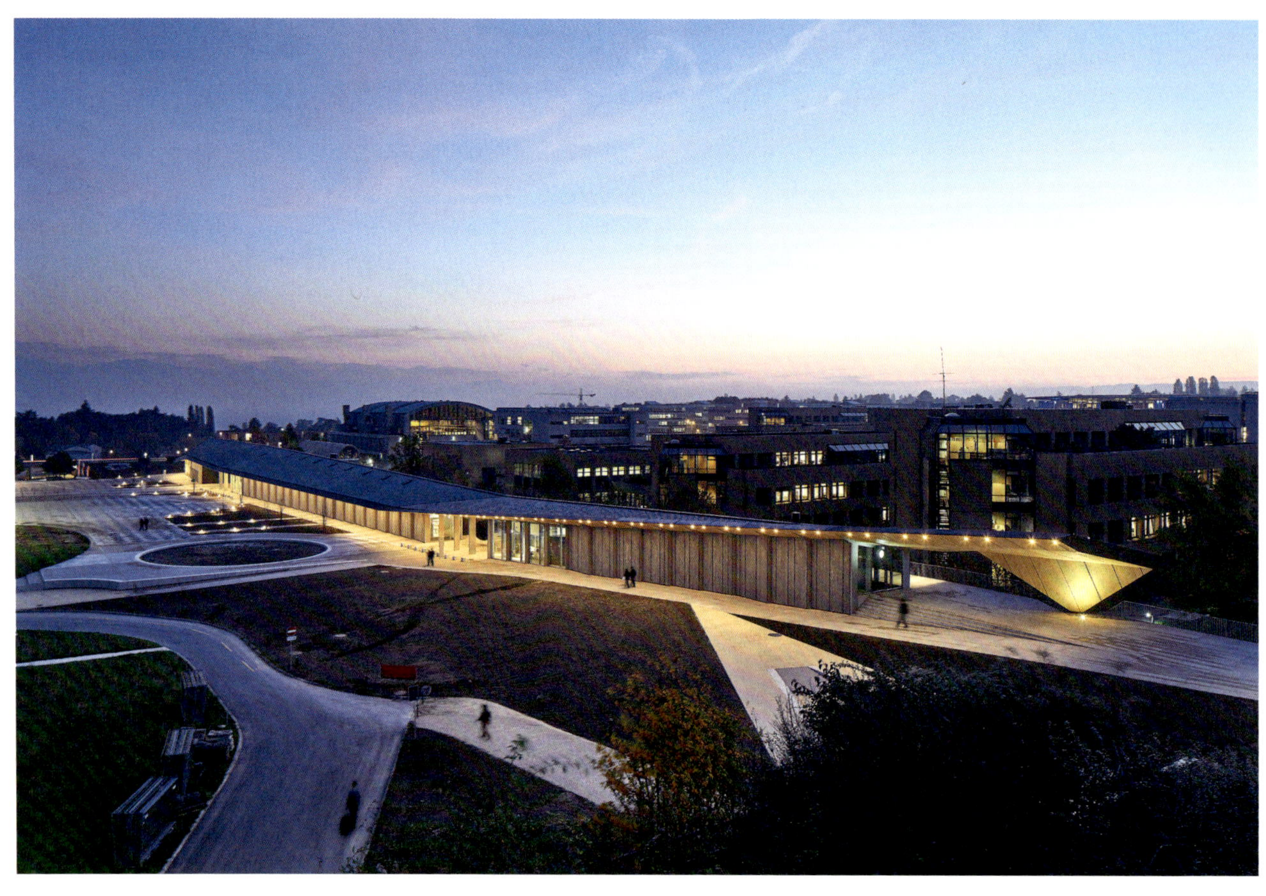

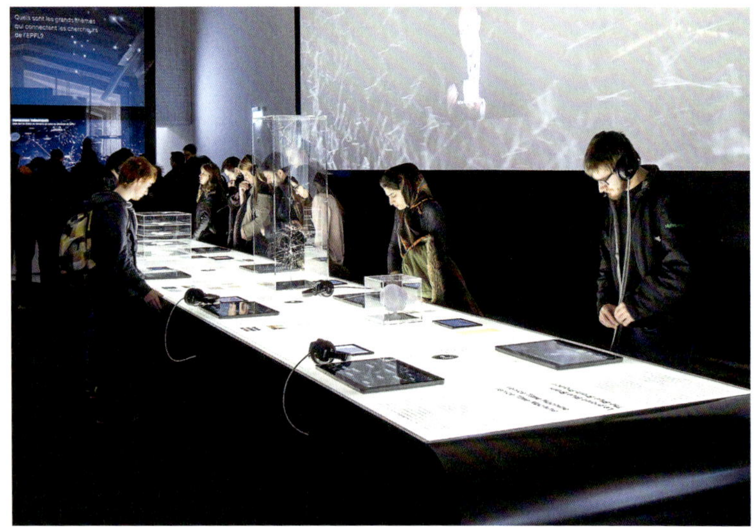

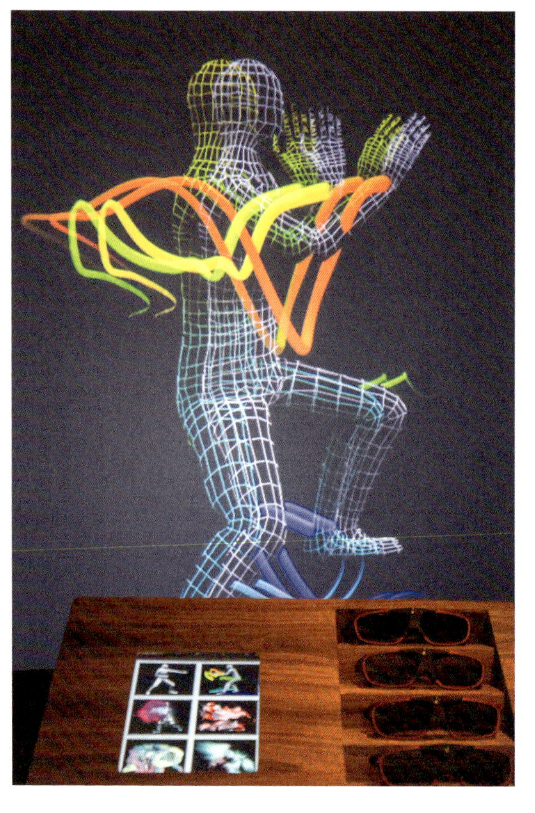

Today, more and more discoveries are emerging at the convergence of bio-technology, nanotechnology, informatics, and data science, as well as the cognitive sciences. Recent advances in big data analysis and the development of new digital tools are pushing the boundaries of this convergence even further toward the social sciences and humanities, creating new opportunities for scientists, engineers, and entrepreneurs of the twenty-first century. Europe—with its rich history and cultural heritage, as well as its competences in science and technology—is the place to explore these new frontiers. In the emerging field of Digital Humanities, Europe can be the leading continent.

University campuses are great environments for exploring new frontiers. Crucial for this exploration is a conducive environment: spaces aimed at providing the opportunity to experiment with this convergence in real time. EPFL strives to provide this environment.

The Rolex Learning Center has paved the way for this evolution. With its gentle and organic architecture, the EPFL landmark building is a place where people meet, learn, and interact. It is a place where architecture is an invitation to innovate, to be disruptive, and to think "out of the box." The Rolex Learning Center could be imagined only by the greatest contemporary architects. Kazuyo Sejima and Ryue Nishizawa (SANAA) have surpassed our expectations.

ArtLab faces the Rolex Learning Center and Place Cosandey, right at the heart of the EPFL campus. The "impossible" mission of bringing art and technology together is embodied by ArtLab, a building designed by Kengo Kuma, the renowned Japanese architect. ArtLab consists of three pavilions linked together by a generous roof, a project Kuma rightfully named "Under One Roof." The three pavilions underline the three dimensions of the Digital Humanities. "DataSquare" explores the world of big data, with the Human Brain Project and the Venice Time Machine as two concrete examples of these scientific developments. Secondly, "Art and Science" is an experimental space for exploring new ways of defining exhibitions of the future. This space is where the public may feel and discover new dimensions at the intersection of the arts, culture, science, and technology. Finally, the "Montreux Jazz Café and Heritage Lab" reflects the commitment of EPFL and the Lake Geneva region to preserve the Montreux Jazz Festival archives, an invaluable legacy inscribed in UNESCO's Memory of the World Register in 2013 that tells the story of modern music and was compiled by visionary Claude Nobs. ArtLab is three pavilions unified into a single place where convergence is both visible and accessible to the EPFL community and to the public at large.

Beyond its inspiring architecture made of wood, aluminum, glass, and tiles, ArtLab is also a research initiative aimed at exploring new venues centered around the emerging field of Digital Humanities. In this respect, ArtLab is an experimental space where EPFL research labs may present their latest work and results. It is a space where new technologies are extracted from the lab and transformed into innovation, prototypes, and concrete user experiences.

ArtLab is the physical and tangible manifestation of this vision of convergence. It is a place at the service of education, research, and innovation, in line with EPFL's core missions. It is a place where one can experience the intersection between science, technology, the arts, and culture. It is a place where new developments in visualization provide opportunities for the public to discover the world of "big data" through concrete projects. It is a place where the public may explore new horizons and imagine the museums of tomorrow.

PATRICK AEBISCHER
PRESIDENT EMERITUS OF EPFL (2000–16)

Top, images from the Montreux Jazz Festival Archives featuring musicians Ella Fitzgerald and Count Basie (top left), Dexter Gordon (right), and Lenny Kravitz with Todd Harold. Bottom, Pierre Soulages, *Peinture, 324×362 cm, 1985, Polyptyque A,* private collection, in the *Noir, c'est noir?* exhibition in ArtLab.

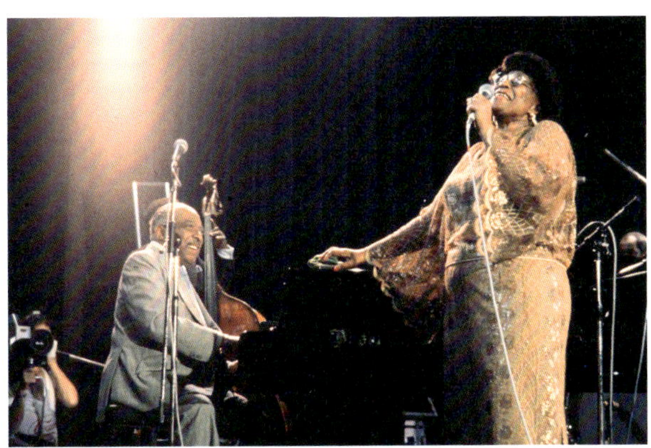

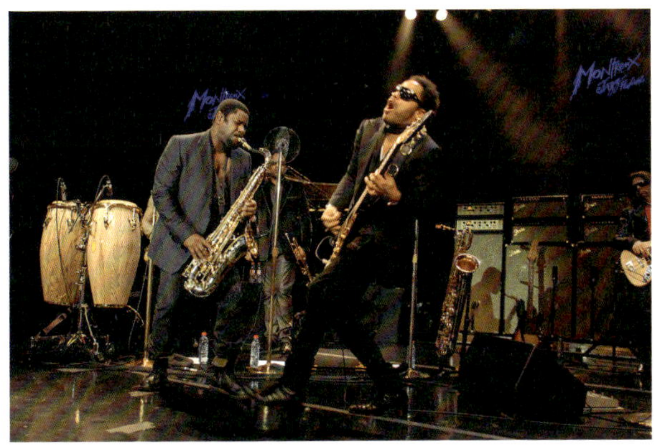

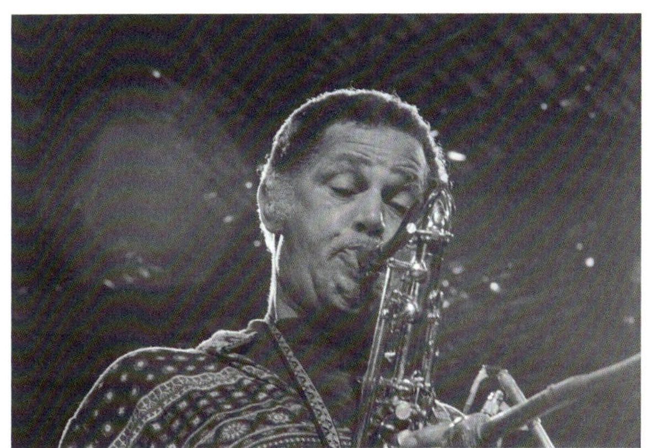

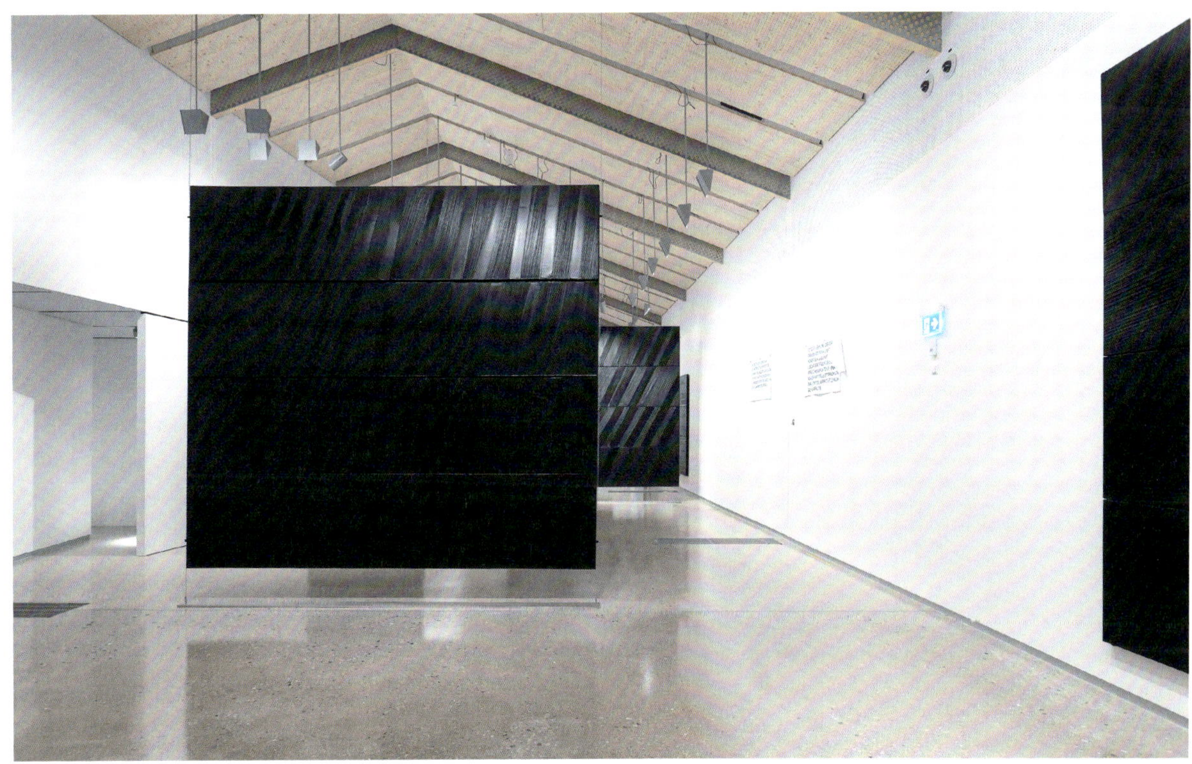

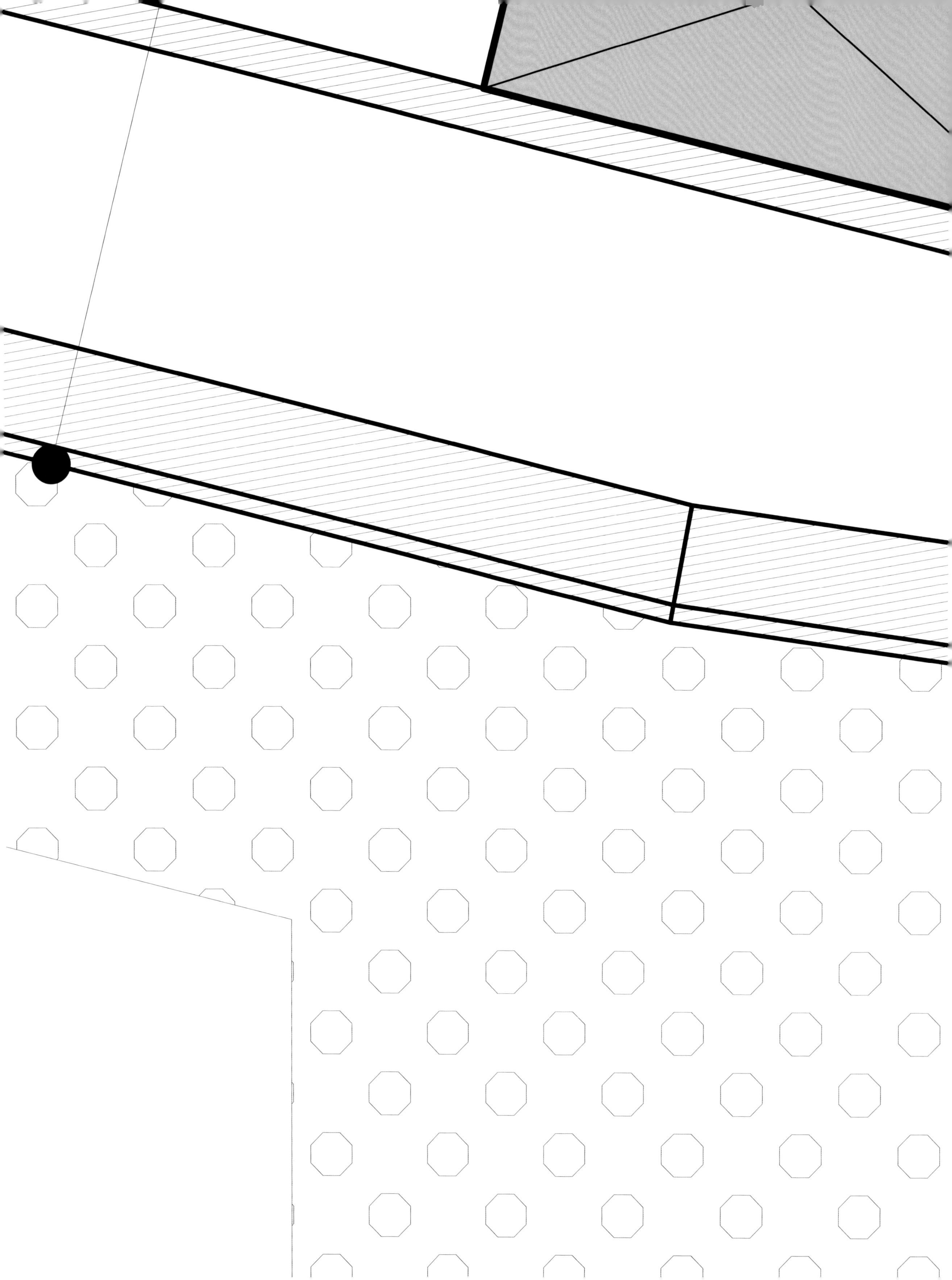

A BRIEF HISTORY OF EPFL

A YOUNG UNIVERSITY

EPFL traces its history back to 1853 and the opening of the École Spéciale de Lausanne, which had a curriculum focusing on chemistry, physics, mathematics, drawing, architecture, and civil engineering. This school became the technical faculty of the Lausanne Academy in 1869. In 1890, the Academy became a university and the Engineering School of the University of Lausanne was officially created. In 1944, the school moved to the former Hotel Savoy on Avenue de Cour in Lausanne. In 1947, its name was again changed to École Polytechnique de l'Université de Lausanne (EPUL). In 1968, the Swiss government passed a law on "Federal Institutes of Technology," creating two such institutions, one in Zurich (ETH or EPFZ) and the other, again renamed the École Polytechnique Fédérale de Lausanne (EPFL), after which the transfer of the latter institution to a new campus outside the city at Écublens-Dorigny was commenced. The University of Lausanne is also located in Écublens, thus EPFL is part of a larger campus with a total of over 20,000 students.

The fifty-five-hectare campus of EPFL has approximately sixty-five buildings, which have been added according to the needs and the development of the institution. The Schools of Basic Sciences, of Architecture, Civil and Environmental Engineering, of Mechanical Engineering, and of Electrical Engineering are located in the modular buildings constructed in the 1970s and 1980s. The Swiss-German architects Zweifel + Stricker laid out the original plan for the campus in 1972. Work began in the spring of 1973, with the first buildings inaugurated in 1978 and the first major phase of construction on the Dorigny campus being completed in 1984. The Zweifel + Stricker plan was arranged in a fishbone pattern with its main axis laid out in an east-west direction. The original buildings are clad in anodized aluminum. The second phase of construction, completed in 1990, was designed by Bernard Vouga, who won the competition that was open only to local architects. Vouga added a diagonal element to the composition, which remained decidedly rigorous in its geometry. Close to the main access to the EPFL campus, the very visible Odyssea Tower building was completed in 1994, formerly occupied by the PTT (Swisscom) but now housing the College of Management of Technology.

Between 1996 and 2002, a third construction program was carried out in the northwestern part of the campus under the design supervision of a group of Zurich-based architects— Dolf Schnebli, Flora Rucha, Tobias Ammann, and Sacha Menz. The Microtechnology Building (BM) was completed in 2000, and the Architecture Building (SG) shortly thereafter. This area was intended to initiate a new north-south axis on the campus related to the public transport line inaugurated in 1991. The SwissTech Convention Center opened further north across Route de la Sorge in 2014. Structures dating from the 1990s house the Schools of Engineering Sciences and Techniques, Computer and Communication Sciences, and a Scientific Park (PSE). More modern additions to the campus house the School of Life Sciences, and the Communications and Architecture institutes. A series of eleven new buildings, EPFL Innovation Park, was added to the southern part of the campus not far from ArtLab beginning in 1991. Of these, two buildings have bio and chemical laboratories and the others provide office space for a total of 55,000 square meters. These spaces are currently used by 120 start-ups, twenty-three larger companies, and twenty service providers.

A number of internationally known architects have contributed to the campus since the Rolex Learning Center—a completely open library by the Japanese architects SANAA—was completed in 2010. In 2013, Dominique Perrault, the architect of the French National Library, completed the multicolored extension of the university's former central library (BI) into the main administration building of EPFL. In 2016, Dominique Perrault also completed the transformation of a building dedicated to Mechanical Engineering and Robotics (ME), which includes the first Discovery Learning Lab that is dedicated to a new approach to the practical work of students. ArtLab, a building designed by Kengo Kuma, which is the main subject of this book, is the most recent significant building to have been created, opening in November 2016. It closes the square formed between the Rolex Learning Center and the ME Building.

EPFL is organized into seven schools and colleges, themselves made up of institutes that group research units (laboratories or chairs) around shared themes. The seven major entities of EPFL are:

→ School of Basic Sciences (Mathematics, Physics and Chemistry), which includes such facilities as the Bio-medical Imaging Research Center (CIBM), the Max Planck-EPFL Center for Molecular Nanosciences and Technology (CMNT), and the Swiss Plasma Center (SPC);

→ School of Engineering (Mechanical Engineering, Micro-technology, Electrical Engineering and Material Science), which also encompasses other entities including the Institute of Bioengineering (IBI);

→ School of Architecture, Civil, and Environmental Engineering, including the Institute of Architecture (IA), Civil Engineering Institute (IIC), and Environmental Engineering Institute;

→ School of Computer and Communication Sciences, which deals with such subjects as algorithms, artificial intelligence, computer architecture and integrated systems, human-computer interaction, security and cryptography, and signal and image processing;

→ School of Life Sciences, including the Brain Mind Institute (BMI), the Swiss Institute for Experimental Cancer Research, and the NCCR Synaptic Bases of Mental Diseases (NCCR-SYNAPSY);

→ College of Management of Technology, grouping the Swiss Finance Institute at EPFL (CDM-SFI), the Institute of Technology and Public Policy (CDM-ITPP), and the Institute of Management of Technology and Entrepreneurship (CDM-MTEI);

→ College of Humanities, grouping the human and social sciences teaching program (CDH-SHS), as well as two initiatives in Digital Humanities and Area Studies.

Beyond this group of major entities there are seven closely related institutes that include the Swiss Cancer Center, the École cantonale d'art de Lausanne (ECAL) that interacts with the EPFL + ECAL Lab, the Wyss Center for Bio and NeuroEngineering, and the Swiss National Supercomputing Center. EPFL has created a number of satellite institutions and activities in Switzerland, including Microcity (Neuchâtel), the Biotech Campus (Geneva), Energypolis (Sion), and the Smart Living Lab (Fribourg).

The university was also the official scientific advisor of *Alinghi*, twice winner of the America's Cup (2003, 2007). In addition, EPFL contributed to the development of the long-range aircraft *Solar Impulse*, which completed the first circumnavigation of the world using only solar power. And EPFL directs the Human Brain Project, which involves 123 European academic partners with a total budget of over one billion euros.

The number of students studying at EPFL has been steadily increasing since the institution was formed in 1969 under its current name. In 1969, EPFL had roughly 1400 students, as compared with 10,686 at the end of 2017. There are more than 110 different nationalities represented in this group and in 2017, 28% were women.

The school had directors from 1853 to 1969. Subsequent to the creation of EPFL, Maurice Cosandey (director 1963–69) became its first president (1969–78), and the central square of the university is today aptly named after him. His most recent successors have been Patrick Aebischer (2000–16) and the current president Martin Vetterli (2017–). In the 2017 *Times Higher Education* "World University, Young University Rankings" for universities aged fifty years or younger, EPFL is listed as number one in the world. In the broader European rankings from the same source in 2018, EPFL is tenth.

Buildings Added to the EPFL Campus 2000–16
1   ArtLab, Kengo Kuma
2   Place Cosandey
3   Rolex Learning Center, SANAA
4   Mechanics Hall (ME Building), Dominique Perrault
5   BI Building, Dominique Perrault
6   Innovation Park, Richter & Dahl, Rocha
7   SwissTech Convention Center, Richter & Dahl, Rocha

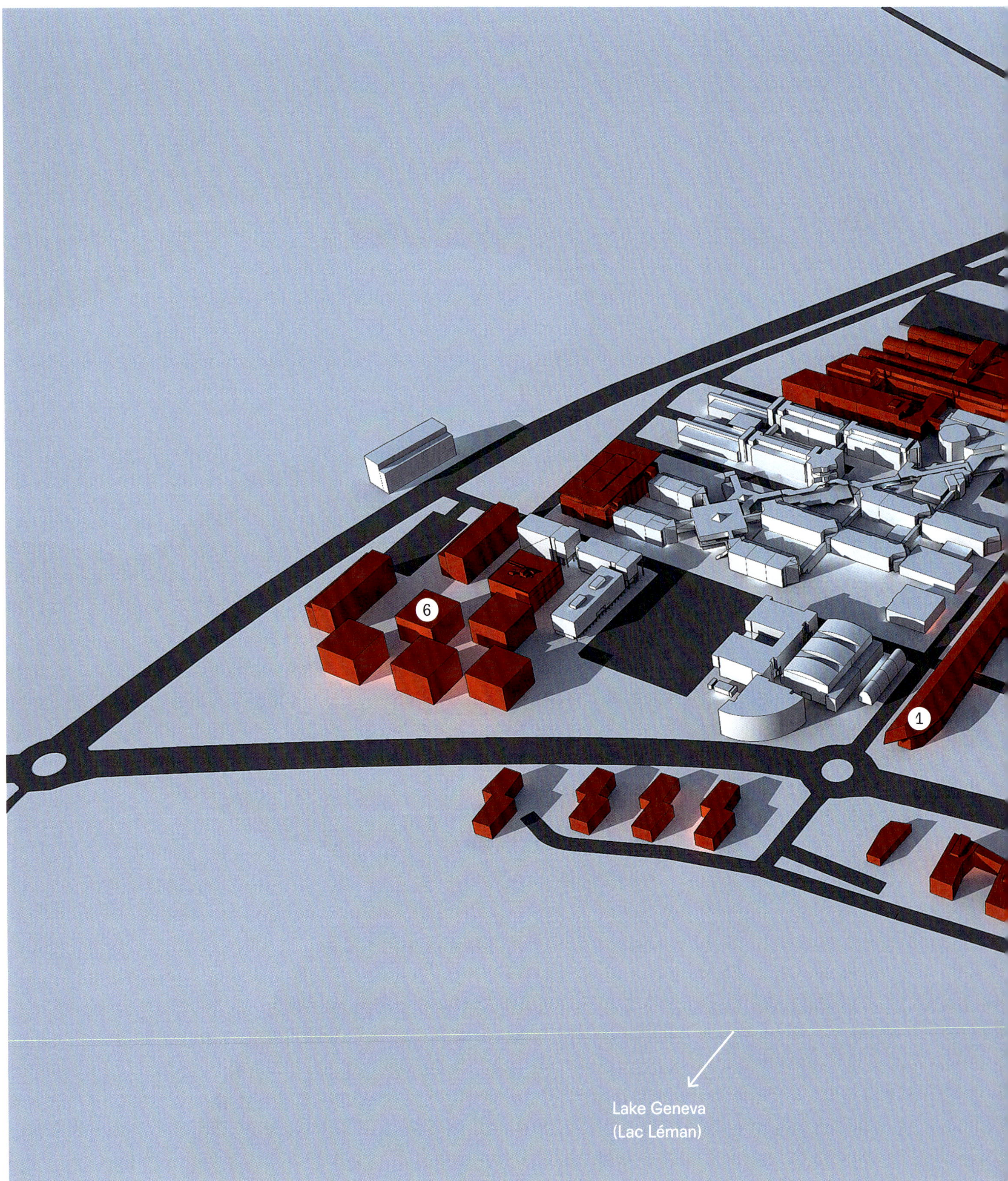

20

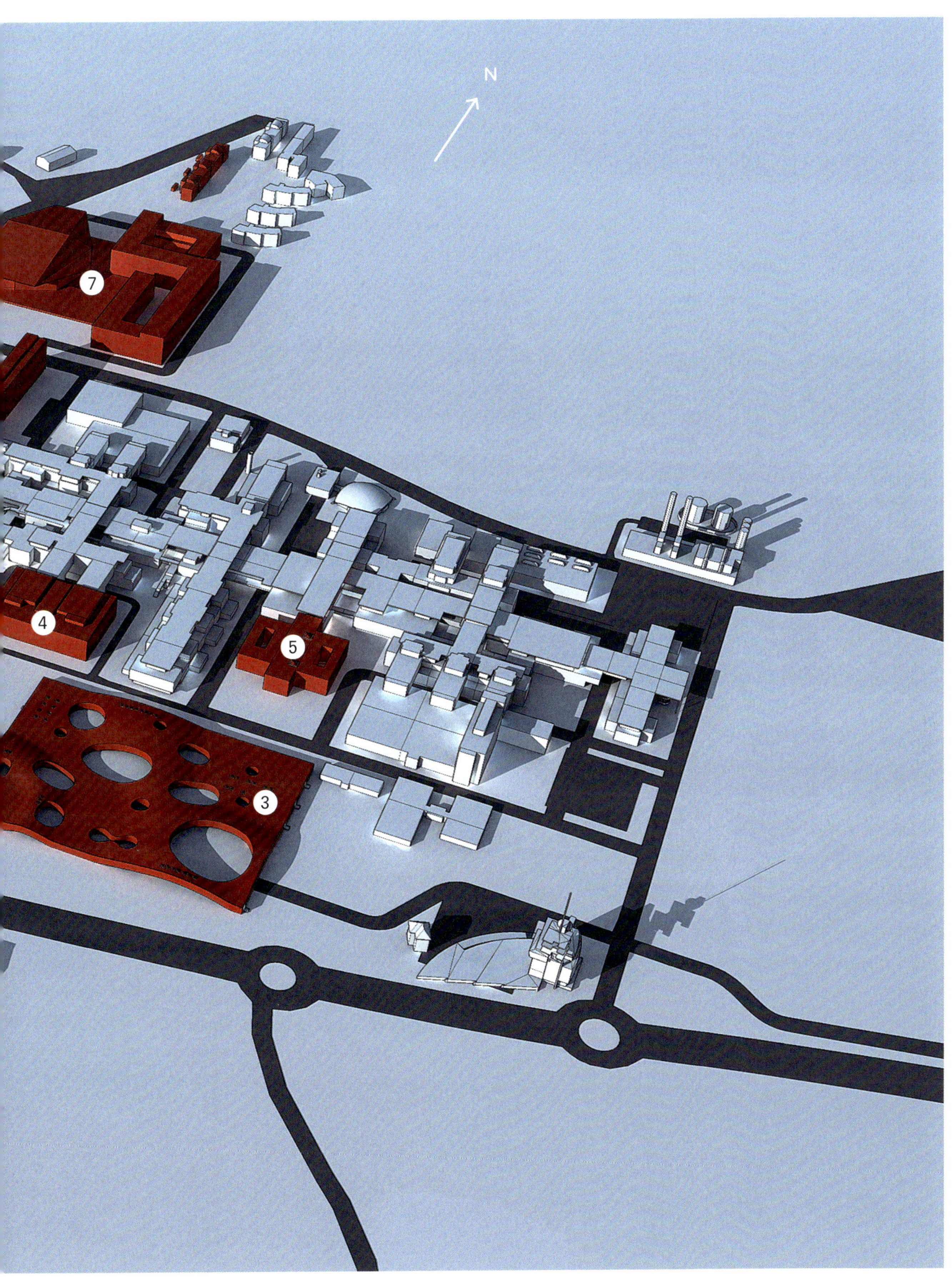

N
7
4
5
3

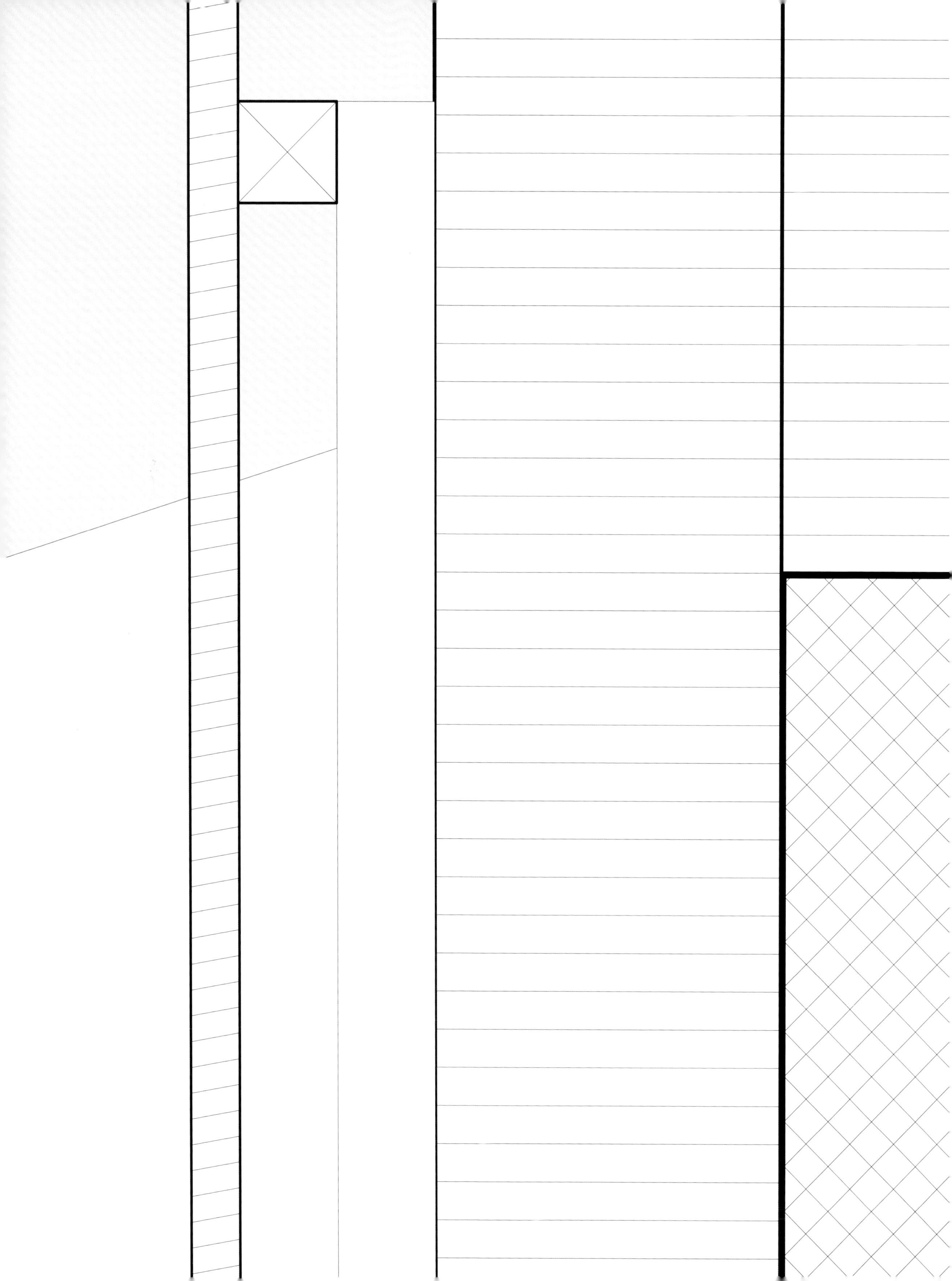

THE HEART OF THE CAMPUS

A TERRITORY
TO CONQUER

The layout of EPFL clearly evolved over time without an overriding scheme, except for the plans of the moment and the available land. Each successive expansion followed a certain logic and awareness of the state of contemporary architecture at the time, and naturally tried to fit into the existing campus and to improve it. The architectural styles that prevailed, even from the outset, tended toward geometric and material rigor. Although logical in the context of a modern, technical university, the architectural decisions taken, overall, generated a relatively arid environment where conviviality and a certain warmth took a back seat to more "rational" goals. A comparison of the EPFL campus as it was prior to 2010, in particular, to other technical universities, such as the University of California, Santa Barbara UCSB, reveals a substantial gap in terms of the amount of space and facilities devoted to leisure and interaction beyond the strictly academic context. UCSB, of course, benefits from the climate of Southern California, but does, nonetheless, put a considerable emphasis on places where students can congregate and organize events, for example. This had clearly not been the case of EPFL prior to the emergence of what is today called Place Cosandey, after Maurice Cosandey, the institution's first president. Located near Route Cantonale that marks the southern boundary of the campus, this broad, largely empty space is beginning to form the heart of the developing university. Largely inspired by the initiatives of the former president of EPFL, Patrick Aebischer, Place Cosandey is today bordered on three sides by new buildings—the Rolex Learning Center (SANAA), the new Building for Mechanical Engineering and Robotics (ME Building, Dominique Perrault), and ArtLab (Kengo Kuma). A reflection of Aebischer's desire to firmly anchor the humanities, or more precisely the interface between technology and the humanities, at the core of the institution, these three buildings are a reflection of a number of elements that make up the institution. The Rolex Learning Center is a place for students to congregate and study, but it is also a library imagined in a form that already takes into account the rising presence of computer and Internet-driven knowledge. The ME Building affirms the central presence of research and science in EPFL. The most recent element in the configuration of Place Cosandey is ArtLab, the long wooden structure designed by Kengo Kuma. As the only wooden building on the campus, ArtLab proclaims a certain difference with the rest of the architecture, even if most of the wood is painted a silver gray. ArtLab is the central location in which science, technology, and culture meet.

As president from 2000 to 2016, Patrick Aebischer took on his task with a decidedly strategic vision. He trained first as an MD (1980) and then as a neuroscientist (1983) at the Universities of Geneva and Fribourg, although this might be unexpected as he is the son of two artists, Emile Aebischer and Joan Aebischer O'Boyle. Emile Aebischer, called Yoki (1922–2012), frequented artists such as the French sculptor Germaine Richier and the painter André Lhote, as well as a number of architects, before commencing his fifty-year career in stained glass, mosaics, and tapestries. Patrick Aebischer's Irish-born mother was a teacher and actress who often played roles in Shakespeare plays. Of this background, he says: "Today I can't travel without taking a detour to see a painting or to hear music. I hesitated as to whether I should take up an artistic career, but I also need the world of science. So I often have very long days."[1] Aebischer worked at Brown University (Providence, Rhode Island) between 1984 and 1992 as a research scientist before becoming an assistant and then an associate professor of Medical Sciences. In 1991, he became the Chairman of the Section of Artificial Organs, Biomaterials, and Cellular Technology of the Division of Biology and Medicine of Brown University. In autumn 1992, he returned to Switzerland as a professor and director of the Surgical Research Division and Gene Therapy Center at the Lausanne University Hospital (CHUV).

Aside from the influence that other campuses across the world, with their almost inevitable symbolic central areas, like Harvard Yard, may have had on him, Patrick Aebischer began, early in his term as president of EPFL, to fashion what would become Place Cosandey, not only for spatial and design reasons but also on the basis of a very precise chain of thought that in many ways characterizes his tenure at EPFL. He states:

> *I thought that the great opportunity of the twenty-first century is to bring content to technology, and not just to develop new technologies. I have been totally obsessed by the idea of converging technologies—the convergence between biotechnology, nanotechnology, informatics, and data sciences, and even the cognitive sciences. I think that digital tools today allow us to make new bridges between the hard sciences, engineering and the humanities, and on to sociology. It was important for me that a school like ours, a comparatively young one, could be placed at a competitive advantage by bringing these disciplines closer to each other. One of my first decisions was to impose courses in the humanities and the social sciences for all EPFL bachelor and master's students (8 to 10% depending on the fields concerned). We relied on surrounding universities that already had structures in place for the humanities and social sciences. To avoid developing nerds and to create people who would be real citizens of the world, we allowed them to choose courses and to tailor content according to their interests, but they had to do some.*[2]

Explaining the creation of the College of Humanities and the corresponding program in social sciences and humanities, Aebischer states: "American universities have less history to some extent than European institutions. You have to explore the areas where you can be unique. I always say that it is hard to find Venice in Nebraska. In culture, we have a gigantic advantage, the raw material is here. Europe has this advantage in cultural heritage, and new technologies allow us to penetrate those and to do new things with them. In the area of digital humanities, Europe can be the leading continent."

These are the underlying currents that began to take built form in the expansion plans that he initiated at EPFL. The first piece in that puzzle was the Rolex Learning Center, of which he says: "Technology was changing and we knew that libraries were changing. In 2000, in addition to the central library, we had about twenty libraries on campus, each one protecting its books, and we knew that this kind of environment was disappearing, everything was going online. We needed a place where people could meet, a place that is conducive to learning—we intentionally didn't call it a library, we were looking for a *learning center*."

He relates his own life story to the continued evolution of the campus in unambiguous terms: "Because of my upbringing, I was comfortable with the world of the arts. I was born into an artistic family, I was trained as a medical doctor, and then I became a neuroscientist and was very much interested in engineering. You have to be a generalist who likes to put things together. It was clear that the campus had to take on an artistic aspect, and the ultimate project was ArtLab. ArtLab is a place where one can experience the intersection between science, technology, the arts, and culture. That was the whole idea behind the building."

As Patrick Aeibischer points out, EPFL had only four presidents in its first forty-seven years of existence. "In this system, presidents last and mark the territory. That is part of the DNA of our school." To those who may have doubted the usefulness of calling on well-known international architects like SANAA, Dominique Perrault, and Kengo Kuma, Aebischer replies: "It has always been philanthropists who pay for these audacious gestures—at least 50% of the price of the Rolex Learning Center and ArtLab… These extra investments add value and visibility to EPFL and augment its capacity to attract the best brains—professors and students. Why do people want to go to Cambridge and to Stanford? Because visionaries dared to create magnificent places where one feels at ease. Look at the new building of Apple (Cupertino, California, Norman Foster), it was imagined as a place that users would enjoy and thus work better. We are not doing anything else." When asked what will remain of his period as president of EPFL in twenty years, he says: "The campus with the Rolex Learning Center, a living, multicultural space that breathes enthusiasm. When I walk through today, I feel that the result of these last seventeen years has gone far beyond what I could have hoped for and imagined."[3]

1 Patrick Aebischer, quoted in "Gens. Patrick Aebischer, chercheur, fils de Joan et Yoki," *Le Temps*, December 11, 1999.
2 All quotes unless otherwise indicated, Patrick Aebischer in conversation with the author, EPFL, March 13, 2018.
3 Patrick Aebischer, quoted in "Il fallait mettre l'institution sens dessus dessous," *24heures*, https://www.24heures.ch/extern/interactive_wch/epfl/#/interview (accessed on March 20, 2018).

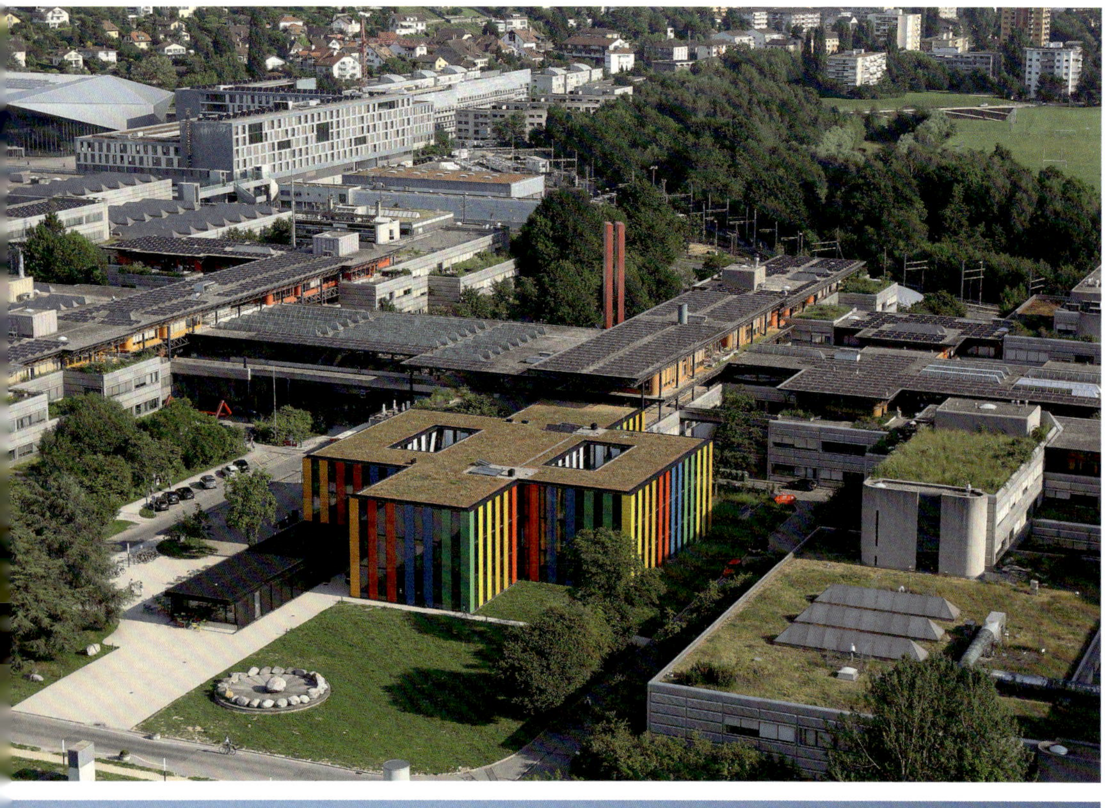

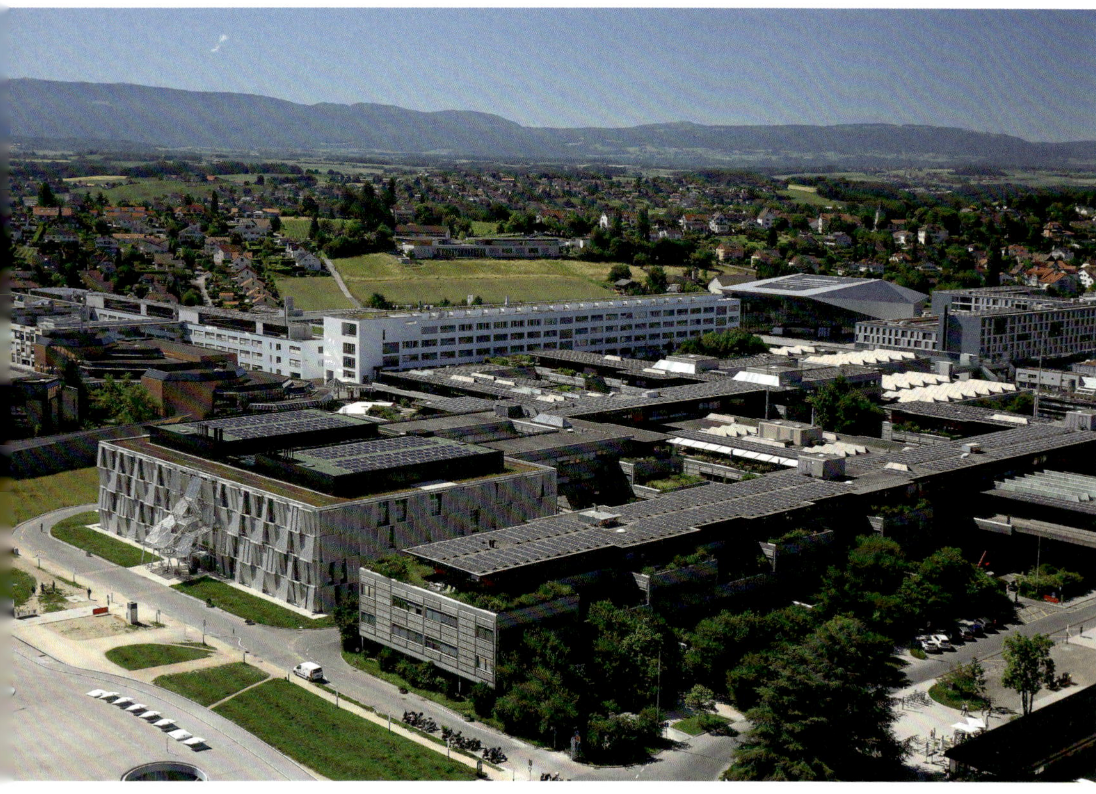

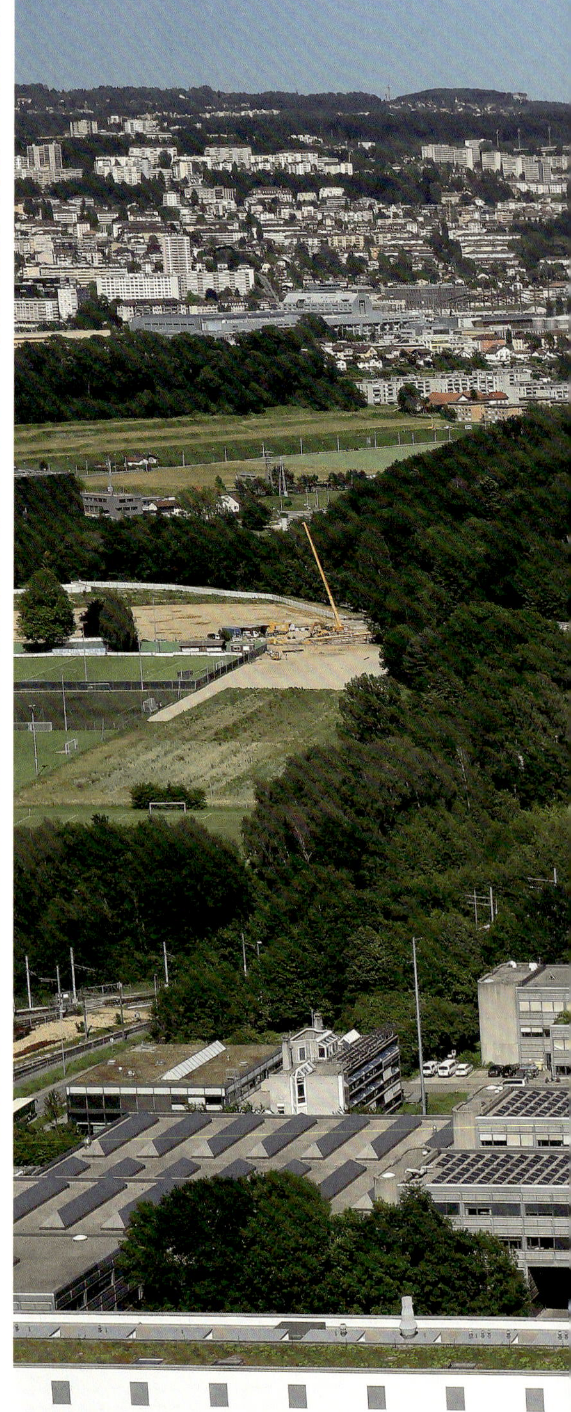

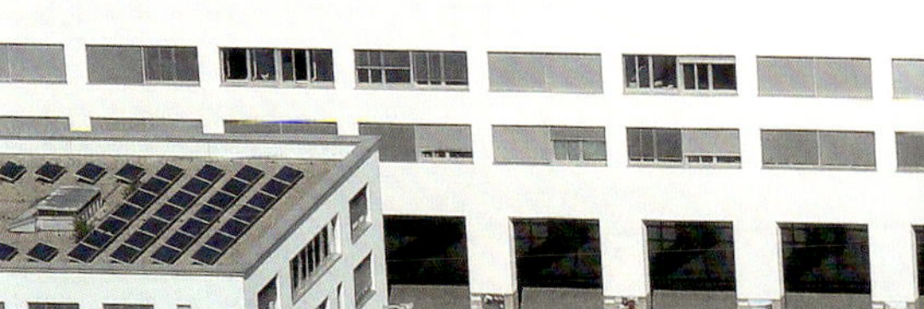

Aerial views of the campus showing the two buildings by Dominique Perrault, the Central Administration Building (BI, top left), and the Mechanics Hall (ME, bottom left).

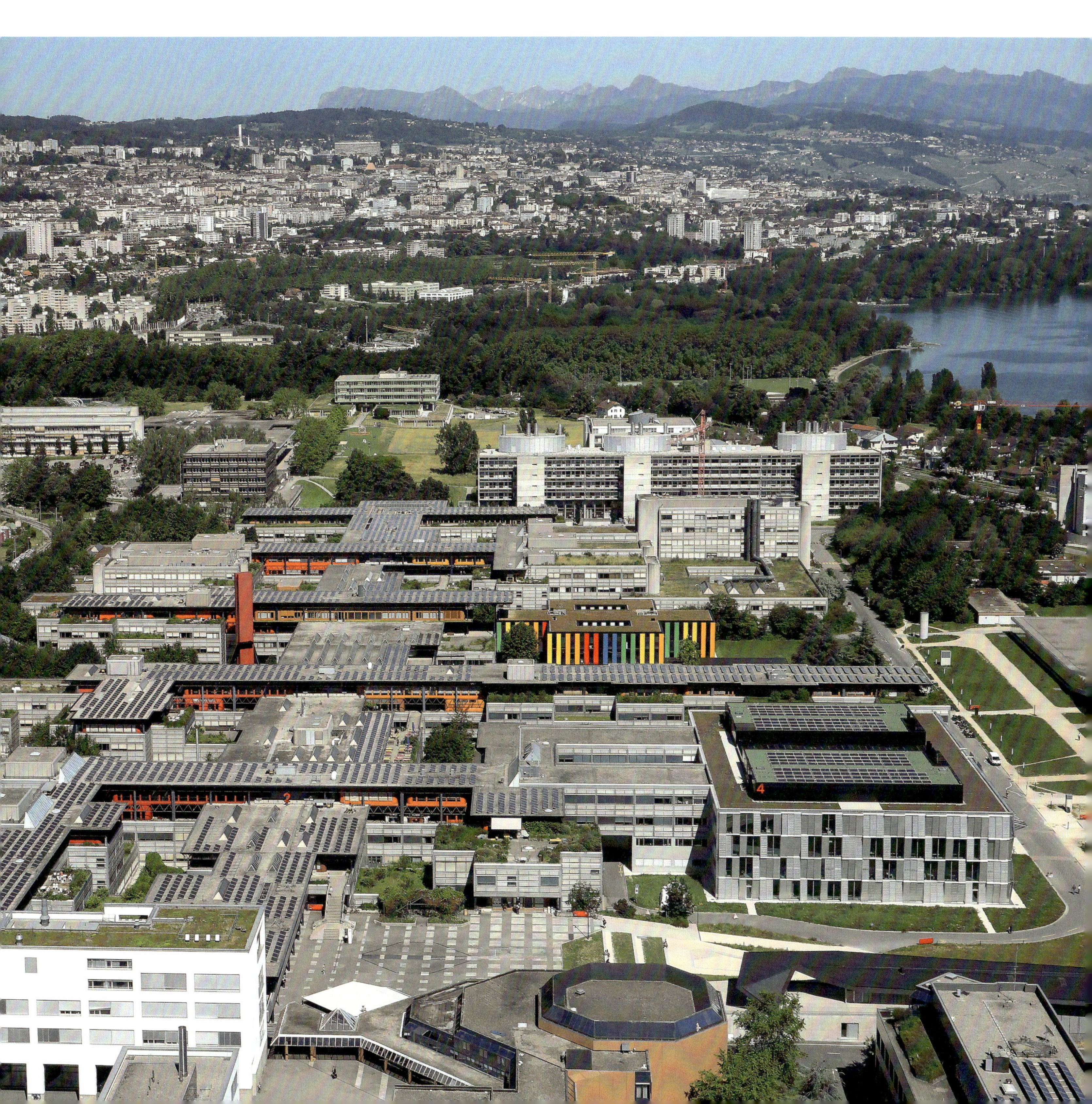

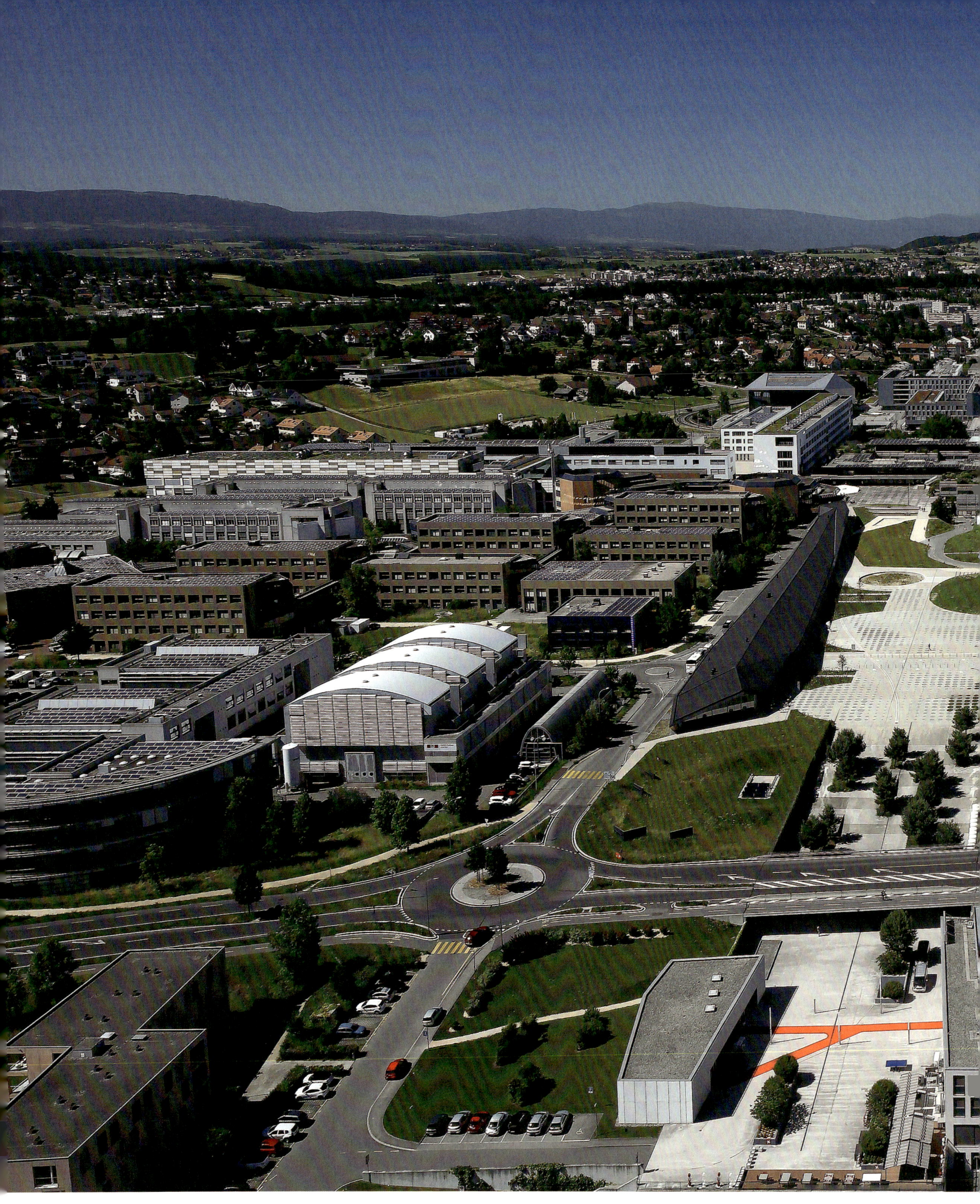

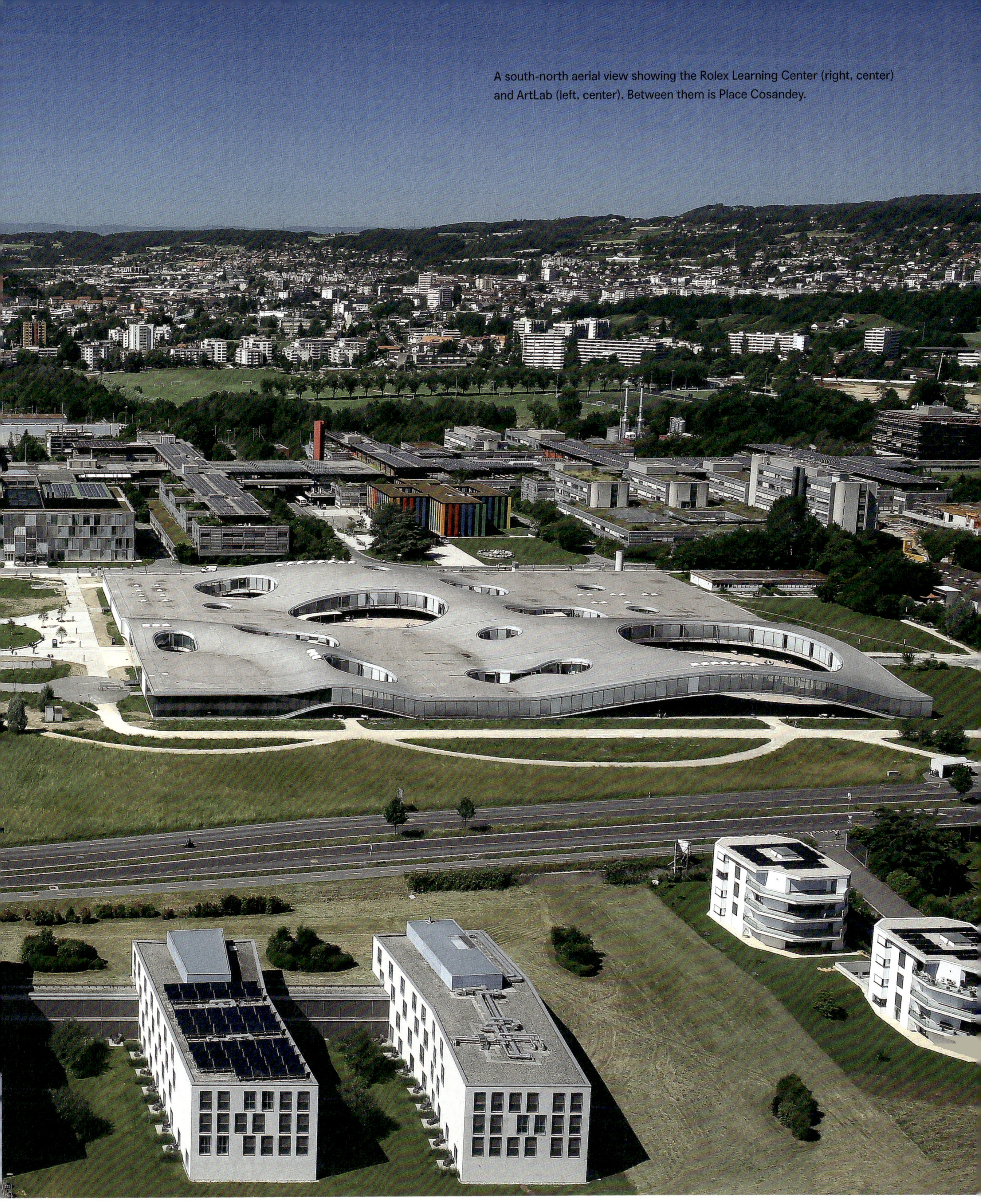

A south-north aerial view showing the Rolex Learning Center (right, center) and ArtLab (left, center). Between them is Place Cosandey.

THE ROLEX LEARNING CENTER

In the spring of 2004, EPFL launched a two-stage architecture competition for a new Learning Center as part of its ongoing development scheme. The competition jury included Patrick Aebischer, EPFL professors Inès Lamunière and Patrick Berger, David Chipperfield, Mike Guyer, Anne Lacaton, and Brigitte Shim. The open competition yielded 181 submissions of which twelve were selected for the second stage. Amongst the firms retained at that point were Abalos & Herreros (Madrid); Jean Nouvel (Paris); Diller Scofidio + Renfro (New York); Herzog & De Meuron (Basel); Mecanoo (Delft); OMA (Rotterdam); Kazuyo Sejima + Ryue Nishizawa / SANAA (Tokyo); Valerio Olgiati (Zurich); and Zaha Hadid (London). The choice of SANAA was announced at the end of 2004.[1] The arrival on the EPFL campus of the Tokyo partnership Kazuyo Sejima + Ryue Nishizawa / SANAA marked a shift in the architecture of the school—toward a higher profile in terms of reputation, even as the architecture they proposed exudes a kind of natural modesty.

SANAA were the winners of the 2010 Pritkzer Prize. The Pritzker jury citation reads in part: "The buildings by Sejima and Nishizawa seem deceptively simple. The architects hold a vision of a building as a seamless whole, where the physical presence retreats and forms a sensuous background for people, objects, activities, and landscapes. They explore like few others the phenomenal properties of continuous space, lightness, transparency, and materiality to create a subtle synthesis. Sejima and Nishizawa's architecture stands in direct contrast with the bombastic and rhetorical. Instead, they seek the essential qualities of architecture that result in a much-appreciated straightforwardness, economy of means, and restraint in their work."[2]

Prior to the EPFL project, SANAA had completed the 21st Century Museum of Contemporary Art (Kanazawa, Ishikawa, Japan, 2004). Another project that has some relation to their Rolex Learning Center is the 2009 Serpentine Gallery Pavilion, a temporary structure erected in Kensington Gardens in London. This event pavilion consisted in a continuous twenty-six-millimeter-thick aluminum roof with an amoeboid plan supported by random, thin, steel columns. Another structure dating from the same period by Ryue Nishizawa further demonstrates the architect's interest in the relation between architecture and landscape: the Teshima Museum (Teshima Island, Kagawa, Japan, 2010) located in Japan's Inland Sea. With its curving, 60-meter unsupported concrete shell design, this building also evokes the mountainous landscape of its site. Nishizawa stated: "Our goal is to generate a fusion of the environment, art, and architecture, and we hope these three elements work together as a single entity."[3]

These projects underline both the architects' interest in landscape and open access, together with a lightness that is not typical of contemporary architecture. The clearly defined lines of much modern architecture are replaced here with flowing curves, reflections, and light. In the Rolex Learning Center, floor and ceiling follow each other in an arching, curving flow that is nearly uninterrupted by internal walls or clearly defined spaces. This design marks a clear break with the otherwise largely rectilinear and purely functional architecture of the campus.

The Rolex Learning Center was inaugurated on May 27, 2010. Located near the main entrance to the campus, not far from the lake, its essentially uninterrupted interior space is open to both students and the public. The Learning Center houses a library with 500,000 printed works, as well as access to 12,000 online journals and over 20,000 e-books. There are four large study areas accommodating 860 students, as well as office space for over 100 EPFL and other employees. The Rolex Forum amphitheater can seat up to 600 people. A café and bar, a food court, and a restaurant are also included in the building. Five external patios have informal seating for visitors and students. The building lifts up along each of its sides allowing visitors to enter through a central entrance. The floor undulations and curved patios gently divide the different programs but also provide connections between them. "The Rolex Learning Center," stated Patrick Aebischer, "exemplifies our university as a place where traditional boundaries between disciplines are broken down, where mathematicians and engineers meet with neuroscientists and micro-technicians to envision new technologies that improve lives. We invite the public into this space to convey the message that working in science is working for the advancement of society."[4]

The architects have explained the significance of the specific relation of the Rolex Learning Center to its environment. Ryue Nishizawa stated: "One of the biggest ideas that we have been trying to develop is… creating architecture like a park. In Lausanne, what we did was to create a very big room, with very many different kinds of programs, open to each other, encouraging communication between them. We also designed the topography to give a very different landscape and character to each area and each program, so that people can find a place where they want to stay. The building has a three-dimensional movement creating open space below it, allowing everybody outside to come directly into the center of the building from all around. The entrance is in the middle of the building. People can stay where they like, as they would do in a park." Sejima goes on to say: "Also, the ceiling and floor basically run parallel. So it's a huge random space, but your view is always cut either by the floor or the ceiling, so you cannot see the edge of the building, which means you always just feel continuity. As an interior experience, you can never imagine the whole building, but just feel continuity. Discussing it now, I realize that maybe this also has some similarity with a reflection; it's a mirror. A mirror, like in the Serpentine Pavilion, allows people to feel they are in a beautiful, large park, whereas what we actually made is, instead, a small park and a canopy."[5]

A public-private financing scheme was the model used for the Rolex Learning Center. The total cost of the center was 110 million Swiss francs, financed partially by the Swiss government and by major Swiss companies. The participation of Rolex in the project is the result of a long-standing relationship with EPFL in materials science research and microtechnology for watch design. Logitech made the initial contribution that launched the architectural competition. Losinger, a member of Bouygues Construction Group and a sponsor, was the principle contractor for the building. Credit Suisse has an open space in the building. Other Swiss partners who contributed to the financing, research, and innovation of the building are Nestlé, Novartis, and SICPA.

The 2010 Pritzker Prize jury citation makes specific reference to the Rolex Learning Center: "The building's many spaces (library, restaurant, exhibition areas, offices, etc.) are differentiated not by walls but by undulations of a continuous floor, which rises and falls to accommodate the different uses,

while allowing vistas across this internal 'landscape for people.' The relation of the building to its context is of utmost importance to Sejima and Nishizawa. They have called public buildings 'mountains in the landscape,' believing that they should never lose the natural and meaningful connection with their surroundings."[6] Ryue Nishizawa stated: "The university people asked us to think about what kind of public space could be nice for the students and the faculty. We found the idea of one room, which doesn't have the definition of 'this is a corridor, this is a classroom, this is where you study, this is where you move.' We decided to throw this kind of definition away. We went to the university and we saw that there are many students walking along the street, talking. They are studying in the street. I also saw that there are many students in the classroom, although it seems as though they are not studying. So I felt that students are people who can study, exchange information, discuss anywhere, even when they move. A bunch of classrooms lined up along a corridor doesn't work so well. One of our ideas is that students can discuss and come up with ideas anywhere, when they study, when they move, or when they drink a coffee. This is the idea we thought would be nice to realize with this building. People can meet." Kazuyo Sejima concludes: "Maybe the space only appears with people. It is just a nondescript (area), but if people meet or start to do something, the space appears."[7] The idea that the space of the Rolex Learning Center "appears" when people come together would seem to be a built translation of EPFL's transformation, where barriers between disciplines become as rare as walls in the architecture of this building.

1   "Learning Center, the Lausanne Example," LIBER
    Architecture Group Seminar – Utrecht, 22–24 March 2006.
2   "Jury Citation," 2010 Pritkzer Prize, at http://www.
    pritzkerprize.com/2010/jury (accessed on March 23, 2018).
3   At http://archinect.com/lian/live-blog-ryue-nishizawa-at-mit
    (accessed on March 23, 2018).
4   Patrick Aebischer quoted in "Rolex Learning Center Press
    Information (EPFL)," revised June 1, 2010.
    At http://rolexlearningcenter.epfl.ch/files/content/sites/
    rolexlearningcenter/files/press%20kit/
    ENGLISH%20Kit2012.pdf (accessed on March 23, 2018).
5   Ryue Nishizawa and Kazuyo Sejima quoted in Hans
    Ulrich Obrist, *SANAA Kazuyo Seijima & Ryue Nishizawa*,
    The Conversation Series 26, Buchhandlung Walther König,
    Cologne, 2012.
6   At http://www.pritzkerprize.com/2010/jury (accessed
    on March 23, 2018).
7   Kazuyo Sejima quoted in Hans Ulrich Obrist, *SANAA
    Kazuyo Seijima & Ryue Nishizawa*, The Conversation Series
    26, Buchhandlung Walther König, Cologne, 2012.

Below, a corner of the Rolex Learning Center seen shortly after the completion
of construction (2009). Right, an aerial view of the same building.

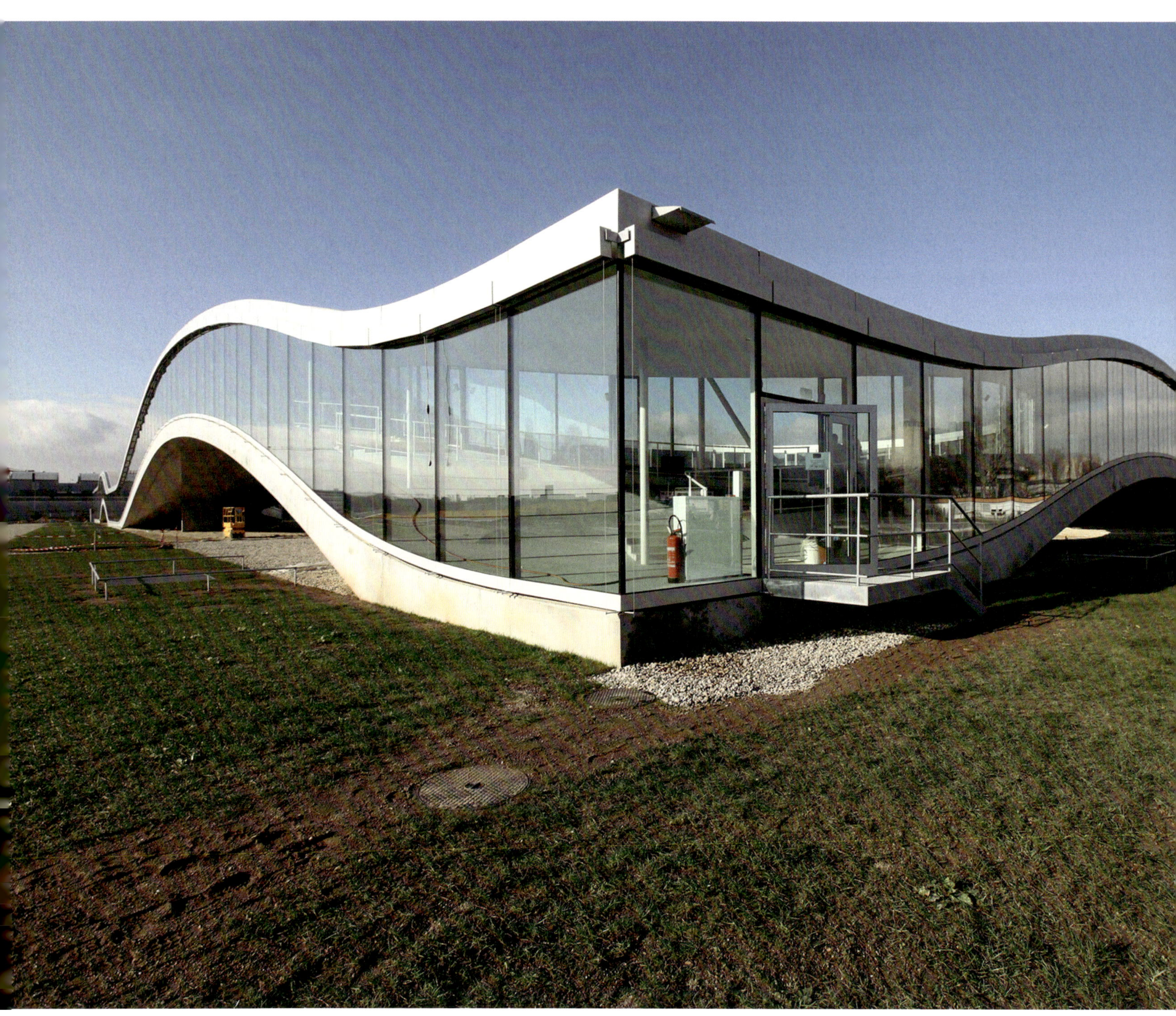

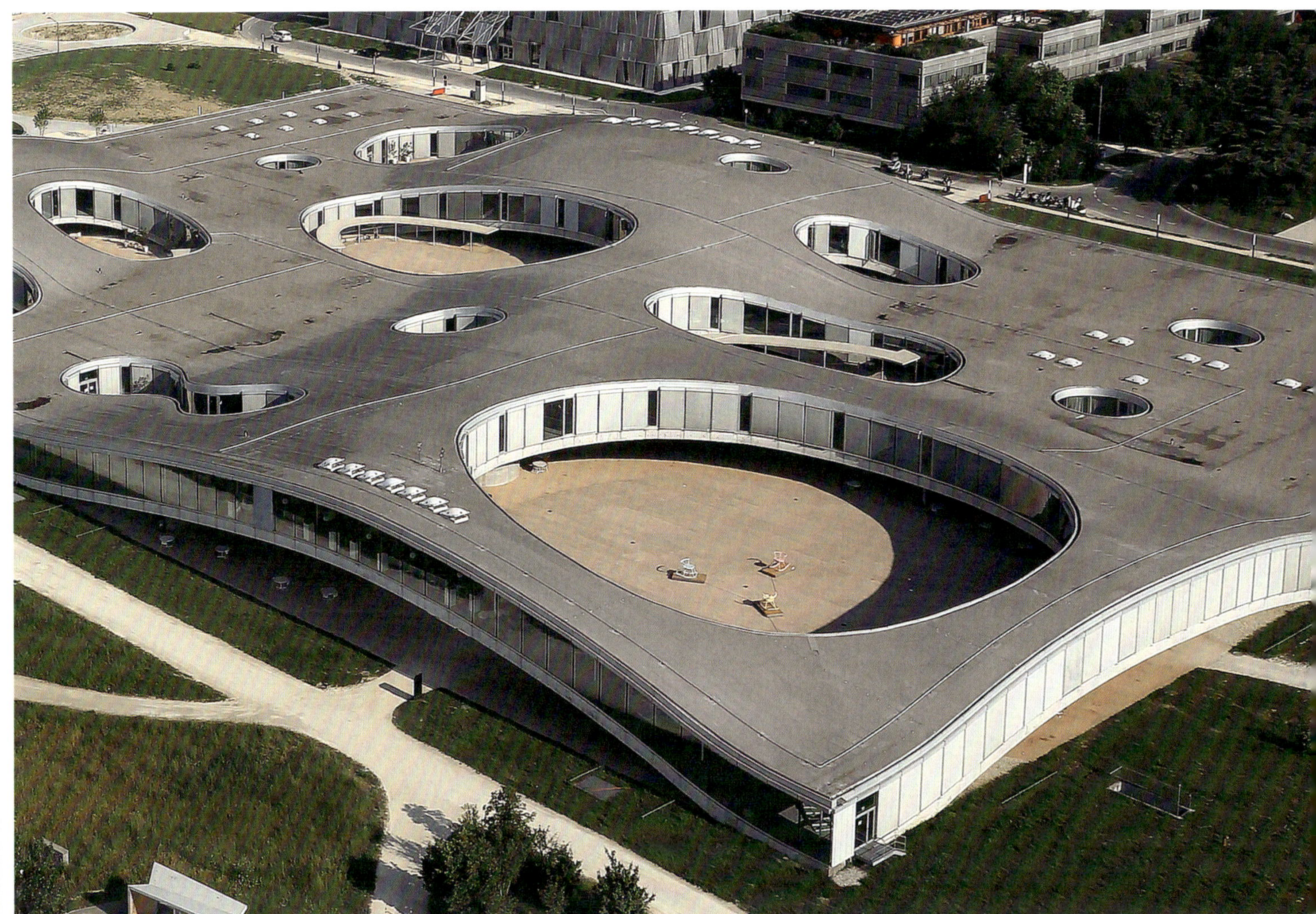

Below, students in the library of the Rolex Learning Center. The generous interior spaces include the Rolex Forum (bottom), which can seat up to 600 people.

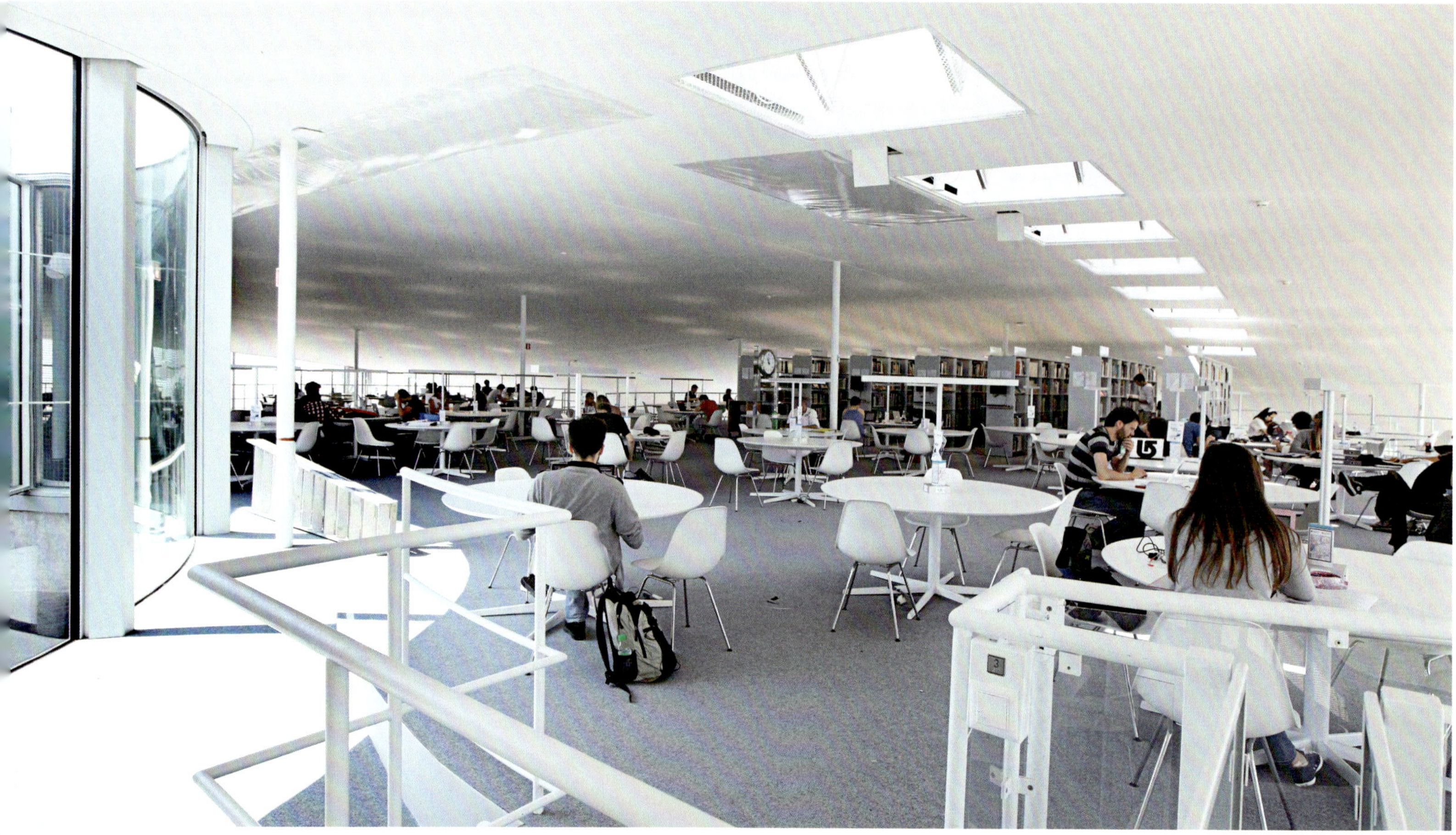

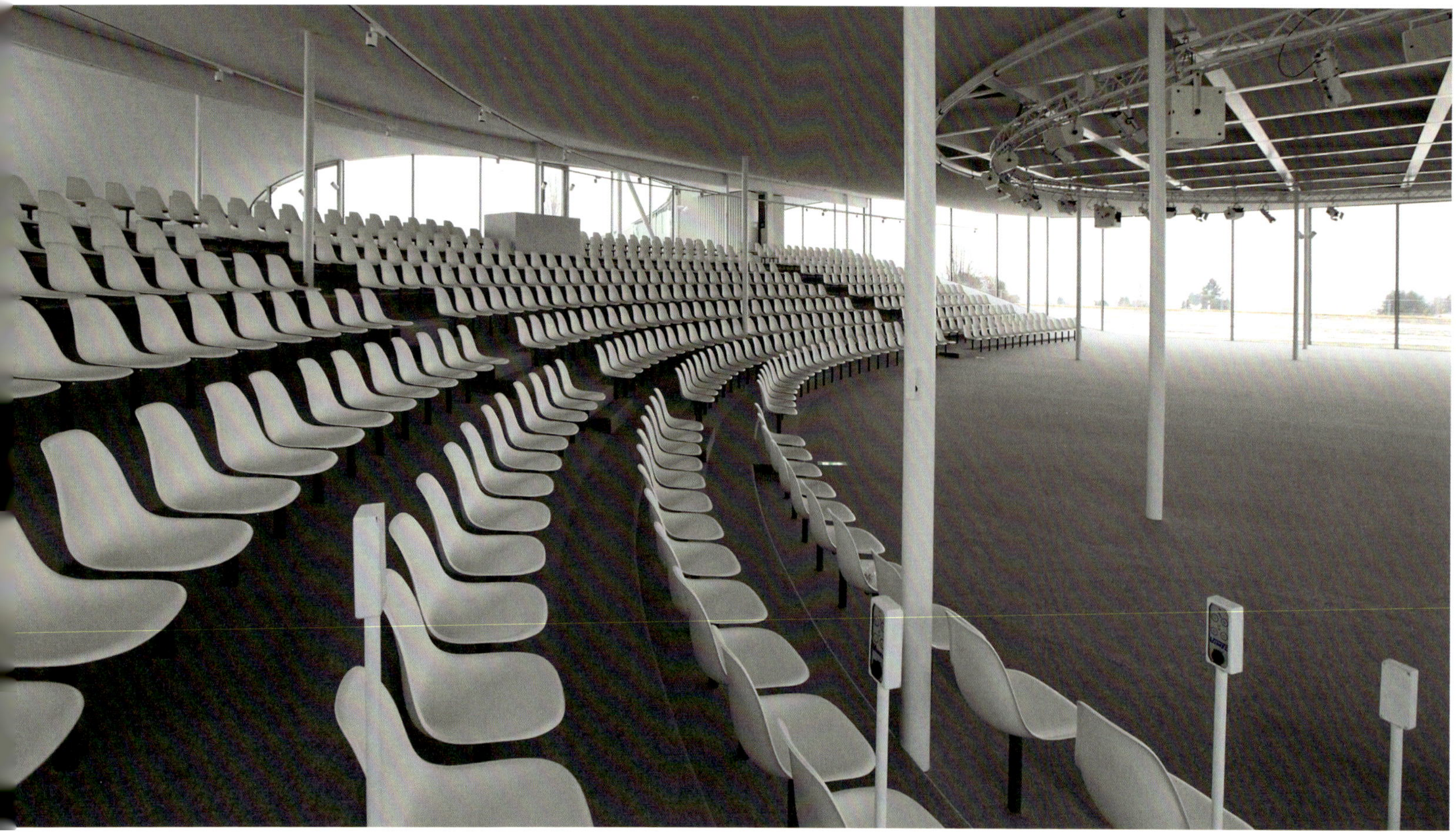

Below, the library space in 2009, and students preparing for exams
in the building, which is open to all.

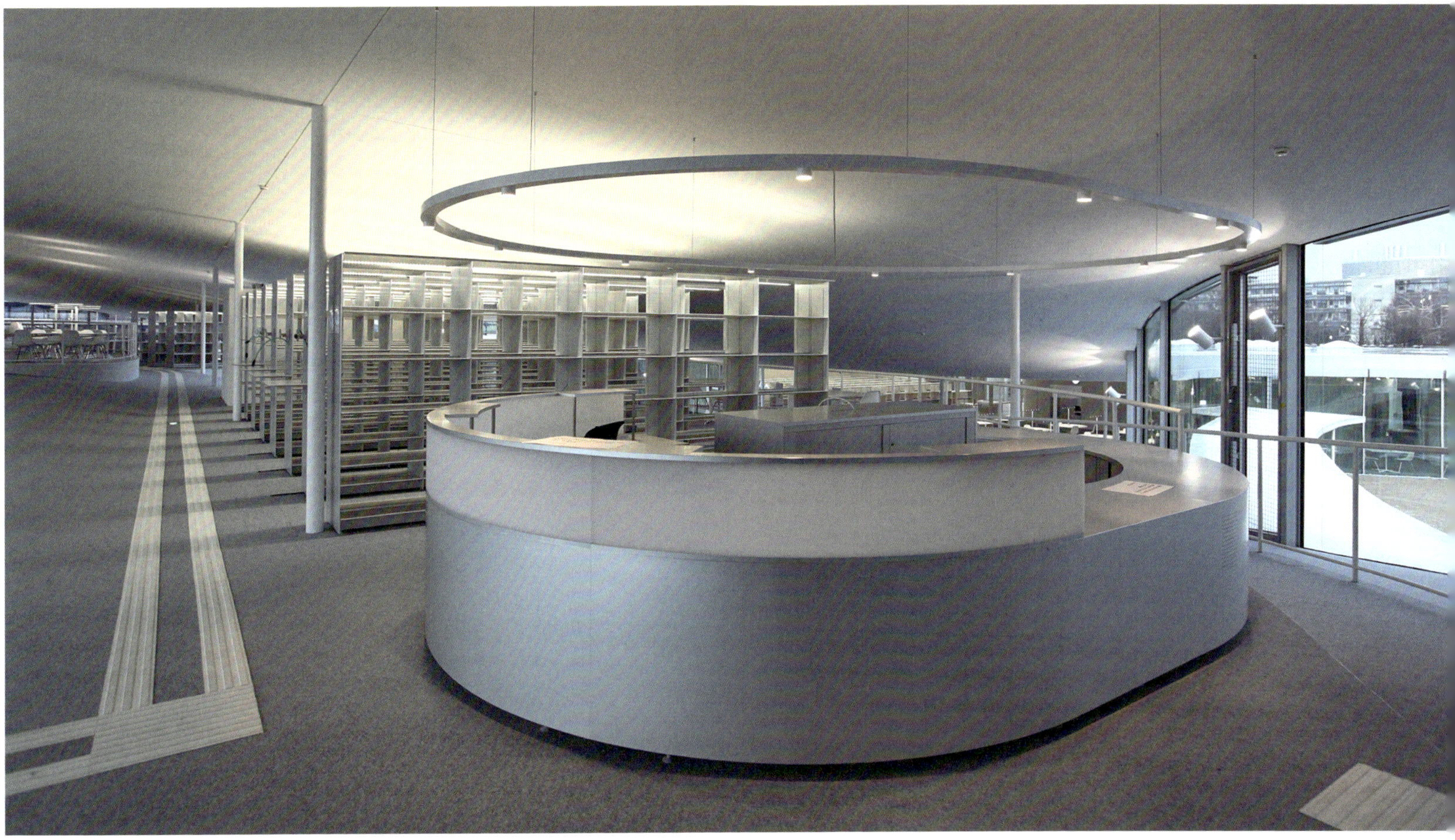

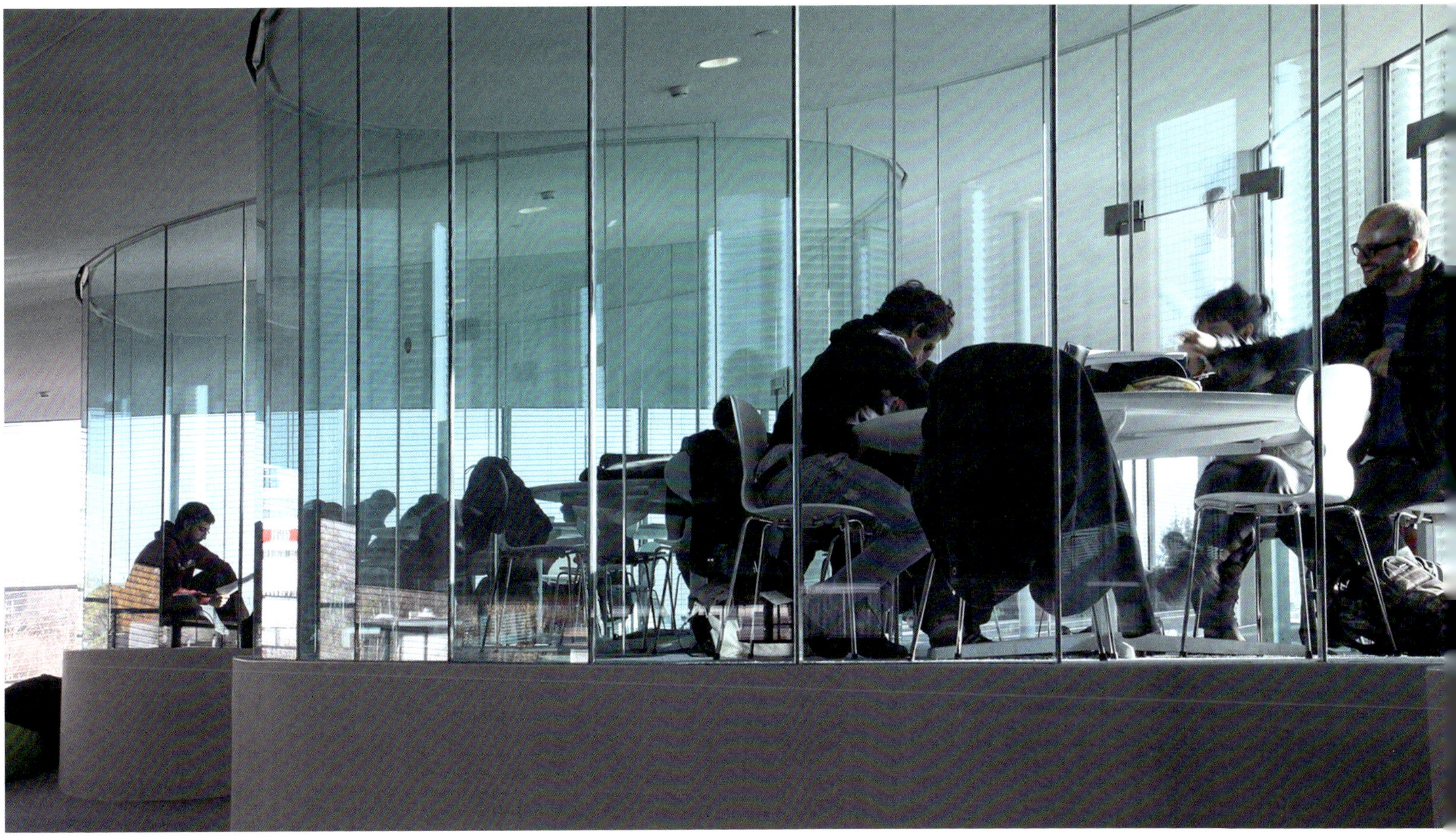

TWO BUILDINGS BY DOMINIQUE PERRAULT

Between 2010 and 2013, the French architect Dominique Perrault, author of the French National Library (BnF, site François-Mitterrand, Paris, 1995), undertook the rehabilitation and extension of the former Central Library of EPFL (the BI Building) into the institution's central administrative offices, including Finance and Human Resources. At the same time, Perrault won the competition for renovating the ME Building (with the construction group Steiner AG) and, also with Steiner, was to design another building on the campus in the same area, the Teaching Bridge, but that project was not carried out. The three projects were all intended to complete the area to the north of the Rolex Learning Center. The Library was reduced to its three-story metal structure after its collection of publications was transferred to the Learning Center. Today's BI Building is located at the intersection of two of the main campus axes—north-south linking the Learning Center to the M1 public transport line and east-west connecting to the nearby University of Lausanne. Perrault added space to the original volume, and created two twelve-meter-high patios into the 5000-square-meter building. It stands out because of its brightly colored, four-meter-high, vertical, enameled-glass panels, alternating with uncolored glass. The base of the building is marked by a black band below the colored glass. The use of bright colors and the insertion of patios and a restaurant affirm the convivial nature of all the new EPFL buildings.

The original Mechanics Hall at EPFL (Halles de mécanique; ME Building) was designed by Zweifel+Stricker, and built in 1977. Dominique Perrault won a 2010 competition (with Steiner AG) for a complete renovation of the building, just after the completion of the Rolex Learning Center. Located directly northwest of the SANAA building, the new four-story structure, completed in 2016, has a rectangular footprint. Although use of the original building as a basis for the project was studied, the solution opted for was a nearly complete demolition, with the exception of the peripheral walls of the basement. A floor area of 19,000 square meters houses administrative offices as well as research laboratories and workspaces for the School of Engineering (STI) and the School of Life Sciences (SV). It also accommodates the first EPFL Discovery Learning Lab, which is dedicated to a new approach to students' practical work. The Lab offers thematic spaces for practical lab sessions that are open to all sections that would like to integrate them into their curriculum. They are adapted for teaching large groups of students, generally at the undergraduate level.

The building has two wings linked by a large central atrium, which, like most of the campus, is open to the public. Its unexpected façade is made up of prefabricated, modular, metal-mesh screen blocks set at various angles on the eastern, southern, and western elevations. Each module is divided into three vertically set panels, two of which slide while the third is set at an inclination of five degrees. A reconstruction of the original metallic façades of the building was created for the north façade as a homage to the Zweifel+Stricker building. The articulated façade of the Mechanics Hall denotes the northern edge of Place Cosandey. It might be noted that this decidedly metallic building marks a material contrast with the glass and concrete employed by SANAA for the Rolex Learning Center. Logically, or by way of further differentiation, Kengo Kuma chose to use wood as a main material for his later ArtLab on the western side of the square.

The Perrault structures, and especially the ME Building, form an unusual northern side to Place Cosandey. Each building here has a different appearance and, aside from these two Perrault buildings, a different architect. Dominique Perrault's architecture is certainly more metallic and "hard" than the two Japanese-designed buildings (Rolex Learning Center and ArtLab) but Perrault thus allows the formation of a successful transition from the coldness of the original campus to the more sensual curving and folded shapes of the newest additions. Perrault's bands of saturated color also make it stand out against the prevailing grayness of the main, older campus further north: this aspect is particularly evident in aerial views.

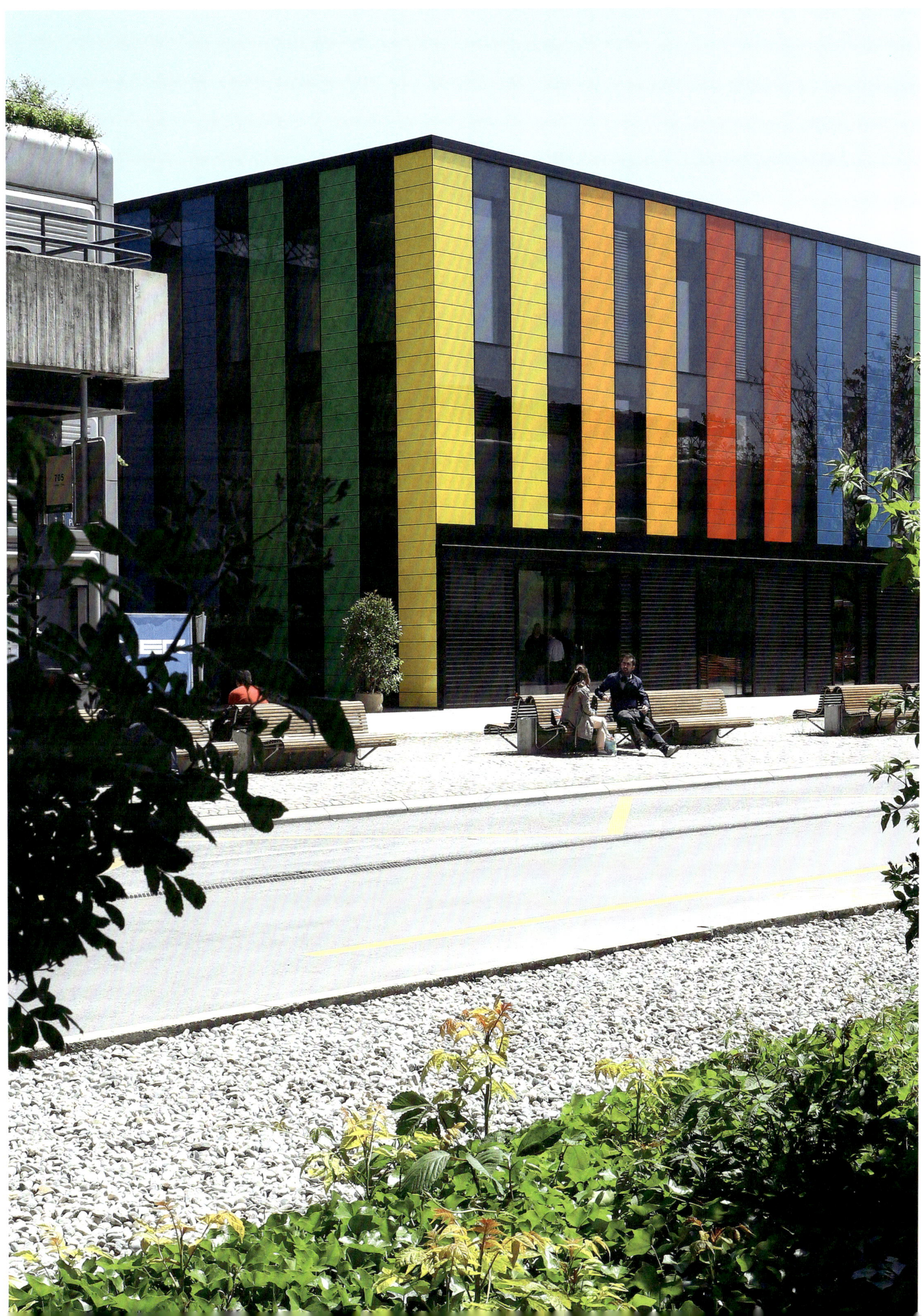

The former Central Library of EPFL (BI Building) became the home of the University's Central Administration after a make-over by Dominique Perrault.

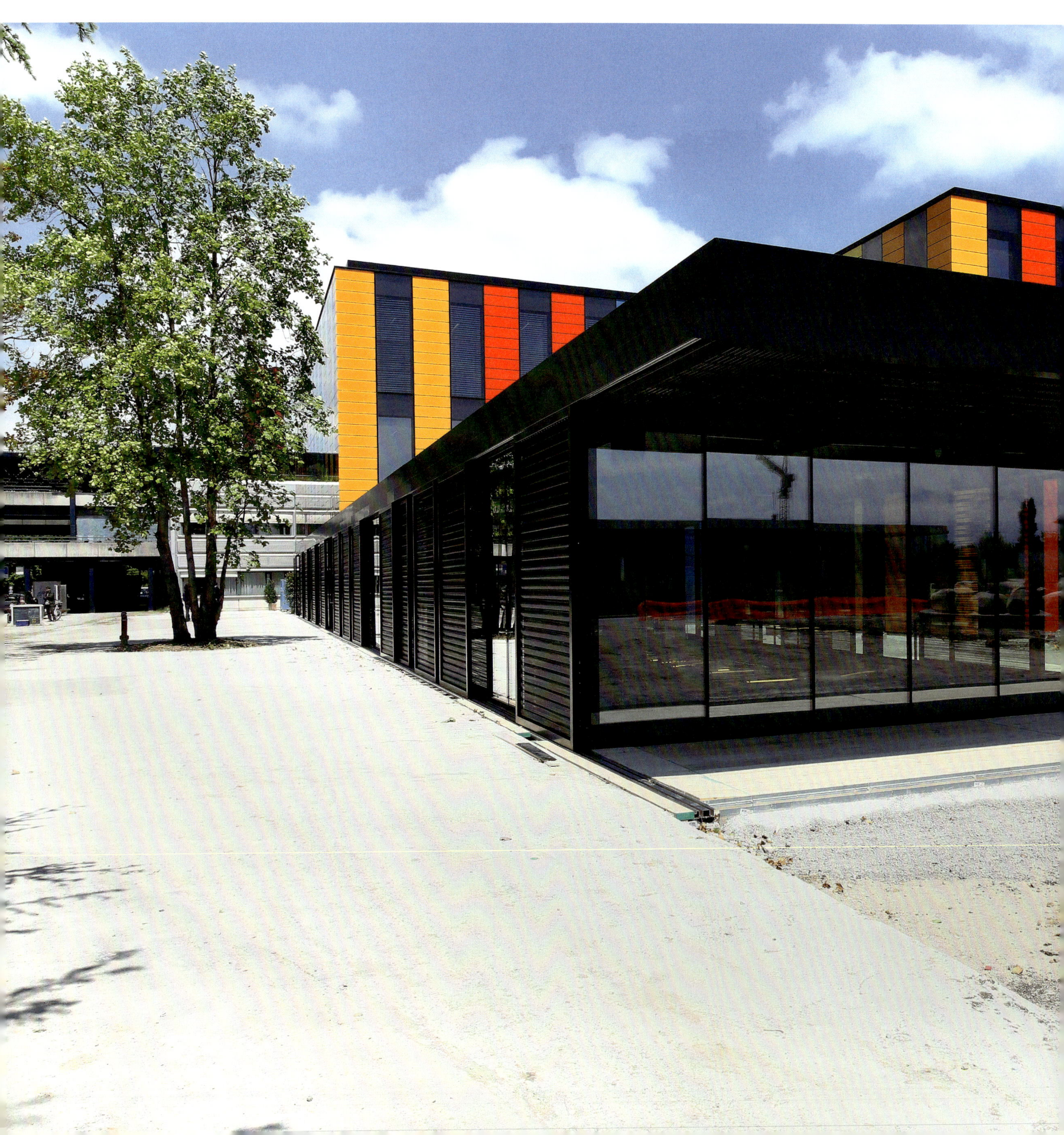

Dominique Perrault created a large, glazed space on the ground floor of the BI Building, sometimes used for exhibitions.

The bright colors chosen by the architect for the cladding are in contrast with the otherwise rather monochrome campus.

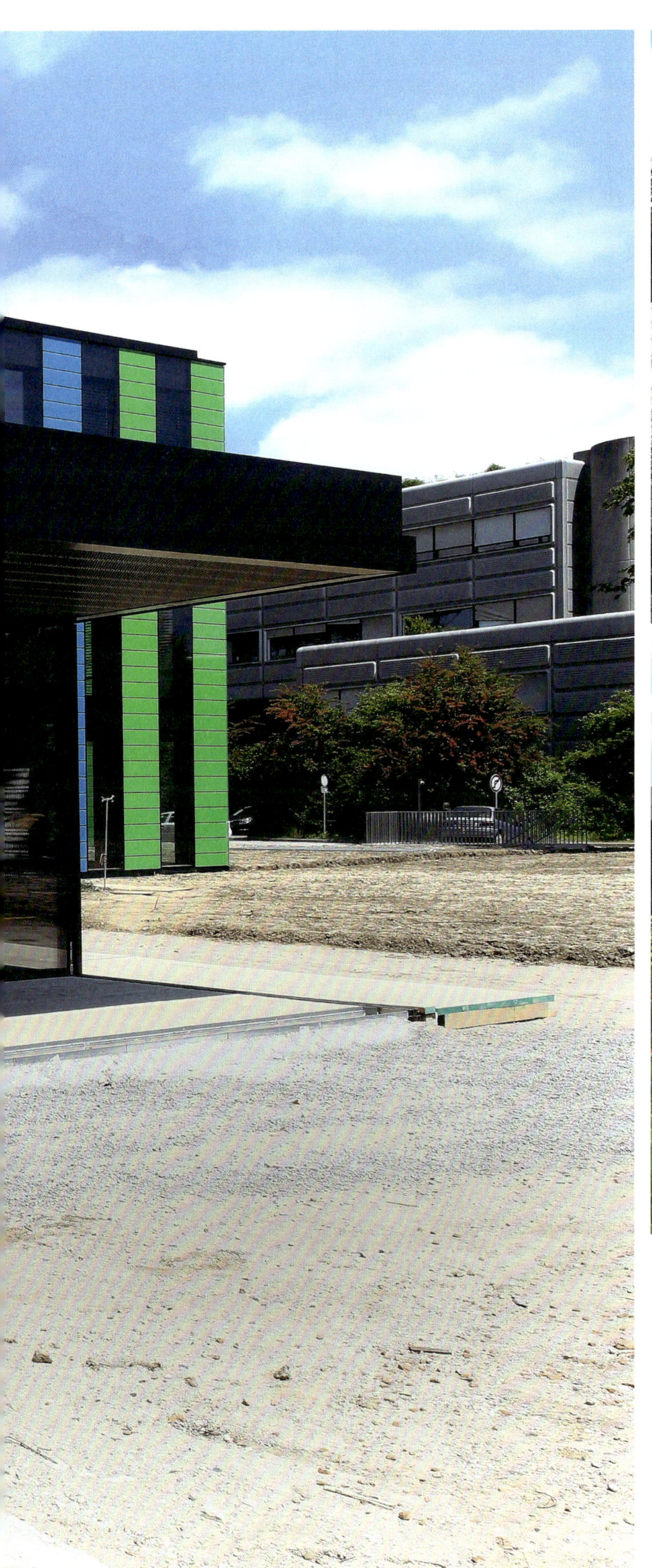

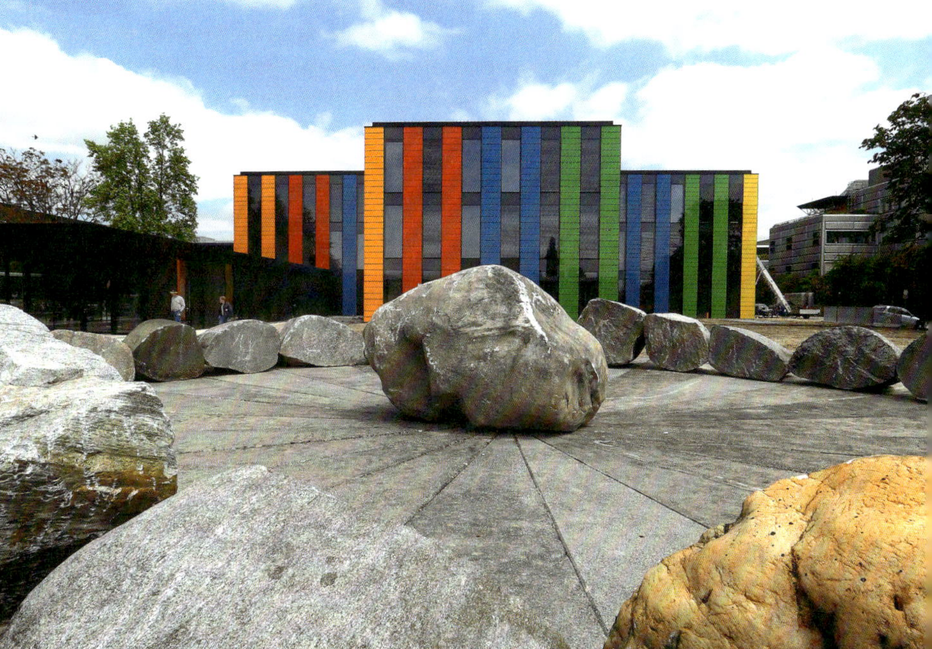

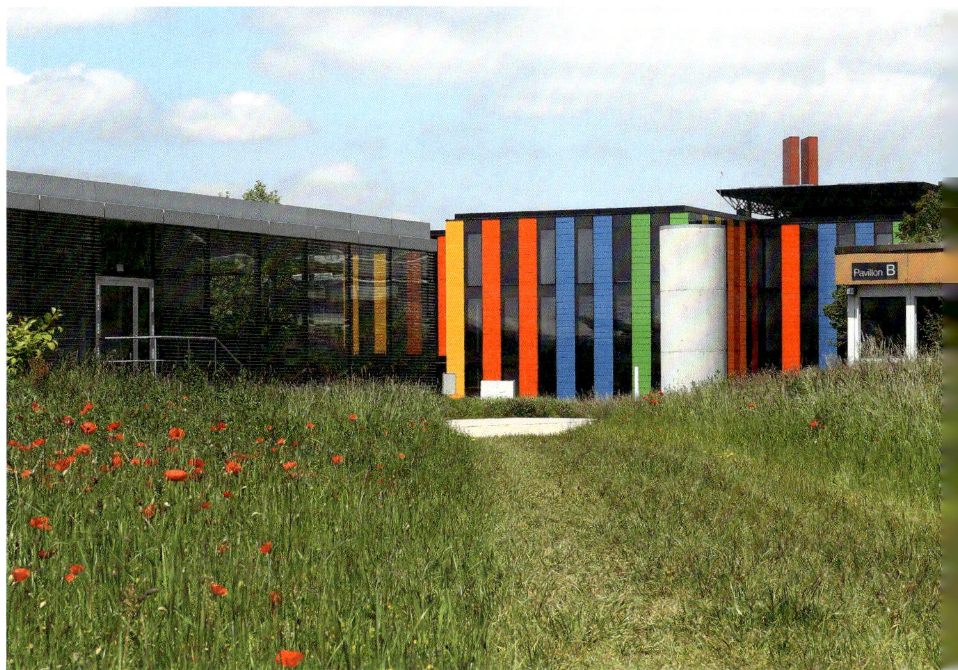

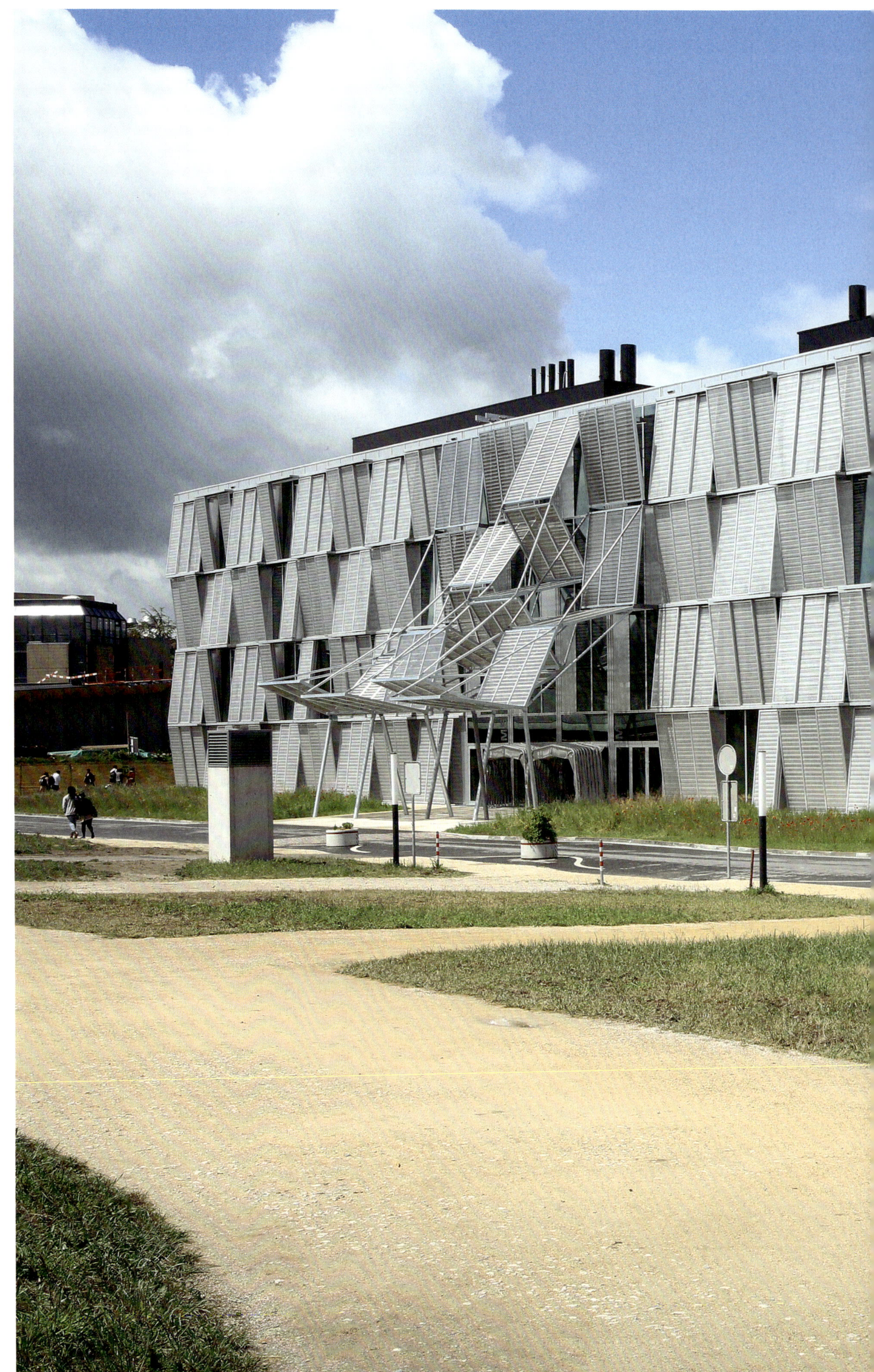

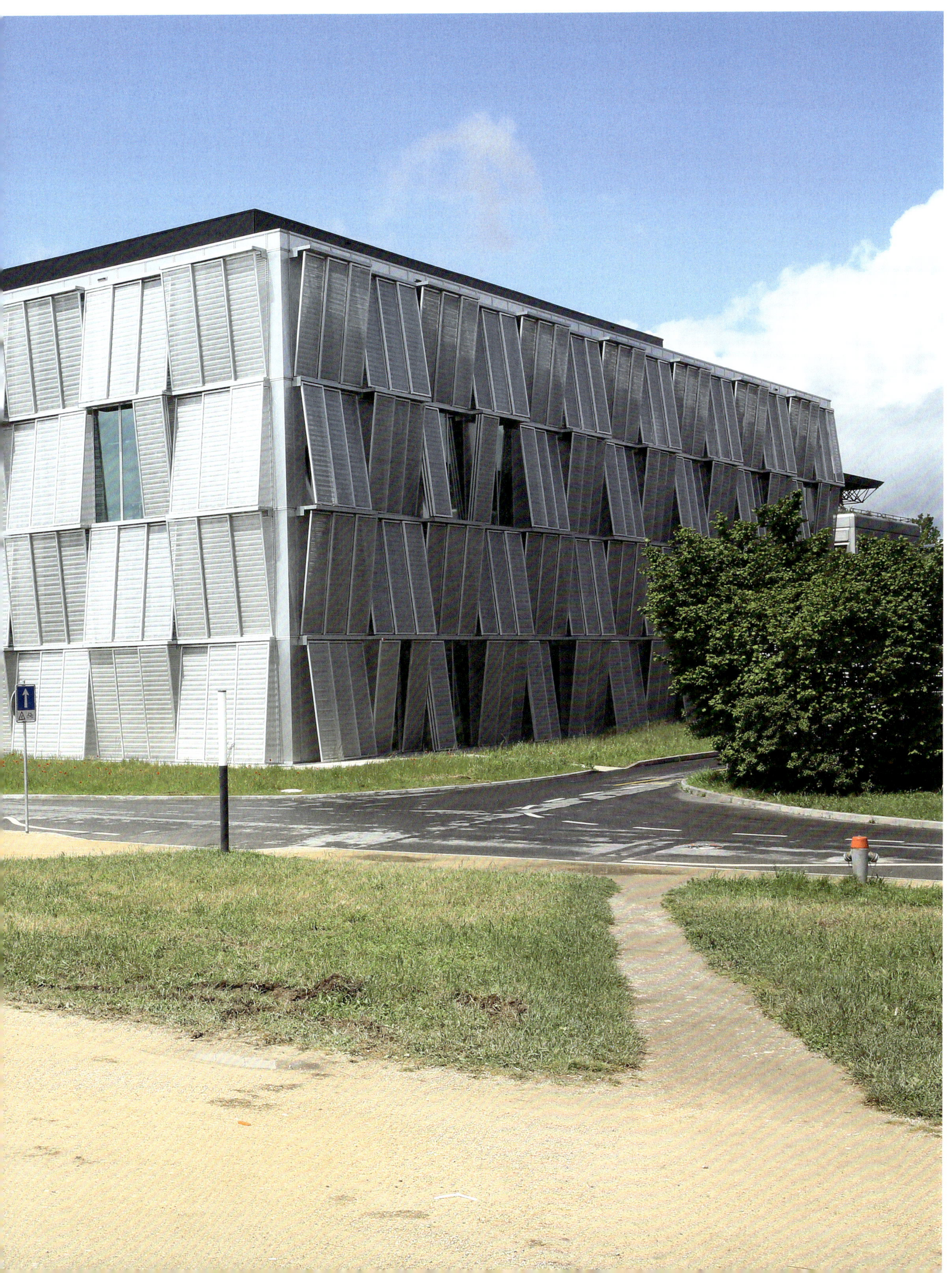

The Mechanics Hall (ME Building) with its distinctive, modular,
metal-mesh screen façade.

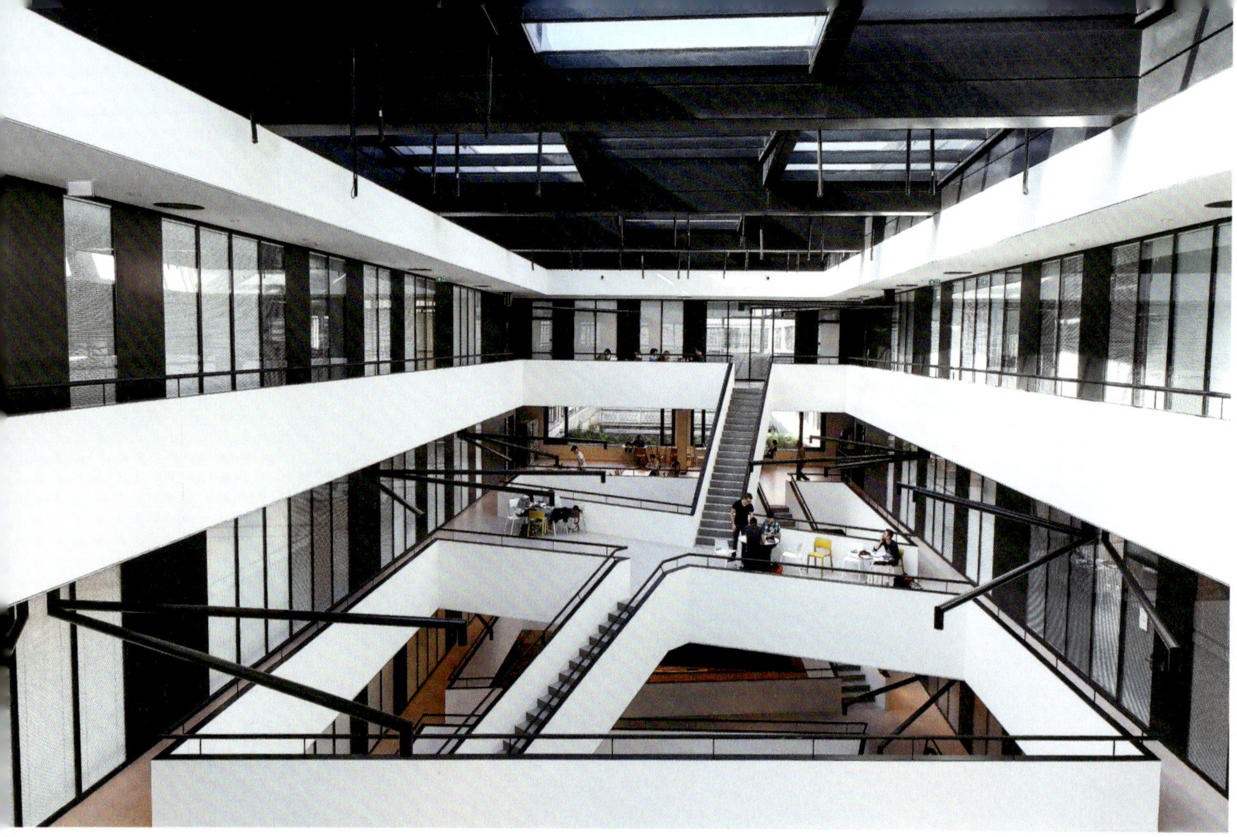

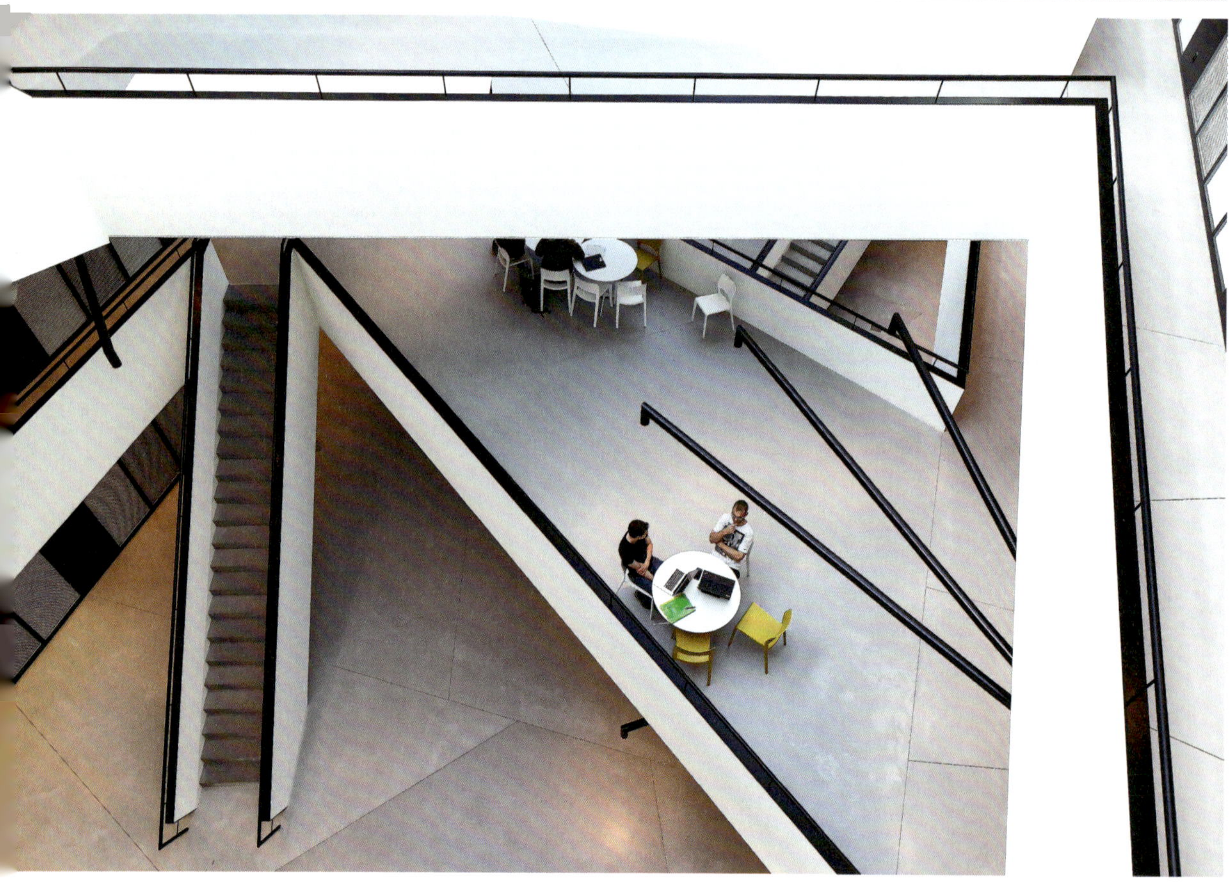

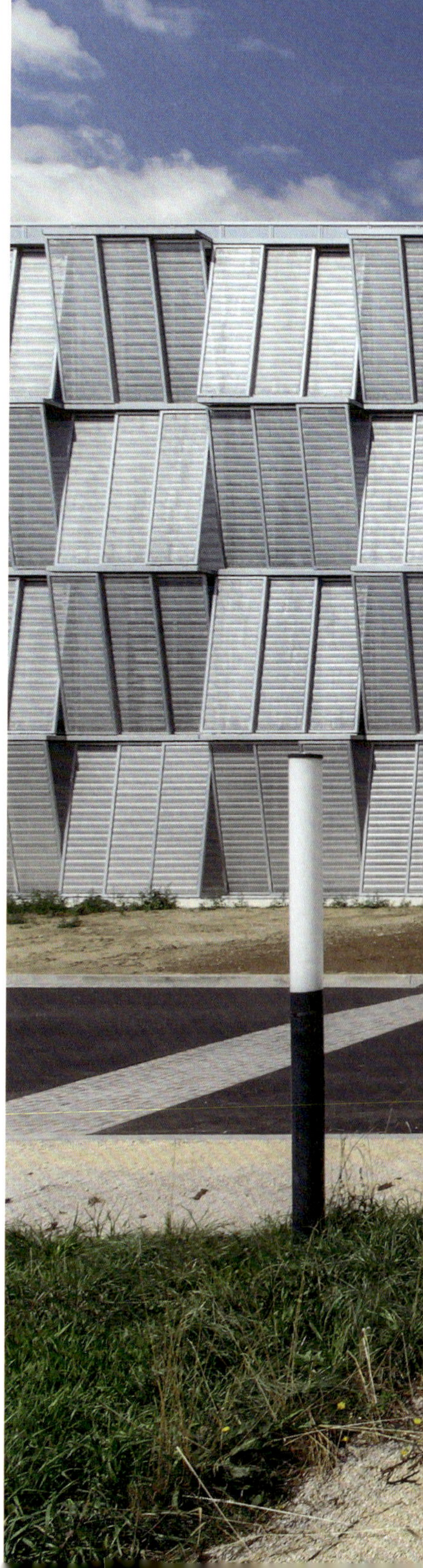

Perrault filled the ME Building with light by creating a generous central
atrium space (left). Below, the main entrance facing Place Cosandey.

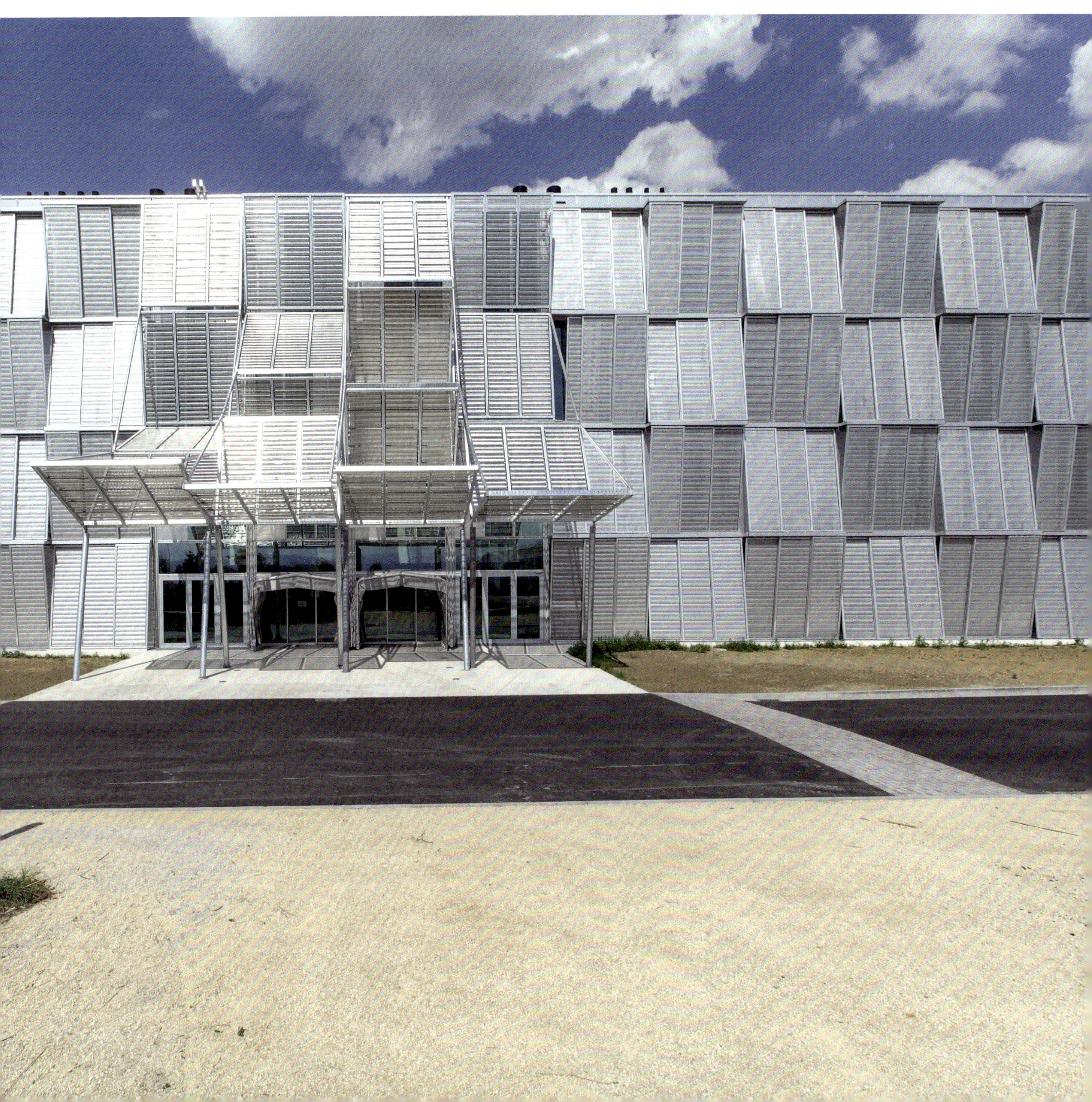

COMPARABLE UNIVERSITIES

Although there are many technically oriented universities in the world, some can more specifically be compared to EPFL, including the five selected here. Each of these universities presents a different profile, in terms of location, specialties, and the mix between technical subjects and the humanities. The presence here of very new universities in Hong Kong or Saudi Arabia testifies to the rise of such institutions on a global basis.

MASSACHUSETTS INSTITUTE OF TECHNOLOGY MIT

The Massachusetts Institute of Technology (MIT) is located in southeastern Cambridge, very close to Boston. Cambridge is also home to Harvard University, making it the American town with the greatest concentration of educational institutions at the highest international level. Founded in 1861, MIT was modeled on European polytechnic universities, and is best known for its physical science and engineering faculties. Economics and architecture have also assumed a significant role in the prestige of MIT, which counts a total of no fewer than ninety-one Nobel Laureates amongst its faculty, researchers, and graduates. It was number one in the world in the 2018 "QS World University Rankings."[1] The current MIT campus, which is linked by a complex system of passageways including the so-called Infinite Corridor (aligned in an east-west direction between buildings 8, 4, 10, 3, and 7), began to take form in 1916 with the completion of some of the first non-industrial reinforced-concrete buildings in the United States. Designed by the architect William Welles Bosworth, these structures have at their center the Great Dome of the Barker Engineering Library and Killian Court, where graduation ceremonies are held, facing the Charles River. Additional buildings on the MIT campus have been designed by major figures of contemporary architecture, including Alvar Aalto (Baker House, 1947); Eero Saarinen (MIT Chapel and Kresge Auditorium, 1955); I. M. Pei (Wiesner Building, 1985, and three other structures); Steven Holl (Simmons Hall, 2002); Frank O. Gehry (Stata Center, 2004); Charles Correa (Building 45, 2005); and Fumihiko Maki (Media Lab Extension, 2009). The California architect Michael Maltzan began work on a new student residence building in 2018, while Nader Tehrani (NADAAA) is working on a complex at Kendall Square. The MIT campus occupies an area of sixty-eight hectares but is set in an urban environment. A plan of the campus shows that it has grown by accretion and not according to any strictly orthogonal scheme. Between 1998 and 2010, MIT renovated more than 81,000 square meters of existing buildings and completed over 241,000 square meters of new construction. In 2017, MIT had an endowment of 14.8 billion dollars.[2]

UNIVERSITY OF CALIFORNIA, SANTA BARBARA UCSB

The University of California, Santa Barbara UCSB, is located near the town of Isla Vista in Southern California on a 414-hectare site adjoining the Pacific Ocean. In 2017–18, the total enrollment of the university included 21,574 undergraduate students and 2772 graduate students. The origin of the institution can be traced back to the Anna Blake School, founded in 1891 for training in "home economics and industrial arts." Renamed the Santa Barbara State Teachers College in 1921, the university initiated curricula in liberal arts, and again was renamed the Santa Barbara College of the University of California in 1944, and finally UC Santa Barbara in 1958. UCSB is thus a public university, and one of ten campuses that comprise the University of California system. Initially located in Santa Barbara itself, the university moved to Goleta, thirteen kilometers away on the site of a World War II Marine Air Base, in 1954, and remains there today. A number of the buildings on the campus were designed by the noted architect William Pereira (1909–85), including the Santa Rosa Hall Dormitory (1954) and the Hoffman Science Center (1959). A College of Letters and

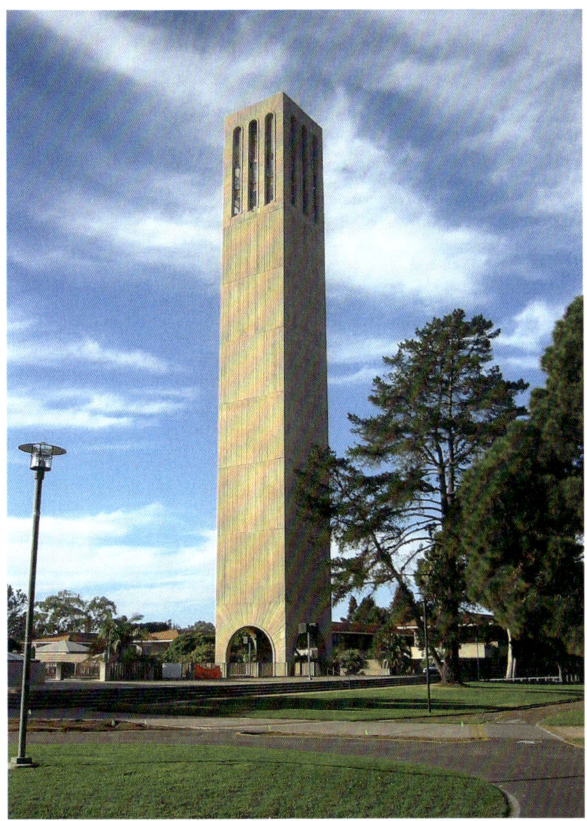

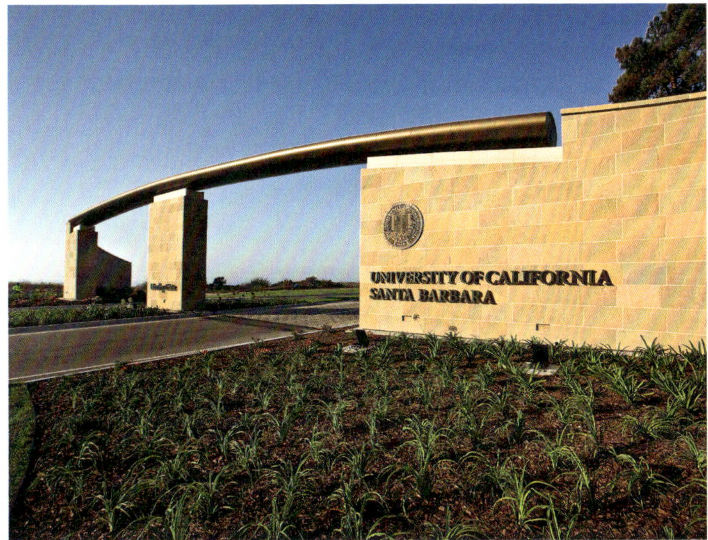

chemistry, physics, and economics. Shuji Nakamura, a professor at the UCSB Materials Department of the College of Engineering, invented the blue LED, considered a major breakthrough in lighting technology and was awarded the 2014 Nobel Prize in Physics.

The UCSB campus is divided into four parts. The Main or East Campus covers an area of 287 hectares and is the site of much of the undergraduate housing and the academic buildings. The UCSB Library, located near the center of the complex on the East Campus, was renovated and extended in 2016, and is the largest public research library in the United States after the Library of Congress. Quadrangles are placed on either side of the Library. The other areas of the university are the Storke Campus including Storke Tower and Plaza, with its fifty-three-meter-high bell tower, and the West and North campuses. These university areas are arrayed around three sides of the town of Isla Vista. A large lagoon at the southern part of the campus is close to the ocean, and has a Marine Biotechnology Laboratory nearby. UCSB has three separate colleges: the College of Letters and Science, which trains professionals in humanities, fine arts, mathematics, and social sciences; the College of Engineering, which focuses on interdisciplinary research on biomolecular and computation science and engineering; and the College of Creative Studies, which is intended to stimulate the creation of original work in music and literature.[3] The university was listed as forty-eighth worldwide in the 2016–17 *Times Higher Education* "World University Rankings."

UNIVERSITY OF CAPE TOWN
UCT

Much like UCSB, the University of Cape Town is a public research university. It has six faculties, devoted to Science, the Health Sciences, Commerce, Engineering, Humanities, Law, and the Built Environment. The university also has a multidisciplinary Center for Higher Education Development. The University of Cape Town was founded in 1829 as the South African College, a high school for boys. It developed into a university between 1880 and 1900 with a rise in affluence due to the discovery of gold and diamonds in the north of the country and the creation of studies in minerology and geology. Between 1902 and 1918, the institution created its Medical School, and introduced engineering courses and a Department of Education. UCT was formally established as a university in 1918, and, in 1928, the institution moved to its present site.

The main area of UCT, called the Upper Campus, is located on the slopes of Devil's Peak, in the mountainous landscape behind the South African city, on land of the Rhodes Estate, named after Cecil Rhodes. A statue of the founder of De Beers Consolidated Mines (1888) and prime minister of the Cape

Science as well as the School of Engineering were created on the campus in 1961. Although it maintained strong credentials in the humanities, UCSB has developed into a "very high activity" research university with twelve national research centers, including the Kavli Institute for Theoretical Physics. In 1969, UCSB became one of the four first nodes of ARPANET together with UCLA, Stanford, and the University of Utah. ARPANET (Advanced Research Projects Administration), initially funded by the US Department of Defense, was the precursor of Internet. Today, the faculty of the university includes six Nobel Prize winners in

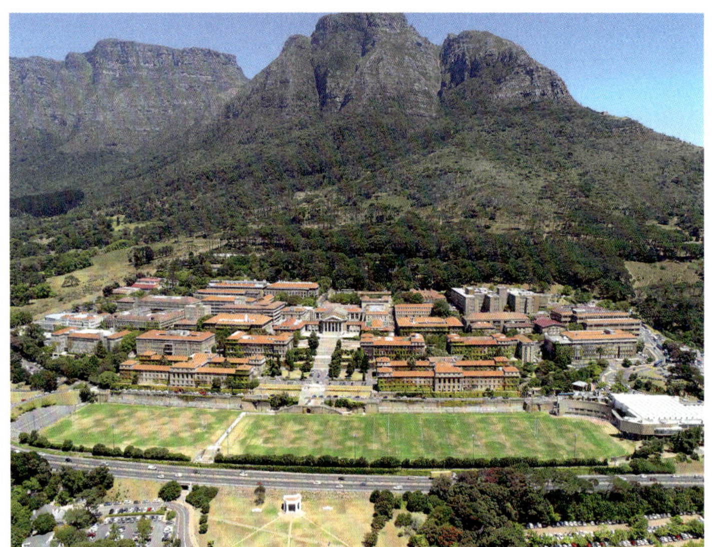

UCT counts five Nobel Laureates amongst its graduates, including Ralph Bunch, the American political scientist and diplomat who won the 1950 Nobel Peace Prize, Aaron Klug winner of the Chemistry Prize (1982), Allan McLeod Cormack, who worked on X-ray computed tomography (1979 Medicine Prize), and J. M. Coetzee, who was a Distinguished Professor of Literature at UCT (1999–2001), and received the 2003 Literature award. The noted heart surgeon Christiaan Barnard (1922–2001), who performed the first heart transplant in 1967, was a graduate of UCT. The fields concerned and these individuals are indicative of the broad interdisciplinary nature of UCT. With 26,357 students in 2014, UCT has the highest international rankings of any African university. It was classed 191st in the 2018 "QS World University Rankings" and 171st in the 2018 *Times Higher Education* "World University Rankings."

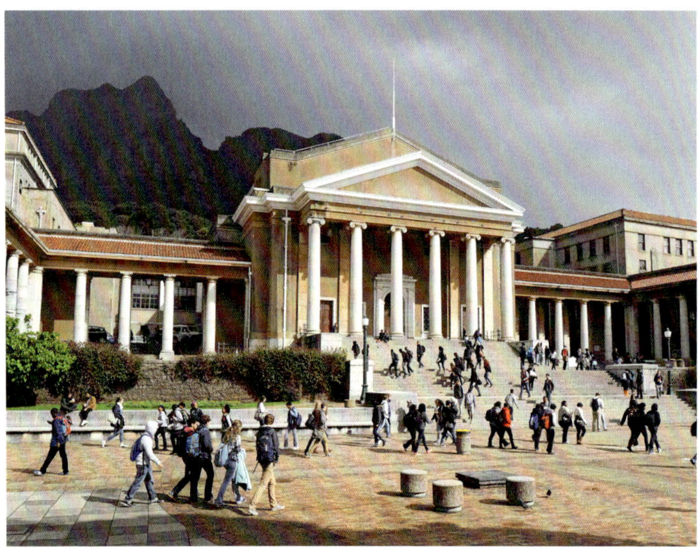

HONG KONG UNIVERSITY OF SCIENCE AND TECHNOLOGY HKUST

Founded in 1991, the Hong Kong University of Science and Technology HKUST currently has about 4800 graduate students and 9300 undergraduates. It has thirteen research institutes, and fifty-four research centers. Its main schools are focused on engineering, science, business and management, and humanities and social science. It was ranked second in the *Times Higher Education* "World University, Young University Rankings" (after EPFL), and has consistently been identified as one of the top young Asian universities. As the institution describes itself, it is "a university that promotes interdisciplinary studies dedicated to educating well-rounded students with a strong

Colony (1890–96) was removed from the campus in 2015 under student pressure. The original buildings of the university were built between 1928 and 1930 and were designed earlier by the architect Joseph Michel Solomon (1886–1926). His vision for the University of Cape Town tended toward classical simplicity: "The center of the composition would be a hall, pillared and domed, the buildings would be large, bold and symmetrical—detail, intricacy, fine effects of light and shade would stand no chance on the foothills of the towering Devil's Peak—the atmosphere would be Mediterranean."[4] The Engineering, Science, Commerce, and Humanities faculties are near the Chancellor Oppenheimer Library, which faces Jammie Plaza along a defined central axis. The Hiddingh Campus is separated from the Upper Campus by sports fields and a large road.

Even as it established itself as a leading research and teaching university, UCT came to be called "Moscow on the Hill" because of its opposition to apartheid between 1960 and 1990. By 2004, about half of UCT's 20,000 students were black.

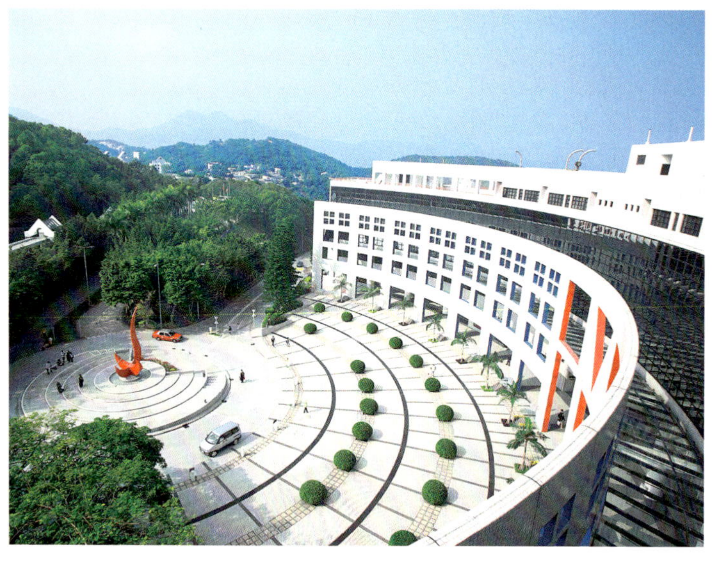

entrcpreneurial spirit and innovative thinking; a university with an Institute for Advanced Study which seeks to become a global premier knowledge hub and incubator of top scientific leaders."[5] It is one of eight "statutory universities" in Hong Kong and is located on a sixty-hectare site in the New Territories of Hong Kong on the northern part of the Clear Water Bay Peninsula, to the east of the city. Set on a sloped site, the university has a central Academic Building with ten lecture halls, classrooms, laboratories, and offices. The Lee Shau Kee Library, at the center of the campus, is a five-floor, 12,000-square-meter facility, with seating for over 3600 students. Its collection includes over 700,000 printed volumes, nearly 350,000 electronic books, and over 50,000 print and electronic periodical titles. Recent additions to the campus include the 18,000-square-meter, eight-story Cheng Yu Tung Building, which connects to the southern end of the existing Main Academic Building and the Enterprise Center (Ronald Lu & Partners). Inaugurated in 2016, it houses an extensive range of teaching and research facilities, including the State Key Laboratory on Advanced Displays and Optoelectronics Technologies, the Robotics Institute, and the WHAT LAB— a laboratory jointly established by HKUST and WeChat and devoted to the study of artificial intelligence.

KING ABDULLAH UNIVERSITY OF SCIENCE AND TECHNOLOGY KAUST

Located on a 1400-hectare campus in Thuwal, Saudi Arabia, 126 kilometers north of Jeddah on the Red Sea, the design and construction of the King Abdullah University of Science and Technology KAUST was initiated in 2006 and completed in just thirty months (2009). The twenty-seven separate buildings with an area of 511,000 square meters were designed by HOK for a community of 25,000 residents and the goal of creating Saudi Arabia's first LEED certified project and the world's largest LEED Platinum complex. The sustainable credentials of KAUST were part of the scheme from the outset in an institute dedicated to the advancement of science and technology. Although the design is modern, it draws on the traditional architecture of Saudi Arabia to reduce energy needs. The overall design is based on traditional Arab cities, minimizing the exterior surfaces that are exposed to the sun, reducing walking distances, and making use of natural light and ventilation. University materials state: "KAUST is committed to innovation in sustainable development and increasing global public awareness about these important issues. The university acts as a living laboratory, demonstrating that environmentally responsible methods of energy use, materials management, and water consumption are viable in the region."[6] The campus has ten research centers that focus on "finding solutions to problems in areas related to water, food, energy, and the environment." The

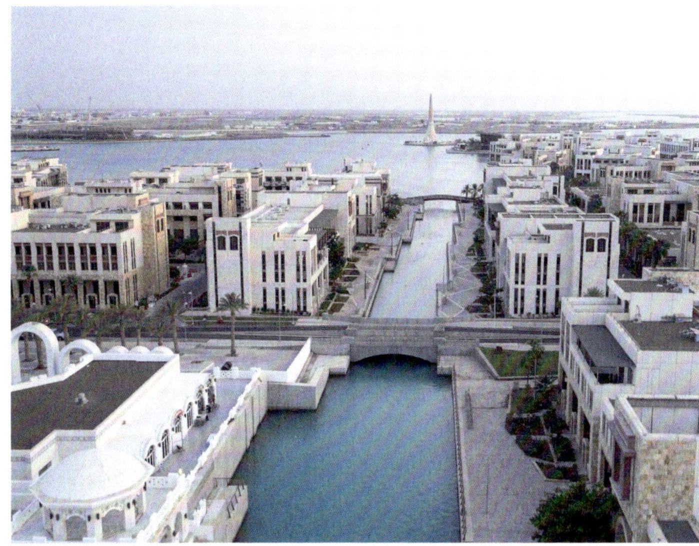

degree programs offered include Environmental Science and Engineering, Marine Science, Plant Science, Applied Mathematics and Computational Sciences, Computer Science, Electrical Engineering, Chemical and Biological Engineering, Chemical Science, Earth Science and Engineering, Material Science and Engineering, and Mechanical Engineering. The campus includes a marine sanctuary, a museum, and research facilities, such as a Supercomputing Core Lab and a Nanofabrication facility, serving a student body of 940 (2016) which has included people of sixty different nationalities. The late King Abdullah bin Abdulaziz Al Saud stated: "Our Intention is to create an enduring model for advanced education and scientific research."

1   At https://www.topuniversities.com/university-rankings/ world-university-rankings/2018 (accessed on March 19, 2018).
2   At http://news.mit.edu/2017/endowment-figures-2017-0908 (accessed on March 19, 2018).
3   At https://www.timeshighereducation.com/world-university-rankings/university-california-santa-barbara#ranking-dataset/589595%20accessed%20on%20March%2020 (accessed on March 20, 2018).
4   At https://www.artefacts.co.za/main/Buildings/ archframes.php?archid=1596 (accessed on March 20, 2018).
5   At http://www.ust.hk/wp-content/uploads/2017/10/ 20170916_HKUST_Folded-Brochure_master_r14_EN.pdf (accessed on March 21, 2018).
6   At https://www.kaust.edu.sa/en/about/green-campus (accessed on March 22, 2018).

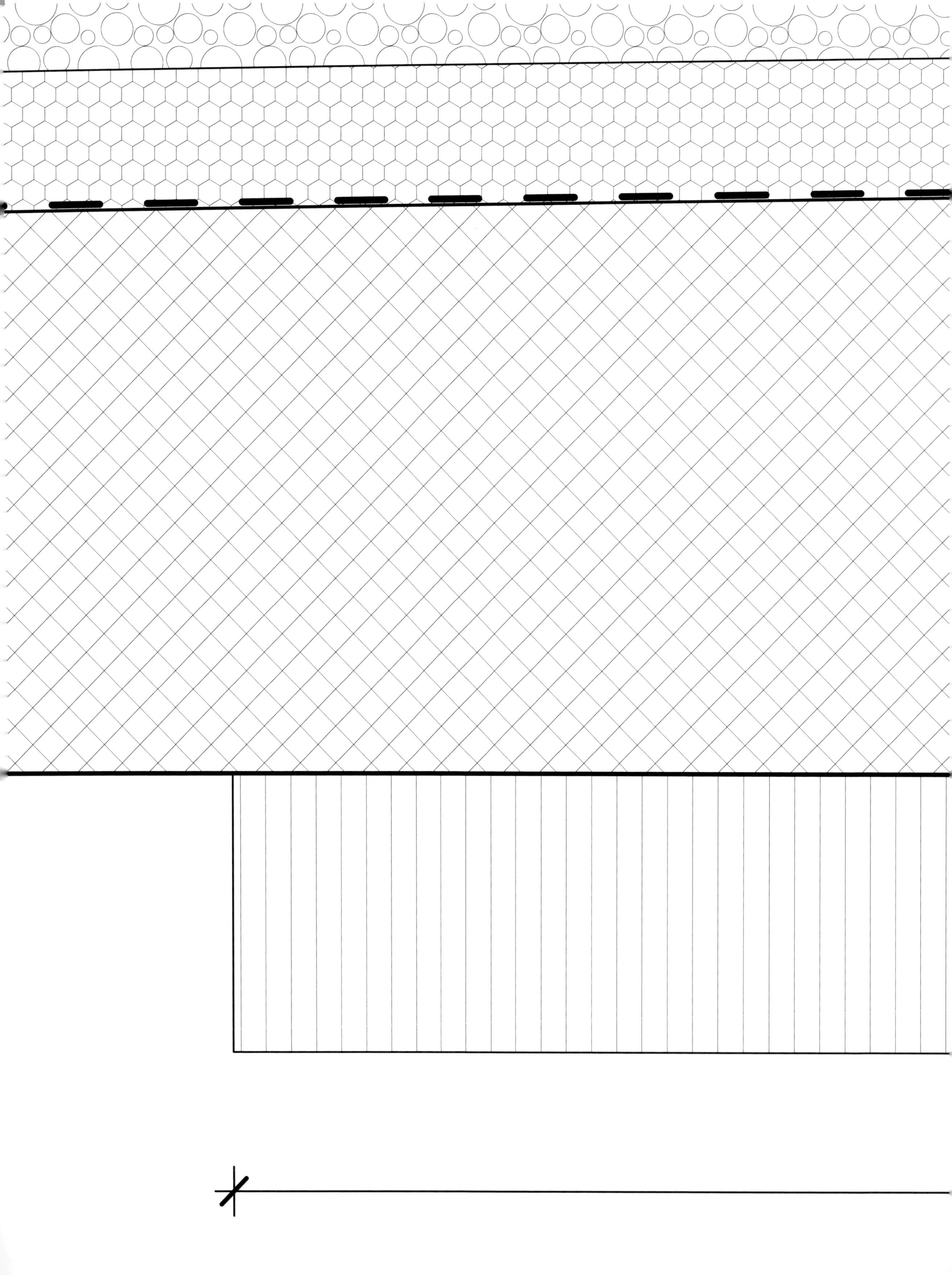

ARTLAB

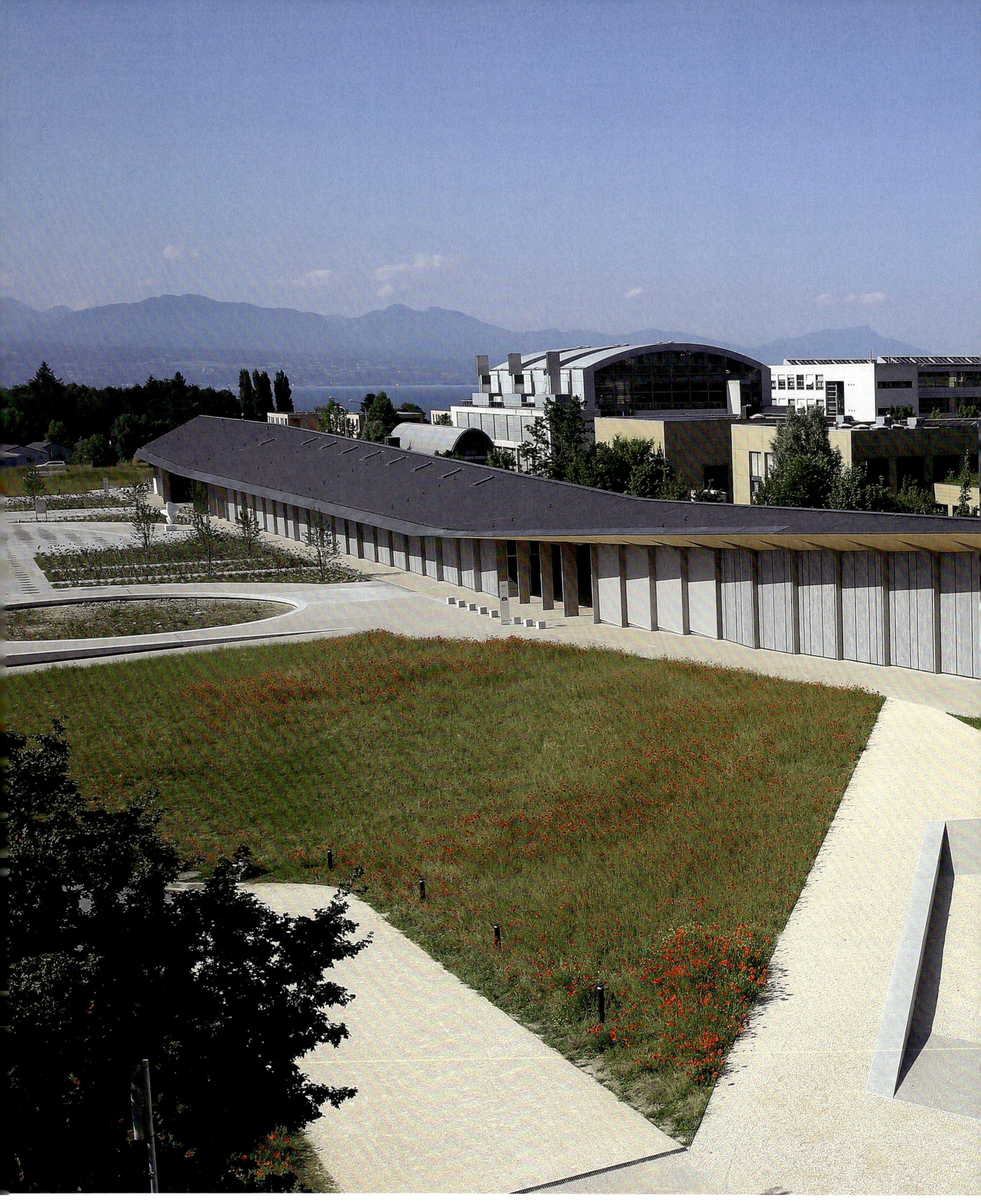

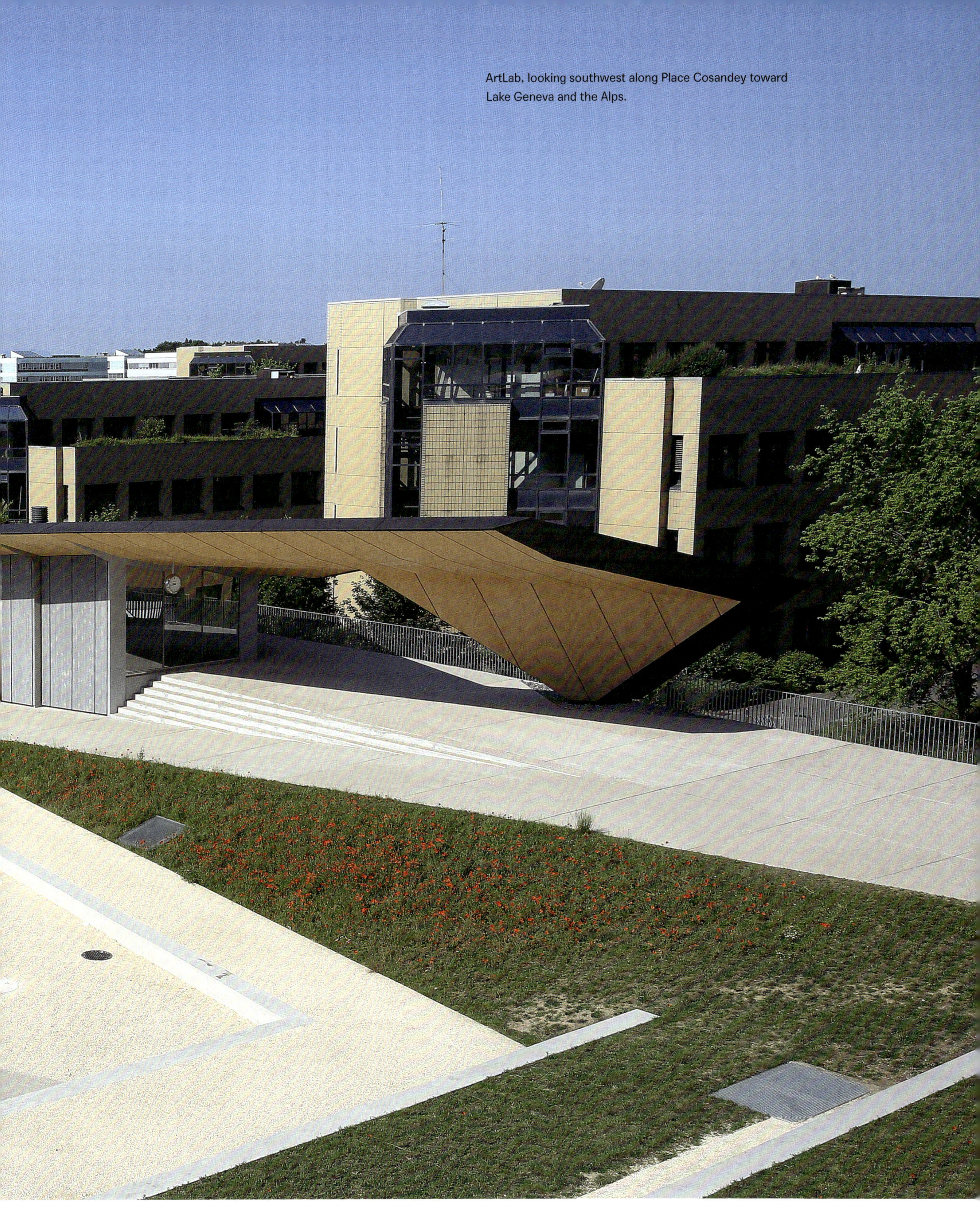

ArtLab, looking southwest along Place Cosandey toward
Lake Geneva and the Alps.

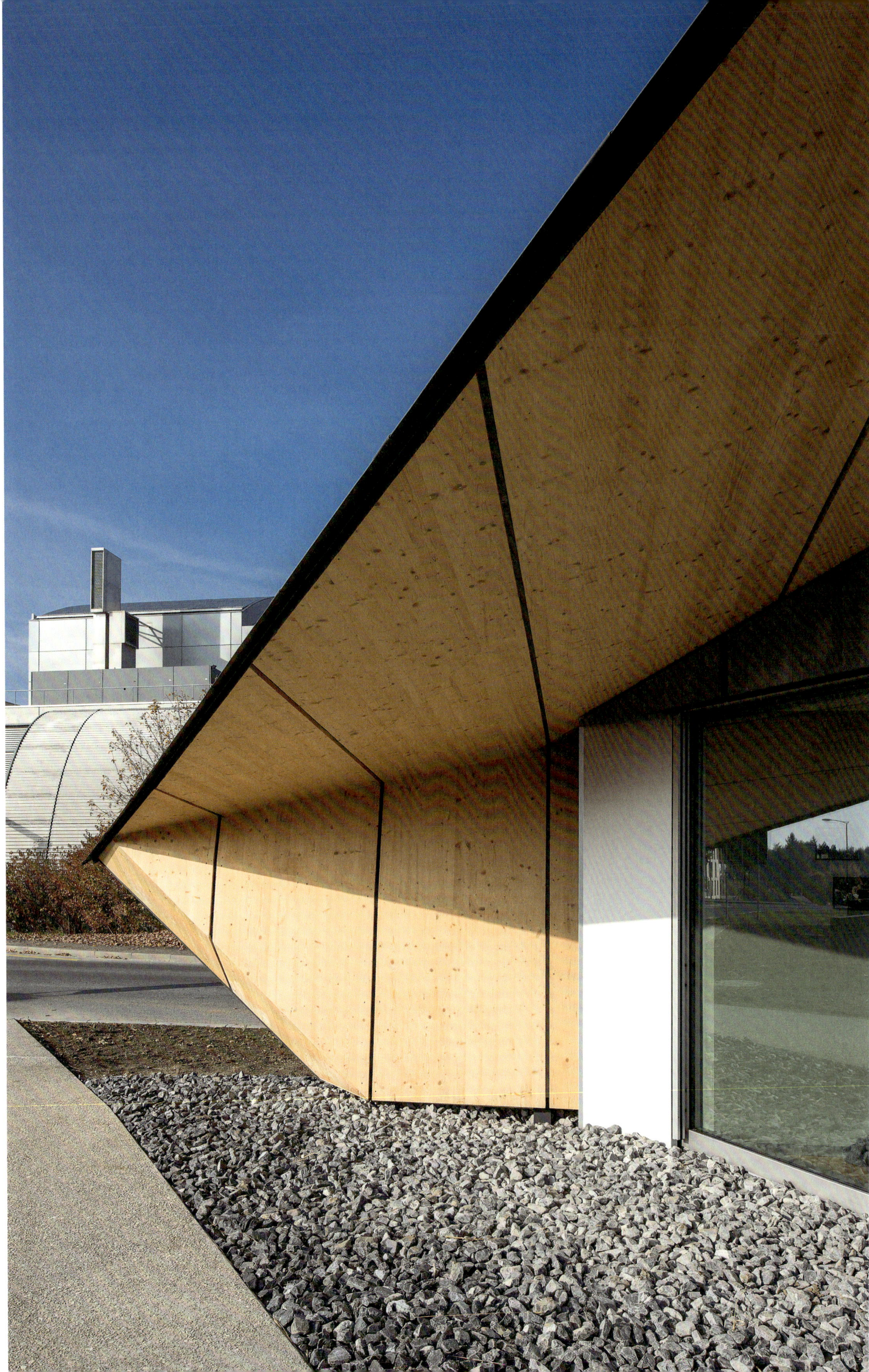

Left, the southern end of ArtLab near the Montreux Jazz Café and, below, the northern end close the center of the EPFL campus.

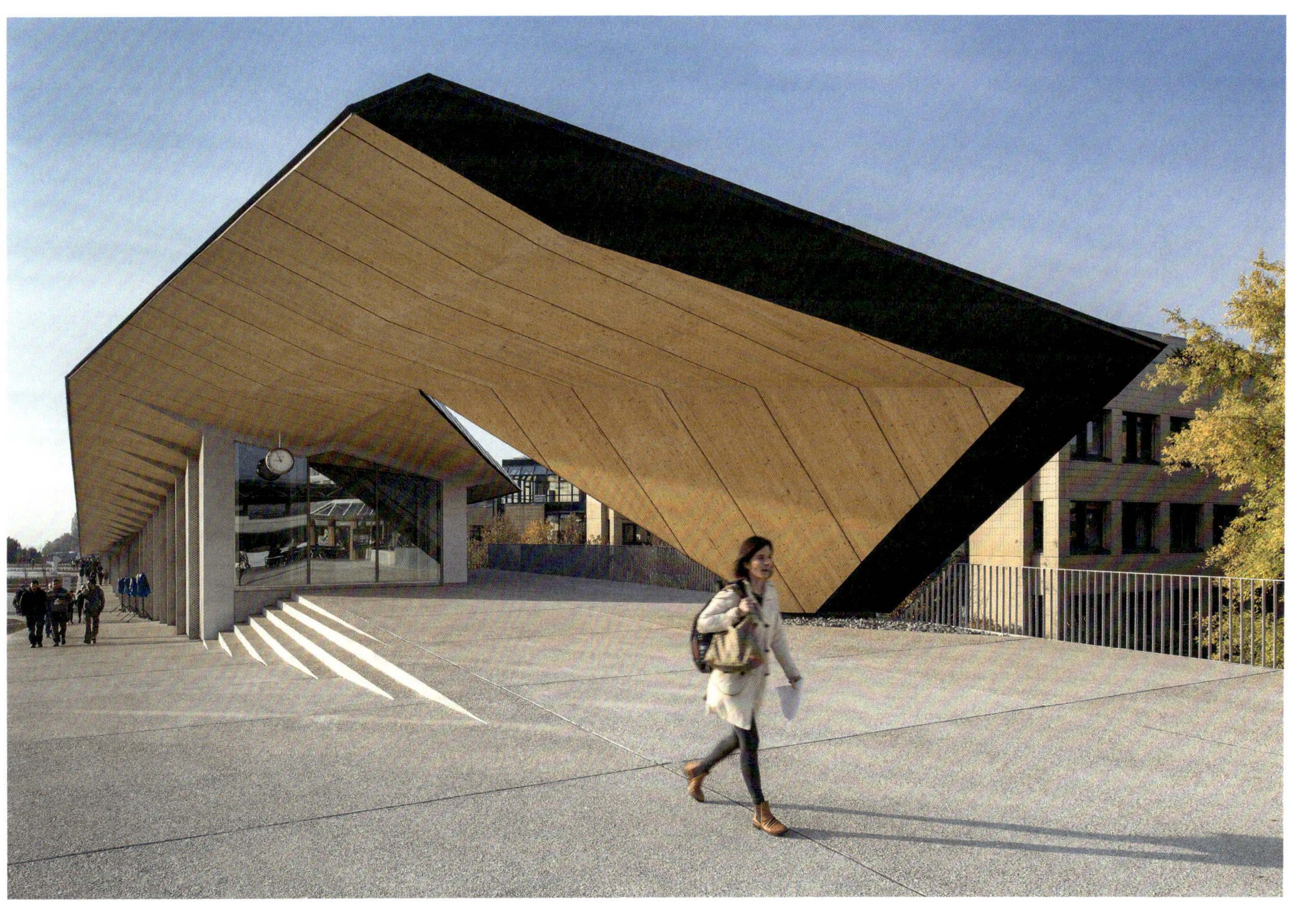

The northern entrance to ArtLab is its highest point and one of the most distinctive details of the architecture of Kengo Kuma.

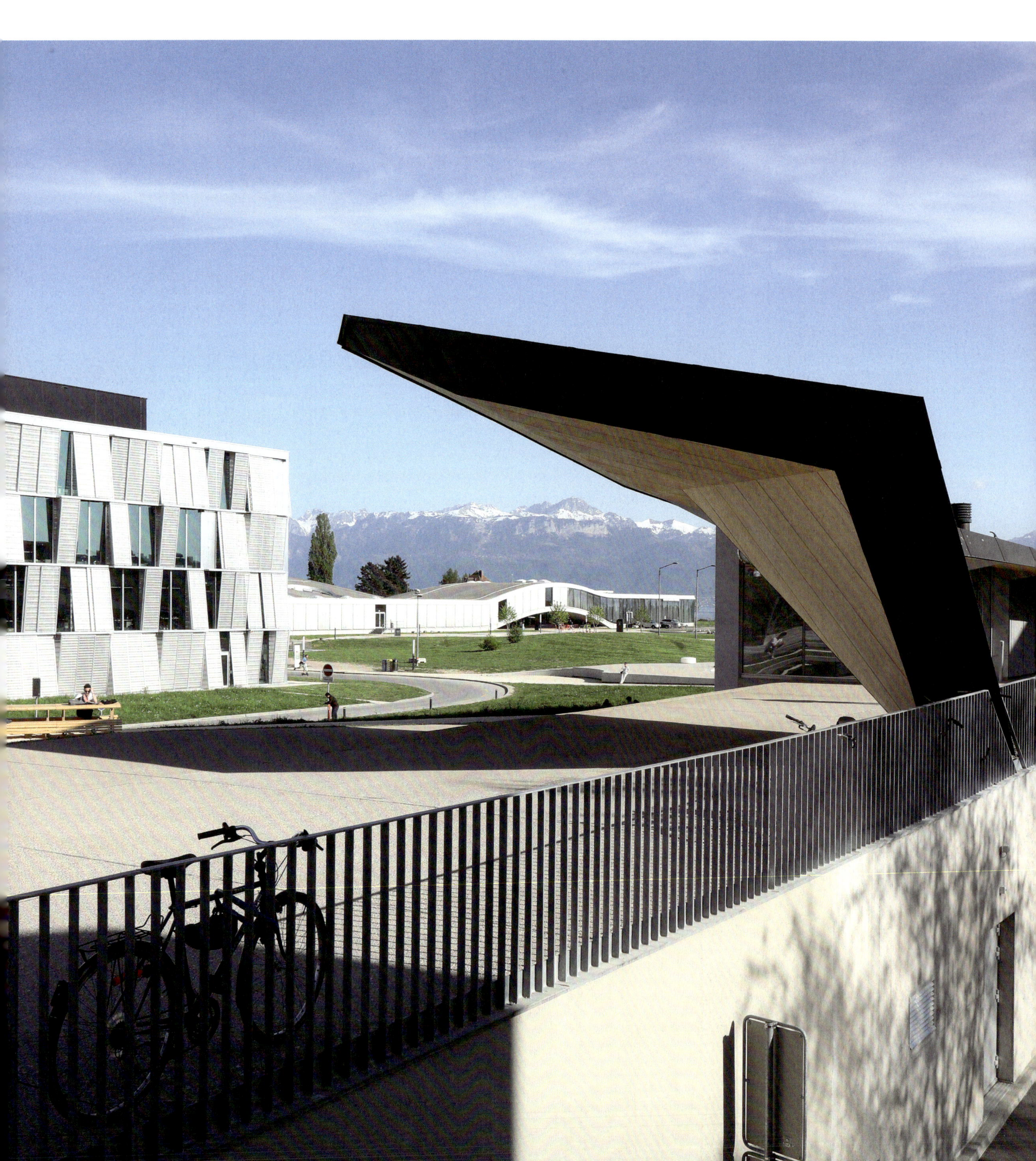

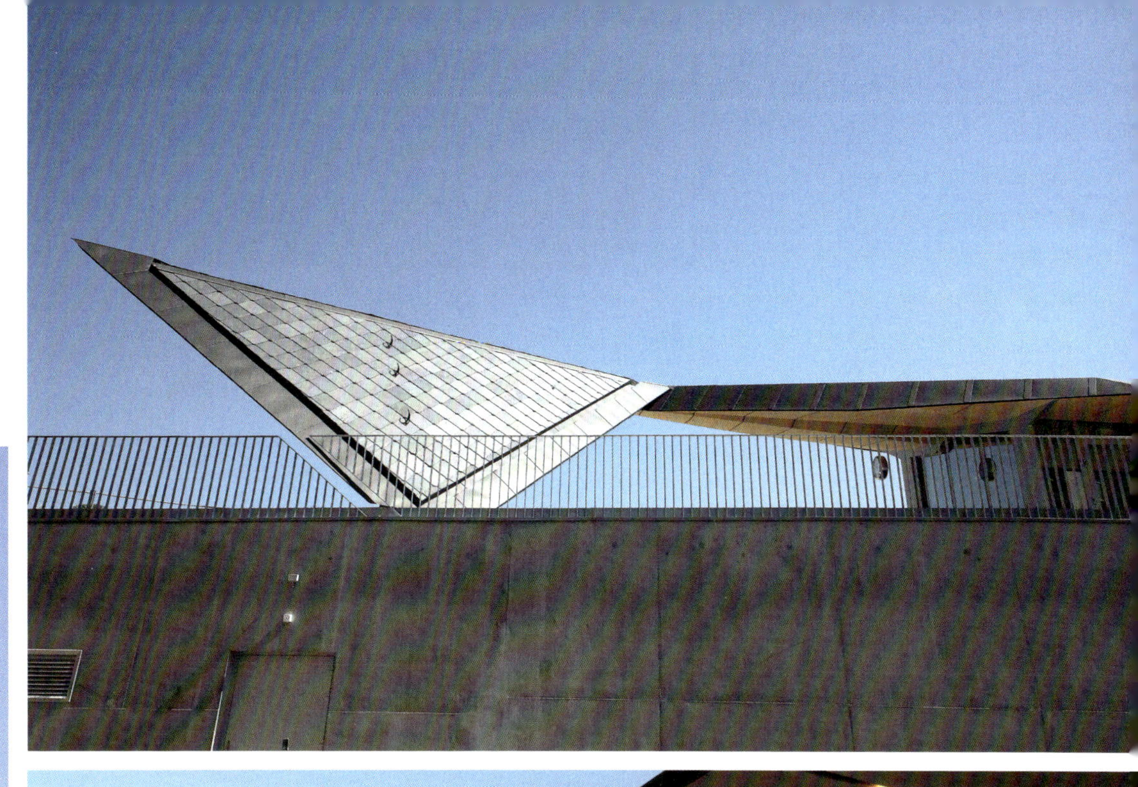

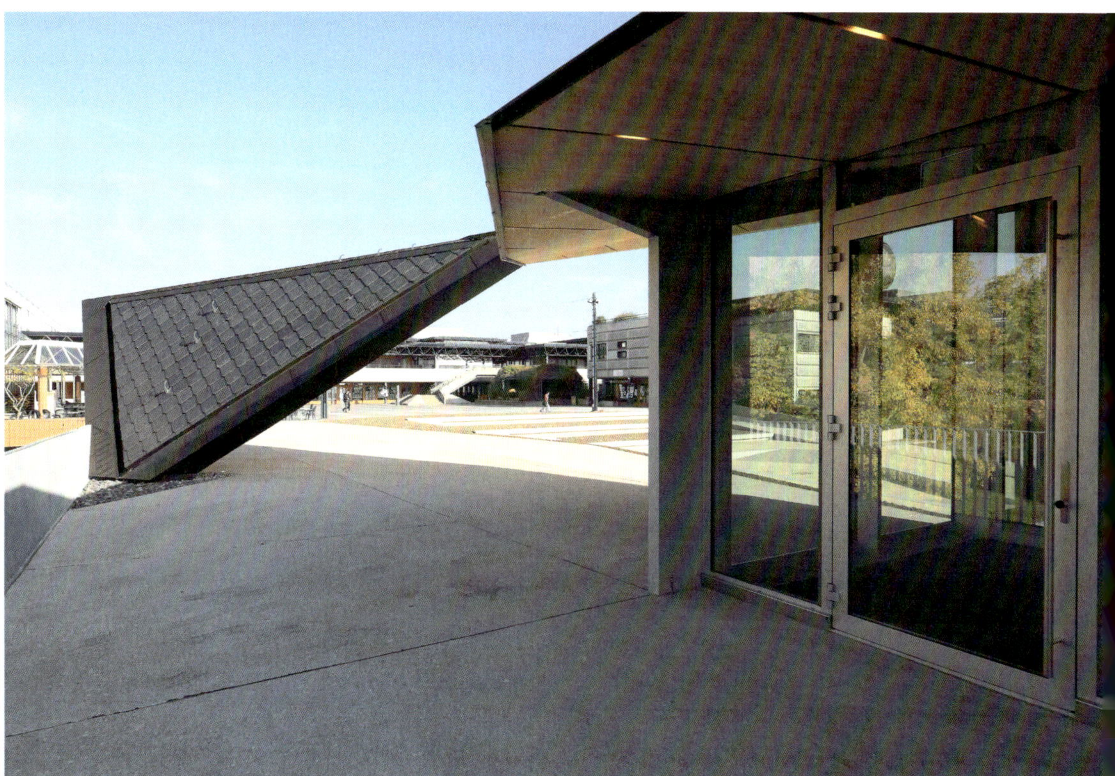

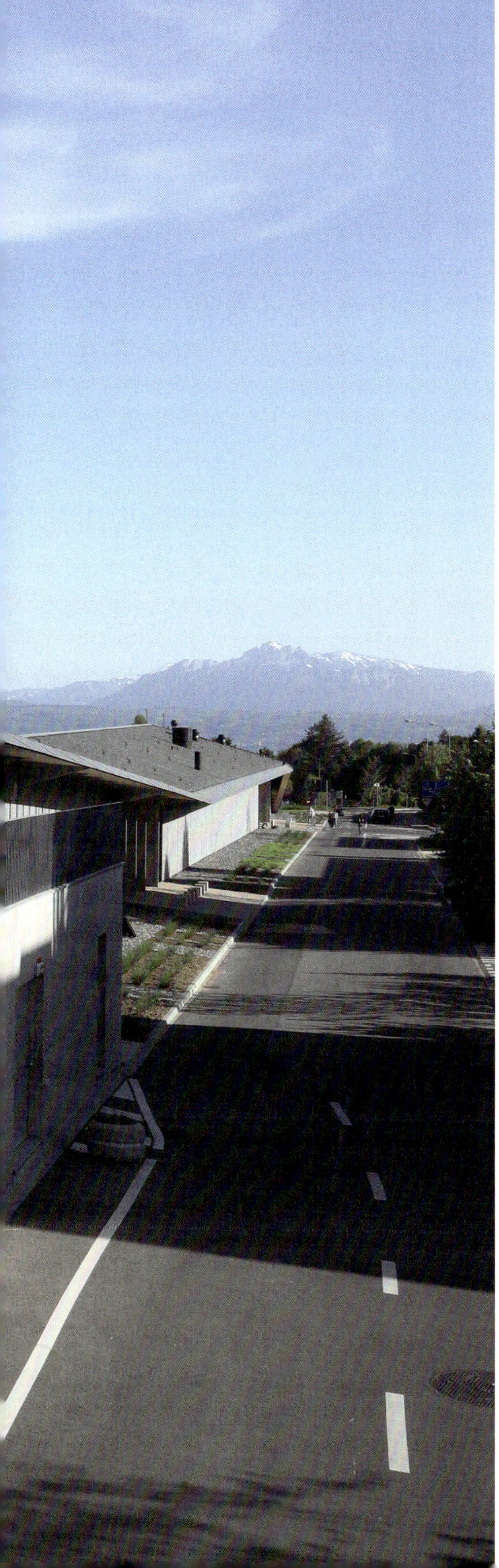

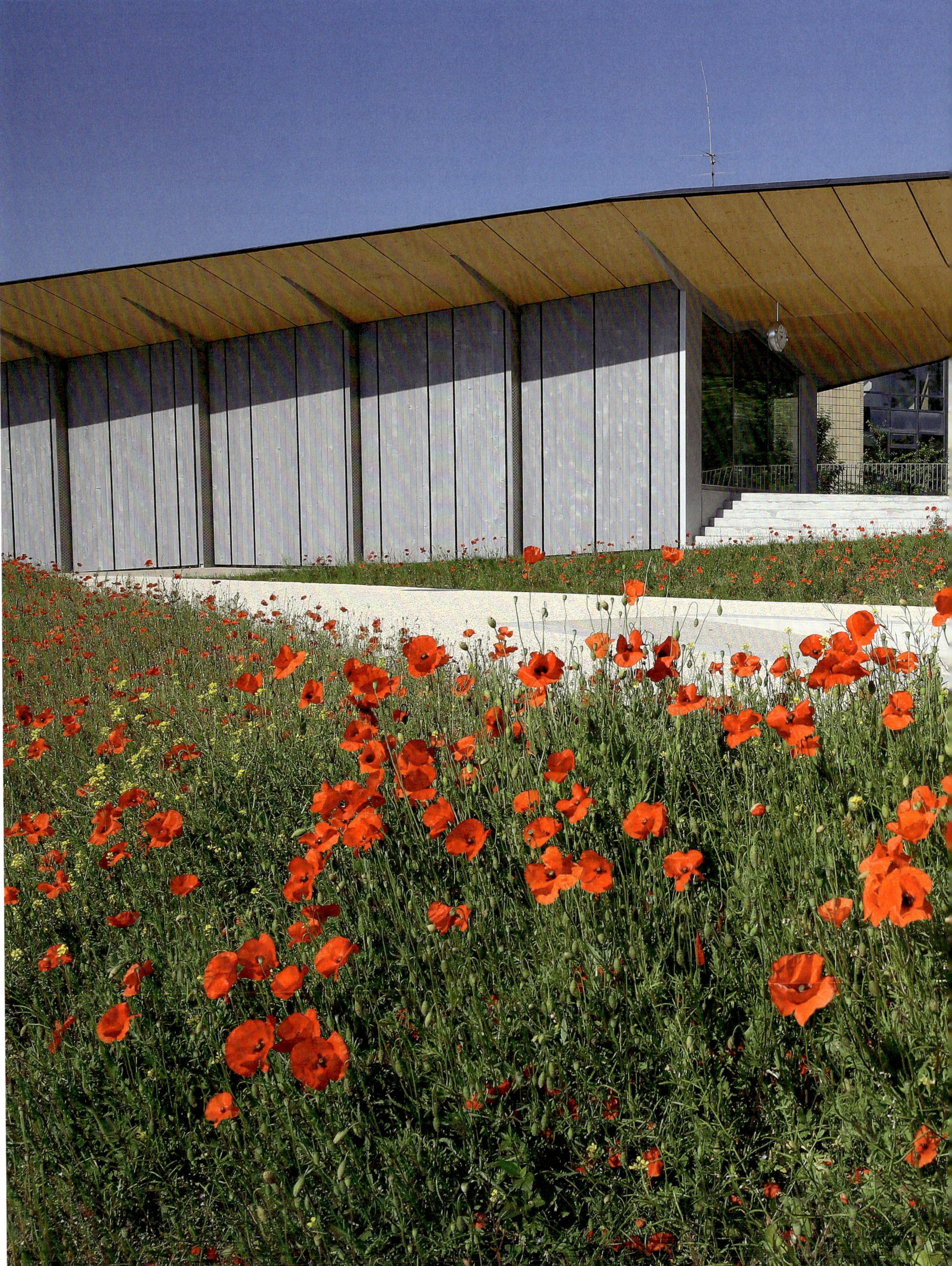

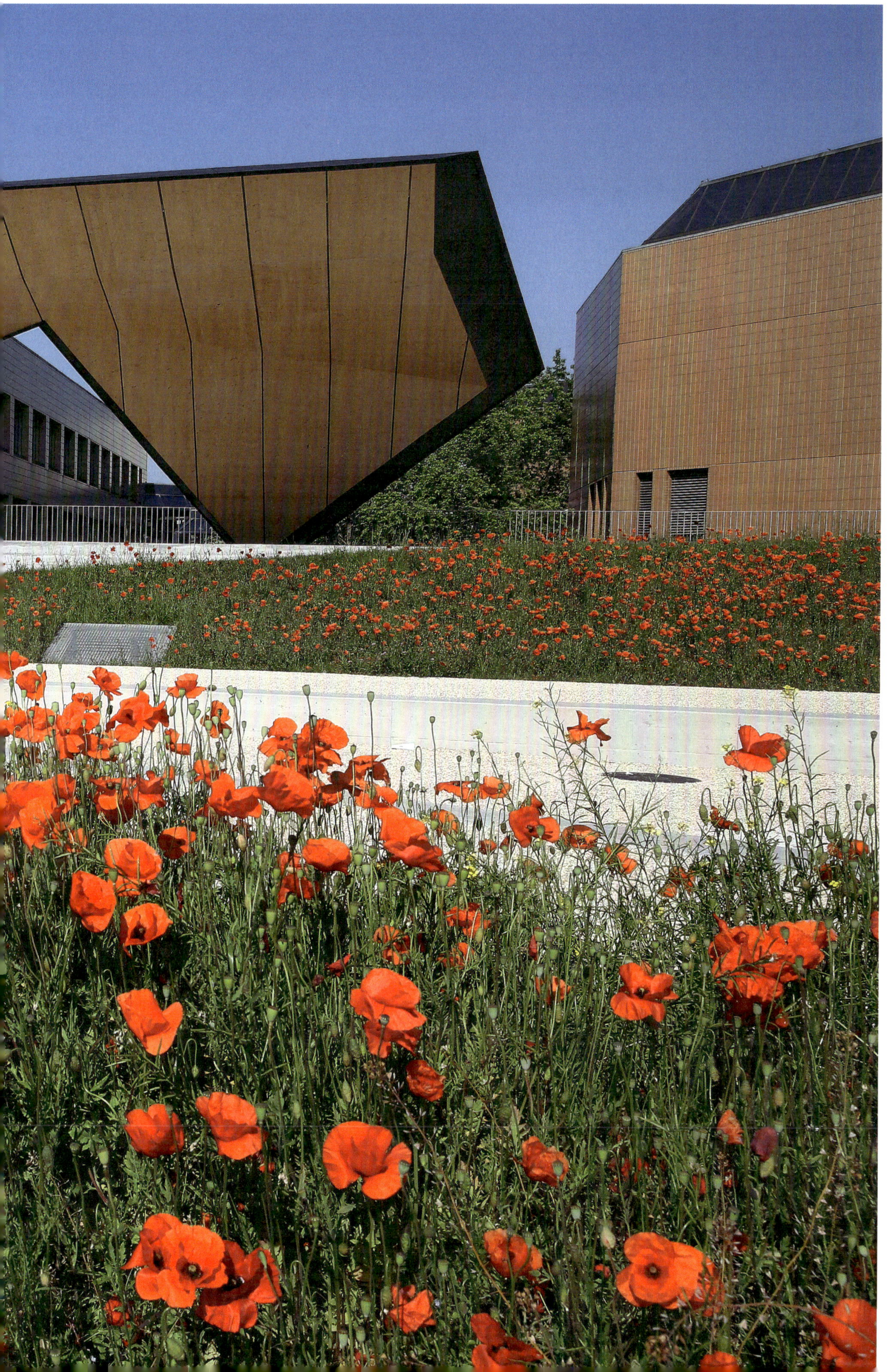

The northern end of ArtLab as seen from the upper part of Place Cosandey.

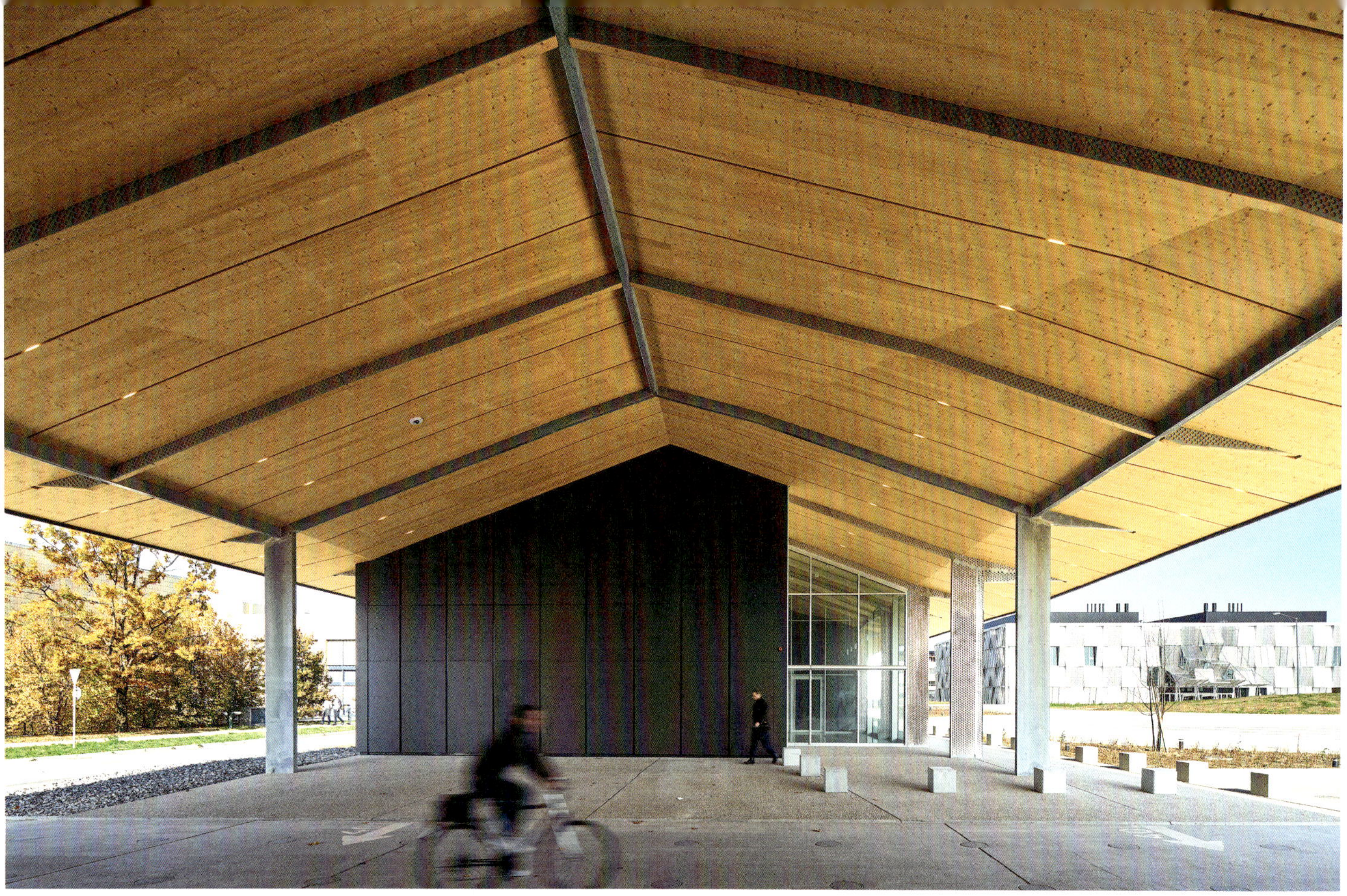

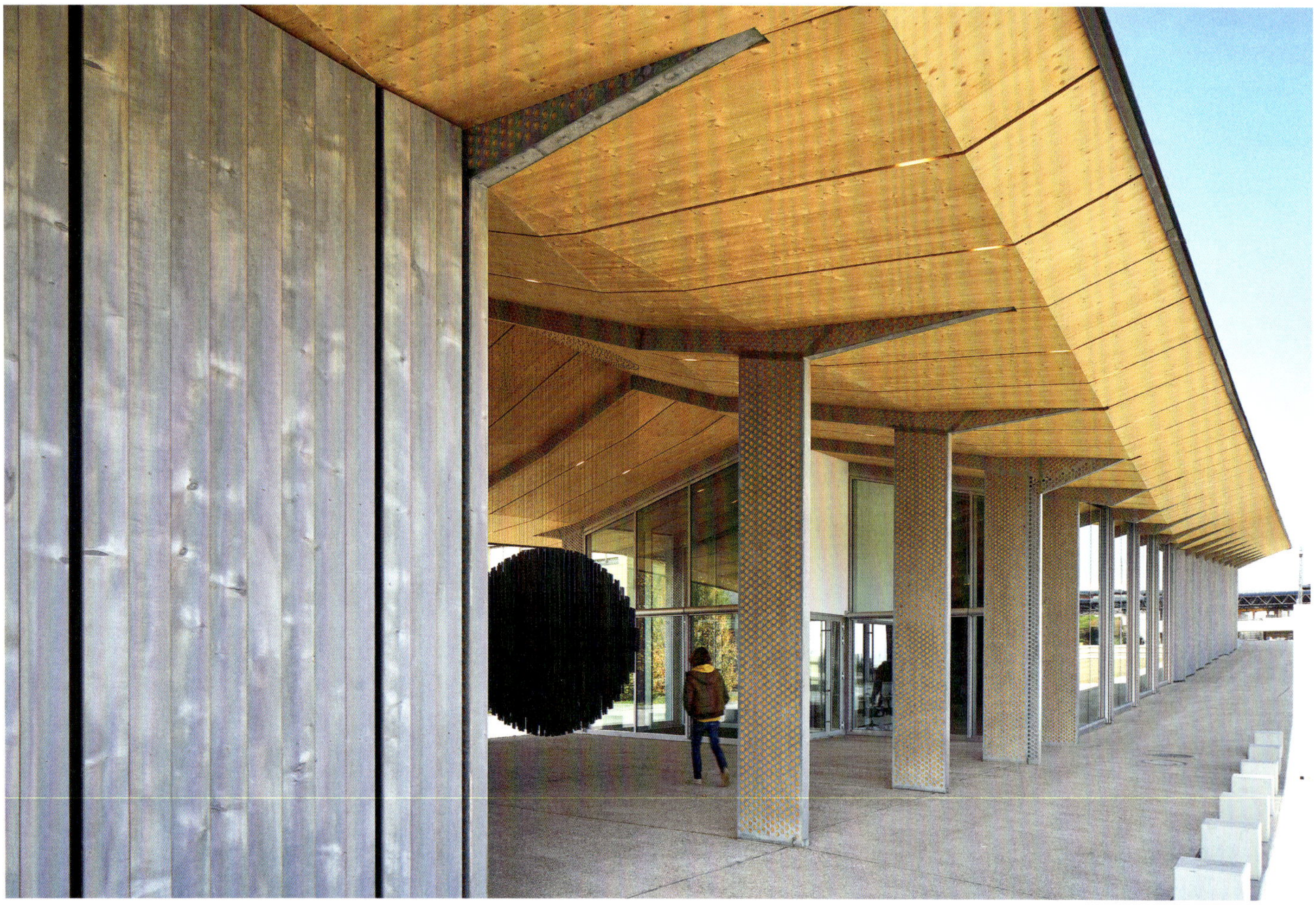

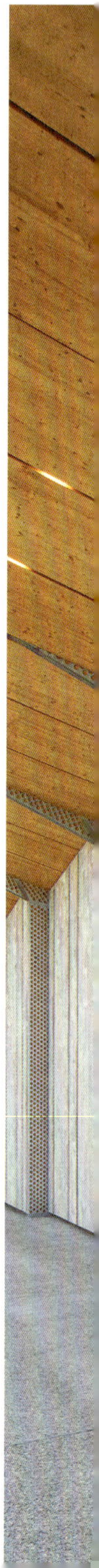

The untreated wood beneath the roof of ArtLab contrasts with
its gray-tinted wood-and-metal façades.

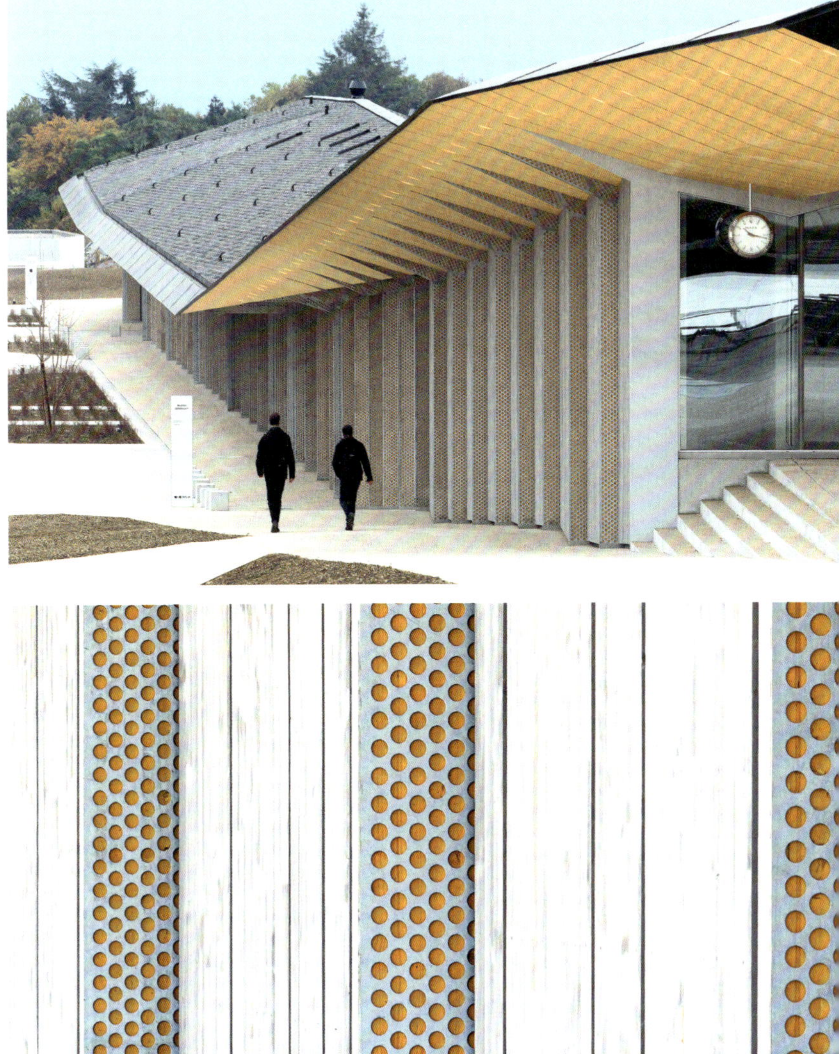

61

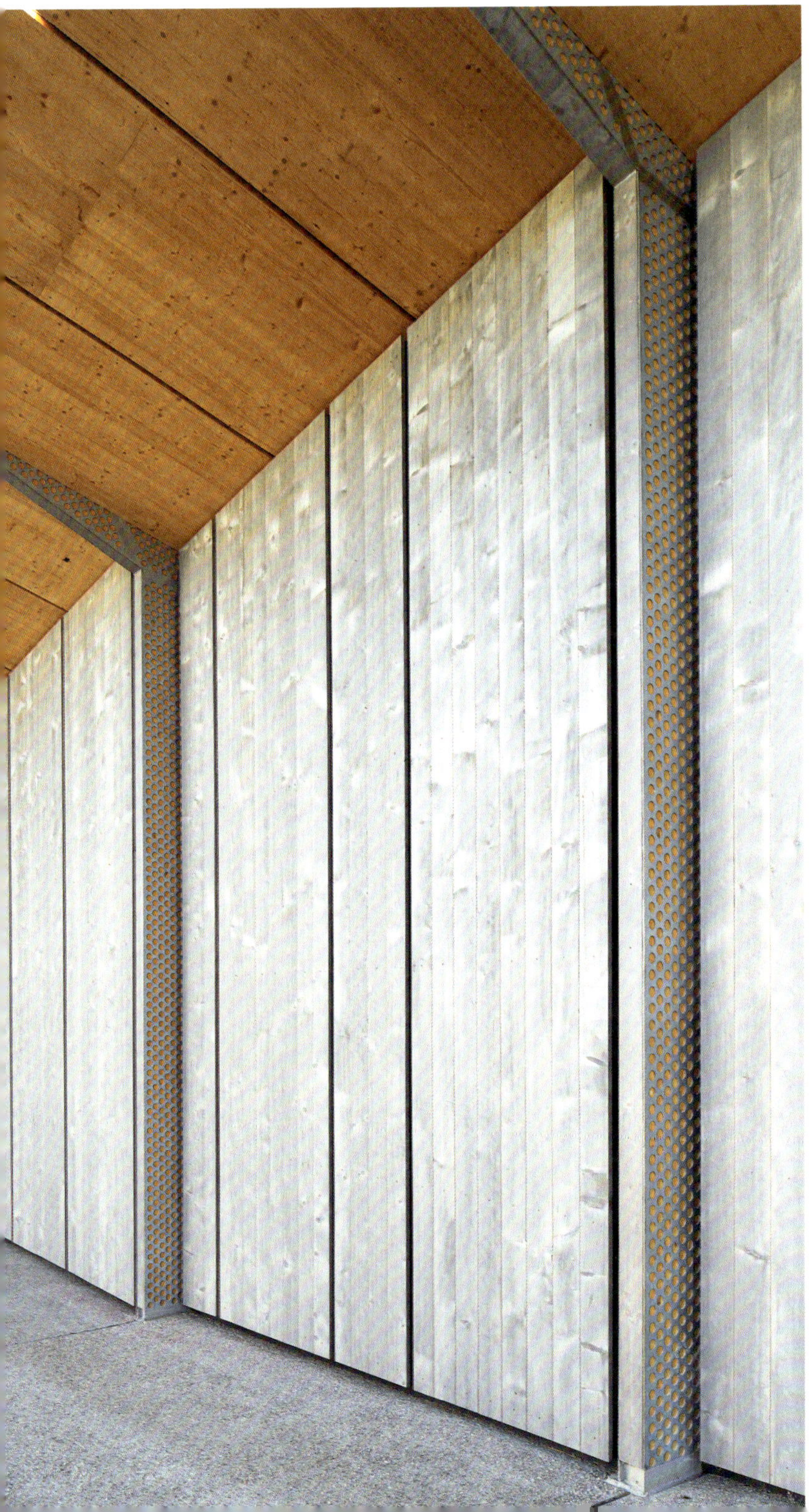

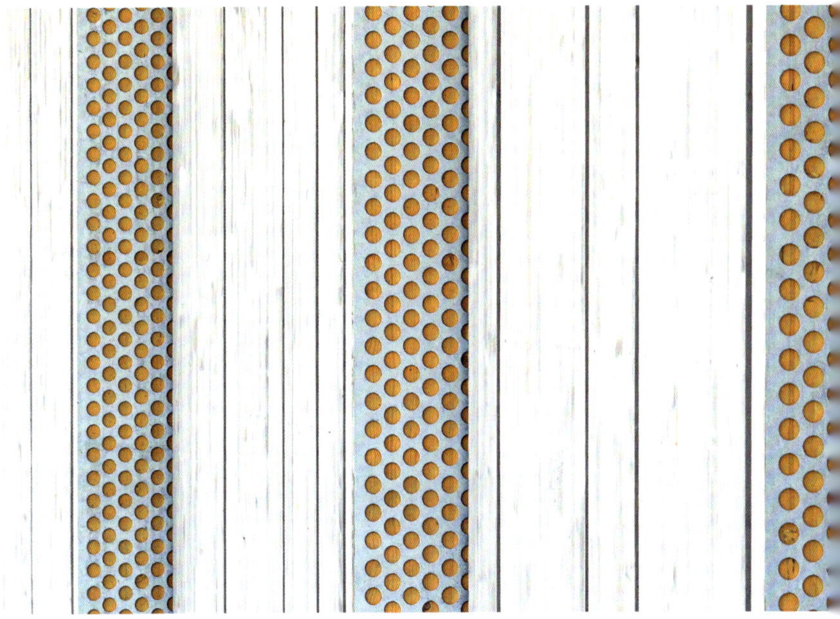

At its southern end, closest to Lake Geneva, the roof of ArtLab folds over the structure and comes down to touch the earth.

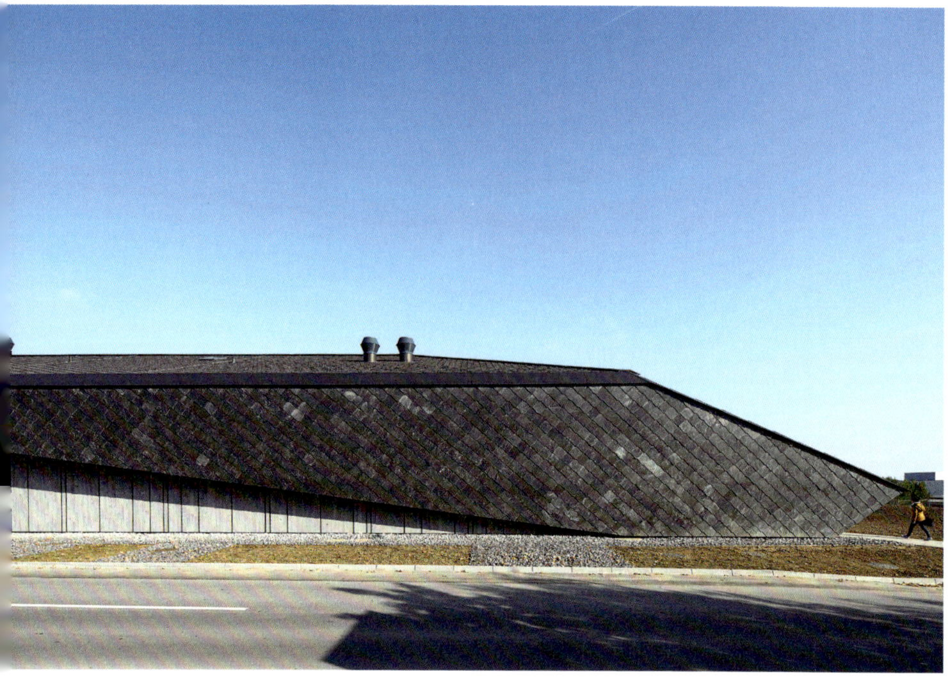

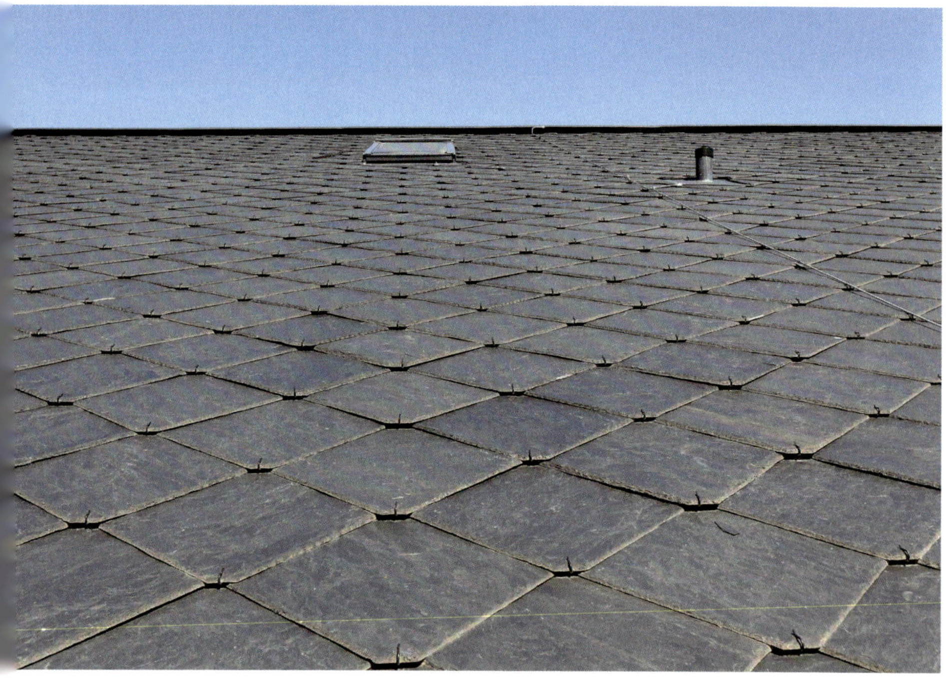

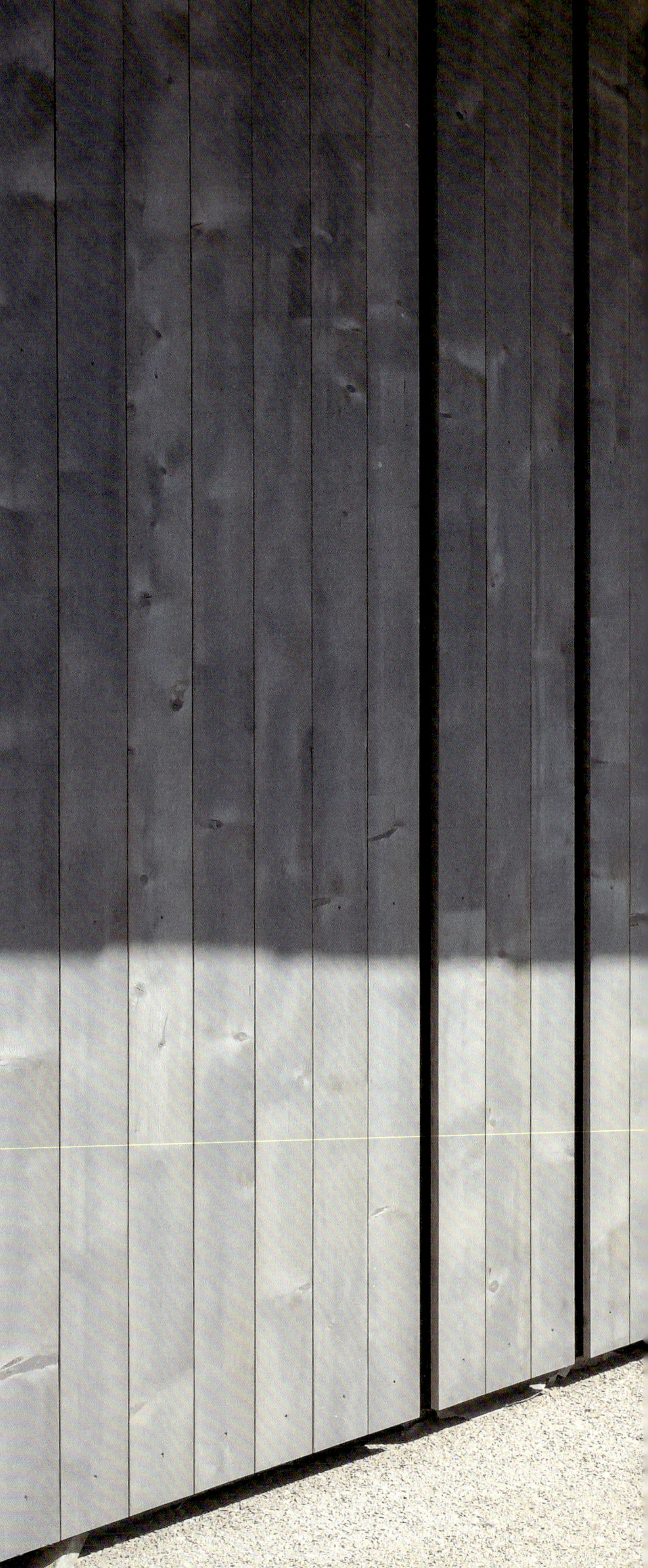

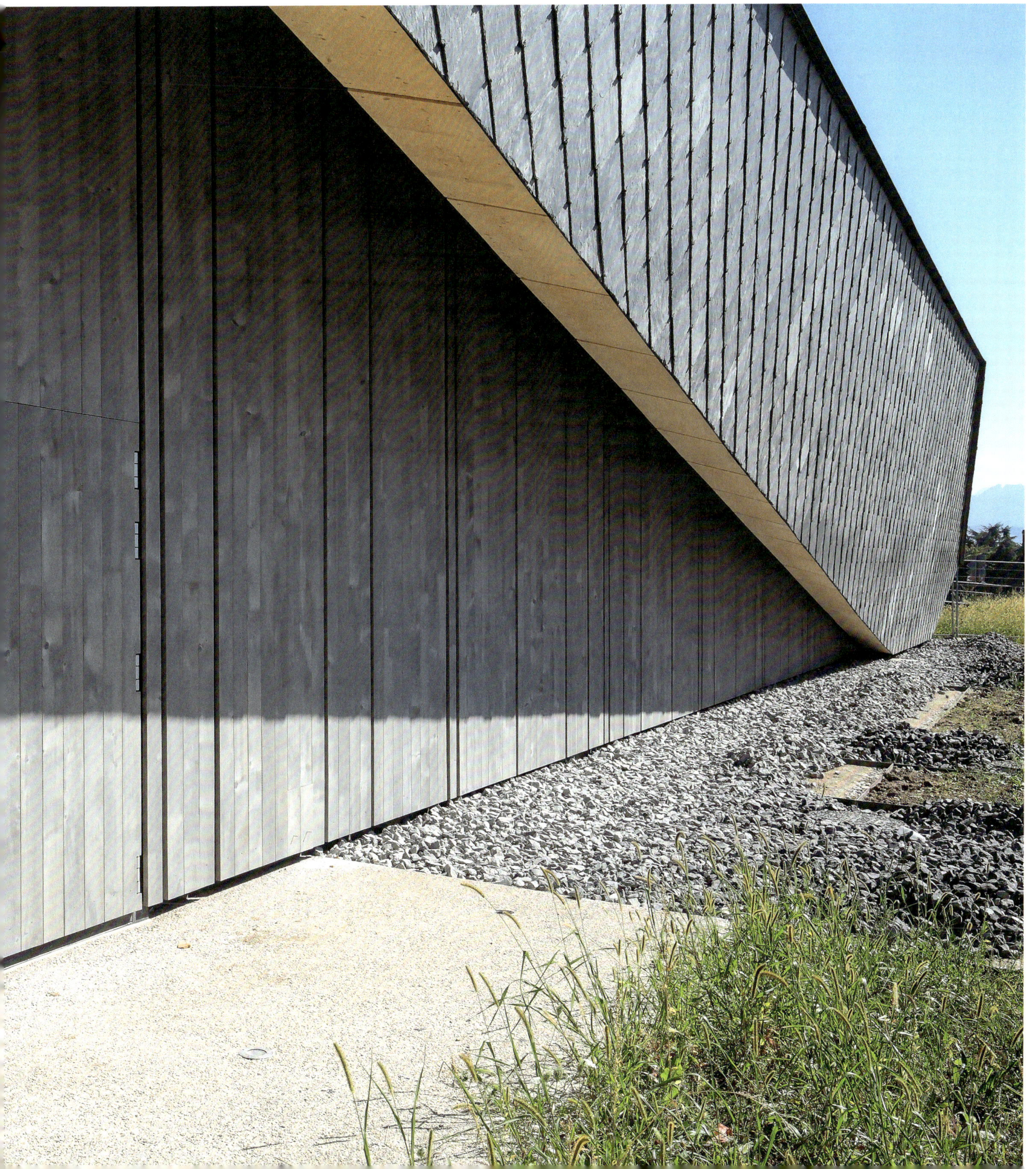

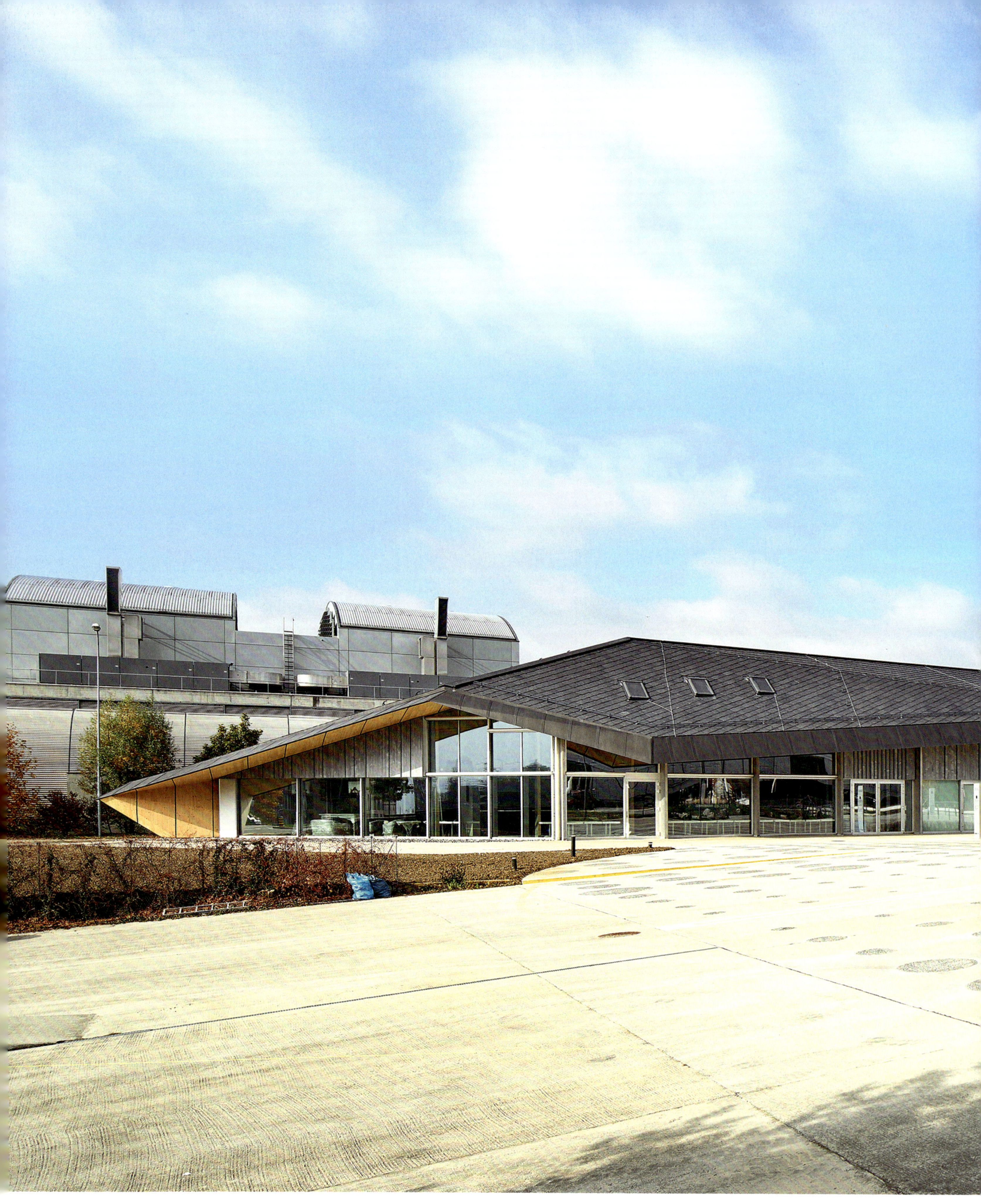

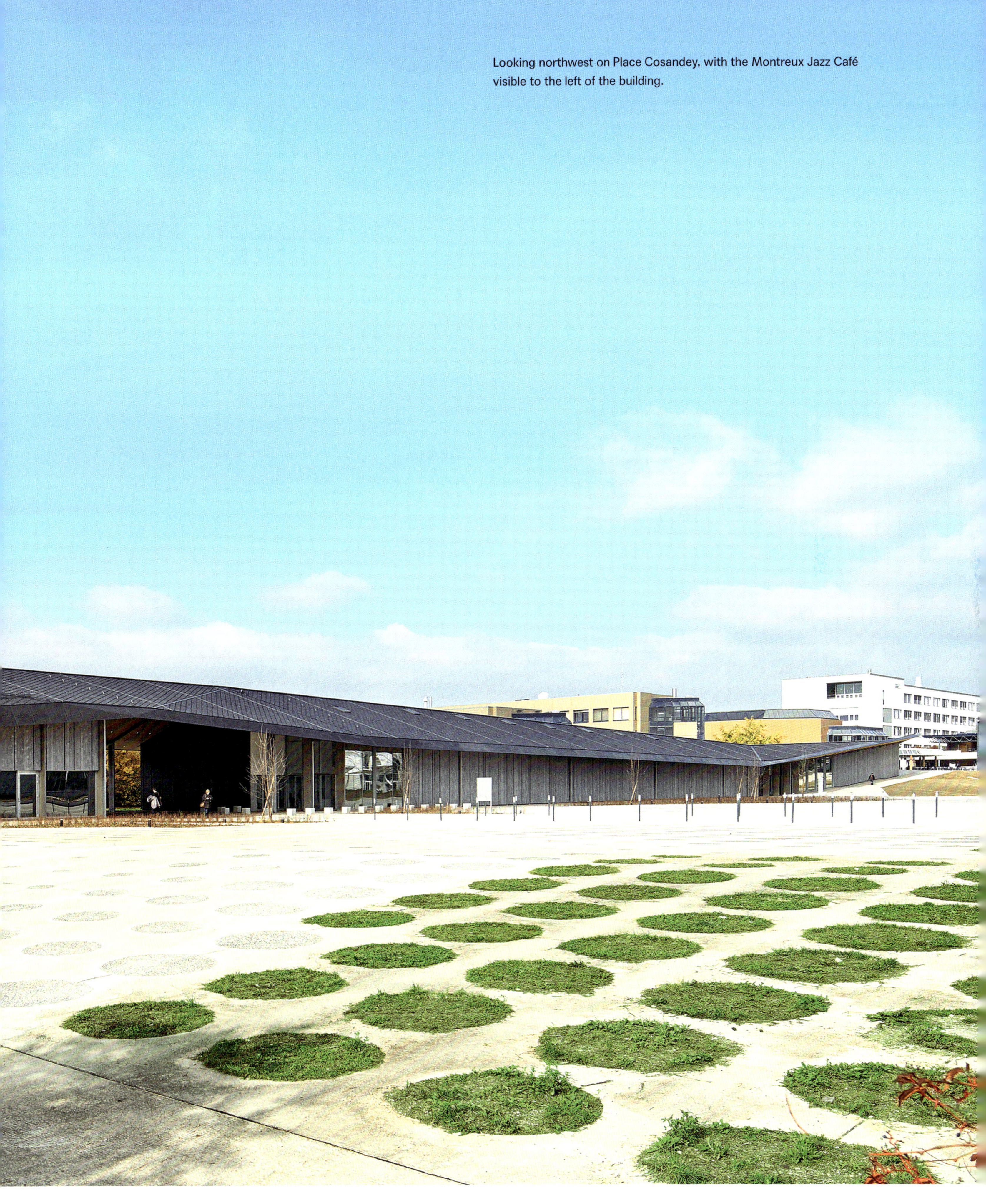

Looking northwest on Place Cosandey, with the Montreux Jazz Café visible to the left of the building.

Top, the northern entrance to ArtLab seen from below.
Bottom, the Montreux Jazz Café at the other extremity of the building.

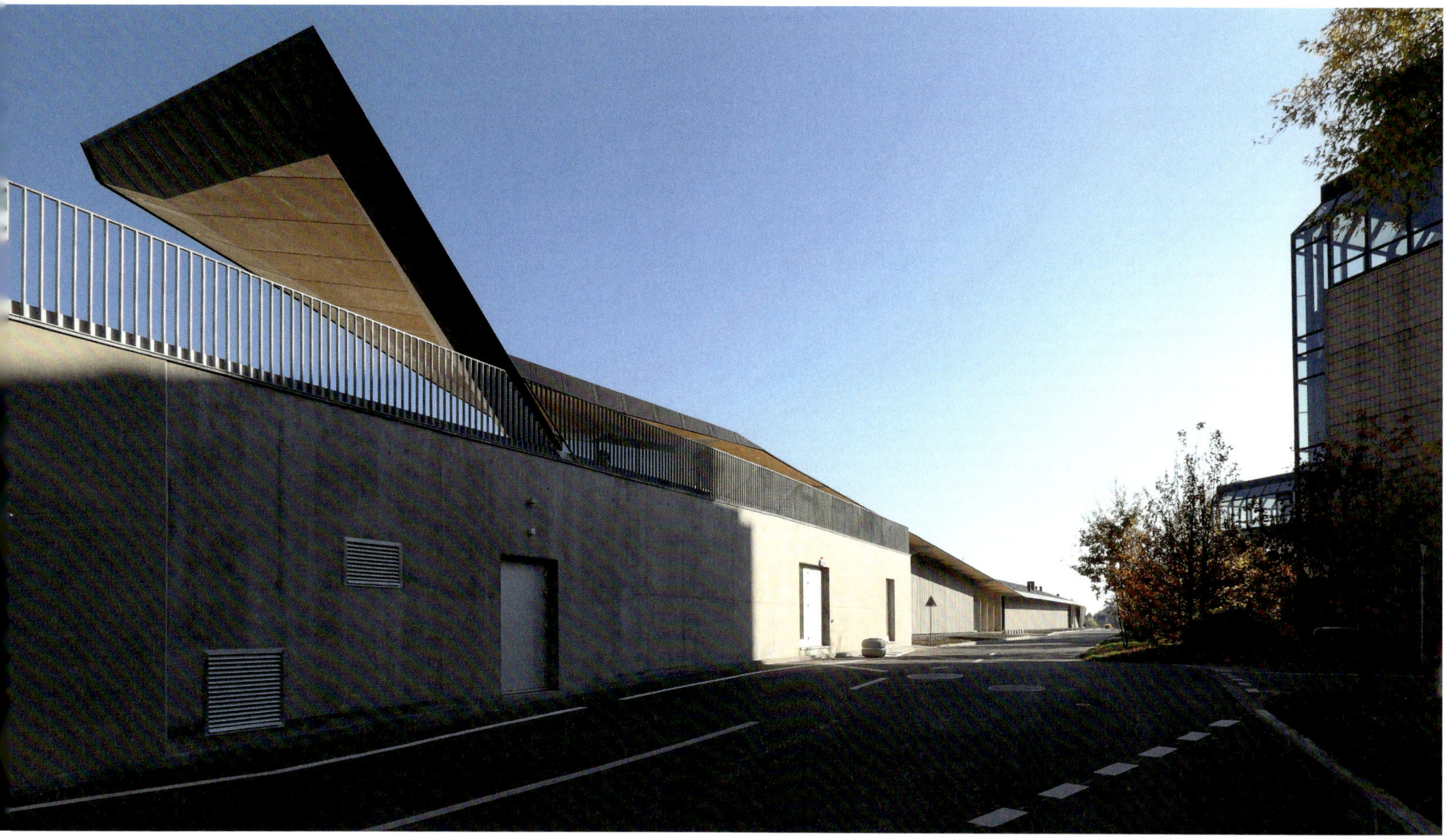

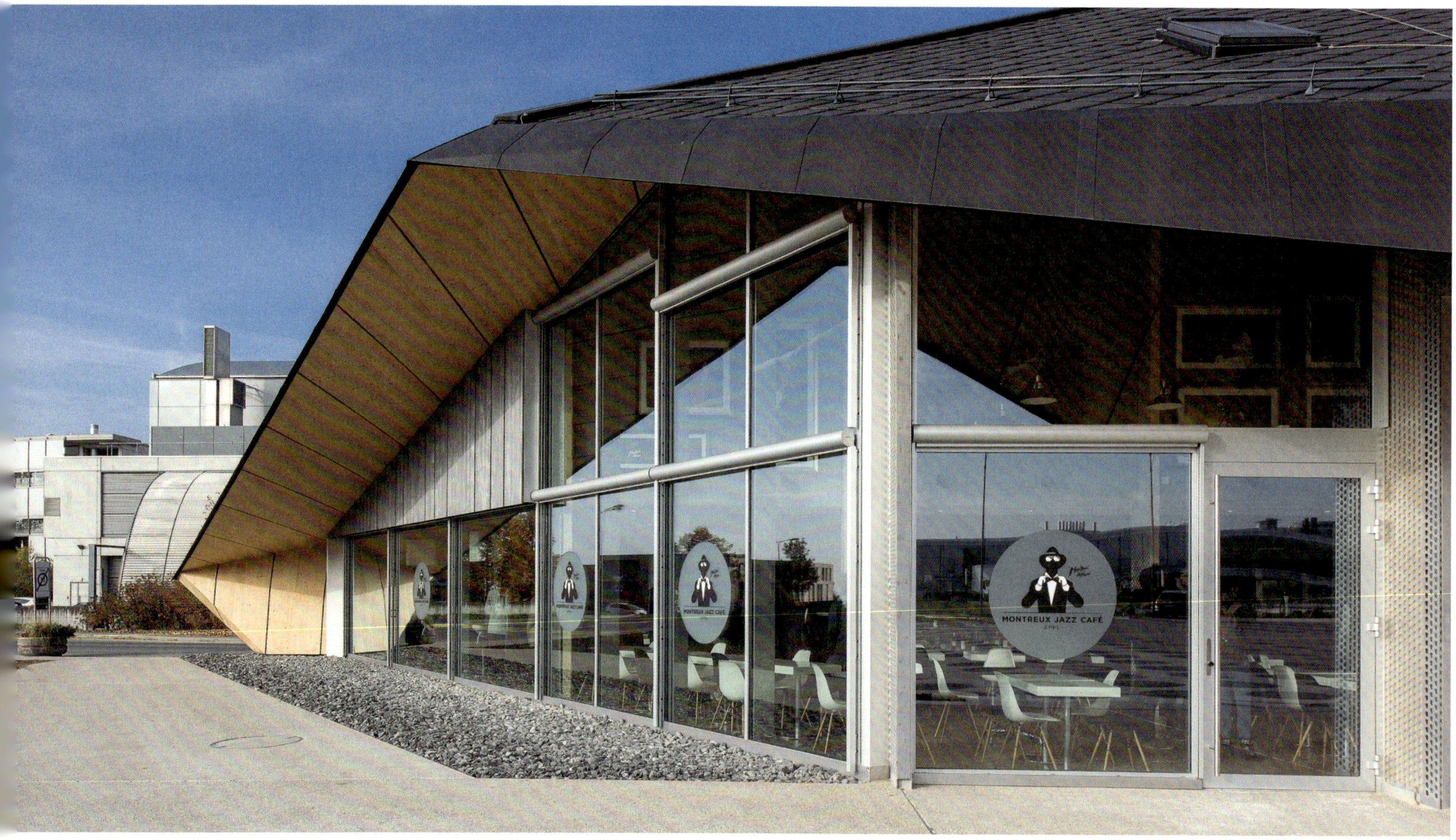

Top, looking at ArtLab from Place Cosandey. Below, a view through one
of the two passageways of ArtLab toward the Rolex Learning Center.

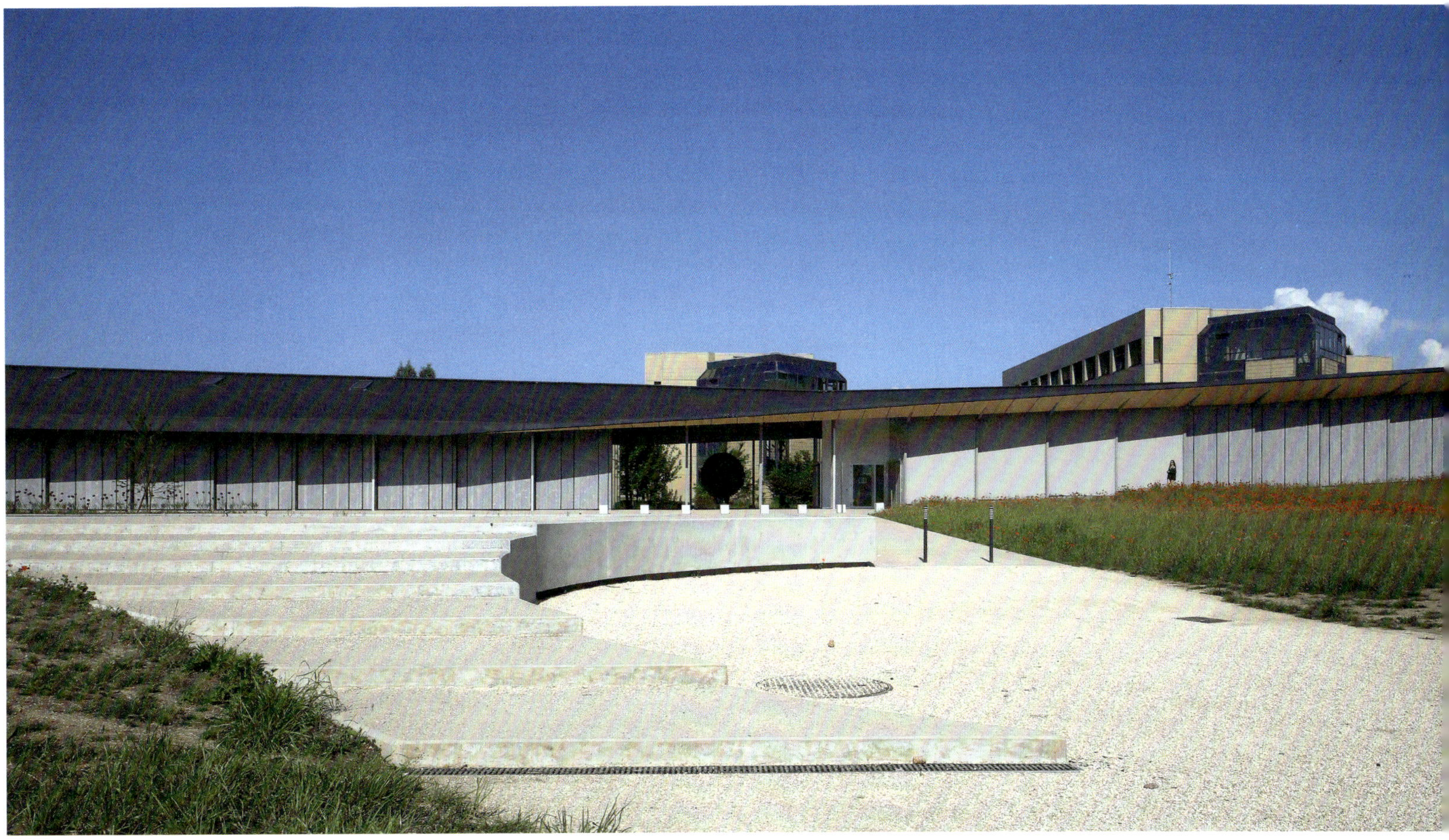

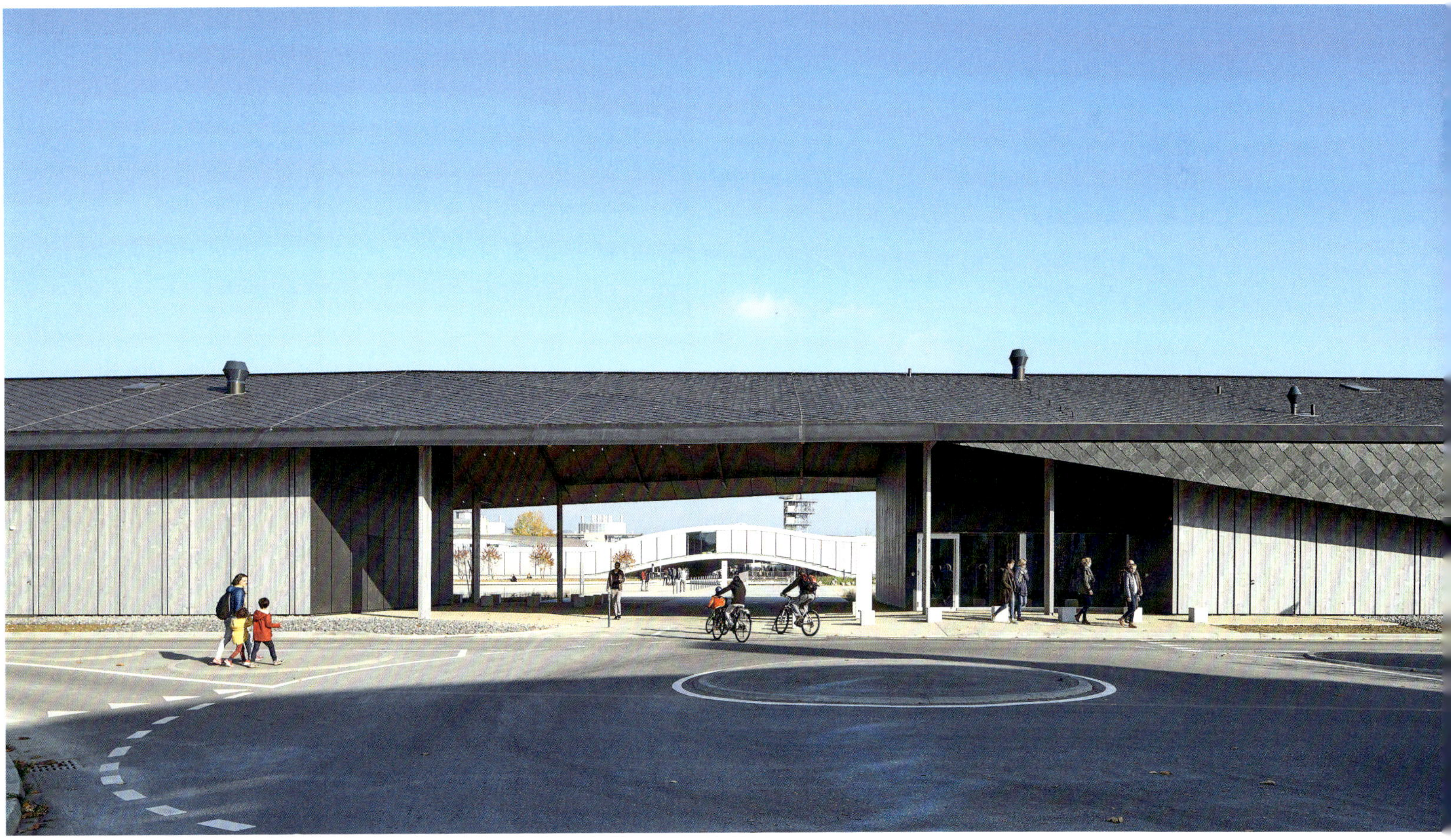

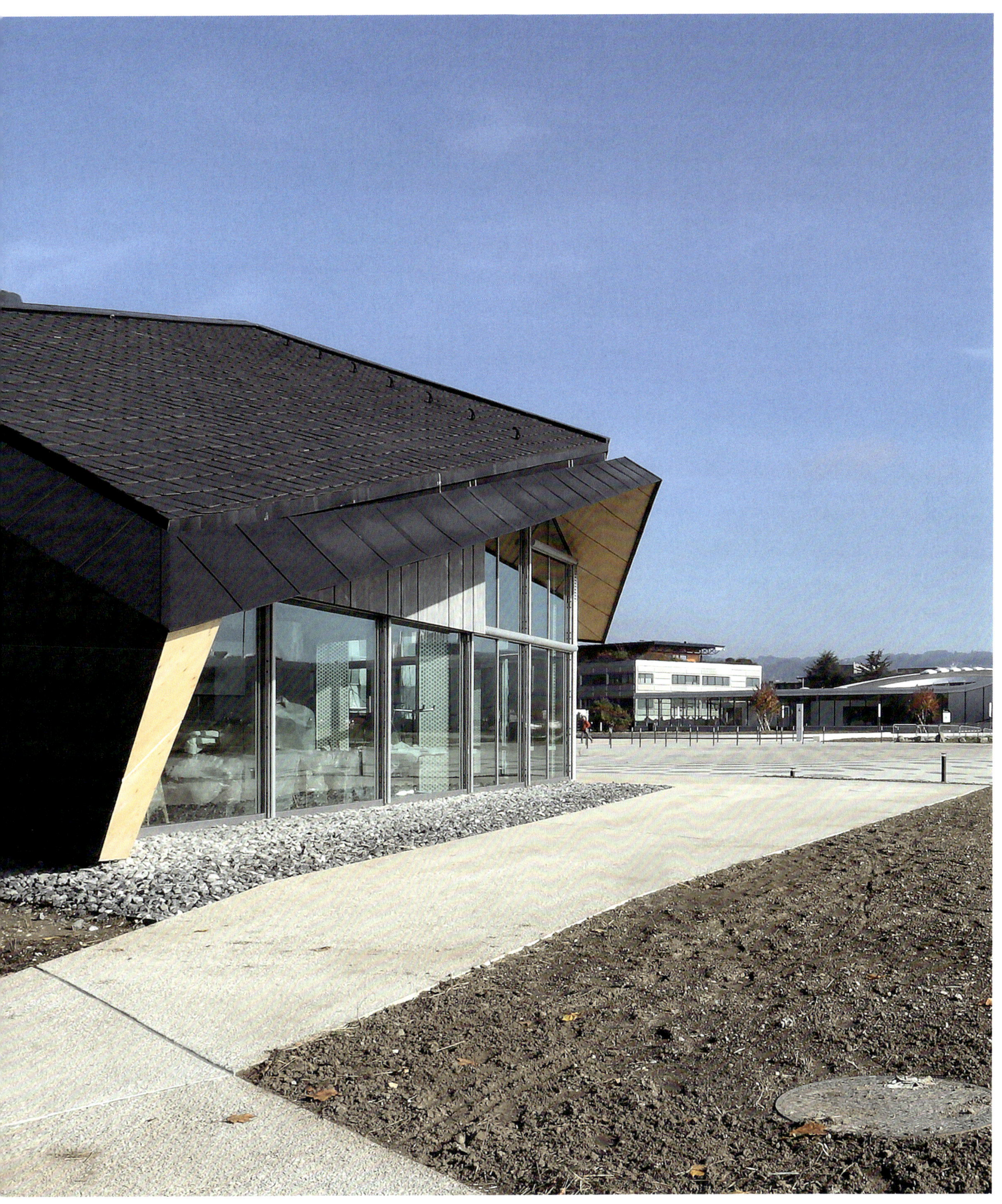

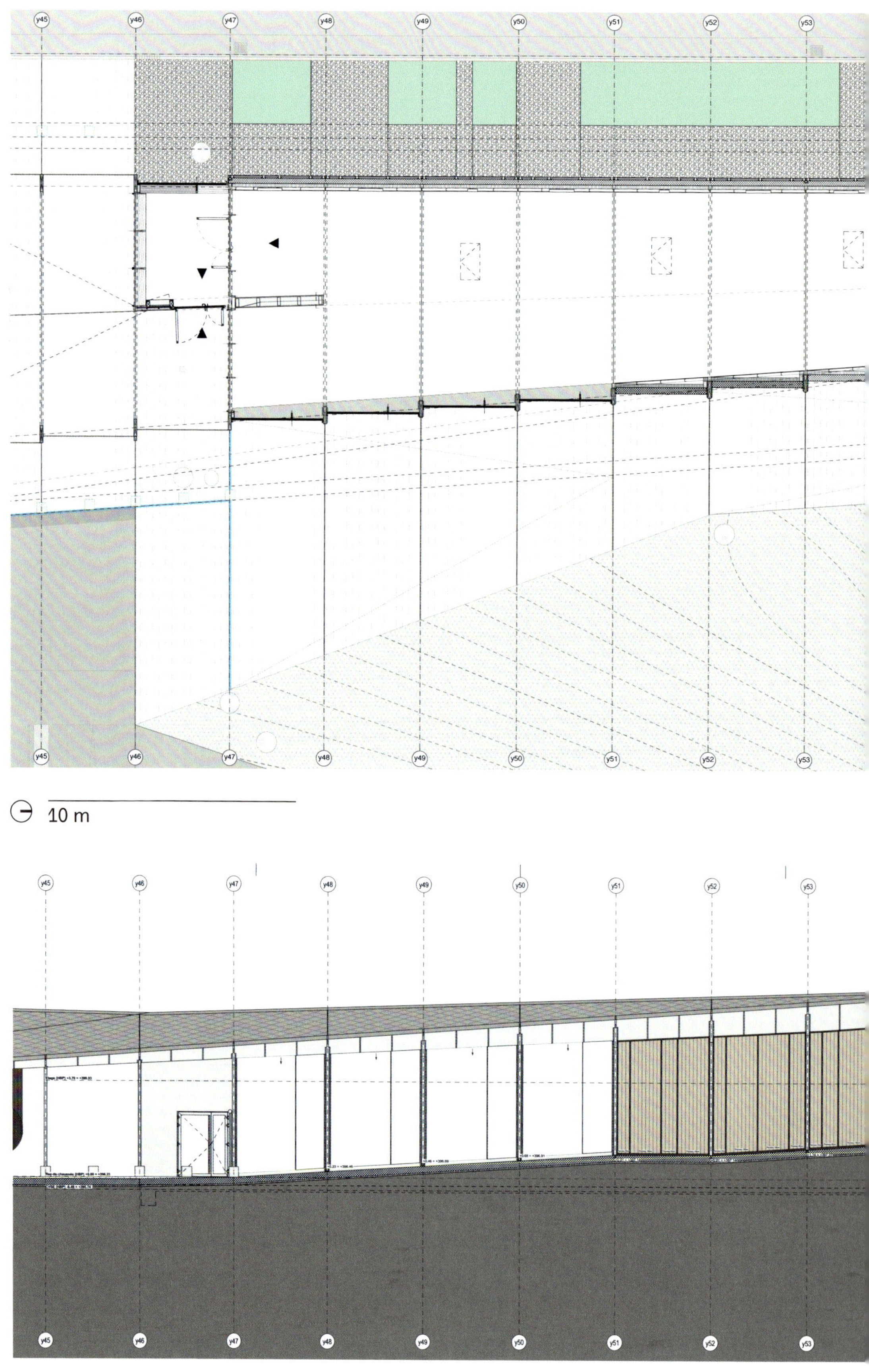

y45 y46 y47 y48 y49 y50 y51 y52 y53
10 m

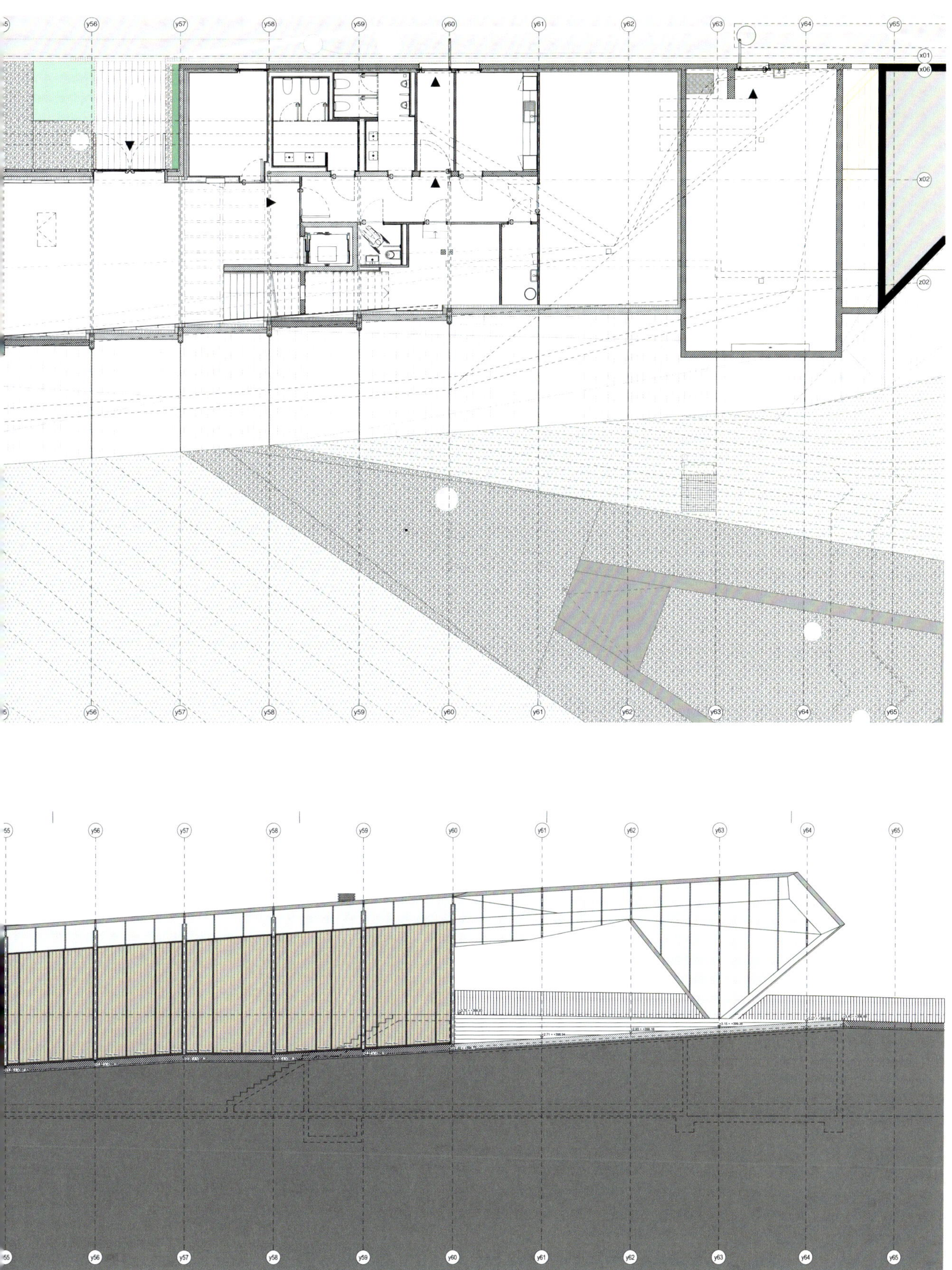

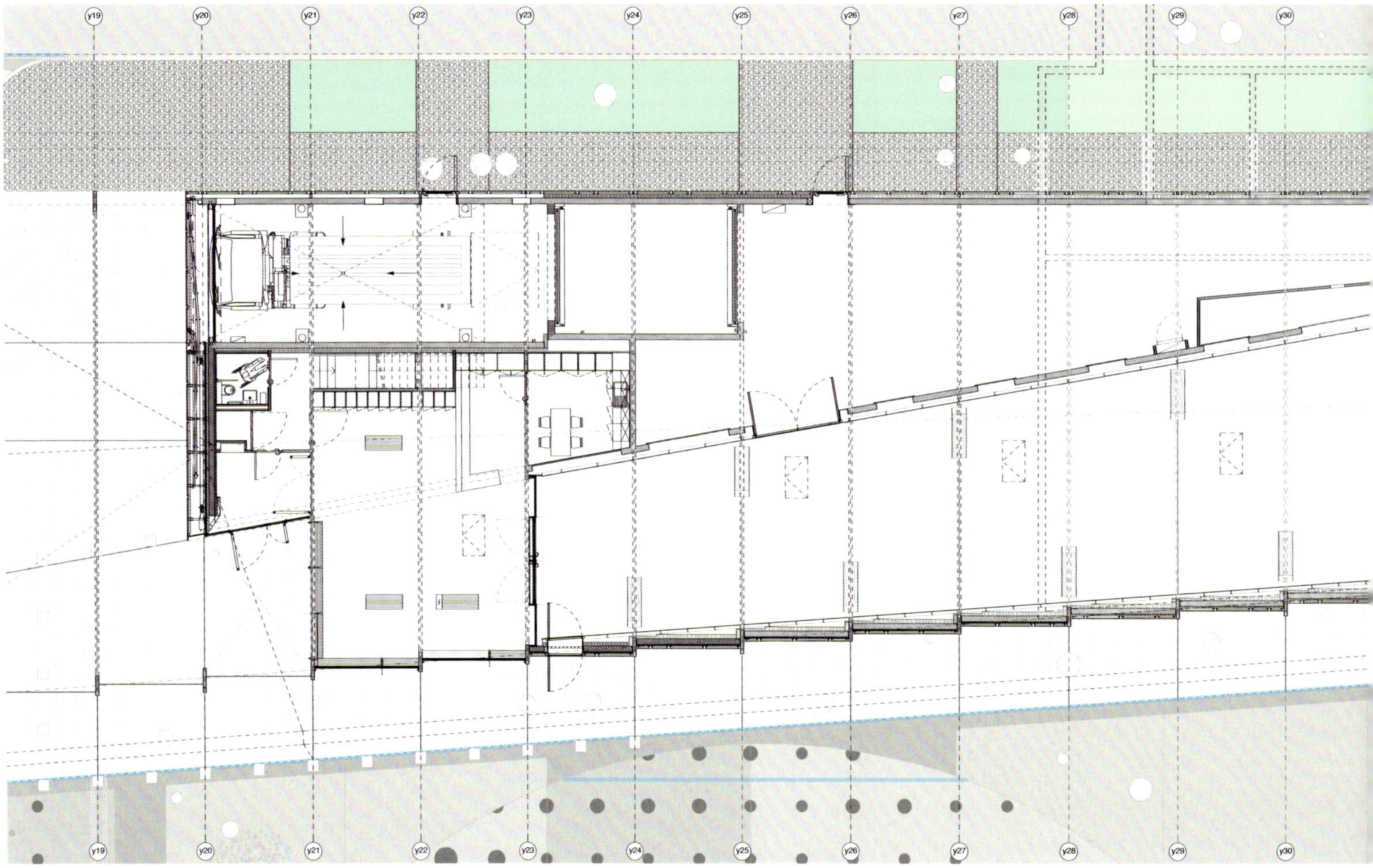

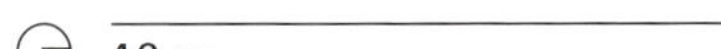

10 m

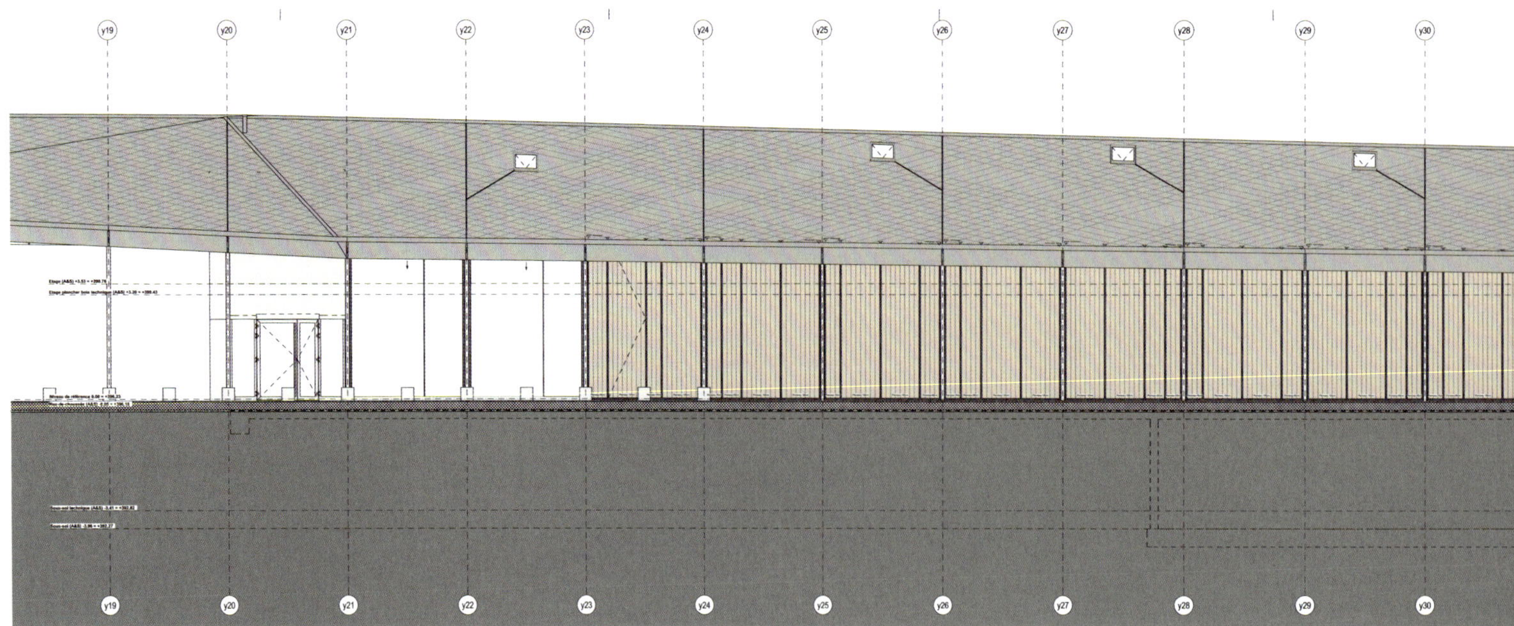

Again, plan and section show the rather closed walls of the building,
and its low profile as opposed to a slightly wider volume.

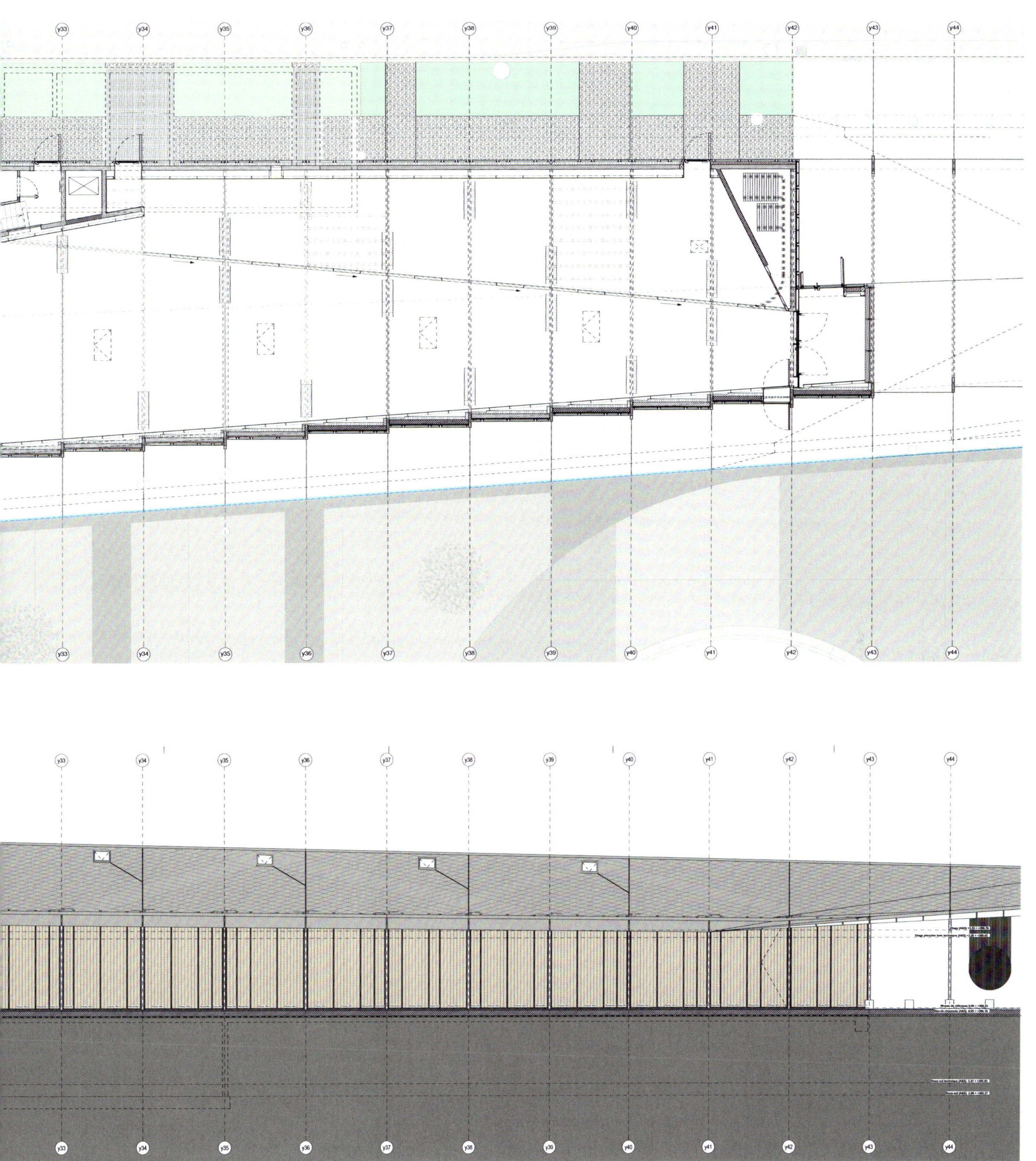

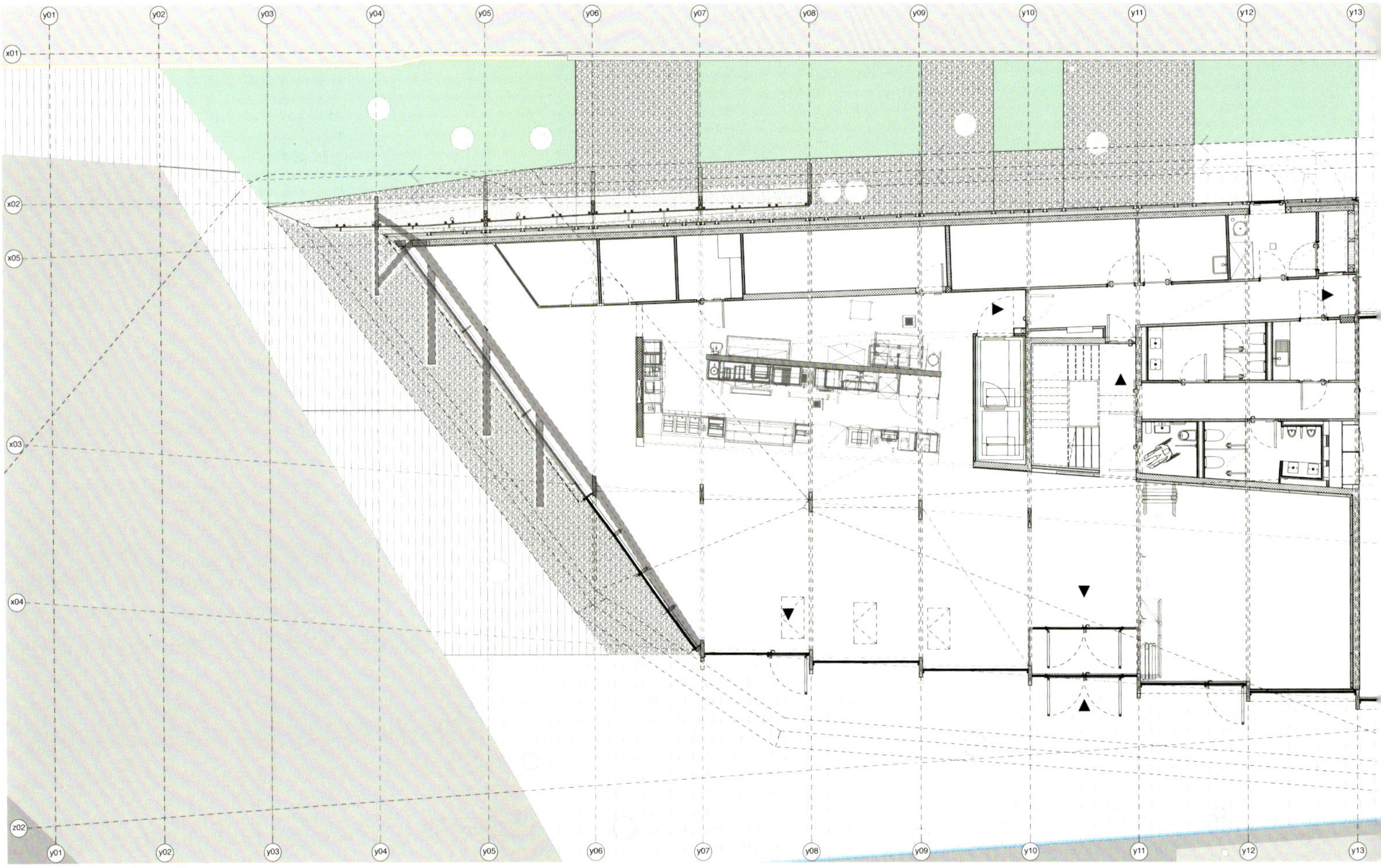

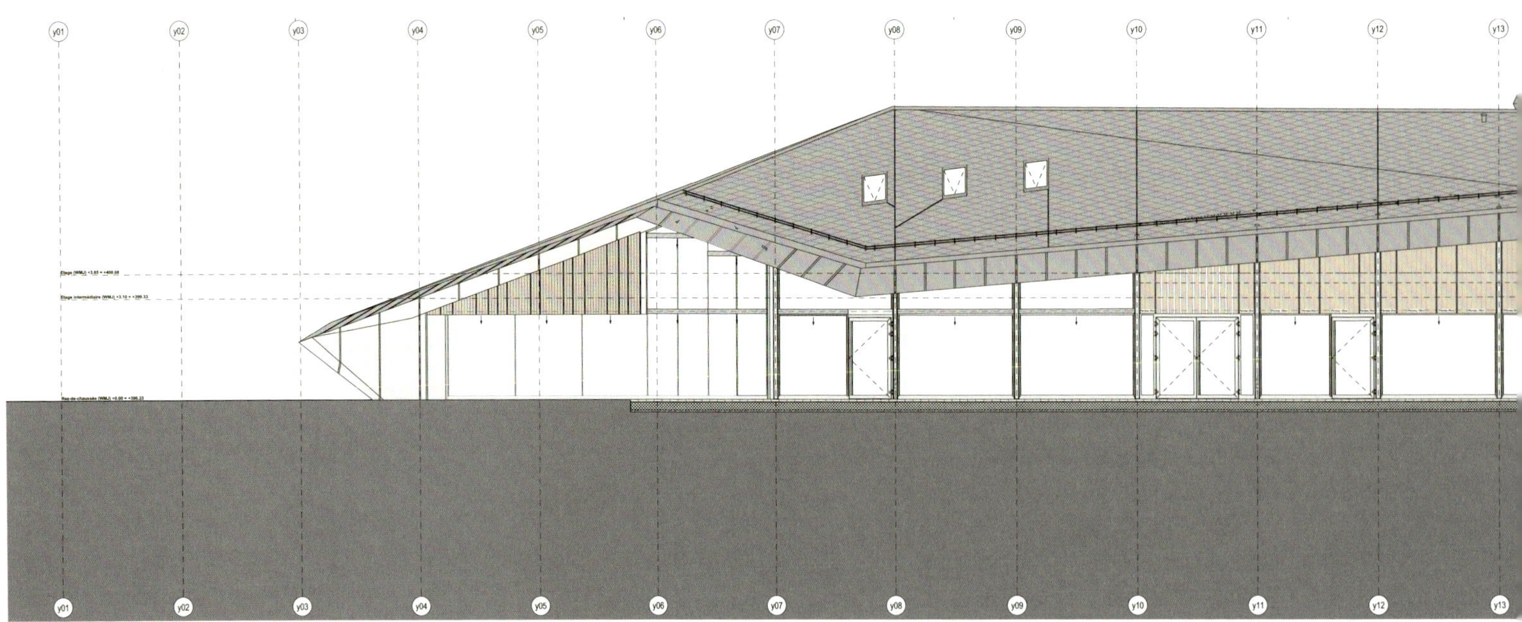

10 m

Below, a section drawing of the southern façade.
Left page, plan and elevation of the eastern façade.

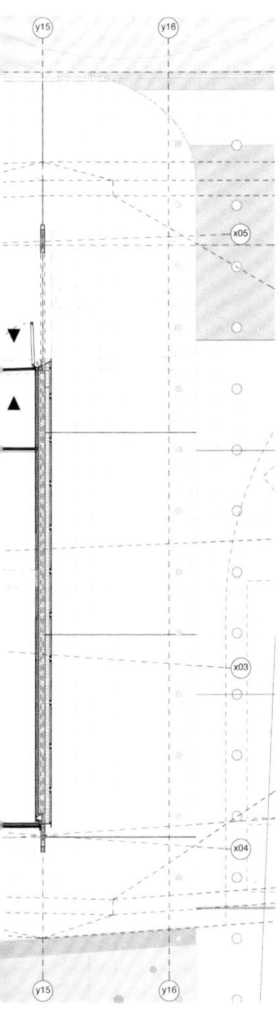

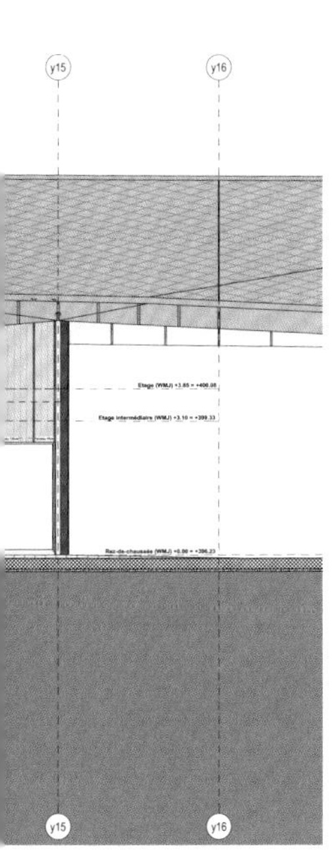

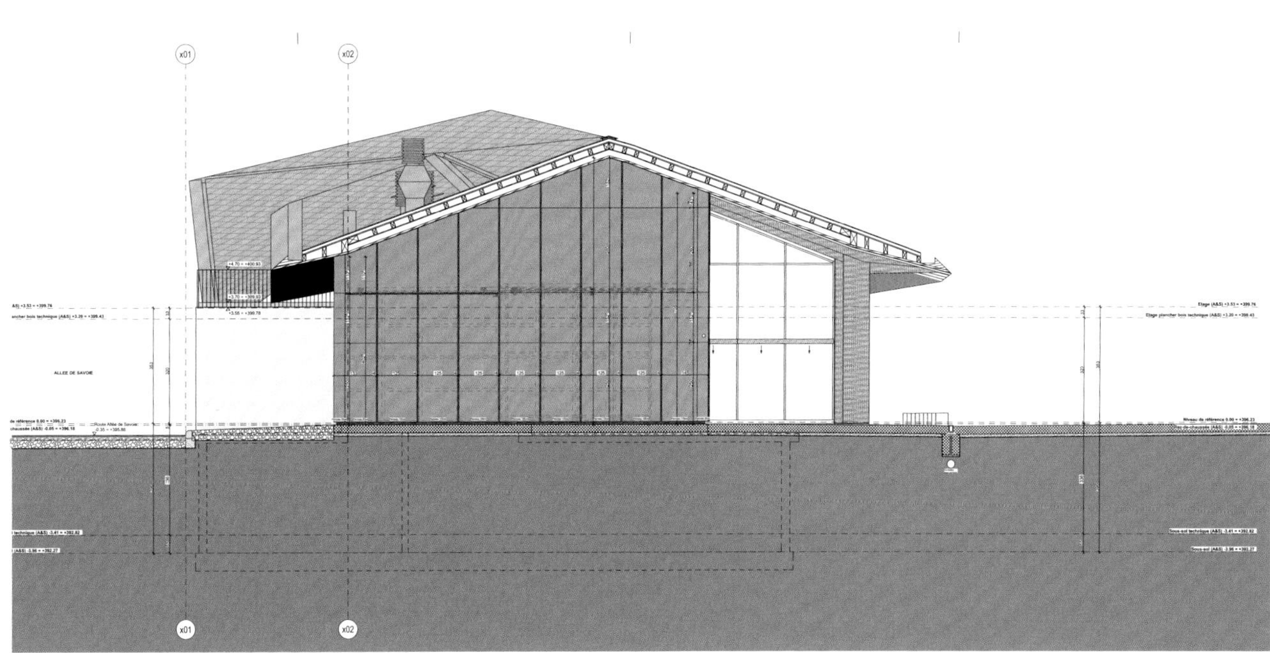

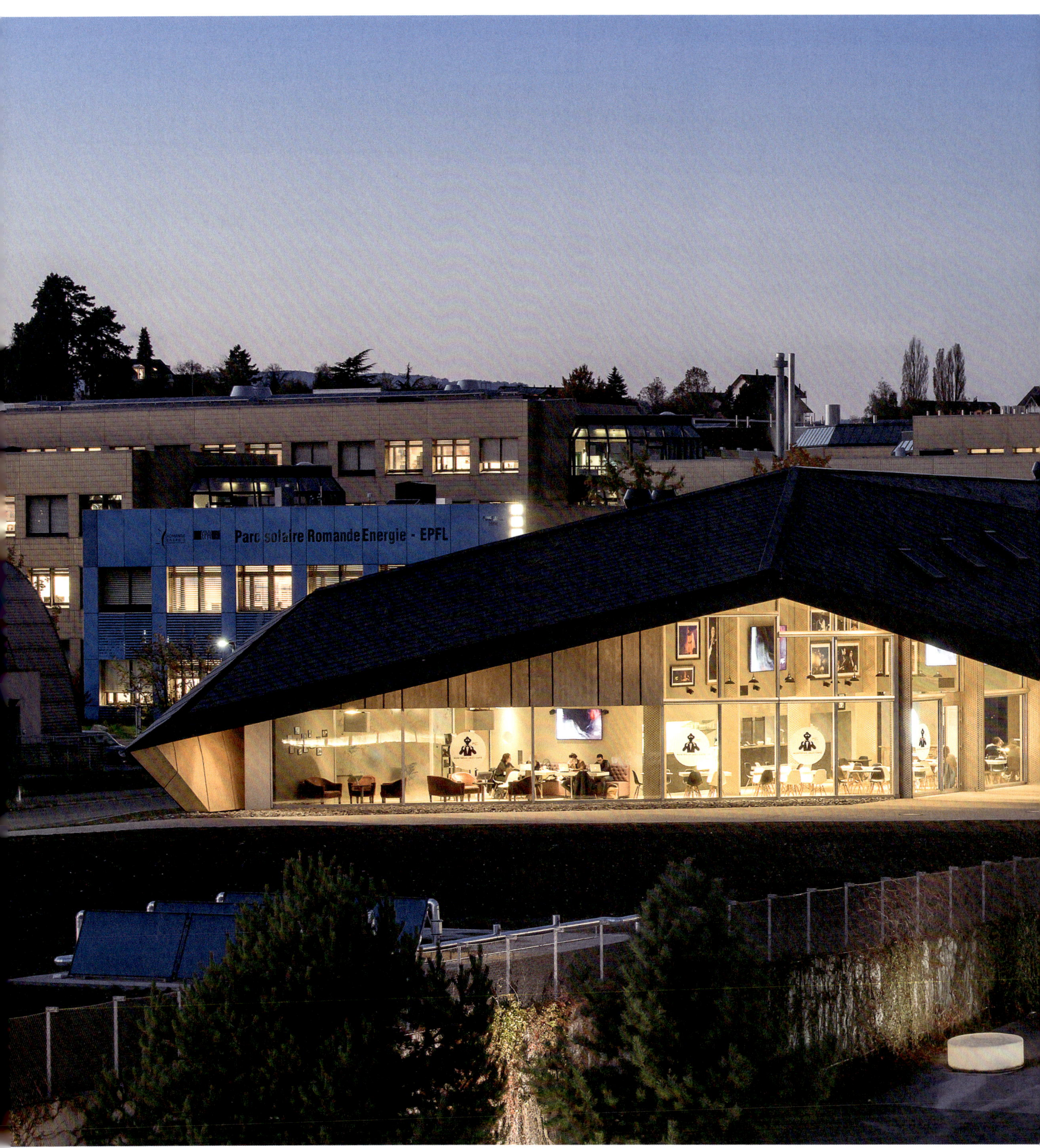

Parc solaire Romande Energie - EPFL

An elevated view of the entire building, looking north with
the Montreux Jazz Café in the foreground.

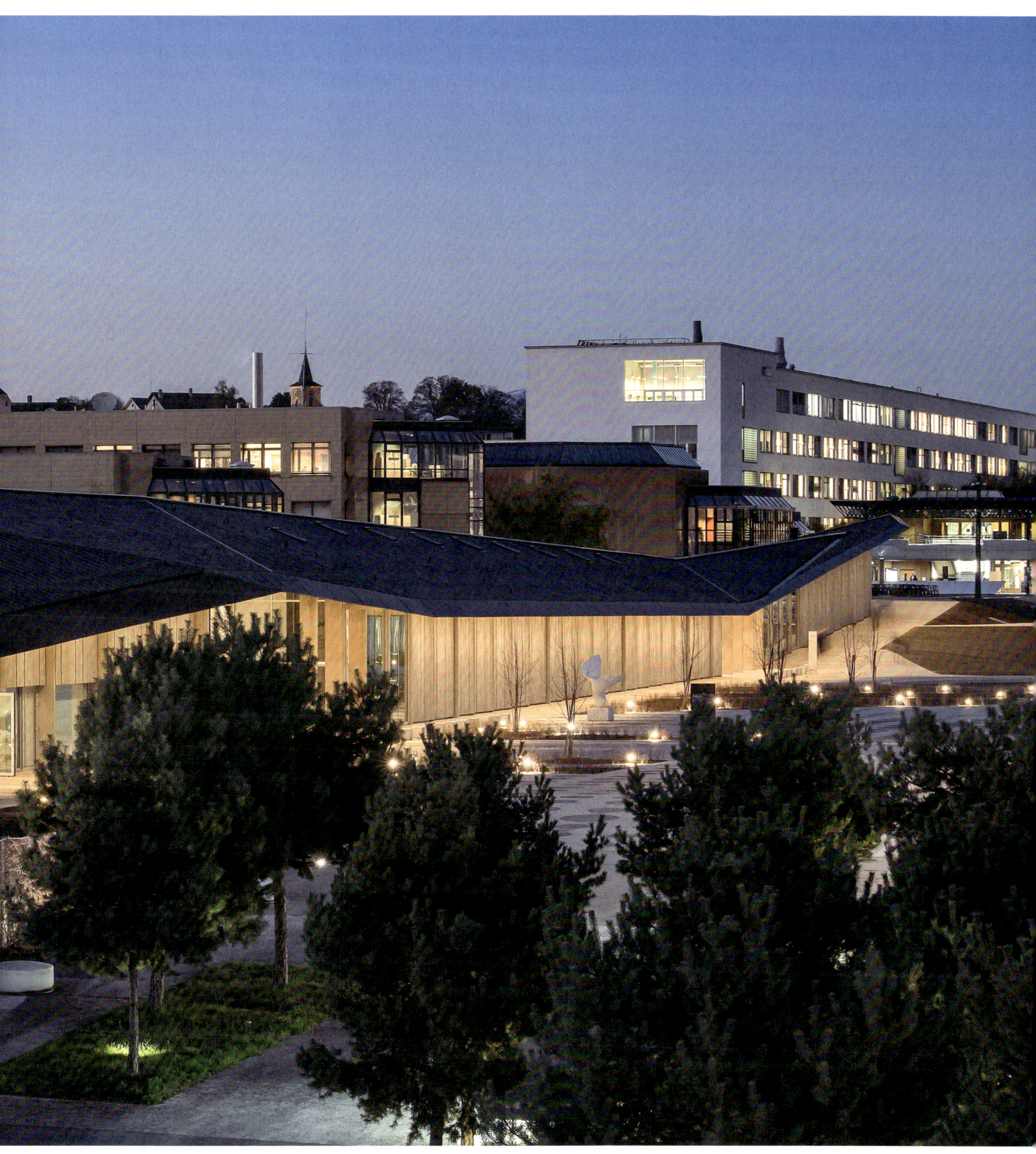

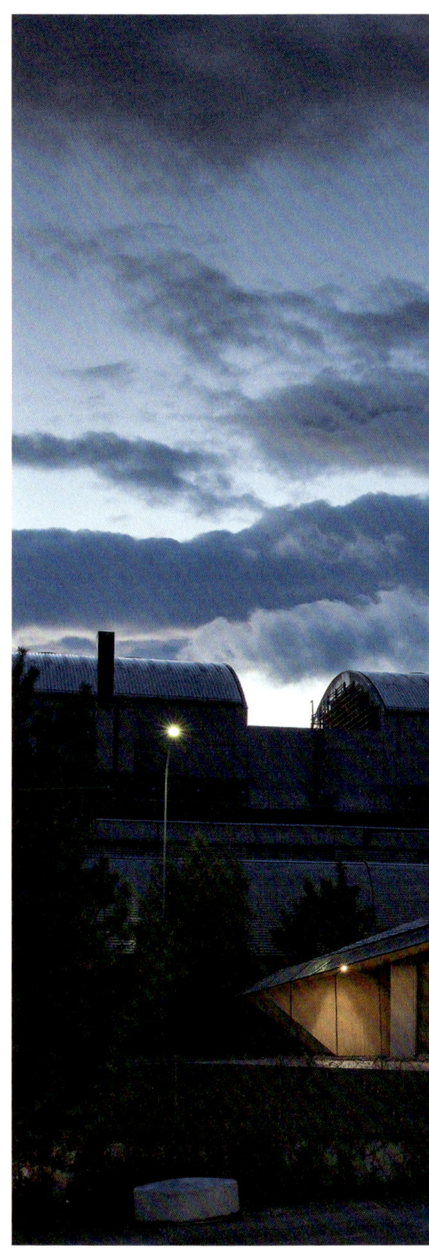

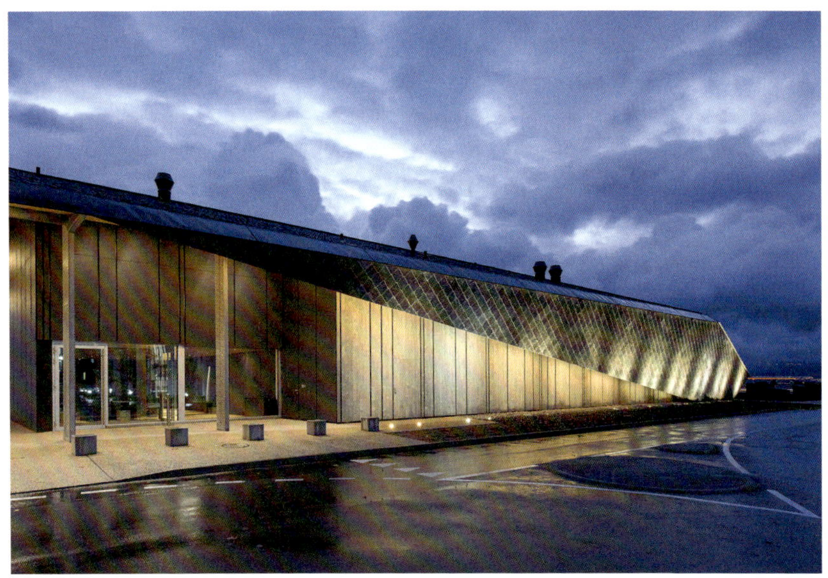

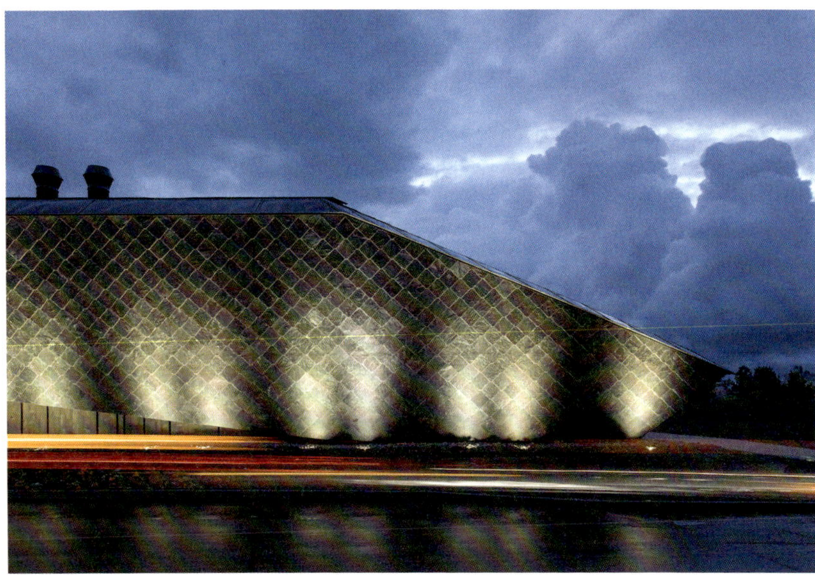

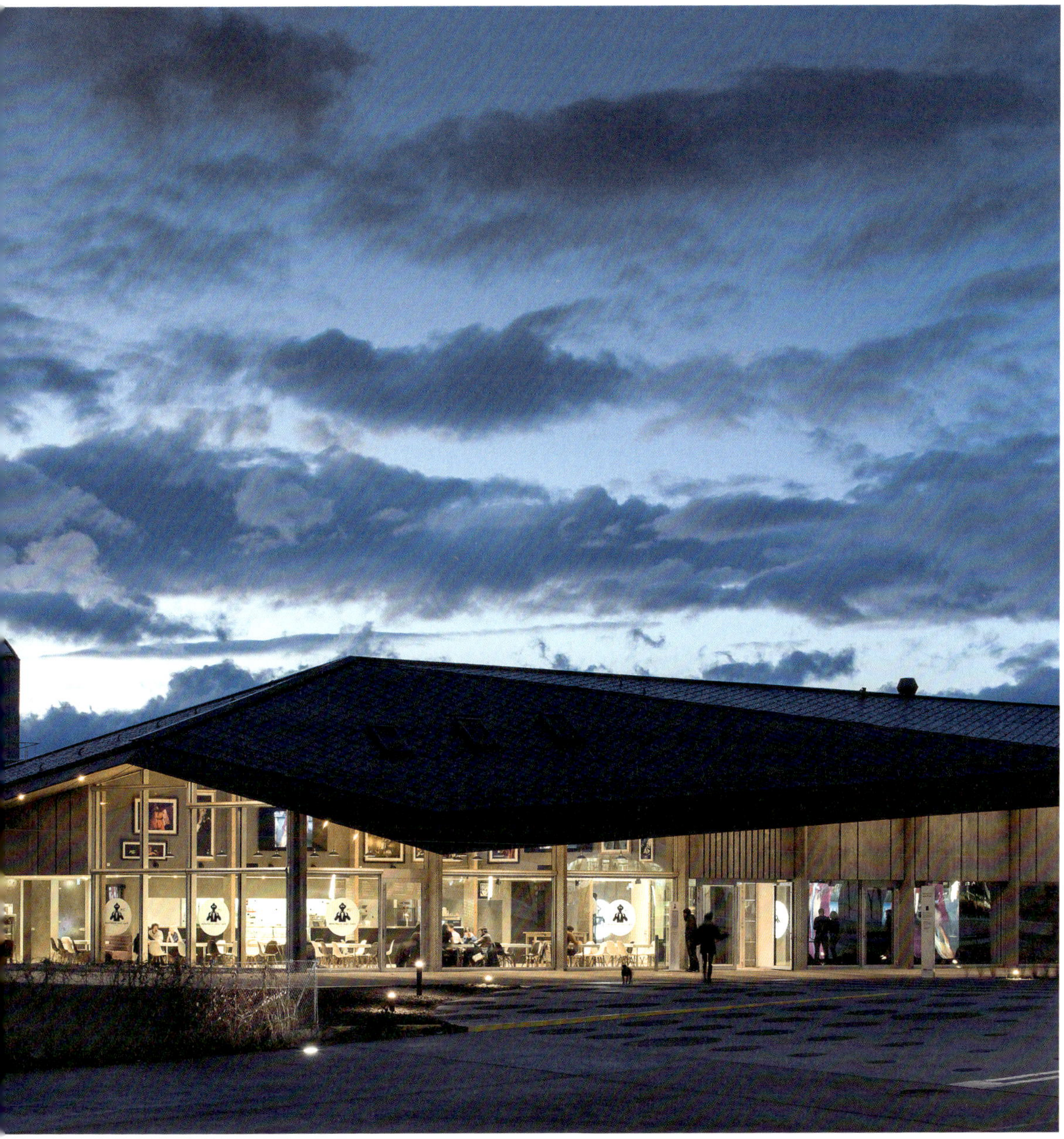

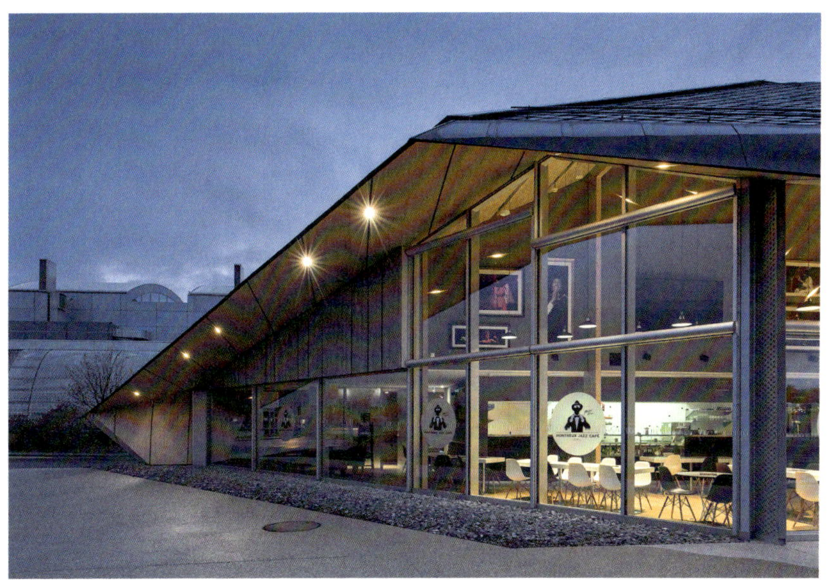

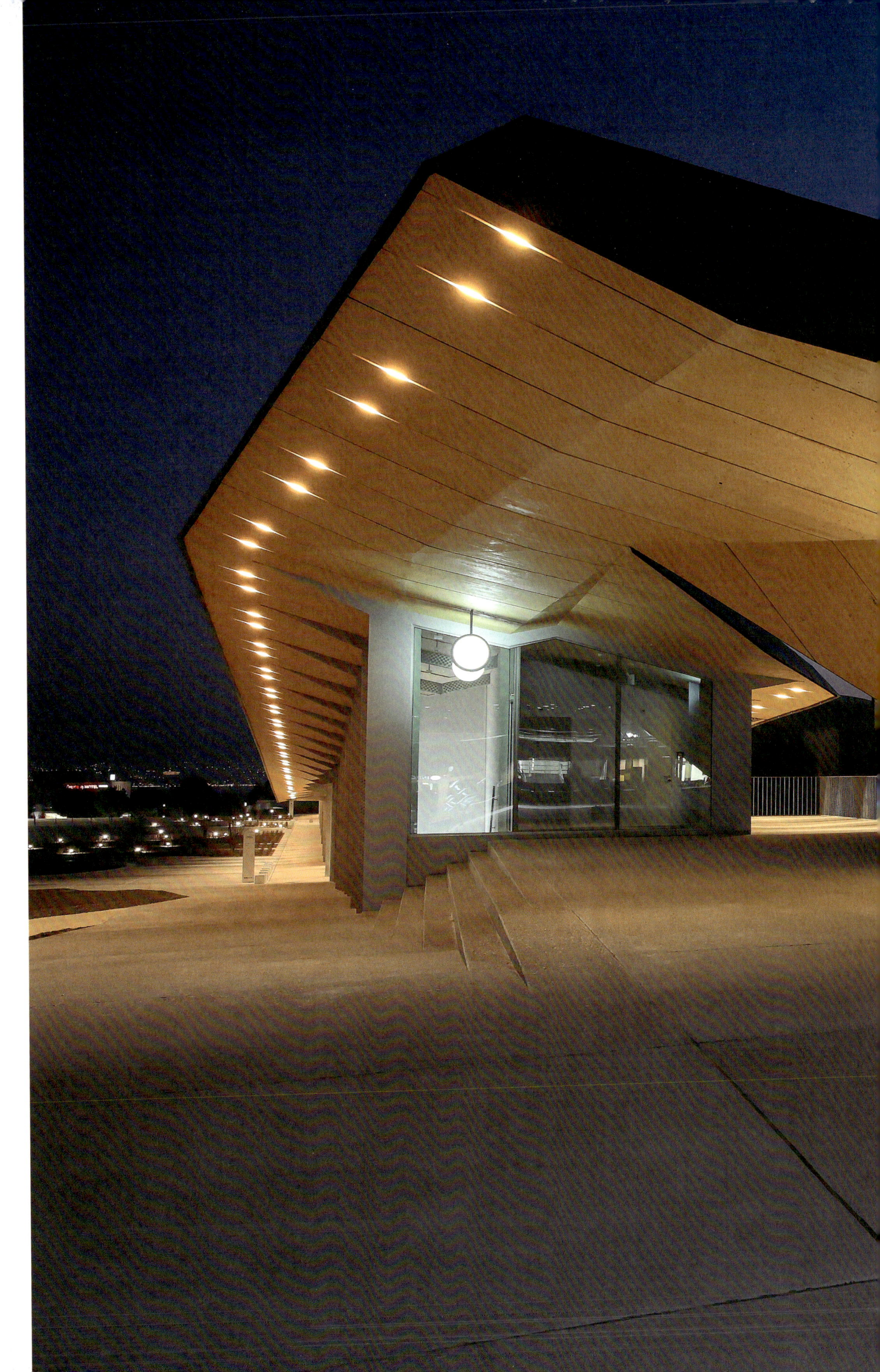

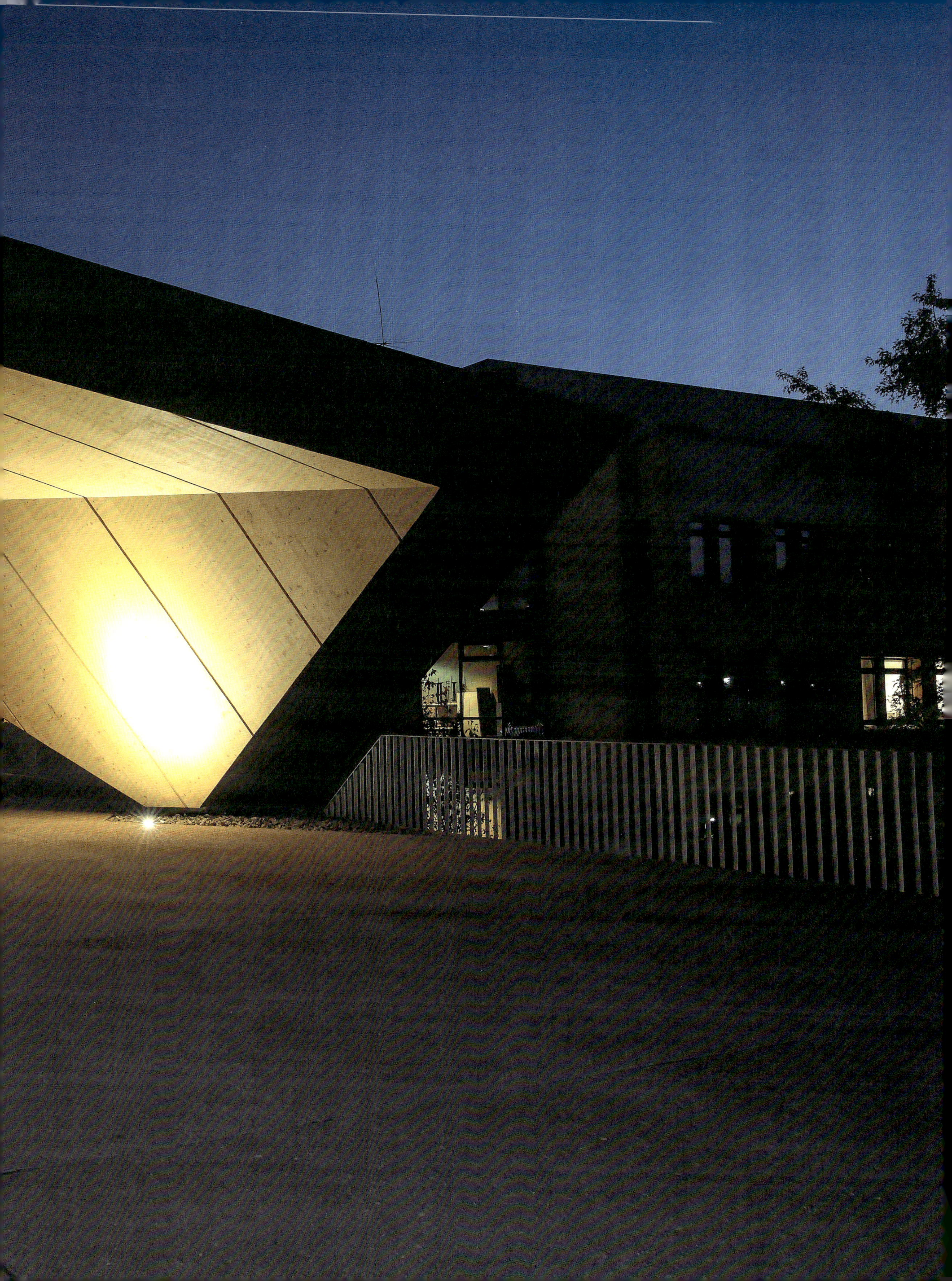

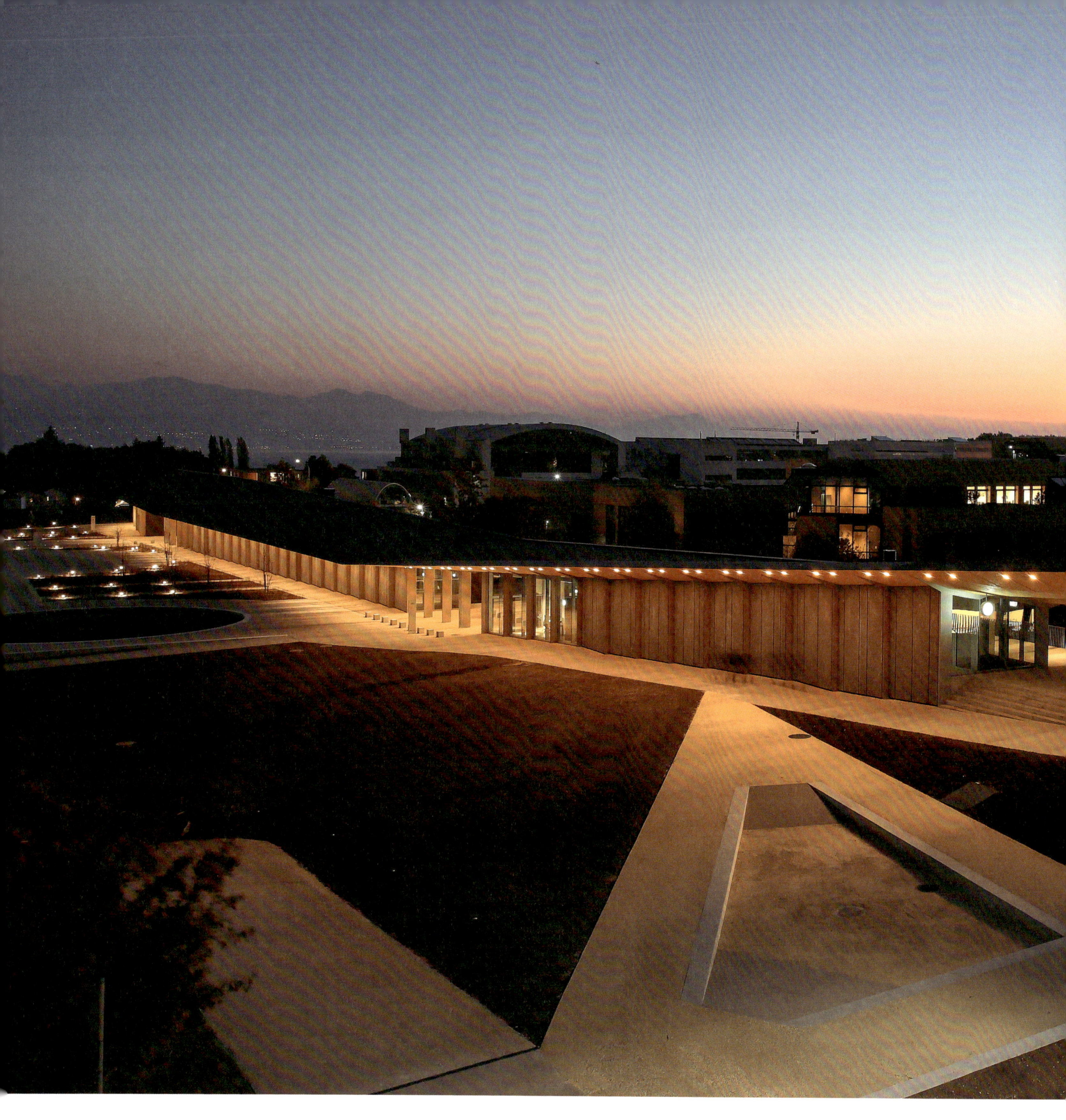

The entire building seen looking southwest, with Place Cosandey on the left. Below, the southern and northern ends of ArtLab.

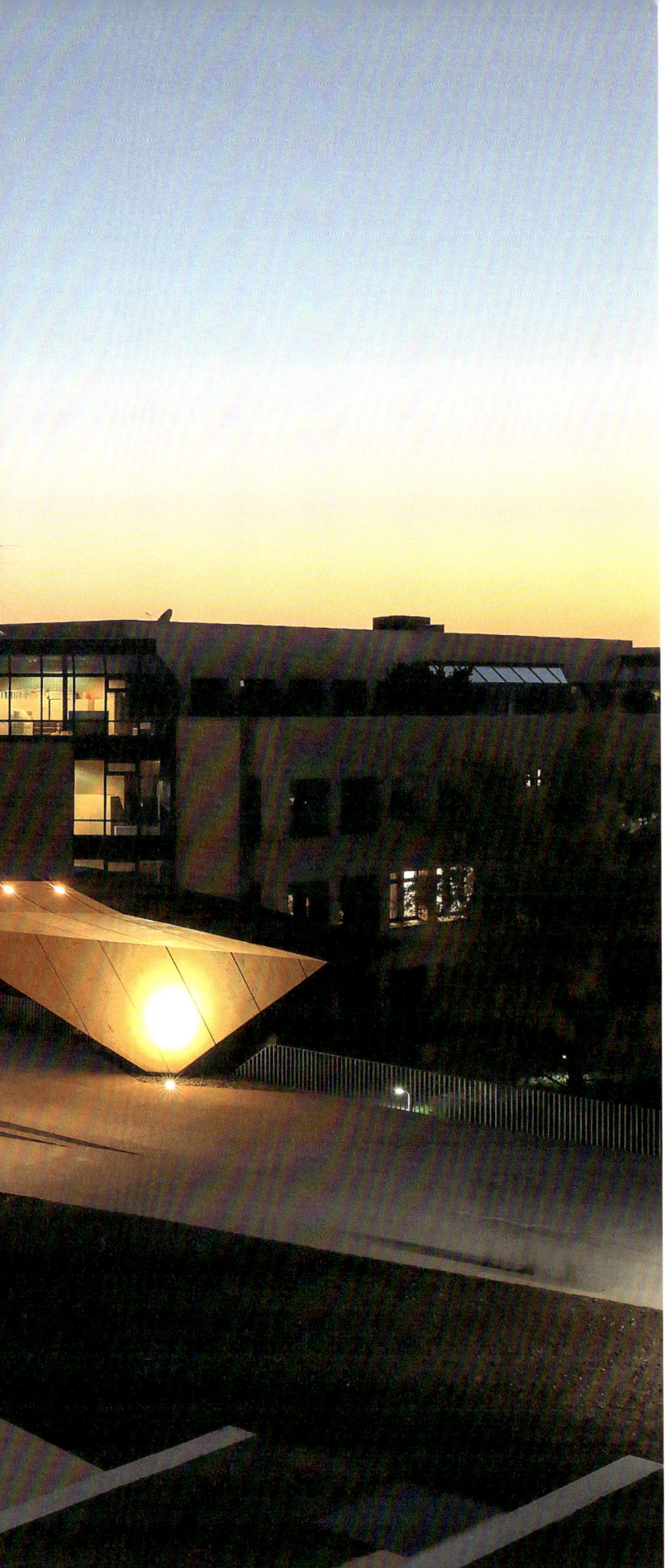

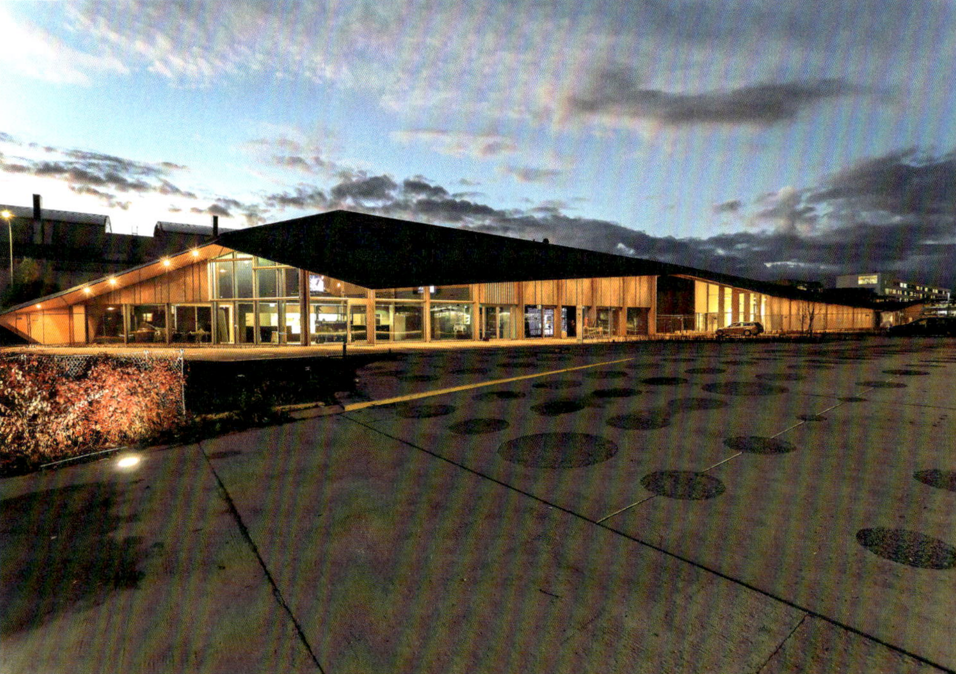

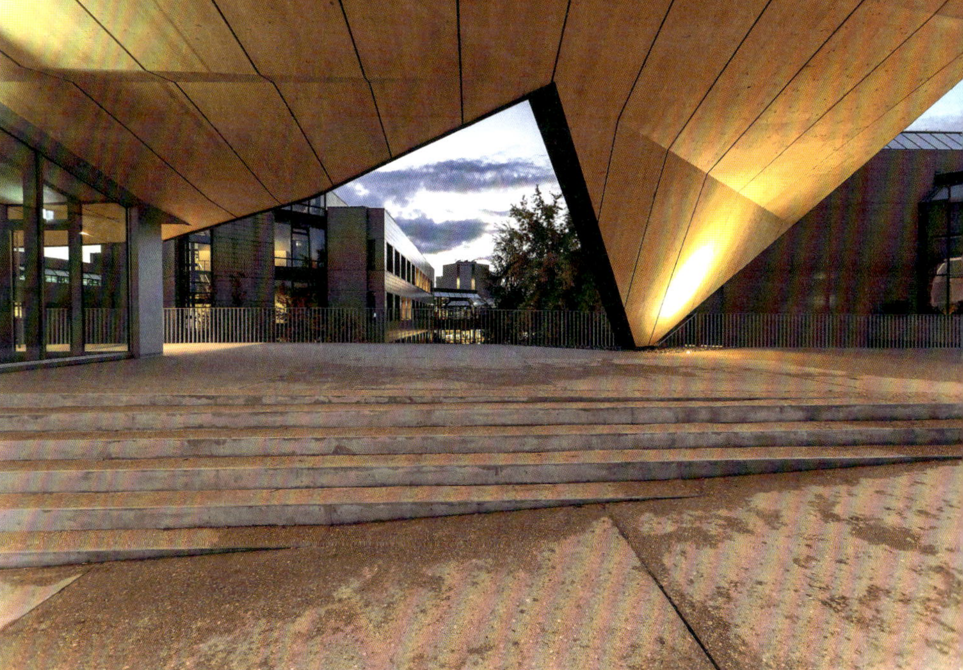

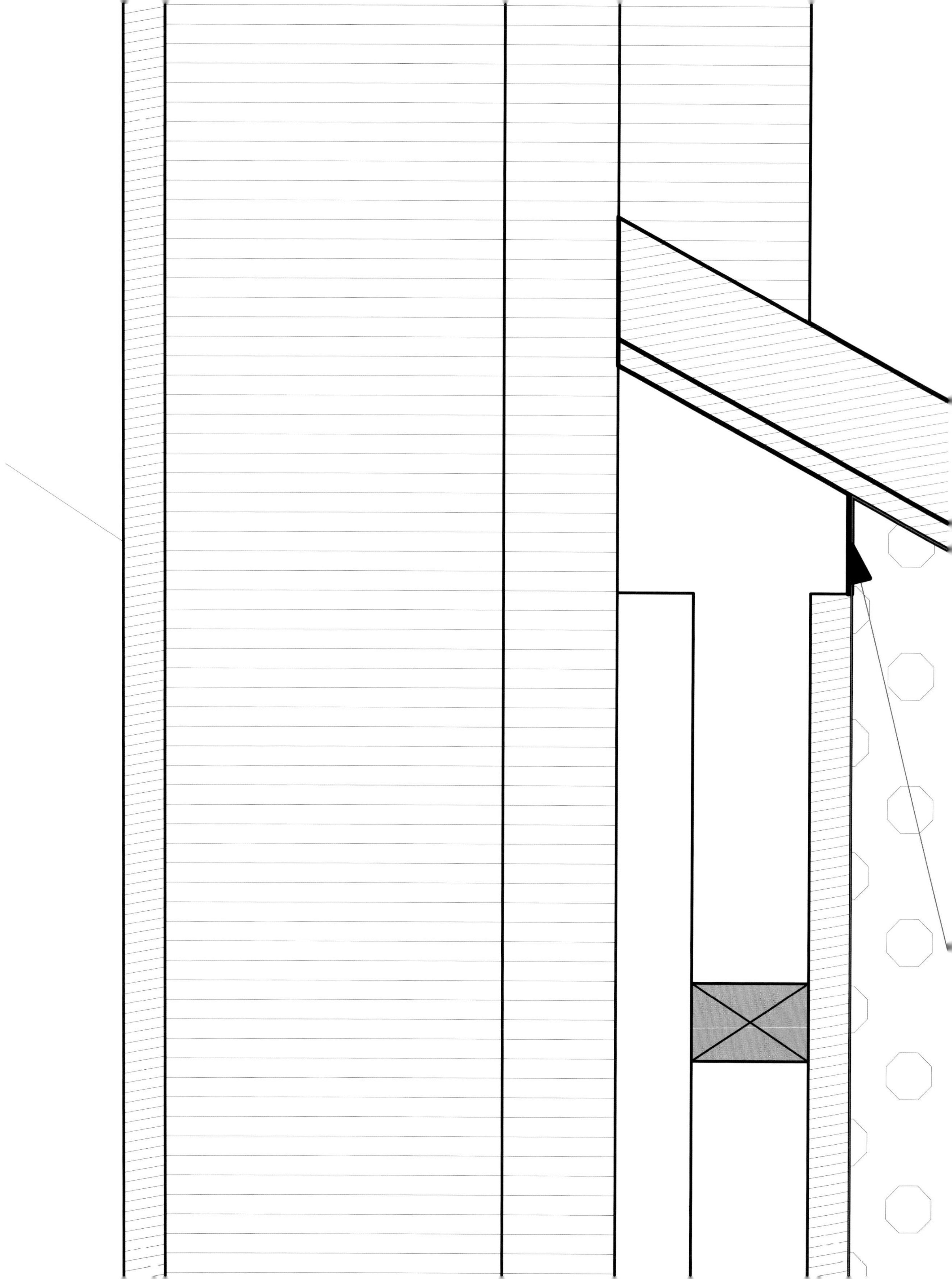

KENGO KUMA

THE FLOW
OF TIME ITSELF

Kengo Kuma was born in 1954 in Yokohama, situated to the south of Tokyo. He graduated with a master's degree from the Department of Architecture of the Graduate School of Engineering at the University of Tokyo in 1979. Kengo Kuma created the Spatial Design Studio in 1987 and Kengo Kuma & Associates four years later in Tokyo. He has been a professor at the Graduate School of Architecture, University of Tokyo, since 2009. He has also been a visiting professor at the School of Architecture of the University of Illinois at Urbana-Champaign (2007–08), and a lecturer at the Graduate School of Architecture, Planning and Preservation, Columbia University (New York, 1994). He is a winner of the Global Award for Sustainable Architecture 2016, for which his citation read in part: "Kengo Kuma is a true artist who has succeeded in modernizing the traditional methods employed by local craftsmen by working out how to industrialize these so that they survive through the twenty-first century without losing their extraordinary modular flexibility. This patient and continuous work of innovation has been carried out in close cooperation with Japanese craftsmen, in wood, earth, paper, while never losing sight of the contingencies of the contemporary economy."

Kuma has frequently worked on cultural projects, such as the Nagasaki Prefectural Art Museum (Nagasaki, 2005) or the more recent Yusuhara Wooden Bridge Museum (Yusuhara, Kochi, 2010). The architect has also begun to work extensively in Europe, opening an office in Paris in 2008. His FRAC PACA (Marseille, France) and Conservatory of Music, Dance, and Theater (Aix-en-Provence, France), were both completed in 2013. ArtLab, the main topic of this book, was completed in 2016. Kengo Kuma has also created a number of commercial buildings and spaces, such as One Omotesando (Tokyo, 2003); LVMH Osaka (Osaka, 2004); and Tiffany Ginza (Tokyo, 2008). In 2016, he won first prize in the competition for the design of the H. C. Andersen House of Fairy Tales (Odense, Denmark). Early in 2018, Kengo Kuma won the design competition for the new Maritime History Museum in Saint-Malo, France.

Not far from his own offices in the Minami Aoyama area of Tokyo, the Nezu Museum of Art (renovated by Kengo Kuma in 2009) is one of Tokyo's most famous and venerable institutions. Originally opened in 1914 in the two-hectare property of the Tobu Railway president Kaichiro Nezu (1860–1940), the museum is renowned both for its collections of Oriental art and for its Japanese garden. Kengo Kuma replaced a storage area and exhibition space on the street side of the institution with a new exhibition wing. The architect also renovated half of the exhibition areas built in 1990. "We thought of gently relating the new Nezu Museum, situated between an urban commercial district and the woods, through the silhouette of its gradually sloping roof," says Kengo Kuma. A line of bamboo trees "gently opens" the museum to the street. Bamboo veneer and sandstone from China were used for the interior cladding. The overall result sought is to allow "visitors to linger with the works of art in the woods." Kuma refers here in passing to "an urban commercial district." In fact, the Nezu Museum is located at the southern end of the fashionable Minami Aoyama (Omote Sando) street, which has been home to fashion boutiques by Future Systems (Rei Kawakubo, Comme des Garçons), Herzog & de Meuron (Prada), and Tadao Ando (Collezione). Without saying as much, Kengo Kuma strikes a decidedly different note than his colleagues, emphasizing Japanese culture (modern and historical) rather than putting forward international fashion.

A building that Kengo Kuma cites for its relation to his design for ArtLab is the Momofuku Ando Center of Outdoor Training (Ookubo, Nagano-ken, Japan, 2010). He says that the Ando Center is a "roof building" like ArtLab, and indeed the roof of the Japanese structure also comes down to the ground. This building in a forest is intended as a training center for "leaders who promote outdoor activities for young people." The varied functions of the center are all located under a single metal roof. "The image for the design consisted of a freely shaped complex where all of the various activities, including exercise, studying, eating, and sleeping, take place randomly under a long roof in the forest," according to the architects. The roof plates are finished in three different colors "in an attempt to give the structure the diverse shades of the trees in the forest." Finally, Kuma's office explains: "The street-shaped passageway that goes through the interior of the building goes up and down according to the contour of the site, making the building integral with the ground around it and giving you the feeling that you are taking a walk in the forest."[1]

An earlier building by Kengo Kuma, the Nakagawa-machi Bato Hiroshige Museum of Art (Bato, Nakagawa-machi, Nasu-gun, Tochigi, 2000) is also related to ArtLab because of its form and materials. The 1962-square-meter structure is dedicated to works by the Japanese *ukiyo-e* artist Ando Hiroshige and, as Kengo Kuma explains: "I wanted to create a building that represented the unique spatial configuration created in his woodblock prints, and attempted to create three-dimensional space that expresses his overlapping layers. This method uses transparent layers, which is in contrast with the use of perspective to create three-dimensional space in Western paintings, and had a large impact on the architecture of Frank Lloyd Wright."[2] Wooden louvers made with Japanese cedar control natural light in the museum, while long, extended eaves help the structure to achieve a high level of environmental performance. The long, narrow plan of the building and its continuous roof very clearly bring to mind the design of ArtLab, albeit in a specifically Japanese context.

Kengo Kuma has undertaken other work in Switzerland, albeit on a smaller scale. In 2014, he completed the renovation of 700 square meters of hotel space in Vals, near the celebrated Thermal Baths by Peter Zumthor (1996). "The project," explains Kengo Kuma, "was to renovate an apartment for the hotel staff to guest rooms. We aimed for rooms like caves filled with warmth and intimacy. The basic unit is an oak panel of forty centimeters width. The room is covered by the units that extend to the whole space, with one side of the panel overlapping the side of the next one. Lights are set between the panels, which is an attempt to integrate the interior and the lighting. The bed here is not a separate piece of furniture."[3] A further 500 square meters of work was done on the same site, completed in late 2015, with Kuma creating penthouses on top of the existing hotel in this instance. Local Vals stone was used for the floors "creating a ground in the air," according to the architect.[4]

Kengo Kuma won another international competition in Switzerland, in 2017, to design the Grand Morillon student residence at the Graduate Institute of International and Development Studies in Geneva. This 700-bed student residence, together with kitchens, laundry rooms, sport facilities, a library, study areas, and a cafeteria, will form part of a new district that will also house the headquarters of Médecins sans Frontières (Doctors without Borders) and accommodation for international civil servants. The overall neighborhood will include housing, offices, shops, and wooded areas, as well as a tram stop on the new line to Ferney-Voltaire.[5]

Kengo Kuma's most significant current project is the National Stadium for the 2020 Tokyo Olympic Games. This $1.26 billion structure is intended to seat 68,000 people in the athletics mode, and as many as 80,000 for football. Kuma has based his design on the use of Japanese lumber, and the idea that in calling on a form of "natural architecture" it is possible to make buildings a part of the landscape. "I want to go beyond the era of concrete," said Kuma in 2016. "What people want is soft, warm, and humane architecture." The design calls on the form of the pagodas of Kyoto and Nara, with plants adorning the eaves. The concrete curves used by Kenzo Tange for the Yoyogi National Gymnasium (1964) inspired Kengo Kuma to become an architect, but he now sees wood as having become more representative of contemporary Japan. "We will show the model of a mature society in the stadium," Kuma stated. "That's the way to live a happy life relying on limited natural resources from

a small land."[6] References to Tange's buildings for the 1964 Tokyo Olympic Games are significant in that they clearly announced the emergence of an indigenous modernity on a par in terms of quality and inventiveness with that of the West. Prior to this period, Japan had few realizations that could be considered significant on the stage of international contemporary architecture. Taking an opposite tack today, moving to the use of wood as opposed to the concrete that makes up so much of modern Japan, is a gesture that is recognized as significant for this moment and for the future. With the National Stadium, taken on in circumstances that attracted international attention linked to the abandonment of an earlier Zaha Hadid scheme, Kuma has brought his work and reputation to new heights.

Kengo Kuma has used wood as a main material in many buildings, aside from ArtLab and the upcoming Tokyo National Stadium. These include a Starbucks coffee shop at Dazaifu Tenmangu (Fukuoka, 2012), and the Daiwa Computing Research Building at the University of Tokyo (2014). In an interesting essay called *Defeated Architecture*, Kuma explores the differences between concrete and wood as building materials. "With concrete, everything is sudden. A substance that was as fluid as water becomes solid suddenly and irreversibly one day. To go back to where we were earlier, we must pulverize the concrete using enormous amounts of energy and forcibly start over once more. Time was not so discontinuous with wooden construction. A building could be altered a bit at a time, leaving the framework as is. We constructed, fixed, and destroyed a bit at a time. There was no suddenness. There was no temporal disconnection. There was no beginning and no end. We never arrived at a state of completion. Architecture was not a momentary event but the flow of time itself."[7]

1   http://kkaa.co.jp/works/architecture/the-momofuku-ando-center-of-outdoor-training/ (accessed on March 25, 2018).

2   http://kkaa.co.jp/works/architecture/nakagawa-machi-bato-hiroshige-museum-of-art/ (accessed on March 25, 2018).

3   http://kkaa.co.jp/works/architecture/therme-vals/ (accessed on March 26, 2018).

4   http://kkaa.co.jp/works/architecture/therme-suiteroom-vals/ (accessed on March 26, 2018).

5   http://graduateinstitute.ch/home/relations-publiques/news-at-the-institute/news-archives.html/_/news/corporate/2017/new-student-residence (accessed on March 25, 2018).

6   "Olympic stadium architect sees wood as way to change Tokyo's concrete legacy," *The Japan Times*, May 30, 2017. https://www.japantimes.co.jp/news/2017/05/30/national/olympic-stadium-architect-sees-wood-way-change-tokyos-concrete-legacy/#.WrfatWaB1GU (accessed on March 25, 2018).

7   Kengo Kuma, *Defeated Architecture*, Iwanami Shoten, Tokyo, 2004.

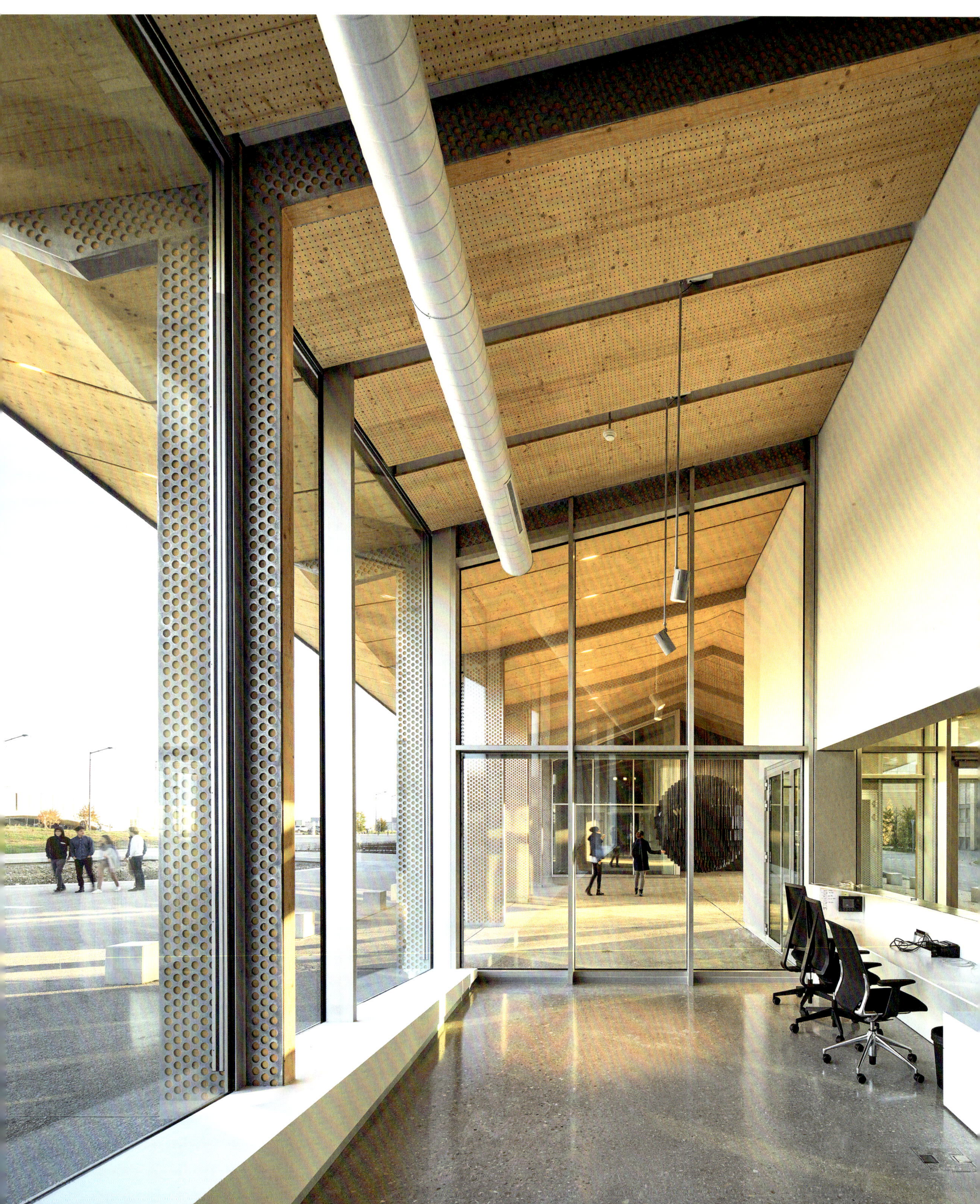
Kengo Kuma wanted the building to be as open as possible.
Right, stairs leading to the northern entrance of the structure.

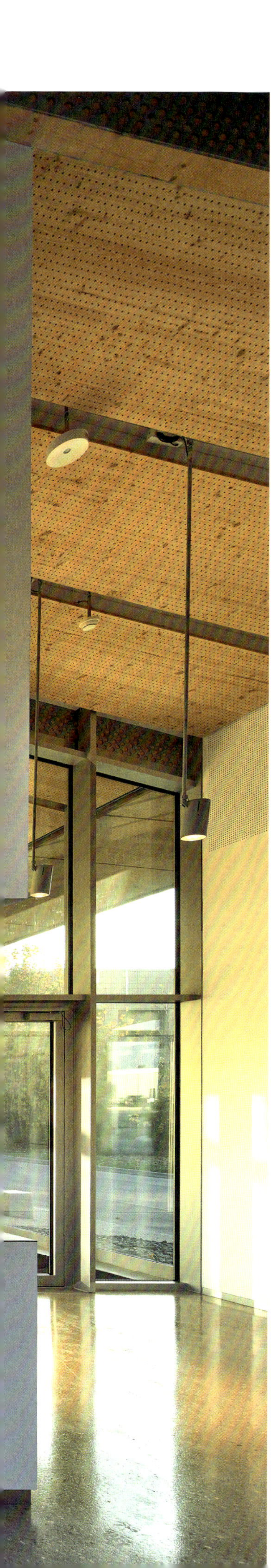

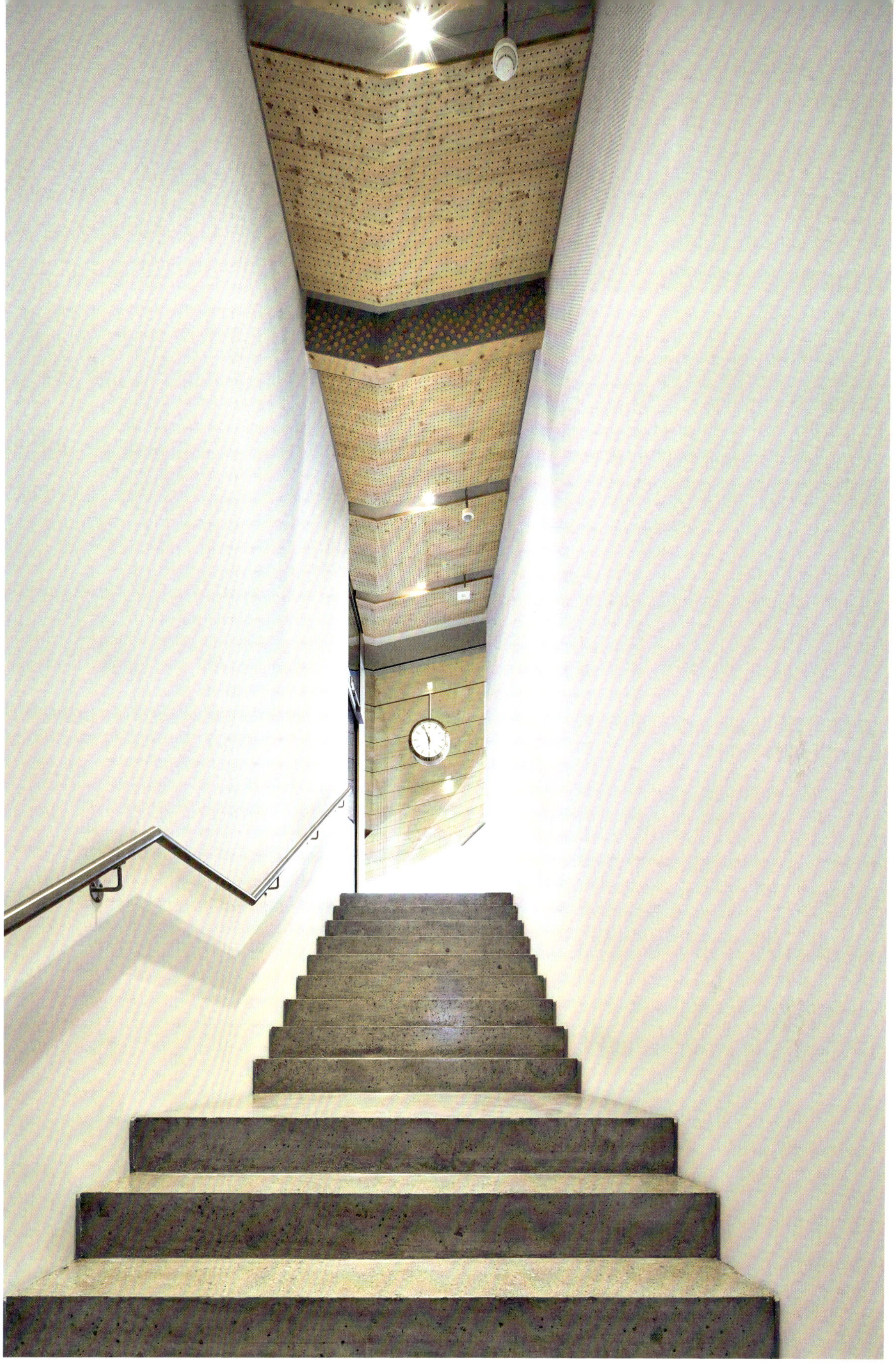

UNDER ONE ROOF

EPFL organized a competition for three pavilions on Place Cosandey in 2012, two years after the completion of the Rolex Learning Center. The clear intention of the competition was to "connect science and culture at EPFL," but also to form the western side of Place Cosandey. The broader project, called Objective: Campus (Objectif Campus), is laid out in detail in the strategic planning documents of EPFL. According to the document "EPFL Plan de développement 2012–16," "the Objectif Campus project is a logical response to the evolution of a campus that is active twenty-four hours a day, 365 days a year. Its goal is to define a clear and coherent vision of the campus for students and staff, but also for the numerous visitors who come to the site." The report goes on to say that the first step of this scheme was carried out in 2009–10 with the creation of Place Cosandey, and to announce the creation of facilities to accommodate the Montreux Jazz Festival archives, a place to present the projects of EPFL, and a "modular and flexible space" dedicated to the interface between the technologies developed by EPFL and culture."[1]

The competition program made clear reference to the "Montreux Jazz Lab," an "Arts and Science Pavilion" and a "Demonstration Pavilion" (space for the presentation of technologies and inventions developed by EPFL) as three distinct entities, although the unifying theme of the initiative was to "build bridges between hard science and the humanities, an area that has been inscribed in the curriculum since 2000." The other finalists in the competition, known for pavilion design in particular, were the Basel firm HHF + AWP from Paris, Harry Gugger (Basel); Made In (Geneva); Barkow Leibinger (Berlin); 2b Architects (Lausanne); FRPO (Madrid); Jakob + MacFarlane (Paris); Carlo Ratti (Lugano); Berger & Berger (Paris); Convergo | Waldvogel & Huang (Lausanne); 168 Saint-Denis (Lausanne); and Kengo Kuma (Tokyo). This list is skewed toward Swiss architects with some French participation, with the notable exception of Kengo Kuma. At the end of 2012, the competition jury chose the Japanese architect Kengo Kuma, whose design differed from other competition entries in that he maintained the program concept of three pavilions but resolved their presence as a single structure under a very long roof. The Japanese architect also gave the building its original name. "Our proposal," he said, "was to bring these three pavilions together under one roof—hence the name of our project, 'Under One Roof.'"[2]

Construction of the project began in August 2014 and was carried out by the general contractor Marti Construction SA. The construction cost was 30.9 million Swiss francs and the cost of equipment, listening booths, and permanent display structures was 4.6 million Swiss francs.[3] Almost half of the 35.5-million-franc cost of the building, including equipment, was financed with private funds and one million Swiss francs from the tech firm Logitech.

In 2012, Kengo Kuma stated:

"This vast project site allowed us to locate the pavilions in many possible locations and configurations. Finally, we decided to gather the three required pavilions into one very long and thin building that would transform the site from being a dysfunctional void into a campus connection hub: the 250-meter-long roof will shelter and go along with the students' walking flow from the north Esplanade plaza down south to their residences several times a day.

The porches provided between the volumes under the roof will be aligned to the main street coming from the West side, leading to the main public parking areas, and to the new tree avenue coming from the East, currently under construction. Therefore, the porches will provide permeability through the building attracting and connecting both these sides of the campus. By transforming the site into a place where students, professors, and visitors will pleasantly pass by every day, enjoying the new cultural activities that will take place under this roof, we are confident that this whole area will become the new center of the campus and will bring a more social and cultural dimension to EPFL."[4]

In keeping with the objectives of the university, Kengo Kuma's ArtLab is clearly an urban gesture as well as an architectural one. It defines the western boundary of Place Cosandey in an elegant and surprisingly light way. One clear reason for its surprisingly light form is that the building is only six meters wide at the north end and sixteen meters wide at the southern end. Its long form gives clear reality to the idea of a strong north-south axis on the campus. It leads in one direction to the rest of the campus and in the other toward the town of Saint-Sulpice, where there is student housing, and the vastness of Lac Léman (Lake Geneva) and the Alps beyond. ArtLab provides a surprisingly modest urban and architectural statement to the campus of EPFL. Despite its manifest presence, the building, which descends a light slope a bit like a snake according to the architect, does not manifest itself as a barrier—because of its two large openings, but also because the roof overhangs the entire façade along Place Cosandey. A concrete walkway provides at least partial shelter from rain along the north-south axis. Rather than a barrier, or a

long-closed building, ArtLab succeeds in creating an impression of great openness despite having few glazed surfaces.

The majority of buildings on the EPFL campus are what Kengo Kuma calls "box" buildings, with several levels and a number of functions. Here, each function occupies a single pavilion with DataSquare, an interactive display space for EPFL-created projects at the north end, the Art and Science Pavilion, an Experimental Exhibition Space in the middle, and the Montreux Jazz Café, which shows the music festival's archived collection, digitized by EPFL, at the southern end. The three volumes are divided by two wide, covered entry spaces that cross through the building and open Place Cosandey to the buildings beyond, including the university's Innovation Park. These entry sequences clearly recall the Japanese concept of spaces that are neither fully inside, nor fully outdoors.

Kengo Kuma calls ArtLab a "roof building" (see the interview, p. 100), meaning that its three volumes are fully linked by a 250-meter-long folded plane roof. The roof, which comes down to the ground at the southern end near the Montreux Jazz Café, is clad in square slate shingles that are set at a 45° angle, giving a more natural effect than pure alignment might have generated. The folded aspect of the roof, which is reflected inside, means that the spaces, including the gallery area, are not fully orthogonal. The exhibition space has vertical walls that are 4.6 meters high. Rather than boxes, the interior spaces of ArtLab are more like flowing, folding, ambiguous volumes, which remain perfectly usable for almost any conceivable future use. There is little natural light inside the building, at the request of EPFL and in order to allow screen presentations and the usual protection of works of art.

Despite its apparent irregularity, due mostly to the appearance of the folding roof, ArtLab was built essentially on the basis of a series of fifty-seven prefabricated frames of different heights, set 3.65 meters apart and erected on a concrete foundation. These frames were made with a sandwich of partially perforated steel plates, glued laminated larch, and clear glue. The thickness of the steel varies according to the loads borne at specific points in the structure. The steel has round openings that allow the enclosed wood to become visible. This sandwich design obviates the potential for the steel employed to become a thermal bridge since wood does not conduct heat, or very poorly. The aged larch employed is painted a silver-gray color on all vertical surfaces, while the wood visible under the eaves of the building is unpainted. Though making the structural system visible is an idea that occurs frequently in contemporary architecture, here the architect achieves a degree of poetic simplicity without disguising the structural reality of the building. The mixture of steel and wood combined with glass and the slate roof is entirely visible but seems more like a purely natural presence than a self-conscious effort to exhibit engineering solutions. Given the budget available and also in keeping with the overall simplicity and continuity of the building, polished concrete was chosen for the floors and white gypsum board for walls and sloping ceilings inside. Kengo Kuma is fully satisfied with the construction and detailing quality of this building. Despite being located in Tokyo, the architect of course visited the site on numerous occasions, but also benefited from the presence of his Partner in Charge, Javier Villar Ruiz. The local architects for the competition phase were the Zurich firm Holzer Kobler, and CCHE Lausanne during the construction, and lighting was conceived by Hervé Descottes (L'Observatoire).

In the competition concepts, EPFL had the idea of three pavilions—essentially for music, the arts, and the "digital humanities" work of the university. The fact that the competition for the three structures was launched simultaneously underlined the idea of EPFL to bring these disciplines together. Kengo Kuma, instead, created a single building to contain the three functions while maintaining the tri-partite pavilion-based structure. At its upper end, the roof of ArtLab rises up in an inviting gesture to students and others arriving from the side of the EPFL Esplanade, heart of the "old" campus. From this point, ArtLab engages in the concerted effort of EPFL directors to make the campus and the university itself an open place. Open to the public, ArtLab also draws a long, but permeable line along the eastern side of Place Cosandey, giving an urban sense to a square that would otherwise be a relatively undefined space. The long folding roof of ArtLab symbolically joins together the three areas of intellectual exploration set down by the university; it speaks in architectural terms to the *transversality* of future education referred to by successive presidents of EPFL. These pavilions are "Under One Roof" not only for reasons of architectural design, but quite clearly because the future holds more and more communication and cross-fertilization between disciplines. At

its southernmost end, ArtLab opens to the landscape with the broad windows of the Montreux Jazz Café, but, importantly as well, its roof bows down to touch the earth. Here, both ArtLab and (finally) EPFL have been integrated into their incredible landscape of Lac Léman and the Alps. The long line formed by ArtLab from the upper Esplanade to this point of communion with the earth also suggests that students and others passing here should lift their eyes and be inspired by the very unity of nature. Despite its unexpected form, ArtLab at once represents an urban gesture, forming the missing side of Place Cosandey, and the embodiment of an intellectual process that engages EPFL in a future of openness and interdisciplinary thought.

1   "EPFL Plan de développement 2012–16," at
    https://direction.epfl.ch/files/content/sites/direction/
    files/EPFL%20Plan%20développement%202012-2016%20
    310811%20fin.pdf (accessed on March 25, 2018).
2   Kengo Kuma, at https://actu.epfl.ch/news/experimental-
    pavilion-to-bridge-
    culture-and-scie-2/ (accessed on March 26, 2018).
3   At https://artlab.epfl.ch/page-134142-en.html (accessed on
    March 25, 2018).
4   Kengo Kuma, at https://www.archdaily.com/801503/
    under-one-roof-kengo-kuma-and-associates (accessed on
    March 25, 2018).

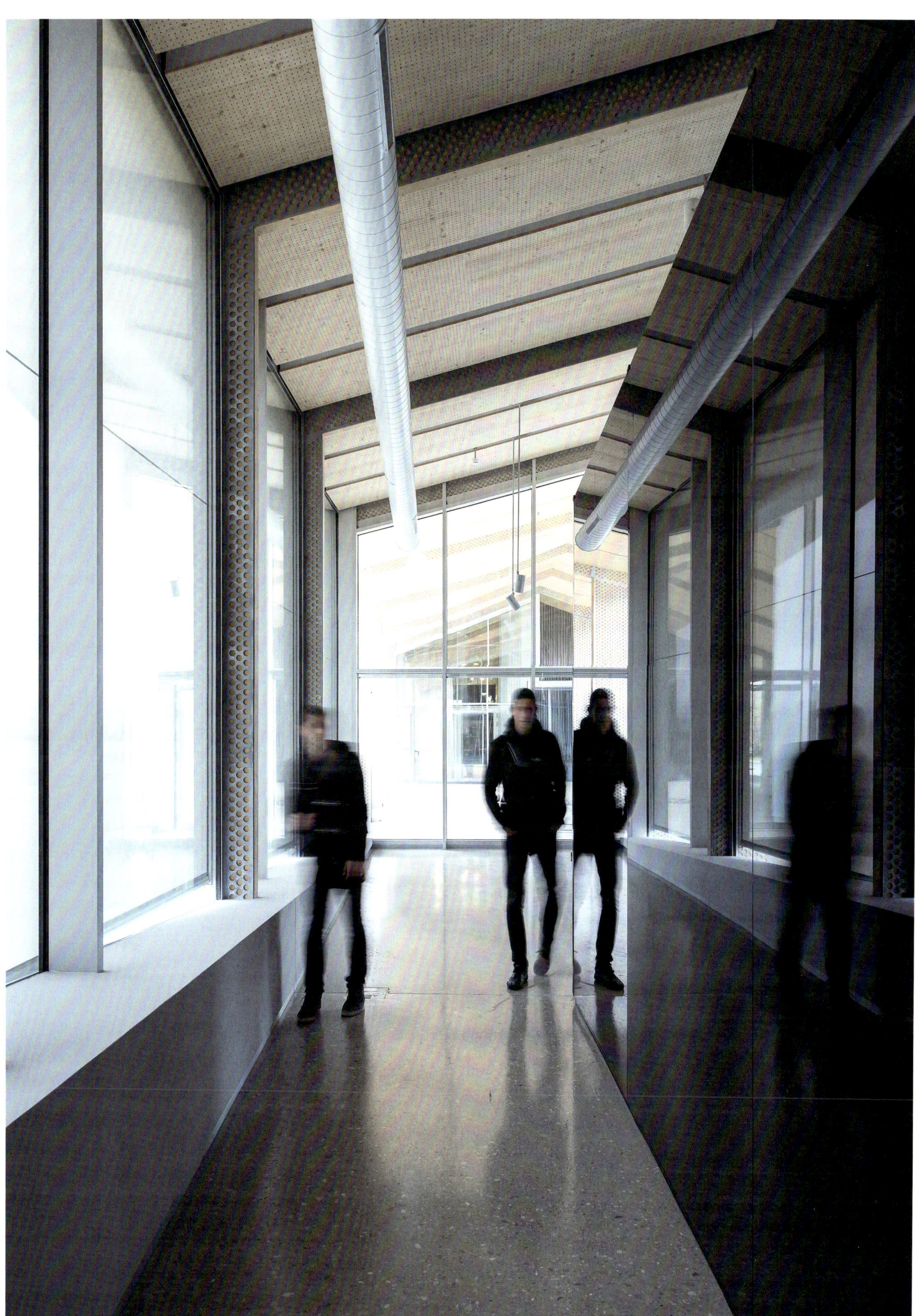

Interior volumes are generous and can readily be used for numerous different purposes.

THREE WORKS OF ART

Within the domain of ArtLab, three sculptures mark the real, permanent presence of art and culture within view of Place Cosandey. Antoine Poncet's *Aileiotrope* (white marble, 270 centimeters high, 200 centimeters wide, 1992; pp. 96–97) was purchased by the Swiss Commission fédérale des Beaux-Arts subsequent to an exhibition on the artist held at the Fondation Gianadda in Martigny. Antoine Poncet was born in 1928 in Paris. A grandson of the painter Maurice Denis, and son of the Swiss painter Marcel Poncet, Antoine Poncet attended the École cantonale de dessin et d'art appliqué, the precursor of ECAL, today one of the partner schools of EPFL, in Lausanne beginning in 1943. Poncet worked in his early years with Jean Arp (1953–55), Constantin Brancusi, and Henri Laurens. Beginning in 1964, he worked in Carrara, at the same time as Henry Moore and Marino Marini. *Aileiotrope* certainly brings to mind the lyrical modern art of Brancusi and Arp; it appears to evoke a bird but does not resolve itself into a fully figurative form. Though it is of relatively substantial size, this sculpture has nothing monumental about it, rather it is lyrical and clearly evokes movement. In this context, standing in front of the silver-gray wooden walls of ArtLab it announces that this is a place where culture is in movement.

A second, even larger sculpture hangs under the eaves of ArtLab near the entrance to DataSquare. Called *Bing Bang*, it is made of burned and patinated oak and nickel-titanium wire (pp. 98–99, 132). It is a 5.9-meter-high sphere with a diameter of 2.5 meters. The wooden strips that form the work are hung on their wires from the high roof of the Kuma building and move when touched, or even in a light wind. The sounds made by gentle collisions of the oak strips are likened by the artist to the first sounds of the universe, whence the title of the work. The artist, Etienne Krähenbühl, was born in Vevey, Switzerland, in 1953 and briefly attended the École cantonale d'art in Lausanne before becoming a practicing artist. Beginning in 1997 and for a period of sixteen years, he worked with Rolf Gotthardt, a professor at EPFL who specialized in shape memory alloys. The art critic Françoise Jaunin wrote of this meeting that "a collaboration ensued that brought the artist, between science and poetry, sensitivity and monumentality, gravity and weightlessness, to push the limits of materials, bringing out movements and sounds from the depths of the earth."[1] The connection between the artist and the work of a professor at EPFL makes the positioning of *Bing Bang*, under the eaves of ArtLab, particularly meaningful.

The third sculpture present at EPFL is indoors, in the boardroom situated between the Montreux Jazz Café and the Experimental Exhibition Space. Called *Pierre au firmament* (Stone in the Firmament), this work by the Lausanne sculptor Yves Dana was given to EPFL by Patrick Aebischer in 2016. When asked to comment on the work, Yves Dana says only: "A stone rises, stretches toward its own sky, is crossed through by a moon. Open in its center so that what is beyond form can appear." Set in a vertical position on a base designed by the artist, *Pierre au firmament* bears an uncanny resemblance to the long, narrow building in which it is located, as though art and architecture in this place could be in perfect harmony.

Yves Dana was born in 1959, in Alexandria, Egypt. In 1961, his family left Egypt, settling in Switzerland. Yves Dana received a degree in Sociology from the University of Lausanne in 1978, then graduated from the School of Fine Arts of Geneva in 1981. He currently lives and works between two places, his primary workshop in the Orangerie in Lausanne, and a second in Pietrasanta (Tuscany); he has worked in iron, stone, and bronze throughout his career. Yves Dana received the Grand Prize of the Fondation Vaudoise pour la Culture for his entire career (2015).

1 Françoise Jaunin, at http://www.3-dfoundation.com/index. php/etienne-krahenbuhl/ (accessed on March 25, 2018).

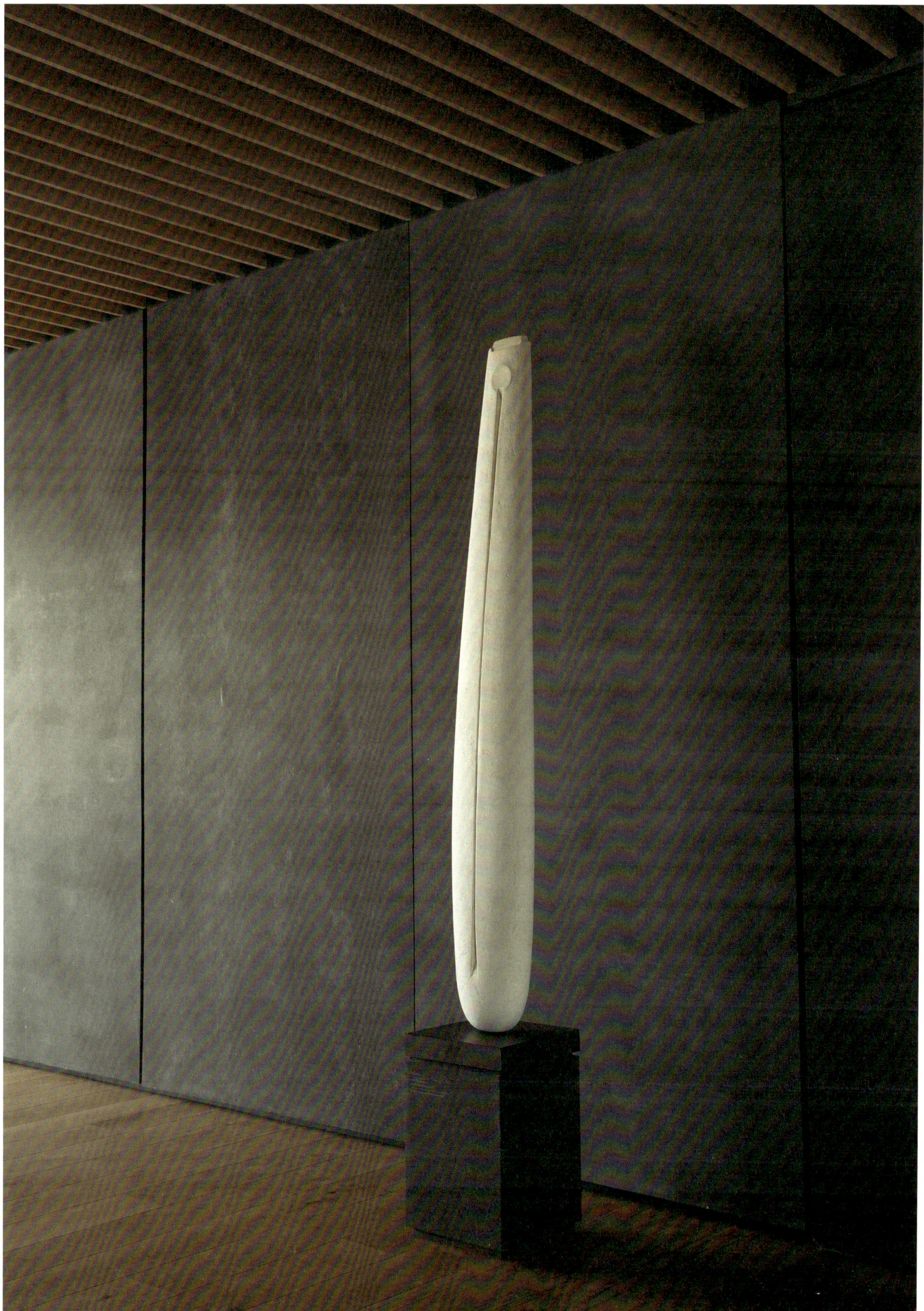

Yves Dana, *Pierre au firmament* (Stone in the Firmament), 2016,
white Sinai limestone, h. 172 cm.

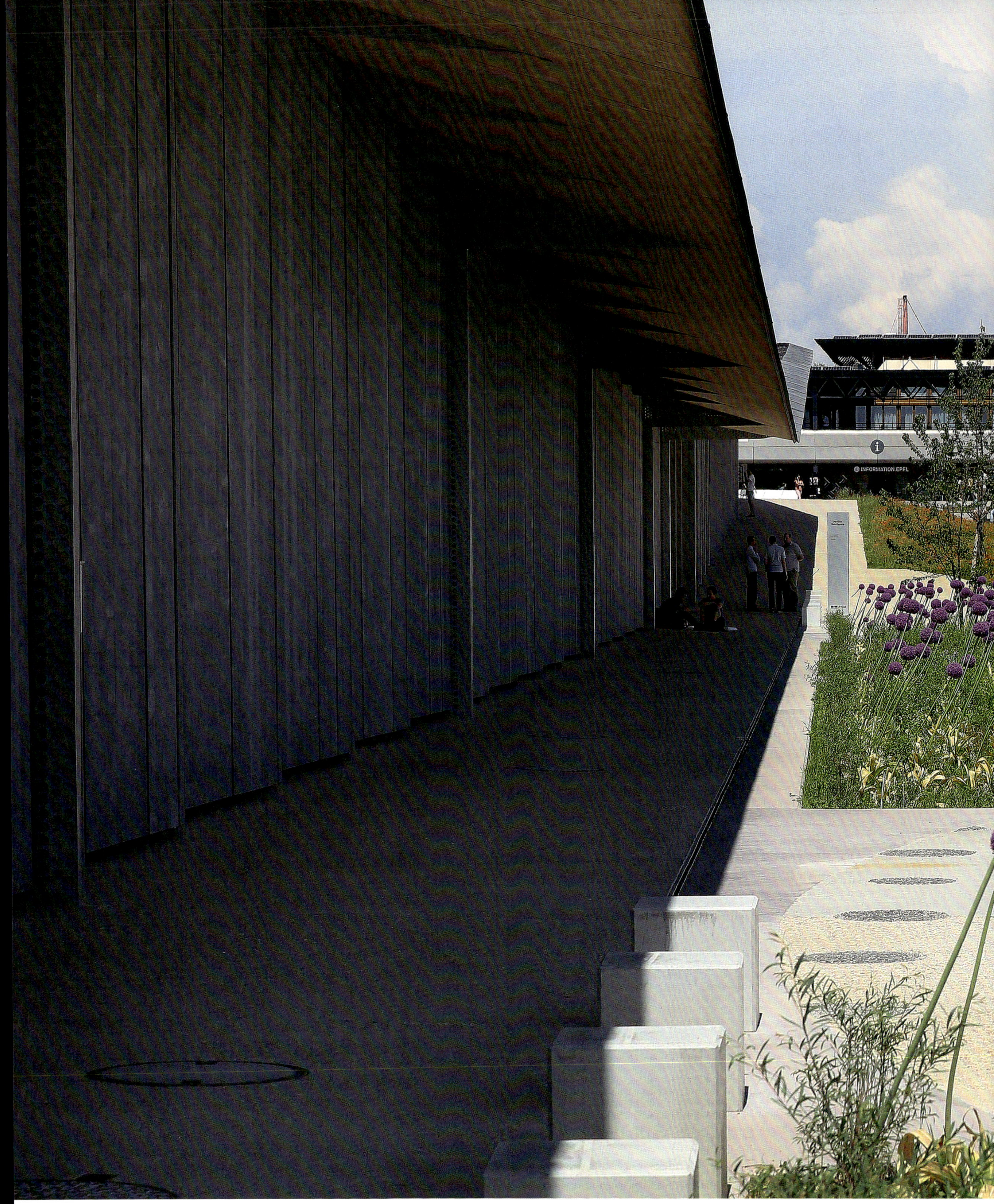

INFORMATION EPFL

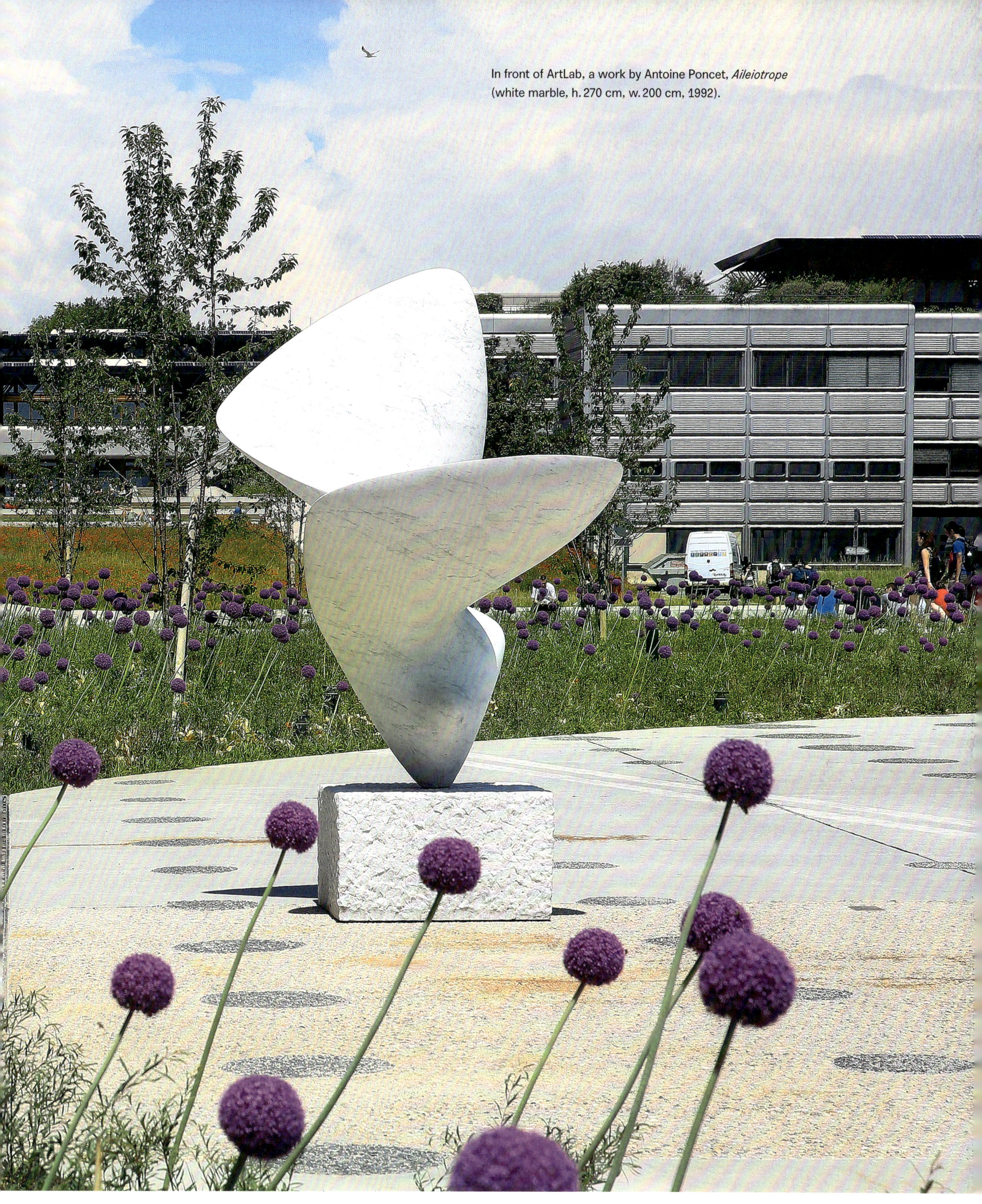

In front of ArtLab, a work by Antoine Poncet, *Aileiotrope*
(white marble, h. 270 cm, w. 200 cm, 1992).

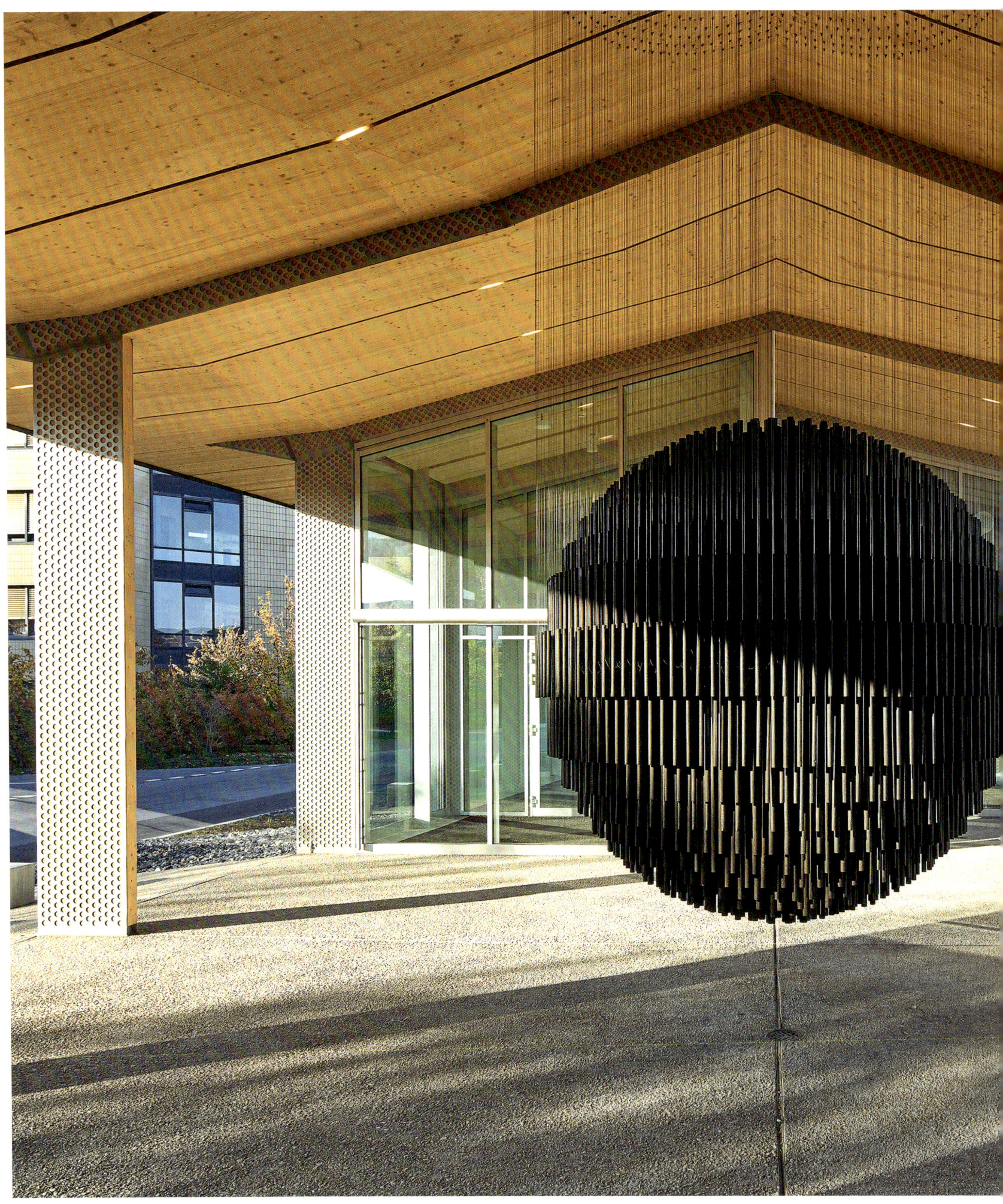

Under the eaves of ArtLab, *Bing Bang* by Etienne Krähenbühl
(oak, nickel-titanium wire, h. 5.9 meters, diameter 2.5 meters, 2016).

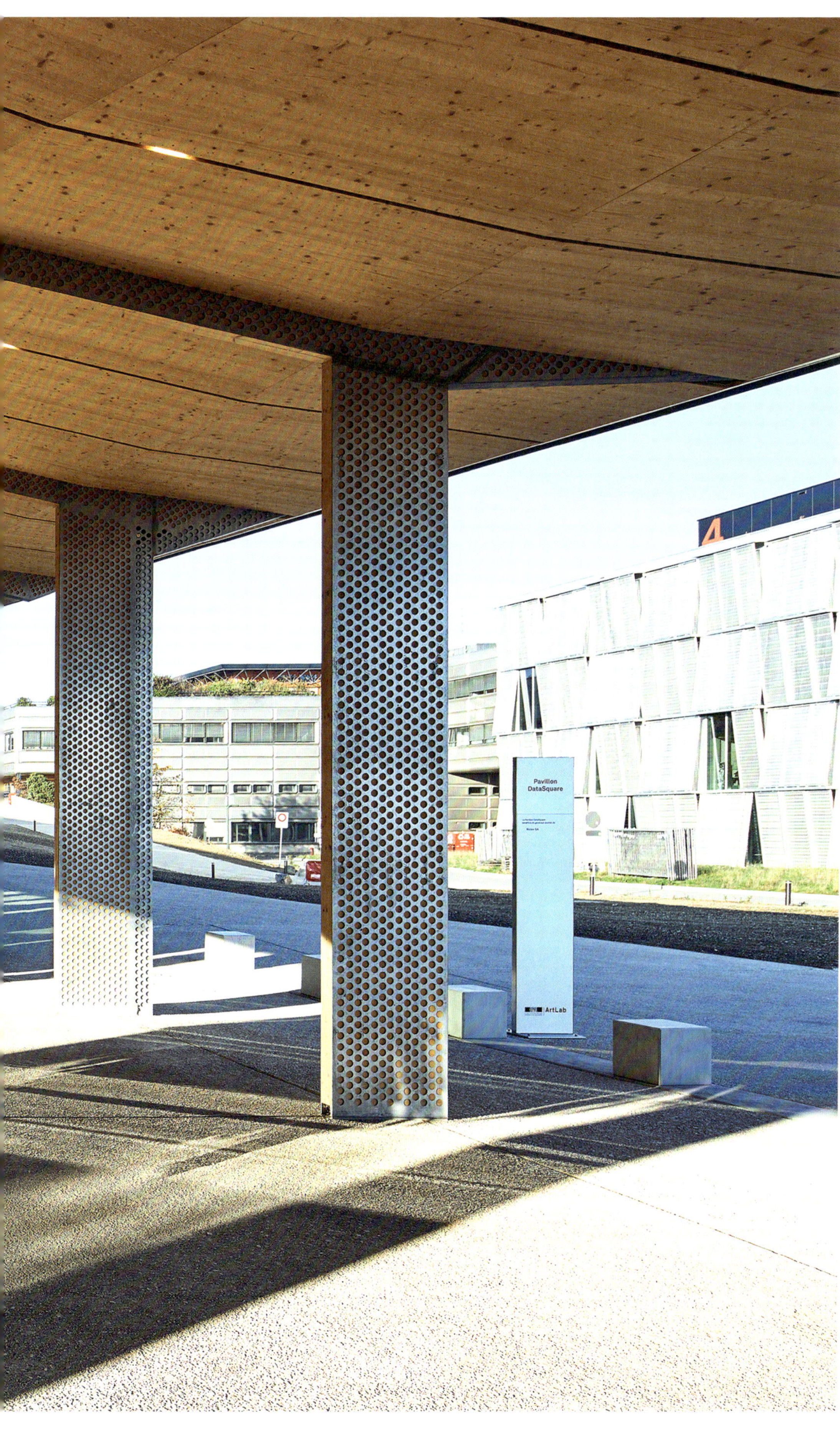

Pavillon
DataSquare

ArtLab

A ROOF BUILDING — INTERVIEW OF KENGO KUMA

How did this project begin? Did you know the president of EPFL prior to that time? [1]

The project started as a design competition, and before that competition I did not know Patrick Aebischer. There was a two-stage competition with documents to be submitted in the first round, and then more precise elements for those selected for the second round. The site was defined by the program, as the border of the square. It was very unusual. I like that kind of long building, and I have created others such as the Hiroshige Museum (Nakagawa-machi Bato Hiroshige Museum of Art, Bato, Tochigi, Japan, 2000).

Did you visit the site before engaging in this process?

I visited the Rolex Learning Center before the competition. I like that building very much. I wanted from the outset to create a kind of response to the center, a type of contrast. The Rolex Learning Center can be imagined as a relatively flat-roof building. There is a lot of concrete and glass in the Rolex Learning Center

and I wanted to search for an opposite solution. I wanted to use natural materials instead of white concrete. I believe that contrast between two buildings that are opposite each other can activate the space that lies between them. The lines of the two buildings serve to define the space. There are also concrete buildings on the opposite side of ArtLab, so I was convinced that I should make a softer, lighter structure.

There are relatively large openings at two points in ArtLab. Did you always want the façades to be quite closed by comparison?

The openings in ArtLab correspond to an effort to respond to the street on the opposite side of the building. At the competition phase, we had more windows. For the museum space, the university did not want to have openings. Step by step, we removed the windows. The idea for the exhibition space was basically to create closed boxes. The idea of closing the building essentially came from the university.

Did you have many conversations with the president of EPFL in the course of the design period?
At the beginning of the project we had discussions with Patrick Aebischer. He came to Japan and saw some of our buildings and liked them. We talked many times about the philosophy of the building and that is to combine art and technology. He strongly believes that the future of the university will be about a mixture of technology and art, in the broader sense.

Was the program for the building clear to you from the beginning? Aside from the reduction of glazed surfaces, were there other changes in the design phase?
The basic use of the three spaces—a café, a museum, and a lab—was clear from the outset. This was in the requirements of the competition. There was originally a roof terrace on the café, but it was removed from the scheme for budgetary reasons.

How much did you have in mind the square that was taking shape between your building and that of SANAA?
Having a square in a university campus is important. Examples such as Oxford and Cambridge show that. It is a communication space of the campus. The EPFL campus had strong axes but no square. Part of my project was to define the square. The creation of the square serves to activate the flow of visitors and students in the campus. That was our starting point.

At first we worked on the design of the space, between the buildings, but that is closely related to the Perrault and SANAA buildings. Finally, it was the decision of Mr. Aebischer that the landscape should be designed by EPFL. We designed the space under the eaves, and that already influences the square. Landscaping is needed to make this space into a real square.

What are your thoughts about being opposite the work of other Japanese architects that you know well?
SANAA and I have already found ourselves with buildings that face each other. The Shibuya Station project concerns one of the biggest public transport hubs in Tokyo. The railway company is demolishing the old station and the East Plaza is being designed by us and the West Plaza by SANAA. There will probably be a contrast between us there as well.

The original campus of EPFL brings to mind an industrial aesthetic, like factories. SANAA also tried to change the atmosphere by employing a certain softness. We tried to change the rigidity by using a folded, sloped roof. That is a kind of implicit criticism of the existing campus.

Why did you choose to use wood as the main visible material for your building?
In some ways, the choice of the wood we used was the most difficult part of the design. We prepared a large number of wood samples and finishes. After a great deal of thought we chose spruce that is painted silver gray. This was my choice, the university did not intervene. The choice was deeply related to the place. We selected wood, but I wanted to create a harmony with what I call the industrial feeling of the campus. I thought that the natural color of the wood would destroy the harmony and that is why I used a grayish paint. It has a little bit of a "technical" feeling. There is a delicate balance between using wood and obtaining the desired harmony.

Is the building intentionally ambiguous?
I think that feeling comes from our design. It is not a "box building" it is a "roof building" and the two for me are based on different philosophies. The box building is clearly defined, but the roof building is more open, more ambiguous. I feel that the building is able to continually change. It is true that the program at the outset was very "soft" as compared, for example, to a classroom building. The idea of a roof building matches what I imagine to be a soft program that would allow for different uses in the future. I have designed roof buildings very often. The Ando Seminar House (Momofuku Ando Center of Outdoor Training, Ookubo, Nagano-ken, Japan, 2010) has a rather similar solution. Parts of the roof touch the ground. There too, the roof covers multiple functions.

How did you deal with the substantial length of the building?
It is a kind of snake coming down the hill. The basic idea is to soften the length of the building. If a structure of this length had a rigid wall, it would probably look like an army building. We wanted to make it softer and to give it some movement.

1   Kengo Kuma in conversation with the author,
     Paris, June 7, 2017.

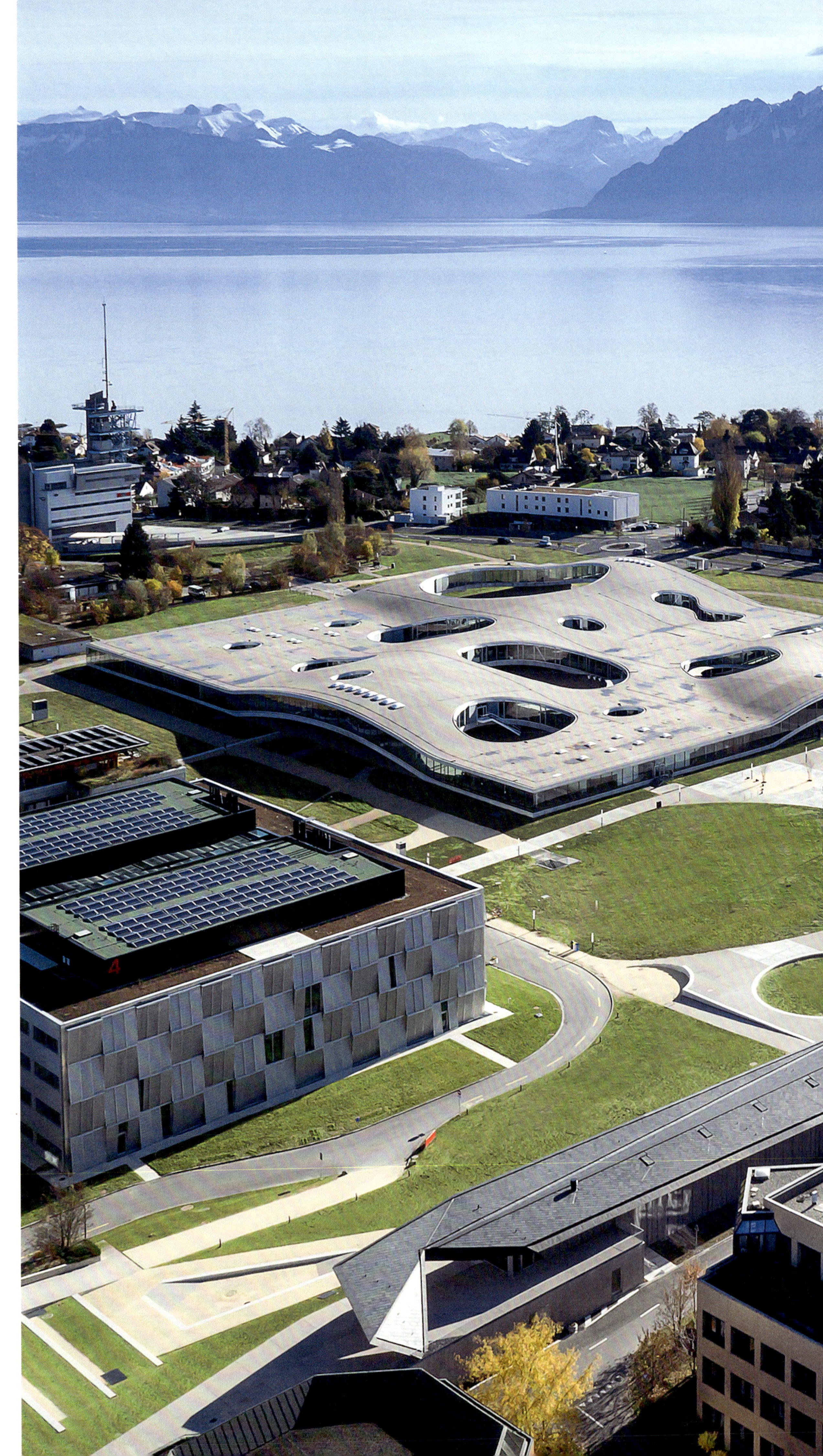

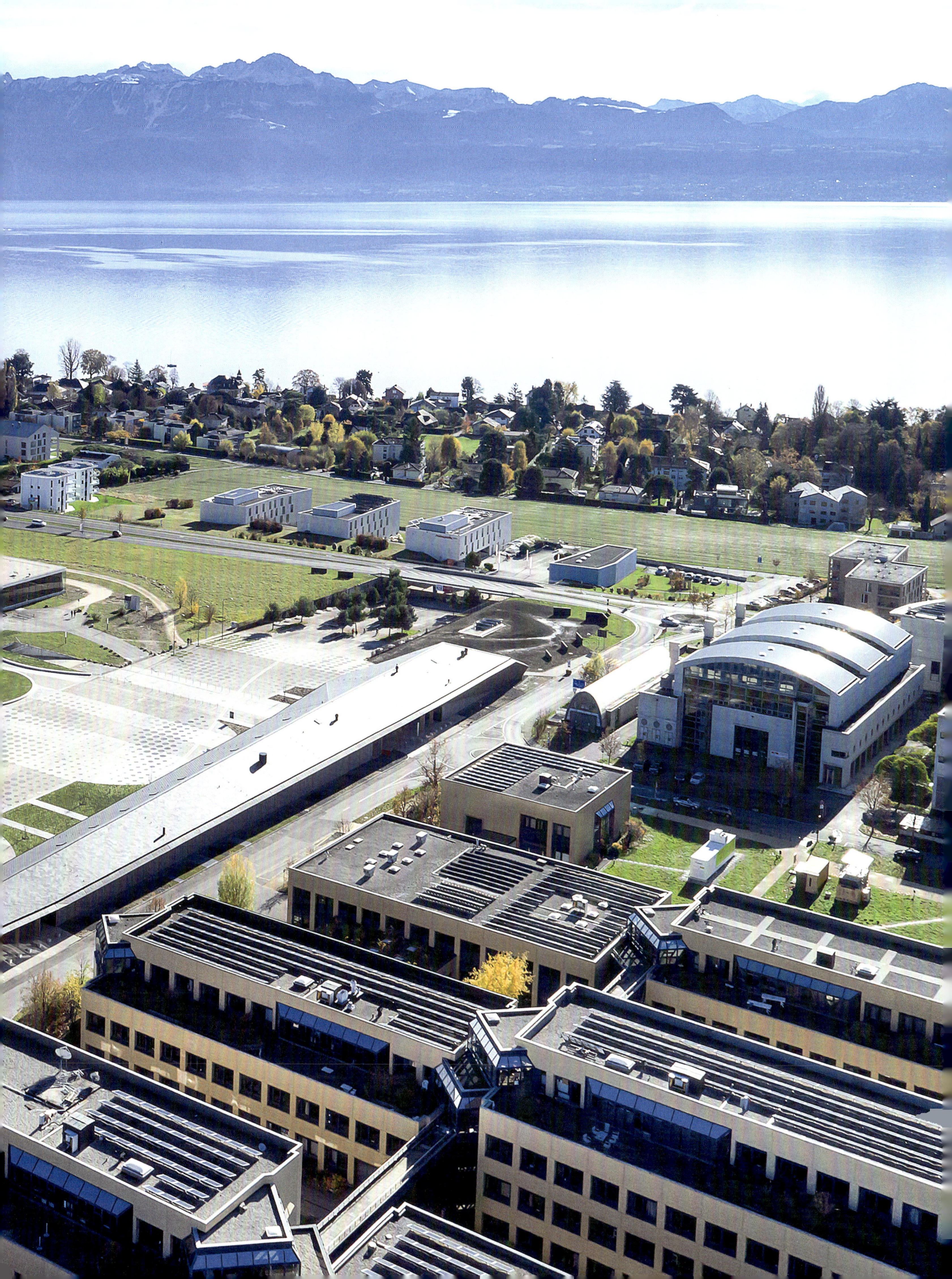

AS BIG AS
ST. MARK'S SQUARE

Dieter Dietz and the ALICE laboratory at EPFL were given the task of designing the space of Place Cosandey between the Rolex Learning Center and ArtLab. They took up this challenge between September and November 2015, in a period of just six weeks. The first part of the work on the square involving the creation of the layout was done in 2016. For administrative reasons, the second and most visible part of the intervention took place in the summer of 2018. Analyses based on participatory GPS localization showed before their intervention that Place Cosandey was rarely used by significant numbers of students. The goal of the landscape architecture design proposed by the students under the supervision of Dieter Dietz and the ALICE team was to enliven the square, to bring life to it in every sense, with recourse to a relatively limited budget. Aside from the goal of increasing the use of the space, Dieter Dietz clearly wished to reconnect EPFL to its site and its mountainous landscape. The rather technological approach taken by the early architects of the campus meant that EPFL buildings were more a series of interconnected geometric blocks than they were in any sense related to their environmental setting. With the Rolex Learning Center, the ME Building, and soon thereafter ArtLab forming the space of Place Cosandey, it was yet another task to actually give life to what EPFL compared to the "commons" areas of other, perhaps more traditional universities, spaces for movement and interaction and events. Giving meaning to what was little more than empty space was the considerable task taken on by Dieter Dietz and his ALICE laboratory, together with the students involved in the project.

Born in Zurich in 1964, Dieter Dietz is an architect based in Zurich and Lausanne, director of the ALICE (Atelier de la conception de l'espace) laboratory at EPFL and founder of dieterdietz.org. His work investigates the nature of architectural space and of *inside-ness* as a fundamental human condition. Projects on habitat, public space, and the city serve as points of departure for his in-depth research connecting landscape, urban environment, and architecture to our embodied existence in space. Work conducted with ALICE and his practice has been awarded with the Swiss Art Award, the London Festival of Architecture Main and Signpost Awards, and the Design Preis Schweiz amongst others.

How did you become involved in work on Place Cosandey?[1]
My lab is, of course, implicated in this project but the idea was also to involve the population of the campus and, in particular, nearly a thousand students. This work is clearly implied in the "Objective: Campus" project. I was originally involved in the Montreux Jazz Heritage Lab, whose goal was to create an immersive environment for the viewing of video from the festival. We were assigned the task of investigating the possibilities that could be offered by Place Cosandey, and the process began with the obvious realization that the space of the square was being used very little. Our survey of students revealed a number of issues, such as a lack of shade. We wanted to create areas and spaces that were not so rigid that they could not be used for purposes other than those originally envisaged, to maintain a sense of openness as it were. A first aspect of the definition of the space was the creation of the large round area between the Rolex Center and ArtLab. A large, rounded, light, wooden bleacher structure with a wooded space behind it was installed in the fall of 2018, and will be able to receive hundreds of people for concerts or even for university lectures, for example. As soon as users go up even two meters in the bleachers, from this vantage point they begin to discover the spectacle of the lake and the mountains beyond. The goals of this project are to bring people together but also to reunite the campus and the landscape. It had almost been forgotten that we are in a splendid landscape that was not visible because of the way the campus was designed.

How is it possible to bring more life to Place Cosandey without a very substantial architectural and event-oriented program?
There is a need for programs to bring people into the space, to bring it to life. In addition to the Montreux Jazz Café, which is, of course, part of the layout, we are creating a "food street" to the north of the square where food trucks come in at lunch time, forcibly bringing new activity to the square, especially in good weather. Long benches and a space called the Poly Grill will be added. We want to add chairs that can be placed anywhere in the space. There is another space called the Green whose use is simply meant to be convivial. With an accumulation of informal spaces, we are convinced that the student presence in Place Cosandey, which is as big as St. Mark's Square in Venice, will increase over time. Although there has not been a specific will to frame views from the square, the conjunction of the work being done and Kengo Kuma's long building does direct views toward the lake and the mountains. We have intentionally left areas, particularly those on the side of ArtLab, relatively free to better allow for the organization of larger events such as the Balelec Festival, an open-air musical event that has been held at EPFL since 1981. The overall project for the square won a prestigious local award—the Distinction de l'Ouest Lausannois—for the creation of a new public space.

1   Dieter Dietz in conversation with the author, EPFL, September 5, 2017. And see https://www.espazium.ch/place-cosandey (accessed on April 28, 2018).

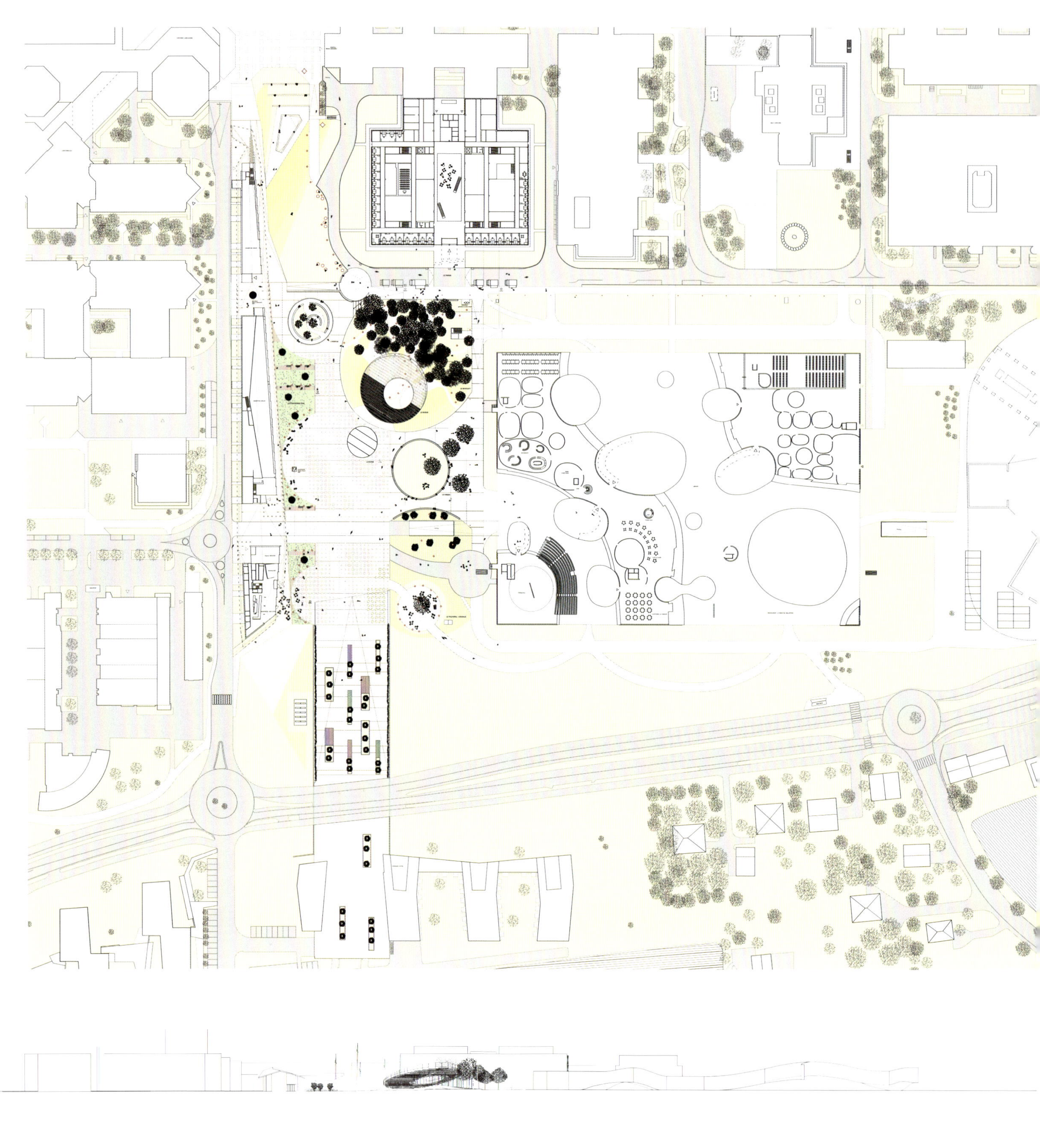

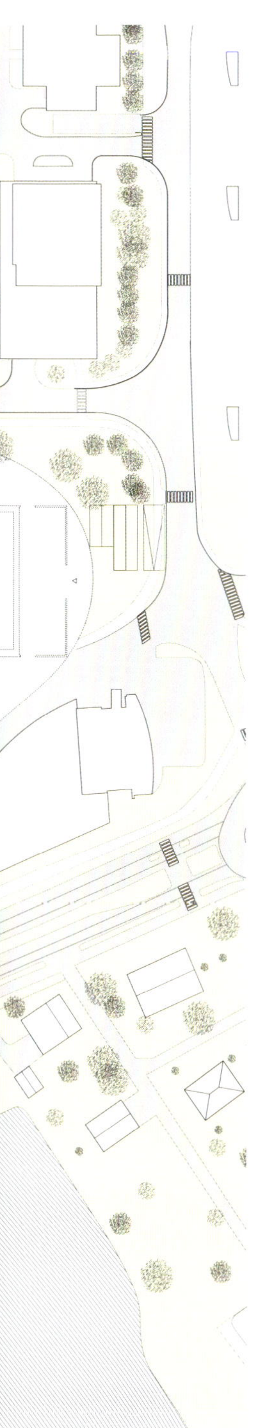

100 m

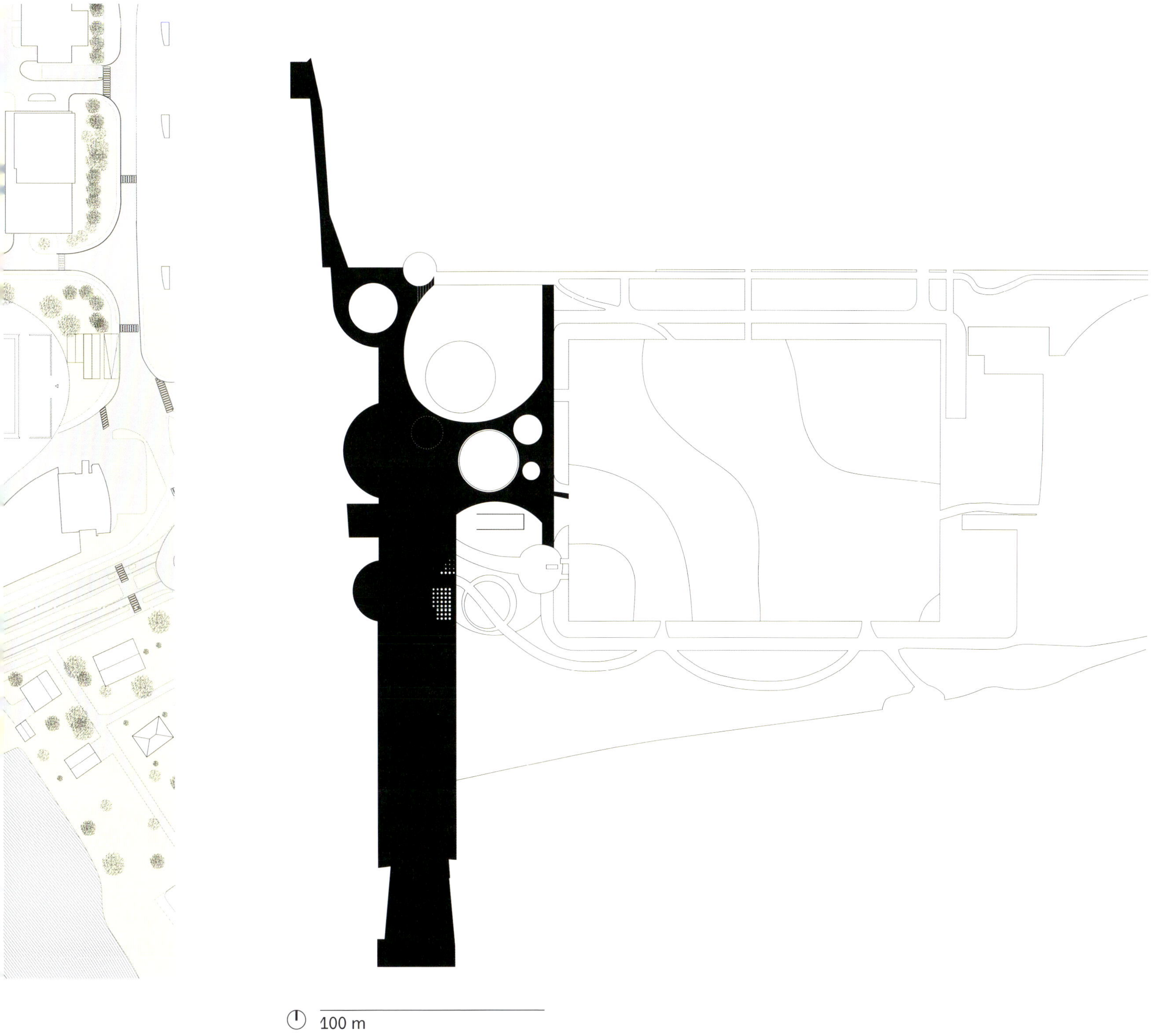

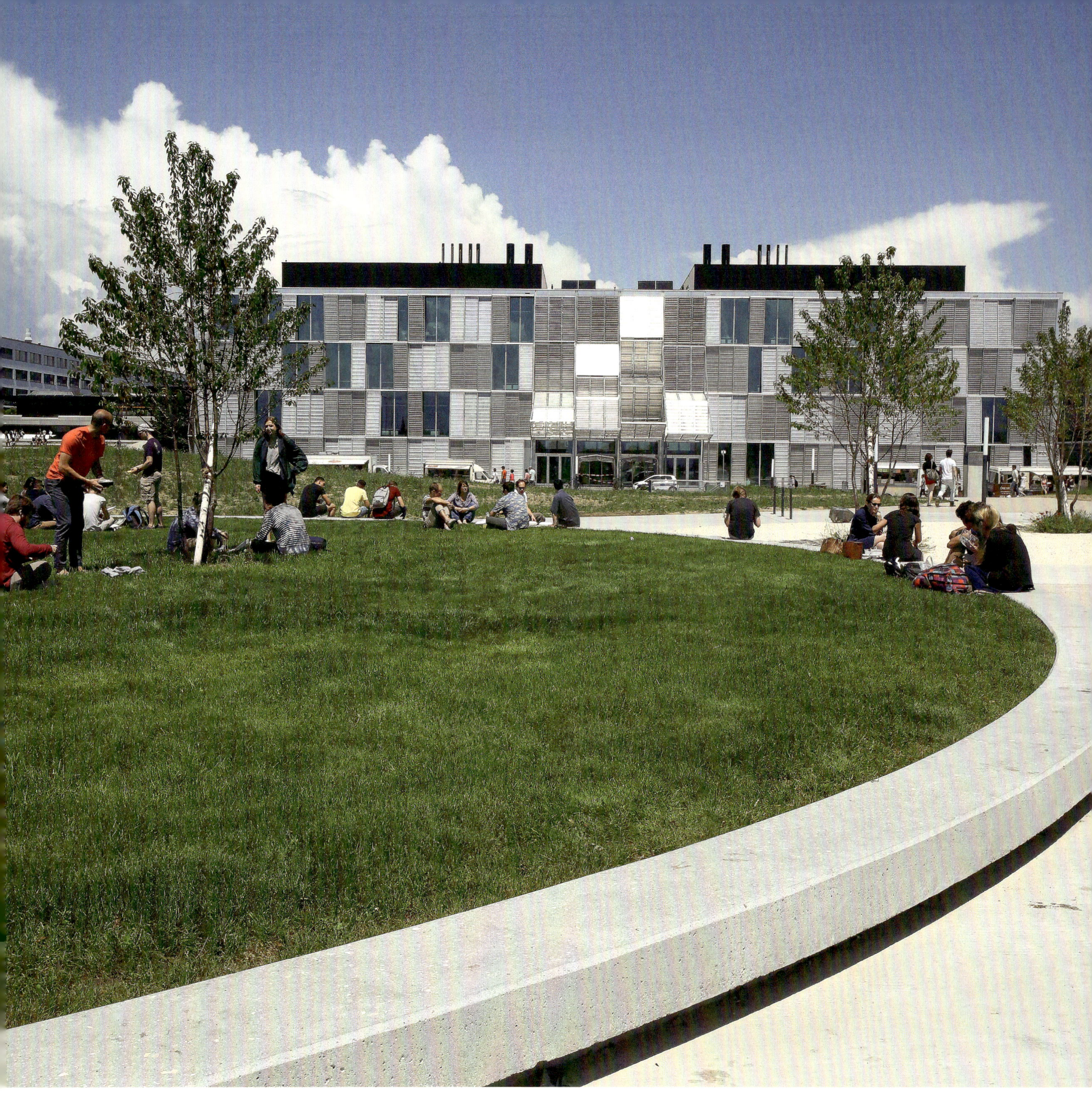

Summer views of Place Cosandey: left, in front of Dominique Perrault's
Mechanics Hall (ME Building) and, below, in front of the Rolex Learning Center.

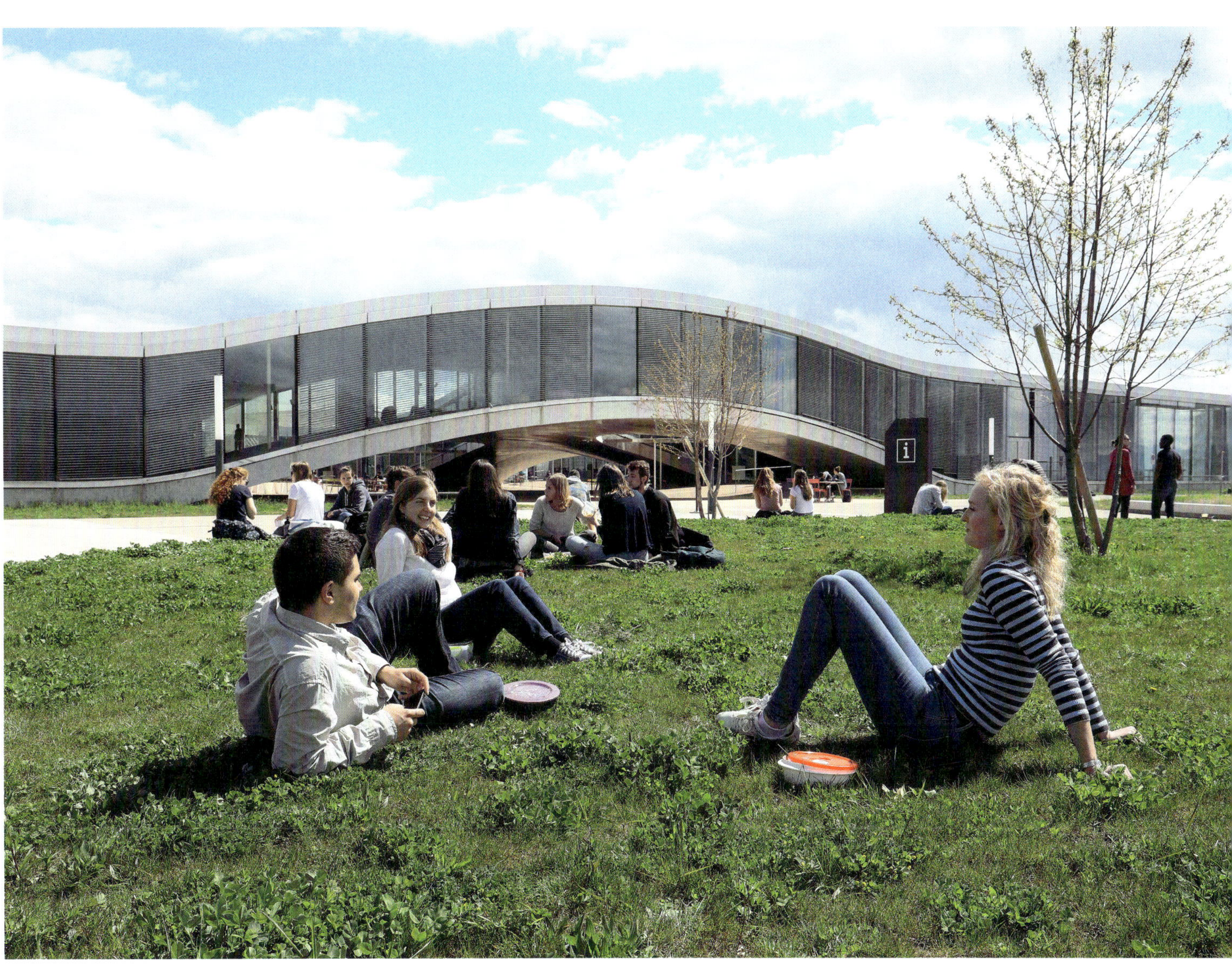

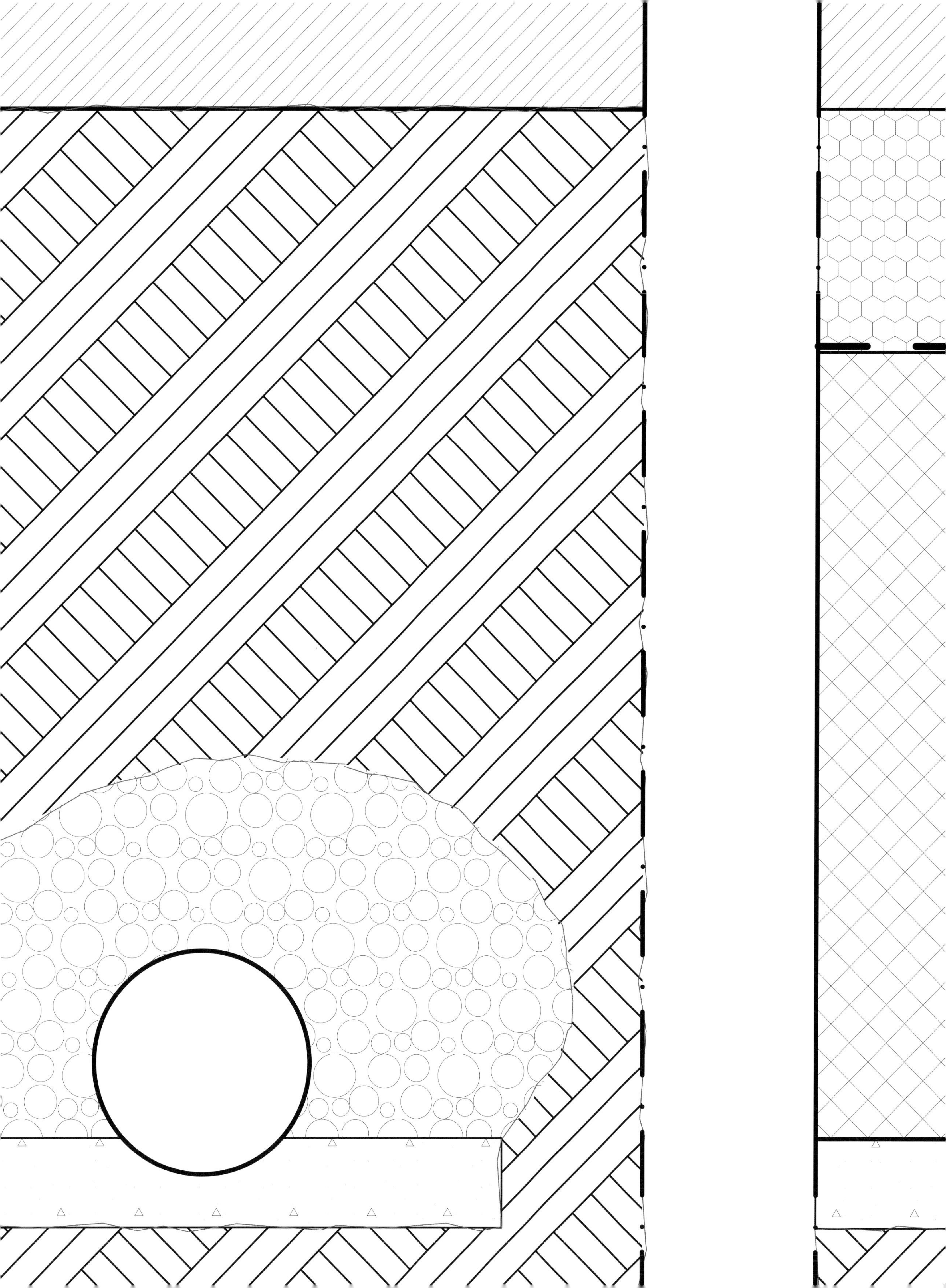

THE CONTENTS
OF ARTLAB

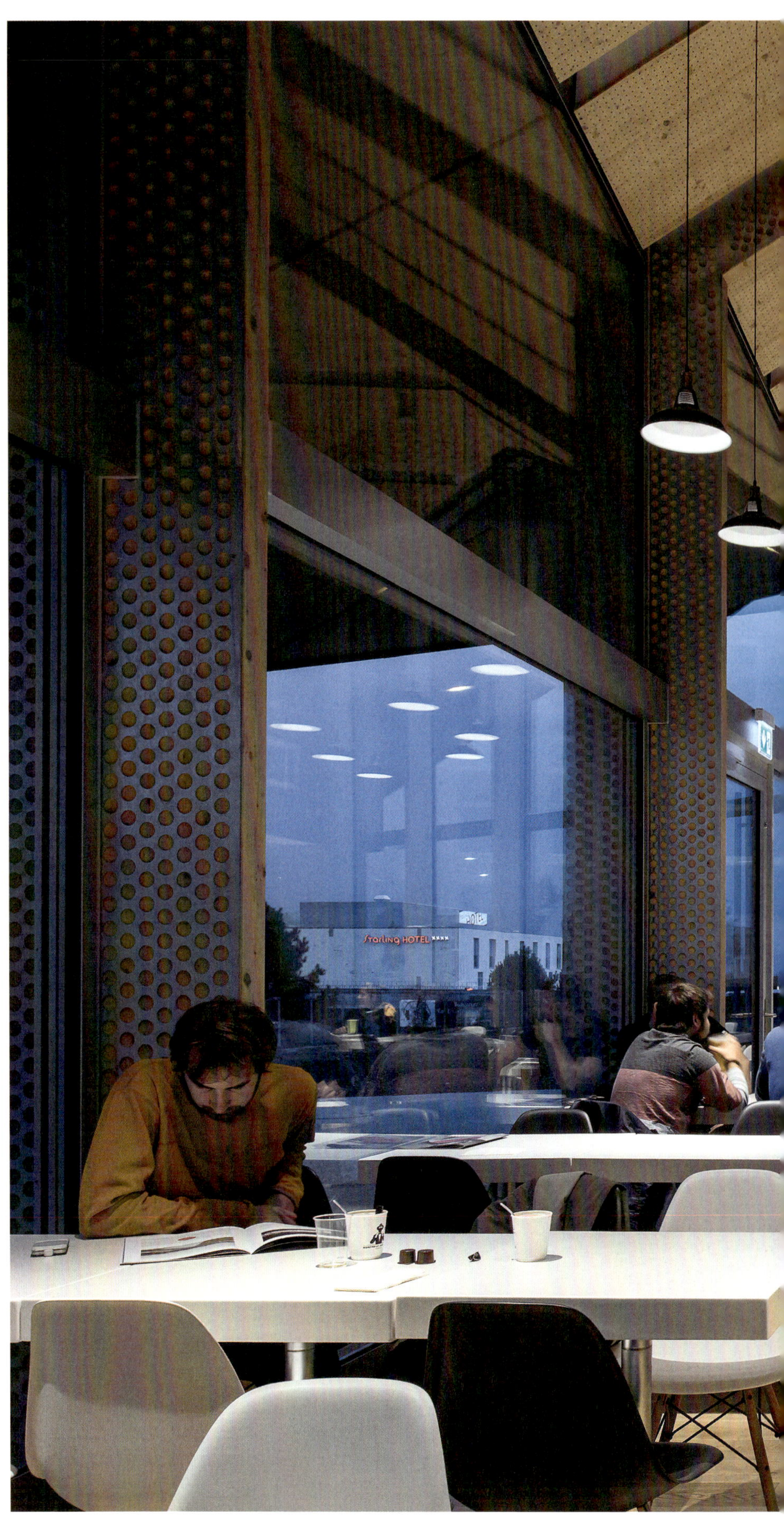
Starling HOTEL

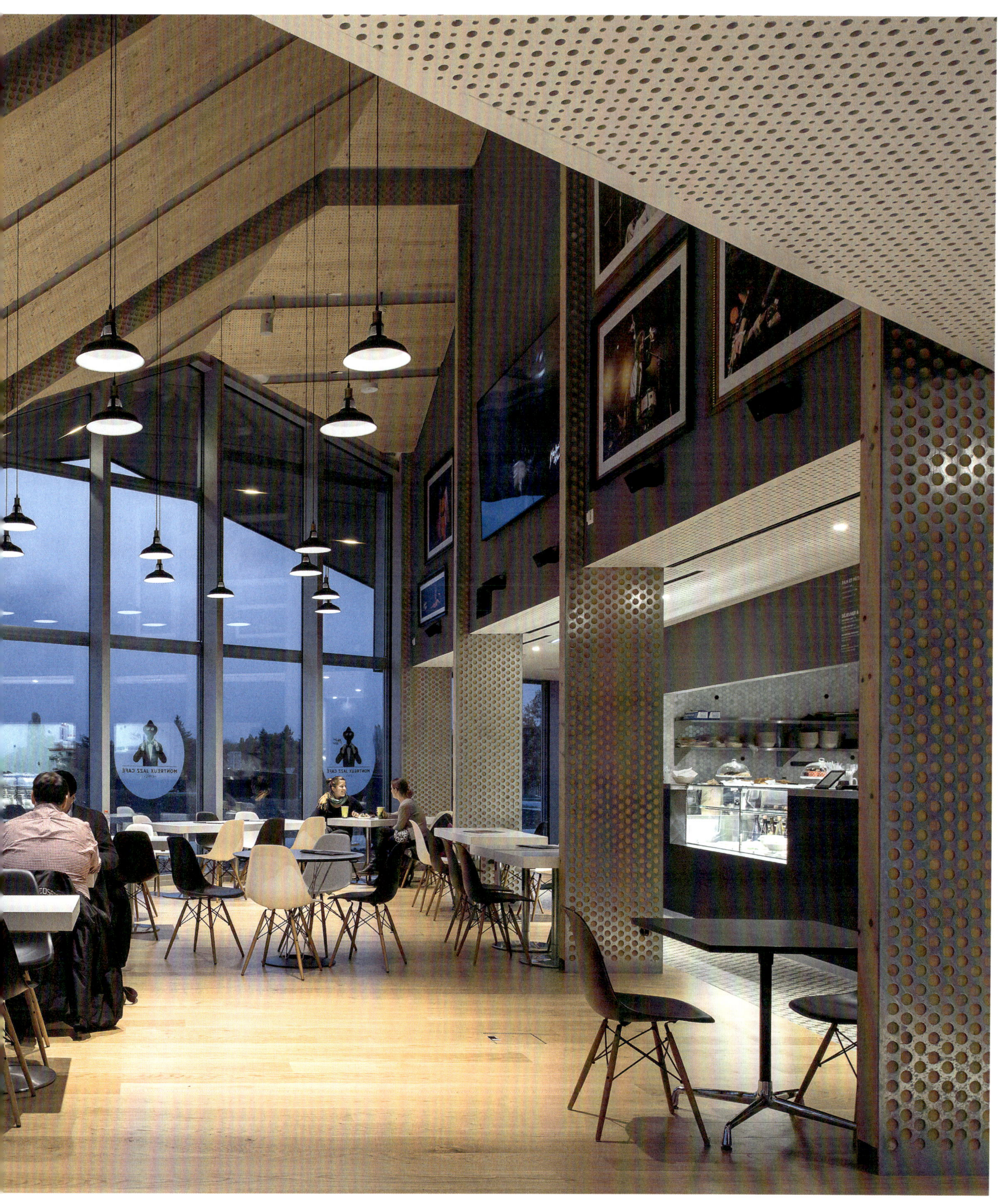

In the Montreux Jazz Café, at the southern end of ArtLab.
Here only the spaces were designed by Kengo Kuma.

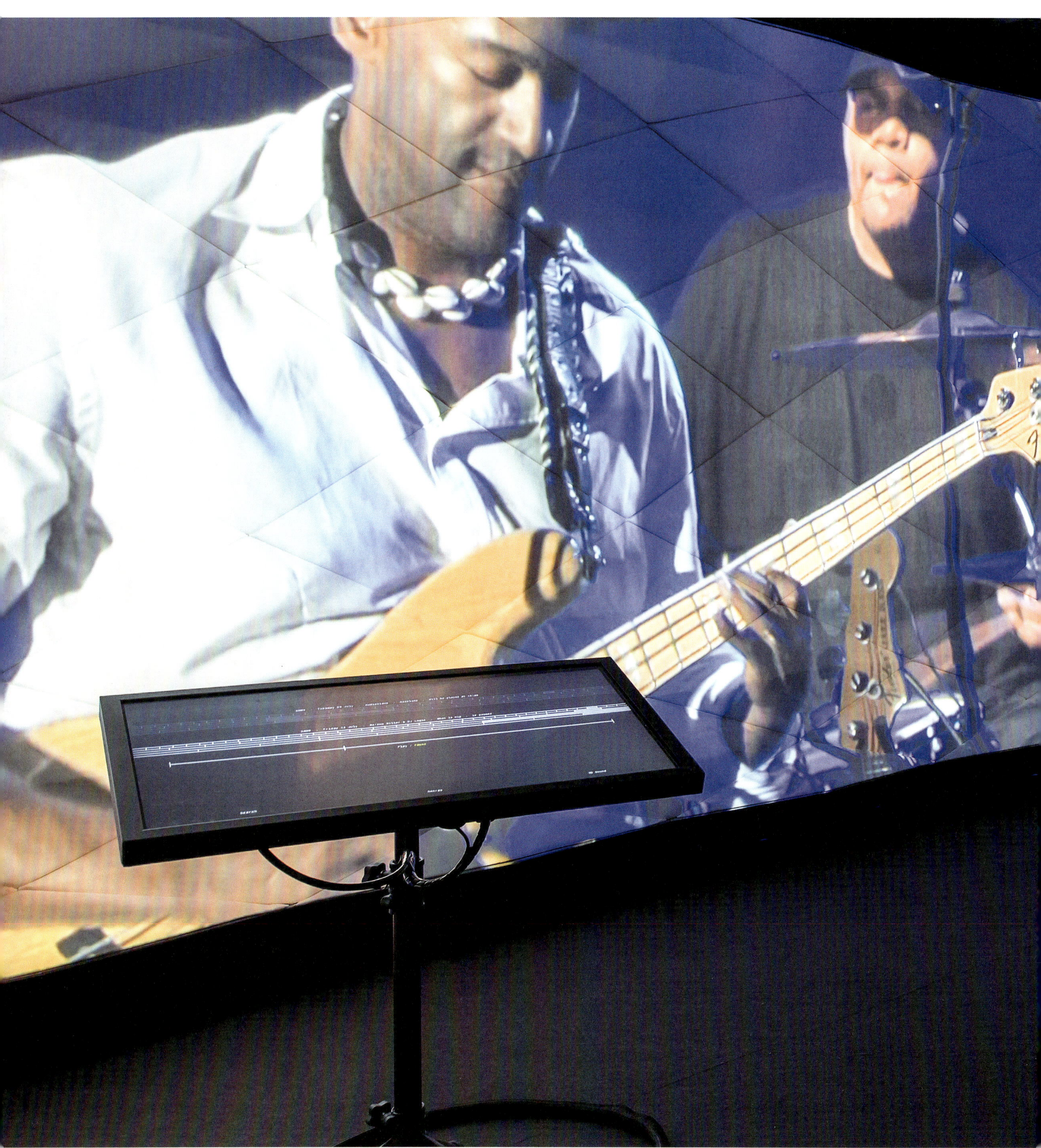

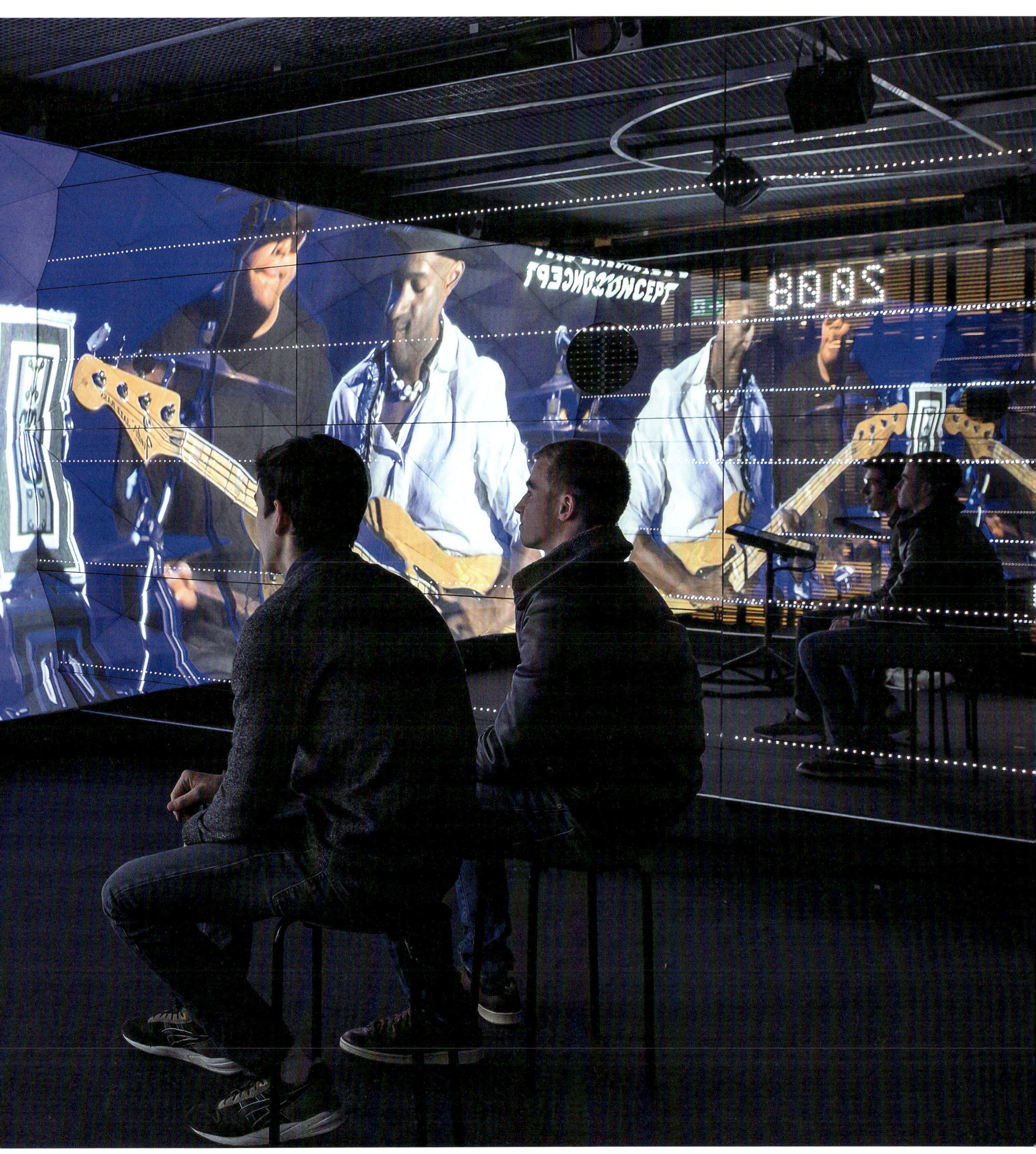

Viewing the archives of the Montreux Jazz Festival.

MEMORY OF THE WORLD

The Montreux Jazz Café forms the southernmost pavilion of ArtLab. With a total area of 895 square meters, it includes an audiovisual immersion space (fifty-five square meters) where the archives of the festival can be seen, and an eighty-seven-square-meter meeting space. The Café has seating for seventy-three people indoors and a further forty on the outdoor terrace that faces the Rolex Learning Center. Besides leading the digitization and preservation of the recordings as part of the Montreux Jazz Digital Project, EPFL designed devices to browse, visualize, and listen to the archives that are available to the public.

The Montreux Jazz Festival was created in 1967 by Claude Nobs, Géo Voumard, and René Langel. Held initially in the Montreux Casino in June, the festival has since branched out to other venues in the Swiss city. It is considered the second-largest international jazz festival after that of Montreal and regularly attracts more than 200,000 people per year. The driving force behind the festival was Claude Nobs (1936–2013), who was previously director of the Tourism Office of Montreux. Under his leadership as general manager, the list of international performers grew substantially, as did the notoriety of the festival. Early in its existence, the Montreux Jazz Festival took on a nearly legendary status in contemporary music when, in 1971, the Casino burned to the ground, inspiring the group Deep Purple, who were in the city to record their album *Machine Head*. The fire triggered their celebrated song "Smoke on the Water," which makes reference in its lyrics to Claude Nobs.

Claude Nobs insisted from the outset that every performance at the Montreux Jazz Festival should be filmed and recorded. As a result, he created one of the most substantial archives of modern music ever compiled. The archives of the Montreux Jazz Festival were recommended for inclusion in UNESCO's Memory of the World Register in 2013. According to the organization listing: "This collection contains… concerts recorded both in audio and video by many of the greatest names in jazz, blues. and rock since the creation of the Montreux Jazz Festival in 1967, by the visionary Claude Nobs. It includes some extremely rare improvised jam sessions and unique footage of performers like Marvin Gaye, who recorded their first and only performance for television in Montreux. Miles Davis played his last performance here, conducted by Quincy Jones, in 1991."[1] The fact that the entire archive of the Montreux Jazz Festival was stored in the basement of the chalet of Claude Nobs created an impetus to safeguard this treasure, but also to make it accessible.

EPFL and Montreux Sounds, curator of the archives, united their efforts to create a high-resolution digital archive of the Montreux Jazz Festivals, with EPFL as exclusive licensee for scientific research and educational use. The goal of this ambitious project, whose initial phase was carried out beginning in September 2010, "is to exploit the know-how and expertise of EPFL for creation of the most technologically advanced high-resolution digital media archive and long-term preservation ever produced."[2] On the EPFL side, the Metamedia Center is a "multidisciplinary and transversal" entity created in 2010 for this project. More than thirty-five projects at EPFL were thus grouped together, in an effort that also involved partnership with other academic institutions. Since 2010, the center has realized the digitization and preservation of more than 11,000 hours of video, 6000 hours of audio, and 180,000 photos.[3] Dieter Dietz and his team (Studio ALICE) conceived the final presentation of the space in the Montreux Jazz Café at ArtLab, where the archives can be consulted. The involvement of the Metamedia Center, directed by Alain Dufaux, and several laboratories at EPFL in the digitization and public use of the Montreux Jazz archives is a clear example of the use of sophisticated technology to organize and render accessible cultural riches, in the spirit of the concepts of EPFL.

Luc Meier, former Project Manager for ArtLab, explains the process and questioning required for this very ambitious project:[4]

What were the technical challenges involved with this project?

The archives of the Montreux Jazz Festival were initially a huge amount of analog material in every format that has existed since the late 1960s, stored in the chalet of Claude Nobs near Montreux. EPFL got involved because of the technical challenge involved with digitization. How could so many different formats be converted into a single digital format? Even when that was done, the result would be a fairly amorphous mass of digital information. It is difficult, if not impossible, to do any kind of search in such an archive without the addition of considerable amounts of metadata (data that provides information about other data). Was it possible to add information about individuals performing more than once in different concerts for example? Beyond the listing of tracks and song names, might it be possible to recognize acoustic kinship between two tracks through harmonies or even moods? In a progressive process, ever more subtle information was used to tag the files. The more metadata that is added, the denser the model is, and the more diverse and interesting the potential paths of navigation. The process starts with raw digitization, then the information has to be organized, often with the help of specialists. Here, the subject is concerts that are collective experiences performed live in defined physical spaces. When the idea of re-broadcasting these concerts arose, it became necessary to imagine the space in which that could be done. What parts of the visual and acoustic elements should be retained for use. This again raises a series of technical questions related to projection of images and sound. Would the process not require 3D sound design or even an effort to recreate the sound of the original venue?

How did the project come about in terms of EPFL's organization?

The project was conceived at the outset under the supervision of Patrick Aebischer with an intent to be based in scientific research, and provide a ground for education for students. The Audiovisual Communications Lab of EPFL is headed by Professor Martin Vetterli, who succeeded Patrick Aebischer as president of the EPFL and was heavily involved in the digitization of the music. There is thus an interaction between highly specialized units already on campus and this new mass of data that is from the area of culture.

What about funding and the commercial implications of such a project?

Because of the strong relation between the region of Lausanne and the Montreux Jazz Festival, it was possible to approach a number of private sources of financing, such as banks or watchmakers, to obtain their commitment and support for this project beyond the public funds available to the university. There is also a commercial aspect to it. This type of work and the research it entails could certainly be of interest in other applications or for cultural institutions at large. Digital technologies permit the better preservation and exhibition of cultural resources. The techniques involved, for example the sound engineering for the 3D broadcasting of the concerts, might then be made available to potential clients. The idea is to be able to replicate the kind of test space that we have built at ArtLab elsewhere. The EPFL+ECAL Lab, directed by Nicolas Henchoz, participated in the development of the immersive environment for the project. This could be in the context of a temporary installation, or people with completely different content could employ the technology. Sound design in an architectural context is a broad and developing field. There is not a specific promotion strategy for the use of these technologies elsewhere, it is rather a matter of opportunities that may arise.

What are the future plans related to this project?

This is a kind of showroom and the effort will also accompany the development of the Montreux Jazz Festival. There are half a dozen other Montreux Jazz Cafés around the world. When they open, local cultural institutions will be made aware of the technology being used. Each year, the new concerts that occur in Montreux will be added to the digital archive. We get pre-edited footage of the new concerts, now in fully digital form. The software chain that goes from issues of raw digitization, to organizing the mass of digital information that is generated, and then going on to publish either in a room like the one in ArtLab, or finding a VR solution for broadcasting, or in exhibition design—these steps apply to any relation between digital technologies and cultural heritage and thus present an interest that can potentially go far beyond ArtLab.

1   At http://www.unesco.org/new/en/communication-and-information/memory-of-the-world/register/full-list-of-registered-heritage/registered-heritage-page-8/the-montreux-jazz-festival-legacy/ (accessed on March 27, 2018).
2   At https://www.claudenobsfoundation.com/pdjm/ (accessed on March 27, 2018).
3   At https://metamedia.epfl.ch (accessed on March 27, 2018).
4   Luc Meier in conversation with the author, EPFL, October 18, 2017.

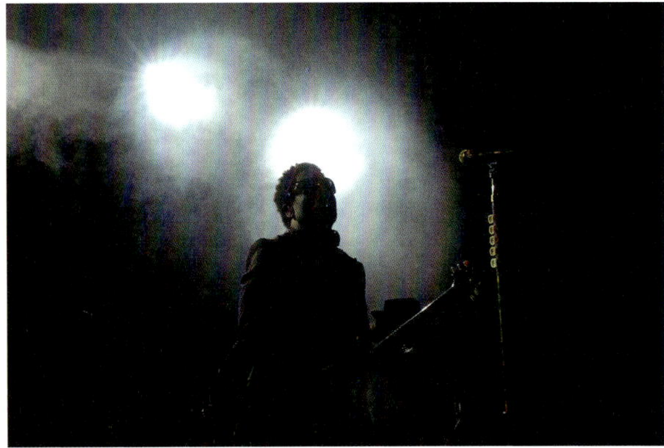

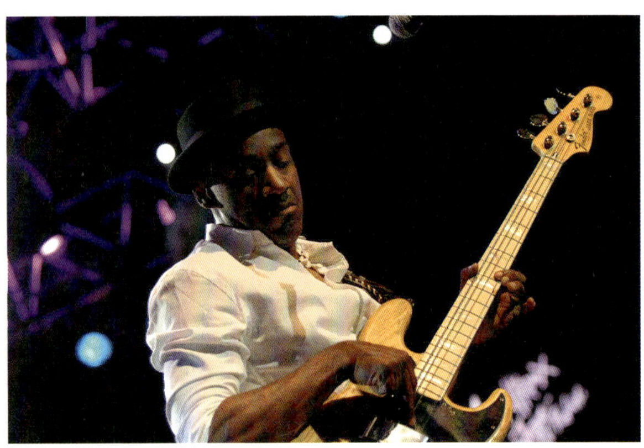

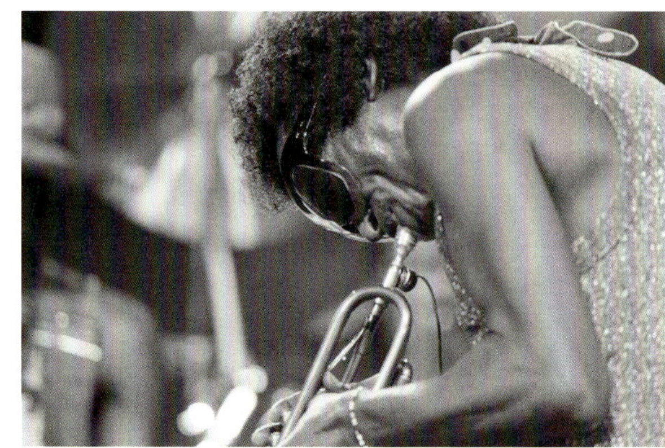

Images excerpted from the archives of the Montreux Jazz Festival featuring musicians such as Ray Charles (right, bottom), and Miles Davis (below and right middle).

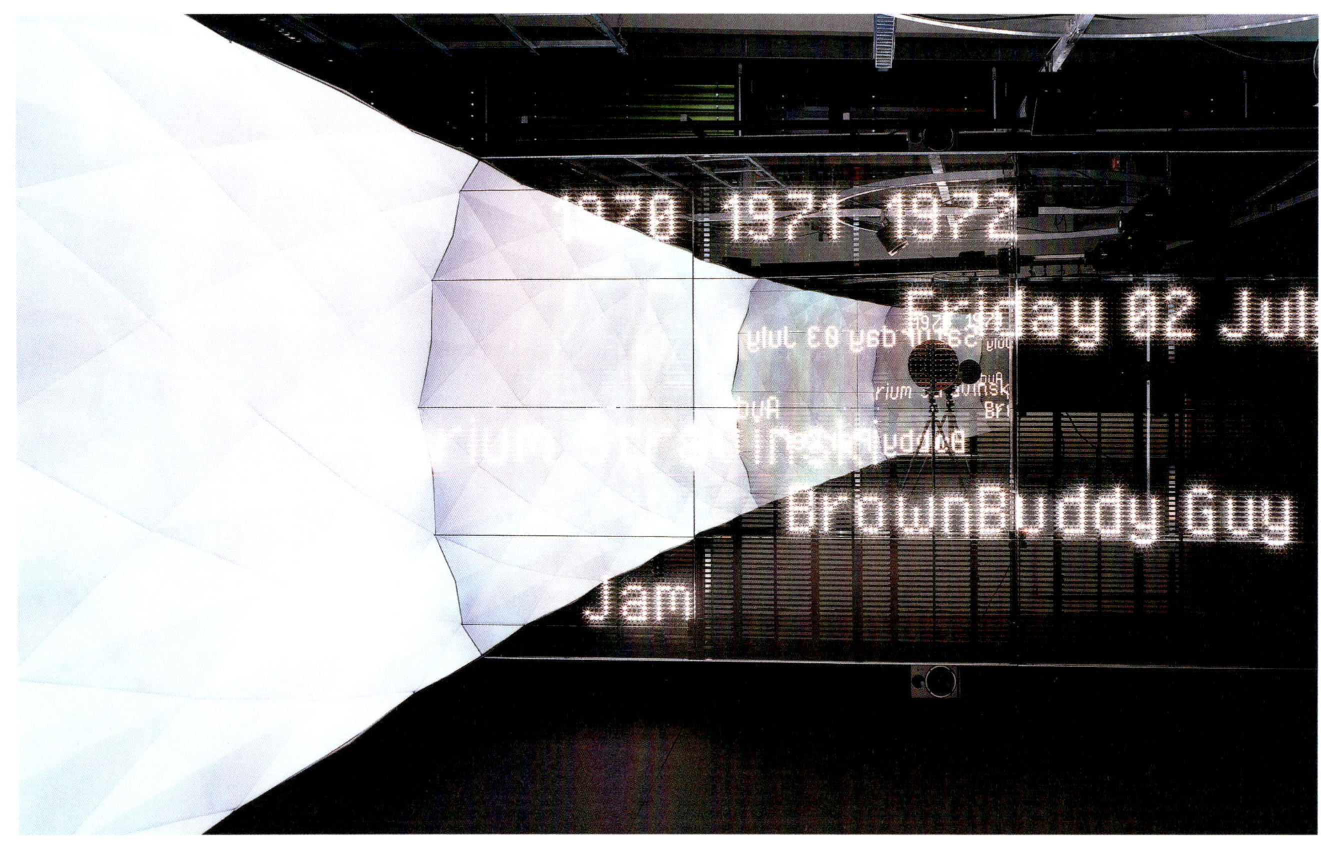

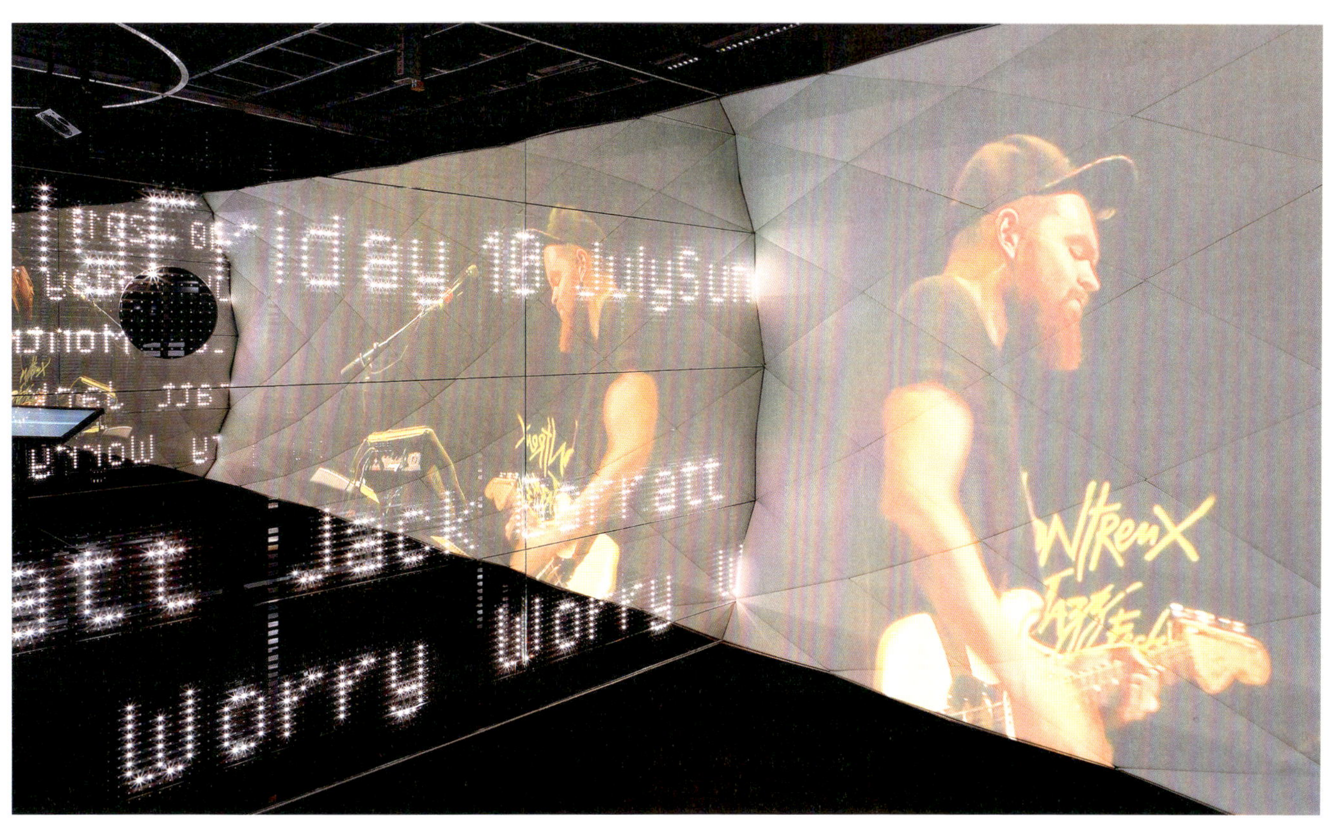

Friday
Worry Worry
WIRENX
Jazz Fed

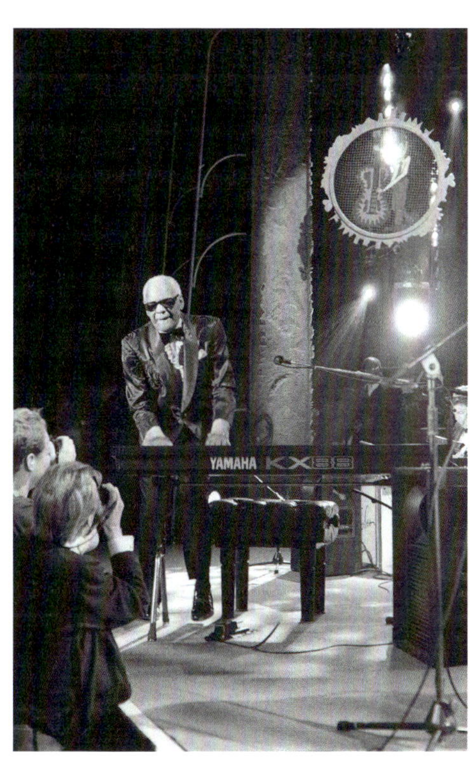

YAMAHA KX

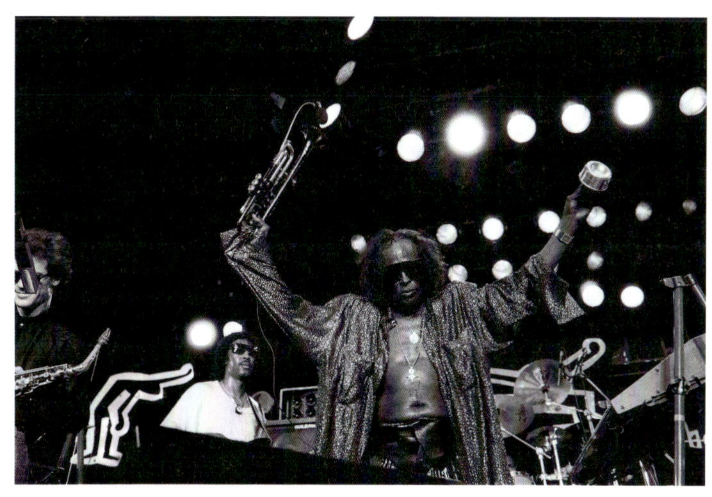

THE EXPERIMENTAL EXHIBITION SPACE

The Experimental Exhibition Space (Espace d'expérimentation muséale), which was developed in partnership with the Fondation Gandur pour l'Art (Geneva), occupies 1838 square meters (618 square meters of actual exhibition space) at the center of ArtLab. The challenge was to investigate the connections that can be created between culture and digital technology and to present the work of the university to the general public. It would seem apparent that the visual arts collection of a museum, for example, could present many of the problems posed by the digitization of the masses of analog materials process for the Montreux Jazz Festival project. This might be all the more true that major institutions typically show less than 5% of their collections in exhibition galleries. Many institutions have started to digitize their collections, but even then, they are difficult to use. The matter of the nature of the required metadata resolved for the Montreux archives can certainly be applied to other art forms. Luc Meier explains:

> *"ArtLab is saying that whatever the type of cultural heritage you are dealing with, if you want to get that mass of information back to an audience you have to go through the questions of how to digitize, how to organize, and how to republish it. EPFL and ArtLab is not alone in this field by any means. The same language is being used by such initiatives as the Google Cultural Institute (www.google.com/culturalinstitute/about/)—digitize, organize, publish. In the Cleveland Museum of Art, the ArtLens Gallery (www.clevelandart.org/artlens-gallery), which is the entrance gallery, is where the entire contents of the museum are digitized and presented. When people come in they have screens filled with images—you click on one and you begin your own exploration. You get a more informed idea of what is in the museum—the information can then inform your physical visit of the museum."* [1]

While all of the spaces of ArtLab basically address the broader issues of how technology and digitization can respond to the world of culture, the central area is more dedicated to visual manifestations than with music or perhaps the "big data" schemes outlined in DataSquare, the third, northern space of the building.

1   Luc Meier in conversation with the author, EPFL, October 18, 2017.

The Experimental Exhibition Space is long and high, offering numerous different possible configurations.

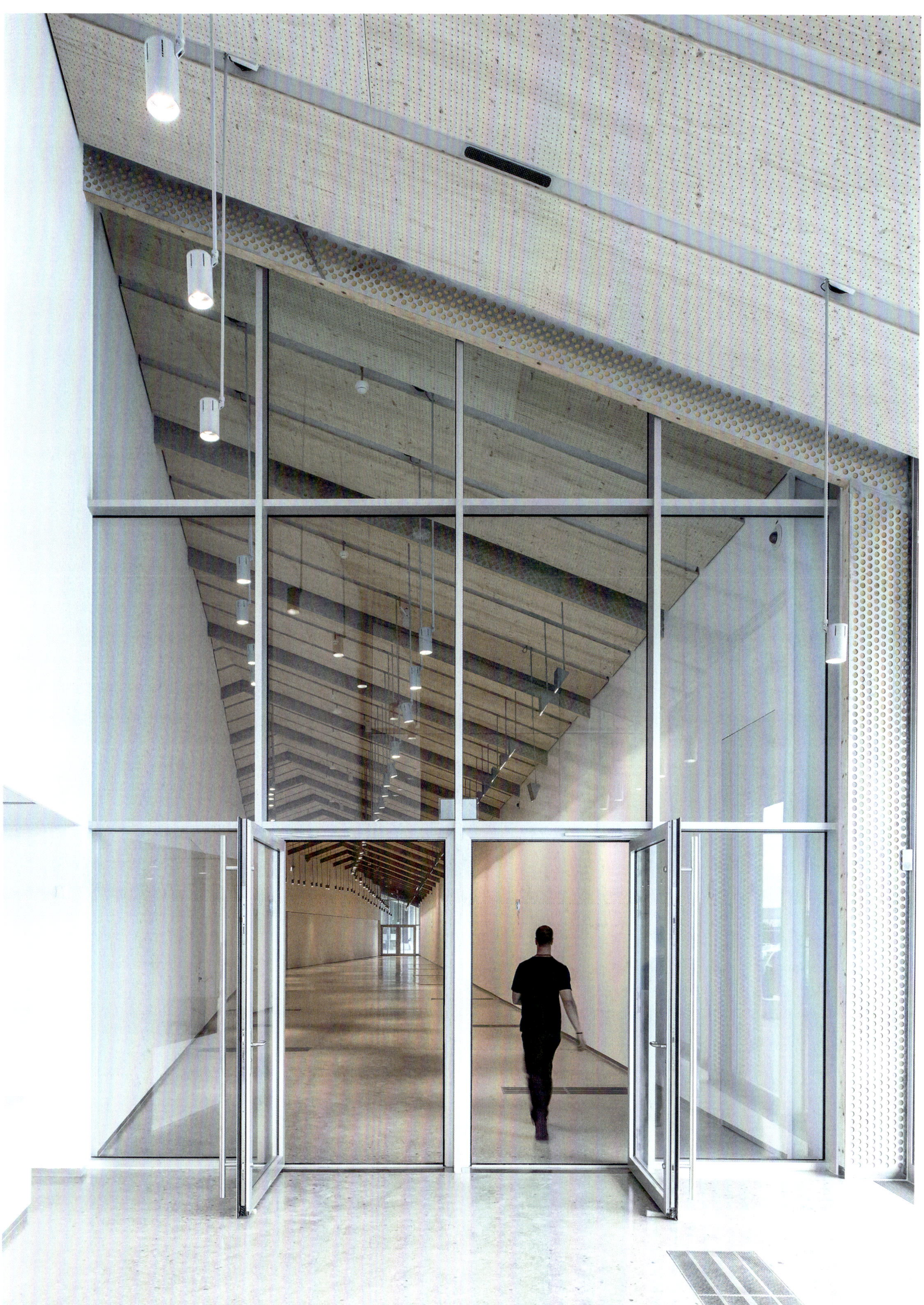

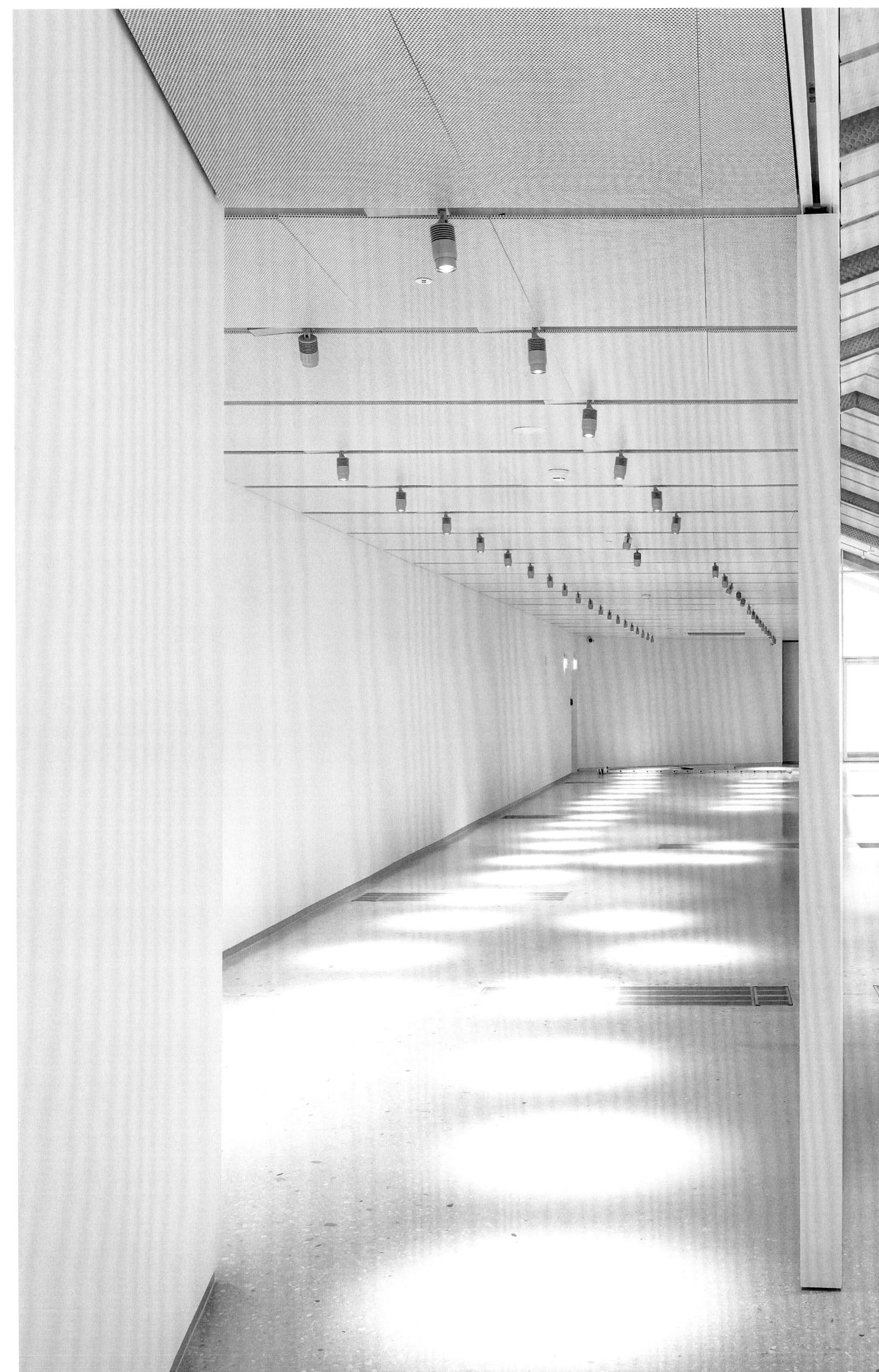

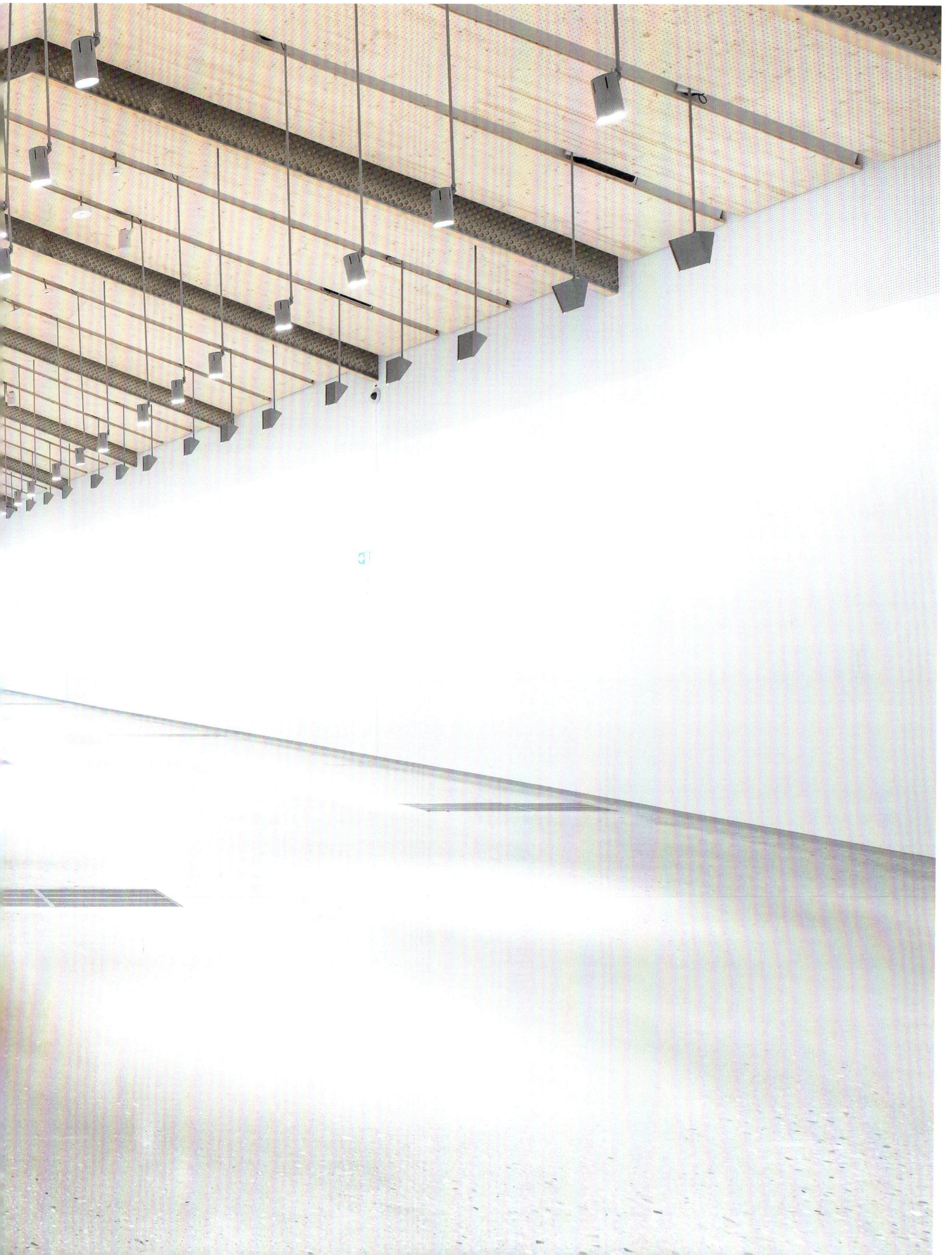

Temporary walls can readily be added to the space and the lighting system can be adapted accordingly.

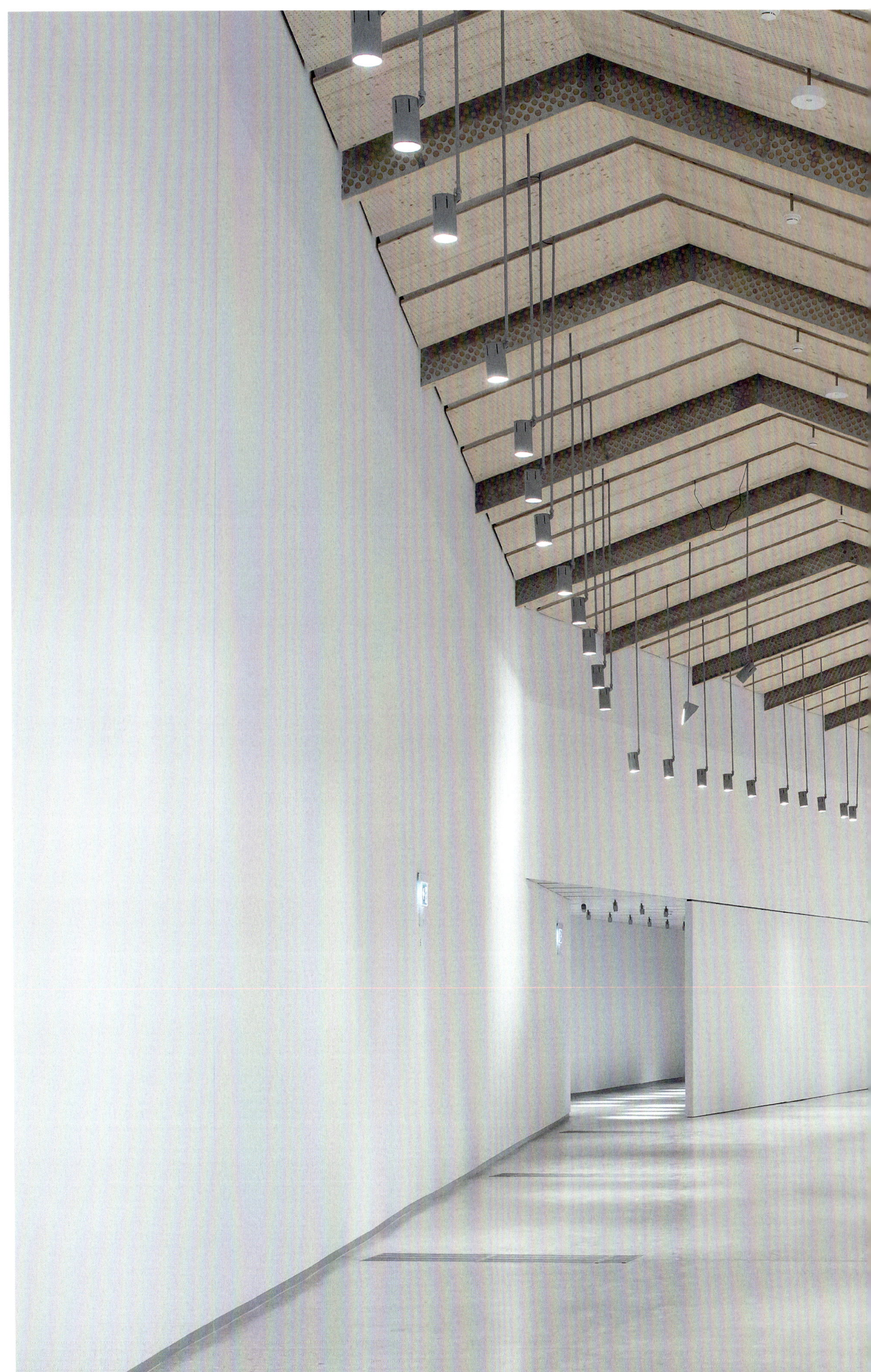

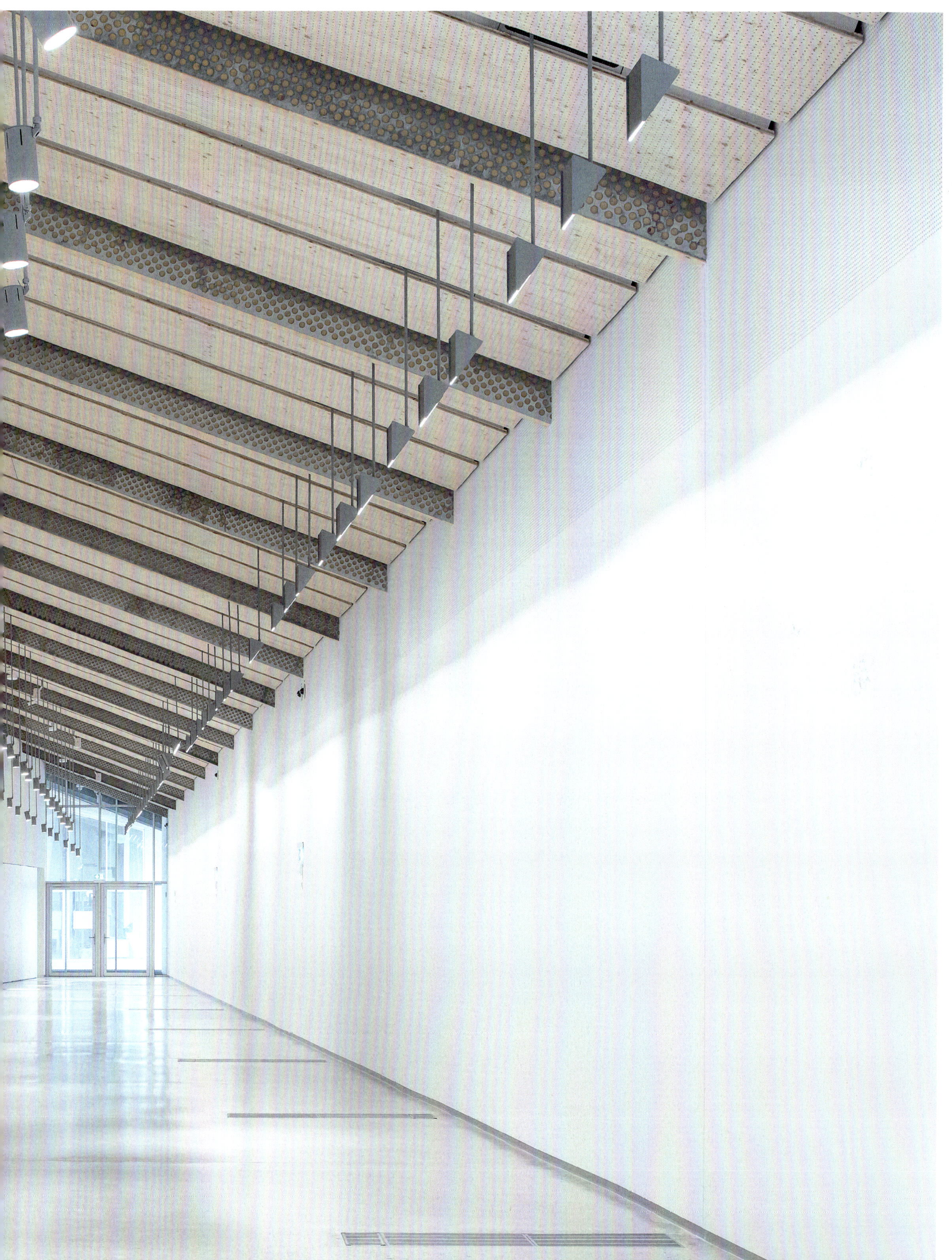

The space forms an important part of the overall snake-like plan of ArtLab,
making a volume that is at once lively and readily usable.

Poster for the inaugural ArtLab exhibition *Noir, c'est noir?* (Black is Black?) focused on the many uses of black in the work of the French painter Pierre Soulages.

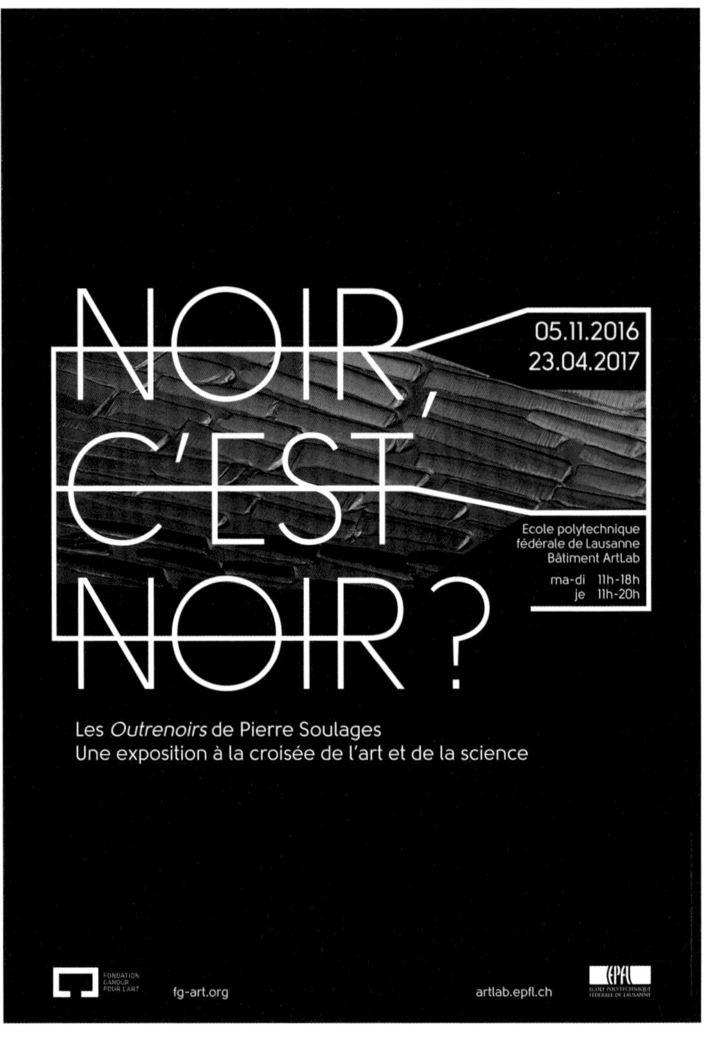

BEYOND BLACK

The initial show held in the Experimental Exhibition Space approached the issues of technology and art from yet another angle. Organized by EPFL and the Fondation Gandur pour l'Art (Geneva), *Noir, c'est noir? Les Outrenoirs de Pierre Soulages* (November 5, 2016 – April 23, 2017) was dedicated to paintings by the French artist Pierre Soulages. Soulages, born in Rodez, France, in 1919 has been called "the painter of black," but he prefers to refer to "the light reflected from black." Two hundred and fifty works by Pierre Soulages are visible in his own museum in Rodez, inaugurated in 2014 and designed by the Pritzker Prize-winning Spanish architects RCR, but the intention of ArtLab was to present his work quite literally in another light. The word *outrenoir* literally means "beyond black." This comment is surely one of the starting points of the ArtLab exhibition, which involved five EPFL laboratories and a number of start-up companies born of their research. Using scientific and scenographic tools to imagine the black paintings of Soulages quite literally in a different light, the show received more than 30,000 visitors and was universally praised.

EPFL's Signal Processing Laboratory 2 (LTS2) and Studio Fragmentin, an interactive design firm formed by students from ECAL (École cantonale d'art de Lausanne), imagined a variable display environment in which an *Outrenoir* painting was surrounded by an animated device that offered several types of lighting (frontal, uniform, tangential, etc.) under the same hanging conditions. A motion detection system allowed one or several visitors to adjust the lighting directly through their presence and their movements.[1] In the same show a virtual reality section conceived by the EPFL+ECAL Lab explored "how interactive virtual immersion performed using 3D computer graphics can expand the understanding and appreciation of an exhibition." In this instance, virtual reality glasses mounted on a fixed pedestal recalled more familiar stationary binoculars that are sometimes available to tourists.[2] Another part of the exhibition was intended to show that as many as thirty-two different black pigments can be used in paintings. Organized by EPFL+ECAL Lab, Signal Process Laboratory LTS5, Gamaya, and Atelier Héritier (Geneva), this area used a hyperspectral camera to capture the visible light reflected by an *Outrenoir* painting, color by color. The collected data was used in an interactive installation that exhibited a "hyperspectral map" of the painting in question.[3] Yet another part of the ArtLab exhibition focused on caustics, which are the result of light rays successively reflected or refracted by a surface and projected onto another surface. This section was created by the EPFL Computer Graphics and Geometry Laboratory (LGG) and a start-up firm called Rayform. Using algorithms developed at EPFL, Rayform produced complex shaped surfaces that "modify the light passing through them to project controlled and detailed images." Another work by Pierre Soulages was used here to demonstrate that the "heart of the work lies in the interaction between surface and light."[4]

Although many exhibition visitors come to see works of art without too many intermediary levels of interpretation, the *Noir, c'est noir?* exhibition at ArtLab certainly went beyond similar past efforts to begin to address the issue of how recent technology can coexist with art and make the experience of viewing art richer and fuller. Though some might have imagined the paintings of Soulages as pure fields of thick black paint, after going to this exhibition, the real complexity of the artist's work and, indeed, of the subtleties and complexities of perception were made more visible. The presence of start-up companies like Gamaya and ARTMYN (see p. 129) immediately evokes the bridges that can be built between art, technology, and other fields. As an example, Gamaya, an EPFL spin-off, employs hyperspectral cameras, like

those present in the Soulages exhibition, to detect the parts of the spectrum reflected by land that the human eye cannot see. Using this type of hyperspectral image allows farmers to make changes in aspects of their work, such as water and fertilizer use, crop yield, and the presence of pests.

The case of Gamaya also emphasizes the kind of funding developed by EPFL around its technological initiatives and some of the resulting start-up companies. Gamaya's launch funding came from Peter Brabeck-Letmathe, a former CEO of Nestle, the Sandoz Foundation, and the Swiss venture capital firm VI Partners.[5]

The example of the work of Gamaya and other start-up firms that originated from the labs of EPFL shows the importance of the type of transversal interaction between disciplines that is, in fact, at the heart of ArtLab and the ongoing plans of the university. "From Leonardo da Vinci, who represented total knowledge, we have reached a time when knowledge is separated into distinct blocks," says Martin Vetterli, the current president of EPFL. "I would not go so far as to say that we all have to become modern Da Vincis, but I firmly believe that in twenty years the separate professions we know today will be different. This is the dimension that we must bring to our teaching to help students in their future careers. The same is true of researchers. The science of data is transversal, for example. It concerns computer science, but also statistics, mathematics, or even medicine. These different disciplines now have to be able to work together."[6]

1   "Bringing an Outrenoir to light," at https://artlab.epfl.ch/
    soulages-experience-three (accessed on March 27, 2018).
2   At https://artlab.epfl.ch/soulages_experience_one
    (accessed on March 25, 2018).
3   At https://artlab.epfl.ch/soulages-experience-two
    (accessed on March 25, 2018).
4   At https://artlab.epfl.ch/soulages-experience-five
    (accessed on March 25, 2018).
5   "This Startup Is Changing Farming with Drones and AI,"
    at http://fortune.com/2016/05/23/startup-gamaya-farming-
    with-drones-ai/ (accessed on March 26, 2018).
6   "Transmission de présidence entre Patrick Aebischer et
    Martin Vetterli," *Alumnist*, no. 5, December 2016.

Noir, c'est noir?, featuring the work of the French painter Pierre Soulages, was the inaugural exhibition held in ArtLab. Seen here, top, Pierre Soulages, *Peinture, 162 × 130 cm, 15 novembre 2011*, private collection.

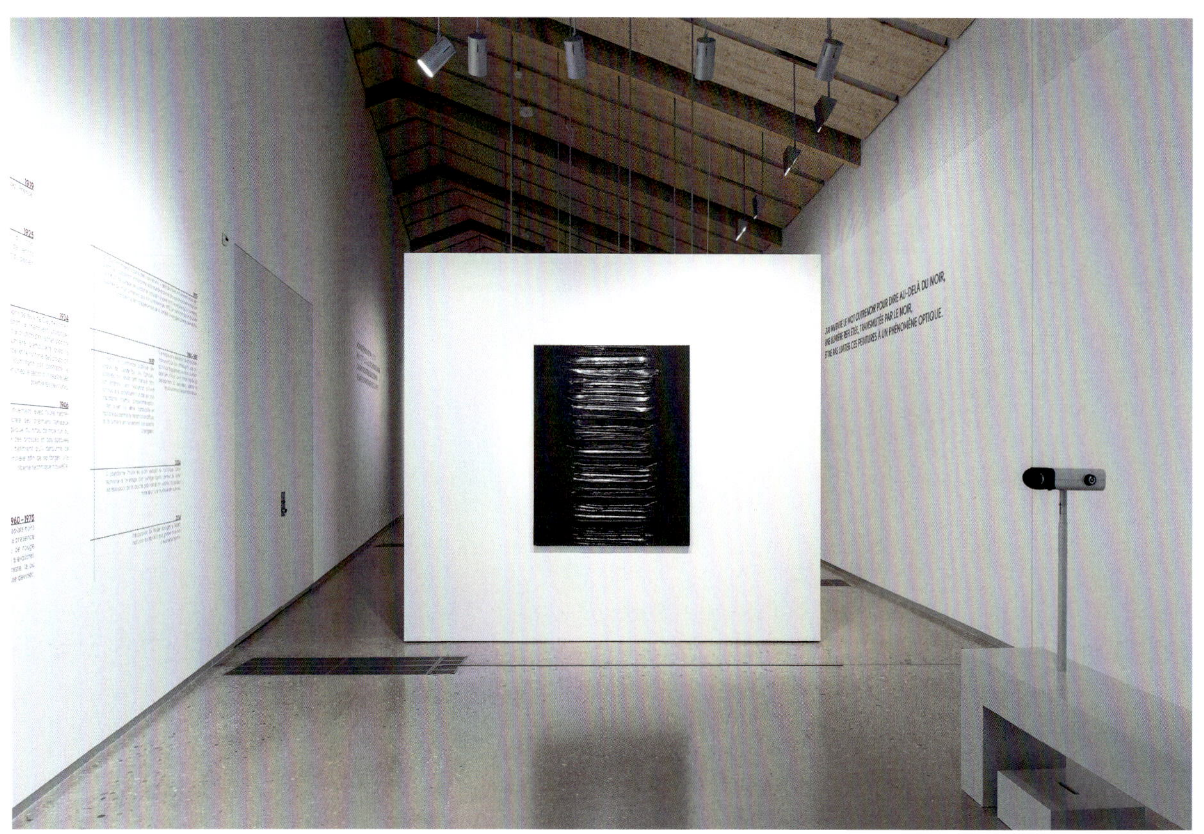

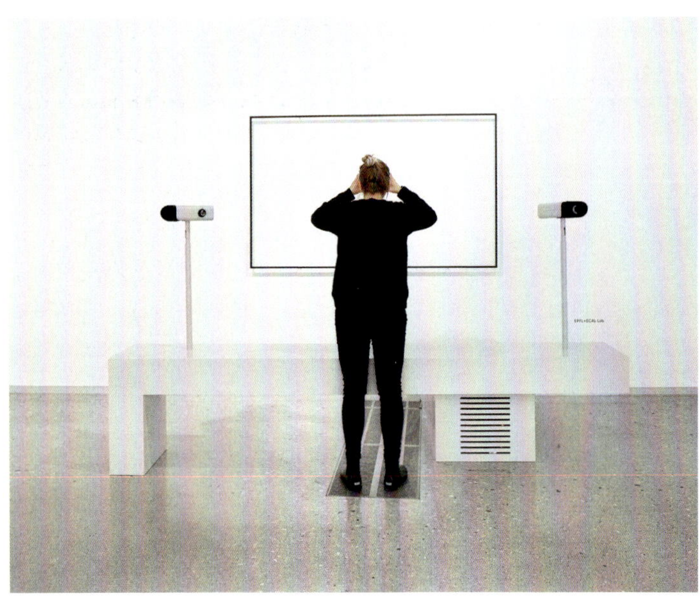

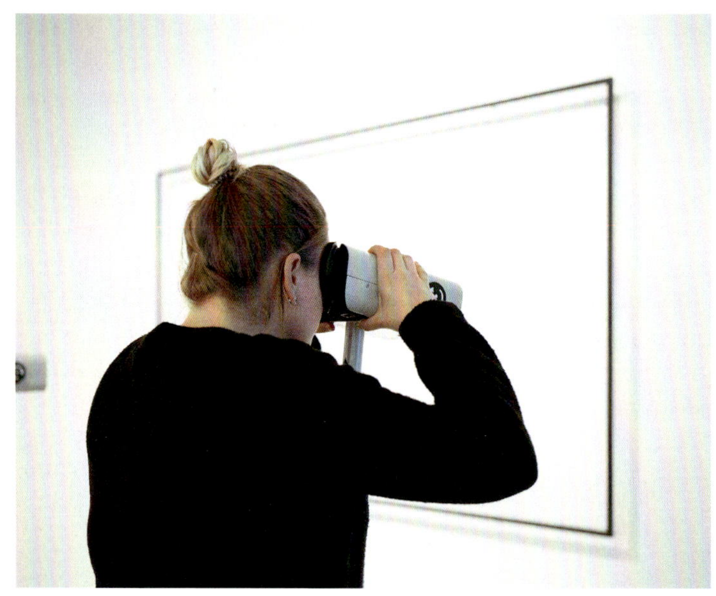

FROM ARTTECH TO ARTMYN

The inaugural exhibitions of ArtLab, and in particular the Pierre Soulages exhibition, were the occasion to see the emergence of a number of new technologies, based on EPFL laboratory work and now being exploited through young, start-up companies such as ARTMYN. Nathalie Pichard, the first director of ArtLab, has since gone on to become CEO of the ArtTech Foundation, which was created in spring 2017 under the chairmanship of Patrick Aebischer.

Nathalie Pichard is an archeologist by education and was in charge of the Musée romain de Lausanne-Vidy (1988–2000). She has been the EPFL General Secretary for Academic Affairs and headed ArtLab from November 2015 to December 2016. The ArtTech Foundation "aims to bring together science, technology, culture, and the arts by stimulating reflection and supporting innovative and pioneering projects." It encourages entrepreneurial initiatives in these areas.

Can you explain the activity of the ArtTech Foundation?[1]
The ArtTech Foundation is a logical follow-up to the work that Patrick Aebischer wanted to do on the relationship between the arts, culture, science, and technology. Following the end of his tenure as president of EPFL, he wanted to put more of an emphasis on the entrepreneurial aspect of this relationship. The idea was to bring the domains concerned together and support the emergence of start-up companies. We have also worked on annual events such as an ArtTech Forum, an opportunity for innovators, researchers, and experts from all areas to come together for conferences, debates, and workshops. Through our links to EPFL we would like to organize exhibitions or events at ArtLab. We have ongoing contacts about this subject with Sarah Kenderdine, who is now the director of ArtLab, and also a member of the advisory board of ArtTech.

What is your relation with start-up companies that have recently been spun off by EPFL?
The start-up companies that worked on the Soulages exhibition show that the work of EPFL labs can, indeed, give rise to commercial applications at the interface between the arts and technology. We also had in mind to bring start-ups like Gamaya, which was originally involved in agriculture and found use for its technology in the *Noir, c'est noir?* exhibition. The goal is also to offer new ways of viewing art to the public, and thus to enter into the domain of art museums all over the world. The case of ARTMYN surely deserves to be known with respect to this type of effort.

The start-up firm ARTMYN emerged from the work of EPFL's Audiovisual Communications Laboratory (LCAV) under the direction of Martin Vetterli. Using a "clean capture structure" (a hemisphere studded with sixty light sources connected to a camera), ARTMYN not only photographs works, but also generates an "explorable" reconstitution in the form of "5D interactive visualization." Their method is to combine thousands of photographs captured with different light sources and spectrums including UV. Beyond the three recognized dimensions, it is possible to change the perspective and digitally alter the emission angle of the light that illuminates the painting. In the *Noir, c'est noir?* exhibition this work was carried out on *Painting 72.5×81cm, May 3, 1985* (oil on canvas 72.5×81cm, Galerie Alice Pauli, Lausanne). The *Outrenoirs* demonstrate the artist's capacity to produce reflections and are ultimately to be considered an exploration of using light as a material. This painting was created on a linen canvas, "mounted on a frame and primed with a thin coating of black gesso to strengthen the mono-pigmented character of the paint layer. The latter is made with ivory black, oil, resins, and a siccative made of lead that makes it possible for the thickly applied oil to dry."[2]

ARTMYN, based in Saint-Sulpice near EPFL, has advanced considerably with the creation of what they call "digital finger prints" for works of art. They say: "Whether for security or insurance purposes, the scanning process extract's each artwork's unique features, the 'DNA' of the artwork (its topography, reflectivity, and colorimetric properties). As the technology reacts to the slightest changes that are invisible to the eye, a second scan protects owners and collectors from potential forgeries."[3] They have worked with Sotheby's, Koller in Switzerland, the Lausanne museums—which are in the course of new construction (MCBA, MUDAC, and Elysée)—and the Martin Bodmer Foundation in Geneva. For the latter, for example, they scanned the Papyrus Bodmer II, written before AD 200 and one of the oldest known manuscripts of the New Testament, and they digitized this significant work in three dimensions.

Although the activity of ARTMYN is currently focused on paintings, the firm is studying the use of similar methods for three-dimensional objects, and even for medical scans of the skin that would allow doctors to see details that are not visible to the naked eye, and to compare images over time.

---

1 Nathalie Pichard in conversation with the author, EPFL, January 19, 2018.
2 Eveline Notter, Gandur Foundation, press release for the exhibition *Noir, c'est noir?* at ArtLab.
3 At https://www.artmyn.com/about/ (accessed on March 27, 2018).

Noir, c'est noir? combined works by the artist Pierre Soulages with systems developed by the labs of EPFL to explore and explain his use of black. Below, two works by Soulages: left, *Peinture, 181 × 145 cm, 13 novembre 2006,* private collection, and right, *Peinture, 117 × 165 cm, 13 mars 2008,* private collection.

Right, Pierre Soulages, *Peinture, 326 × 181 cm, 14 mars 2009,* private collection, in the *Noir, c'est noir?* exhibition.

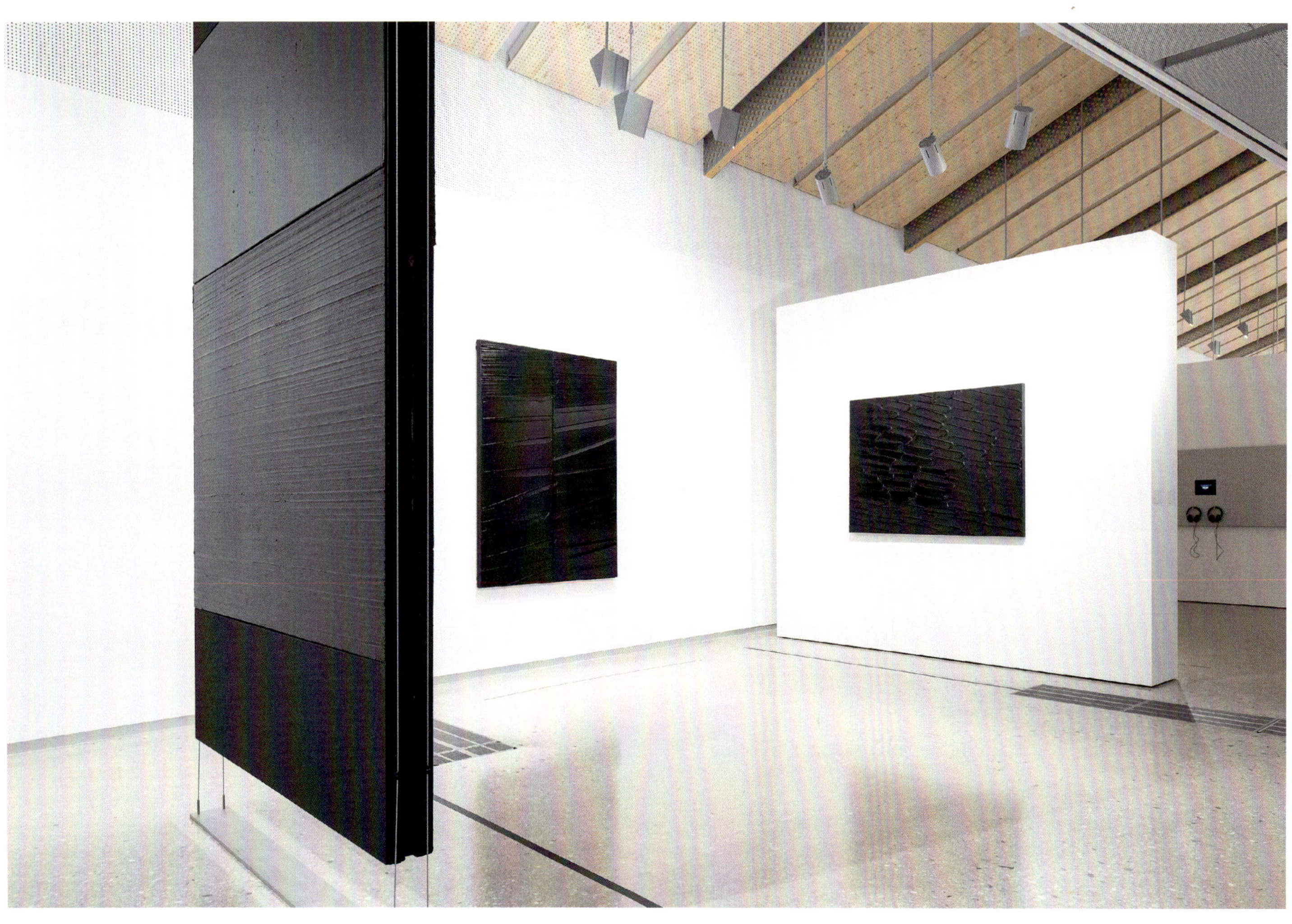

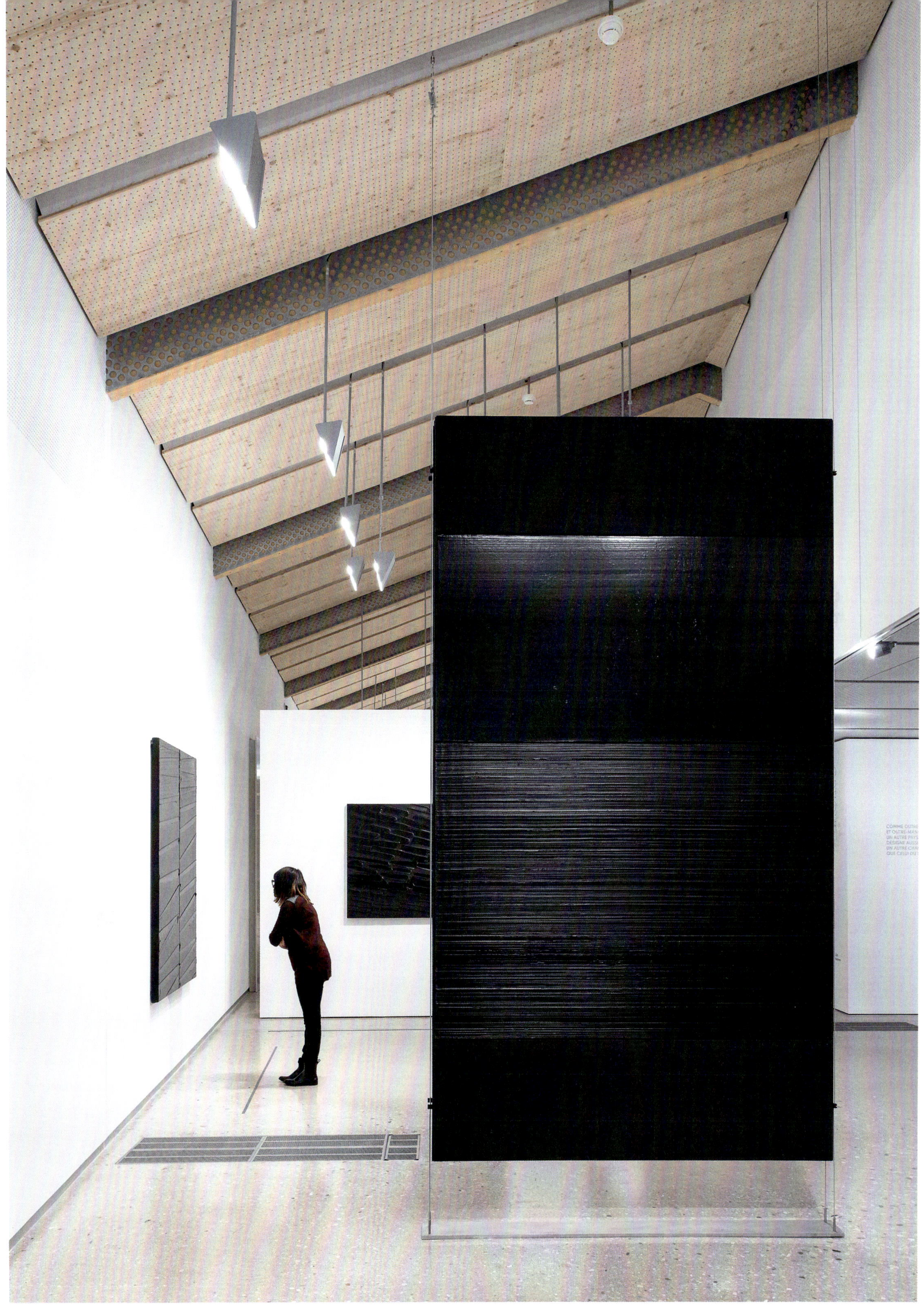

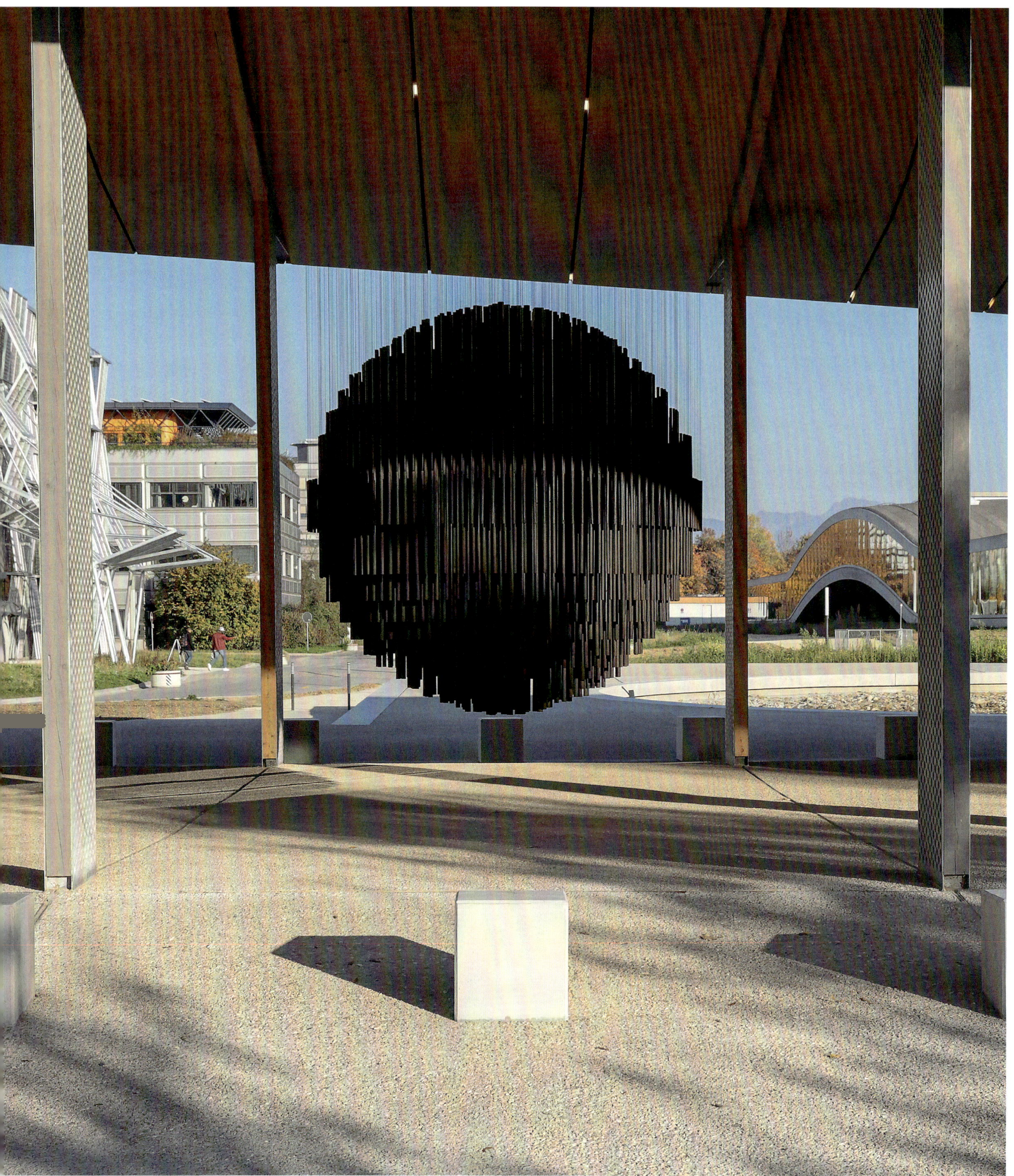

Bing Bang by Etienne Krähenbühl (oak, nickel-titanium wire, h. 5.9 meters, diameter 2.5 meters, 2016).

THE WORLDS
IN DATASQUARE

At the northernmost end of ArtLab, closest to the existing campus, DataSquare is the third pavilion grouped under the single roof of the building. It is presently devoted to a long-term exhibition on big data represented by two major EPFL research initiatives called the Blue Brain Project and the Venice Time Machine. Interactive presentations allow the public to view progress on these projects that share the use of big data to resolve extremely complex problems.

Technological progress has allowed the creation of numerous types of sensors or computer-driven devices that gather nearly astronomical amounts of data about given topics. Simultaneously, data processing has made enormous progress, using algorithms and other inventions to process, store, classify, and share amounts of information that could not conceivably have been used just a few years ago. Big data employs techniques and technologies with new forms of integration that can generate insights from data that is diverse, complex, and on a massive scale. An accepted definition of the phenomena is that "big data represents information assets characterized by such high volume, velocity, and variety as to require specific technology and analytical methods for its transformation into value."[1] EPFL has wholeheartedly taken on the challenges of the new possibilities offered by big data as demonstrated by the two projects presented in ArtLab and other ongoing work.

The exhibition also includes an interface that shows key data about EPFL, in which the school itself can be examined through the optics of big data. EPFL commissioned the Barcelona-based office MediaPro Exhibitions to come up with an original display design. Mediapro is specialized in "interactive installations and last-generation audiovisual technologies (stereoscopic 3D, virtual environments, augmented reality, immersive sound, interfaces)." MediaPro worked closely with EPFL labs, the EPFL ArtLab team, and the campus facilities management throughout the design process. DataSquare has a floor area of 629 square meters with 260 square meters of exhibition space and shares with the other elements of ArtLab a high, folded ceiling that corresponds to the form of the building's long roof.

1   Andrea de Mauro *et al.*, "A Formal Definition of Big Data Based on Its Essential Features," Library Review, Vol. 65, 2015, at https://www.researchgate.net/publication/299379163_A_formal_definition_of_Big_Data_based_on_its_essential_features (accessed on March 29, 2018).

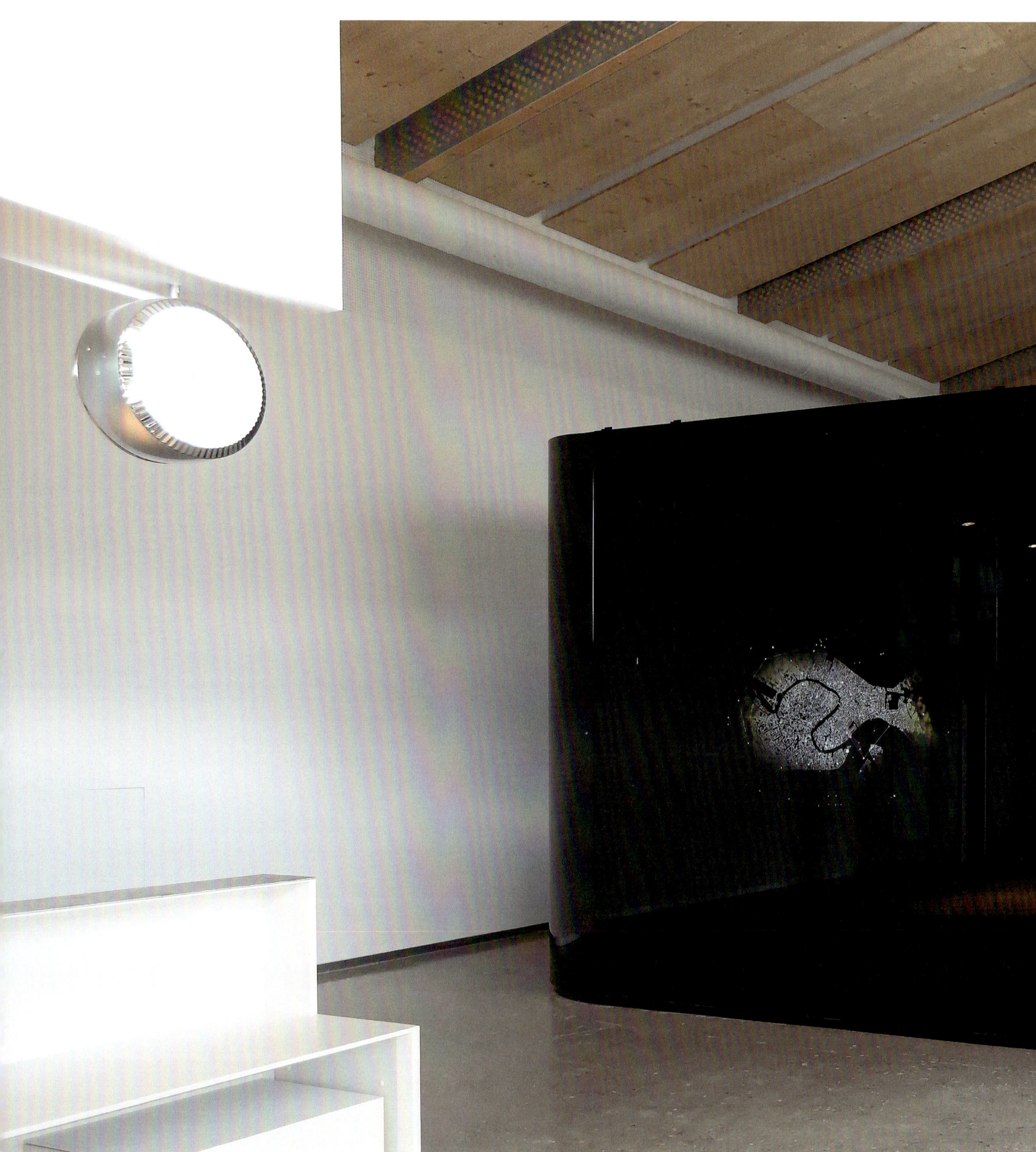

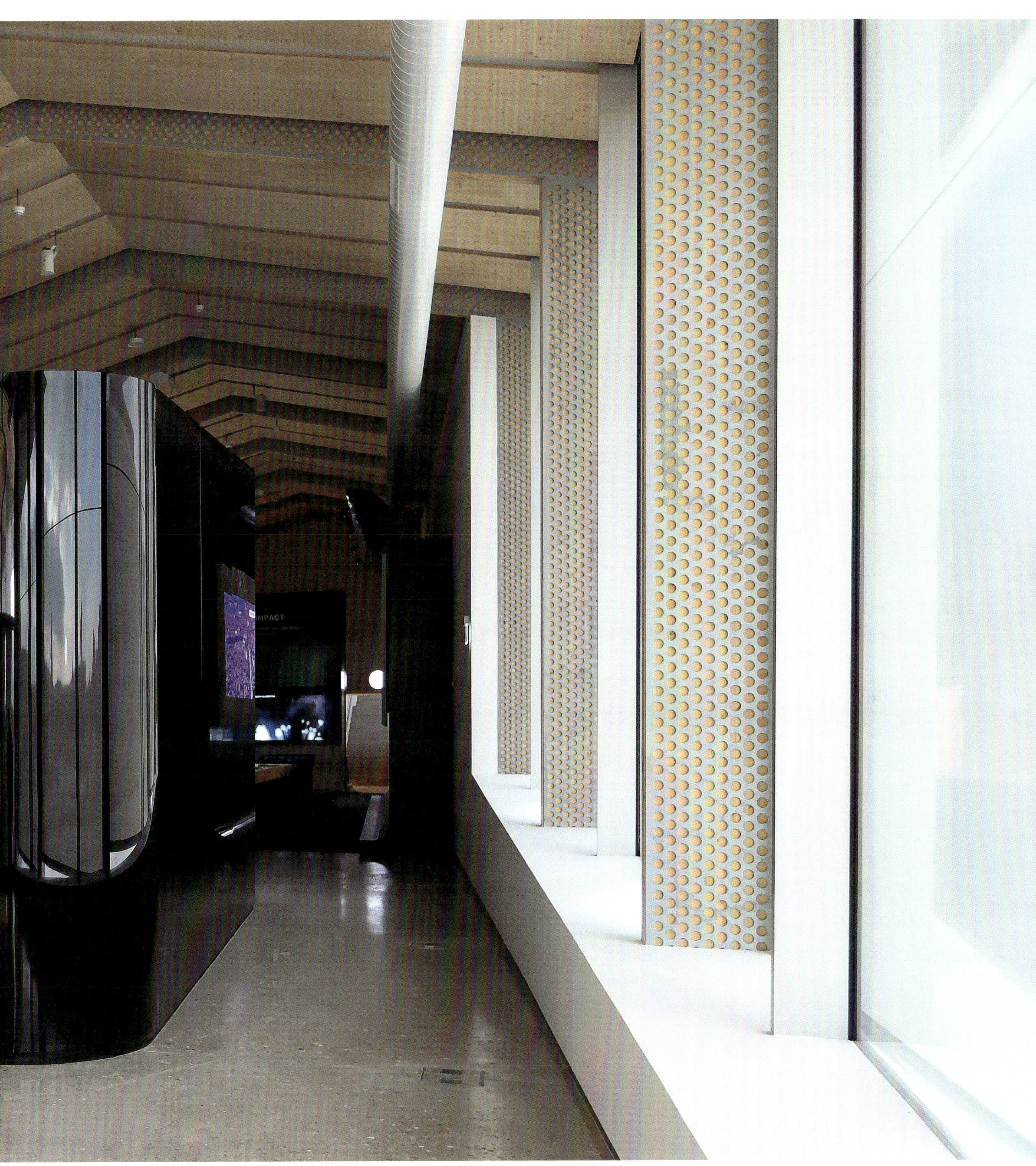

Inside the high-technology exhibition space of DataSquare.

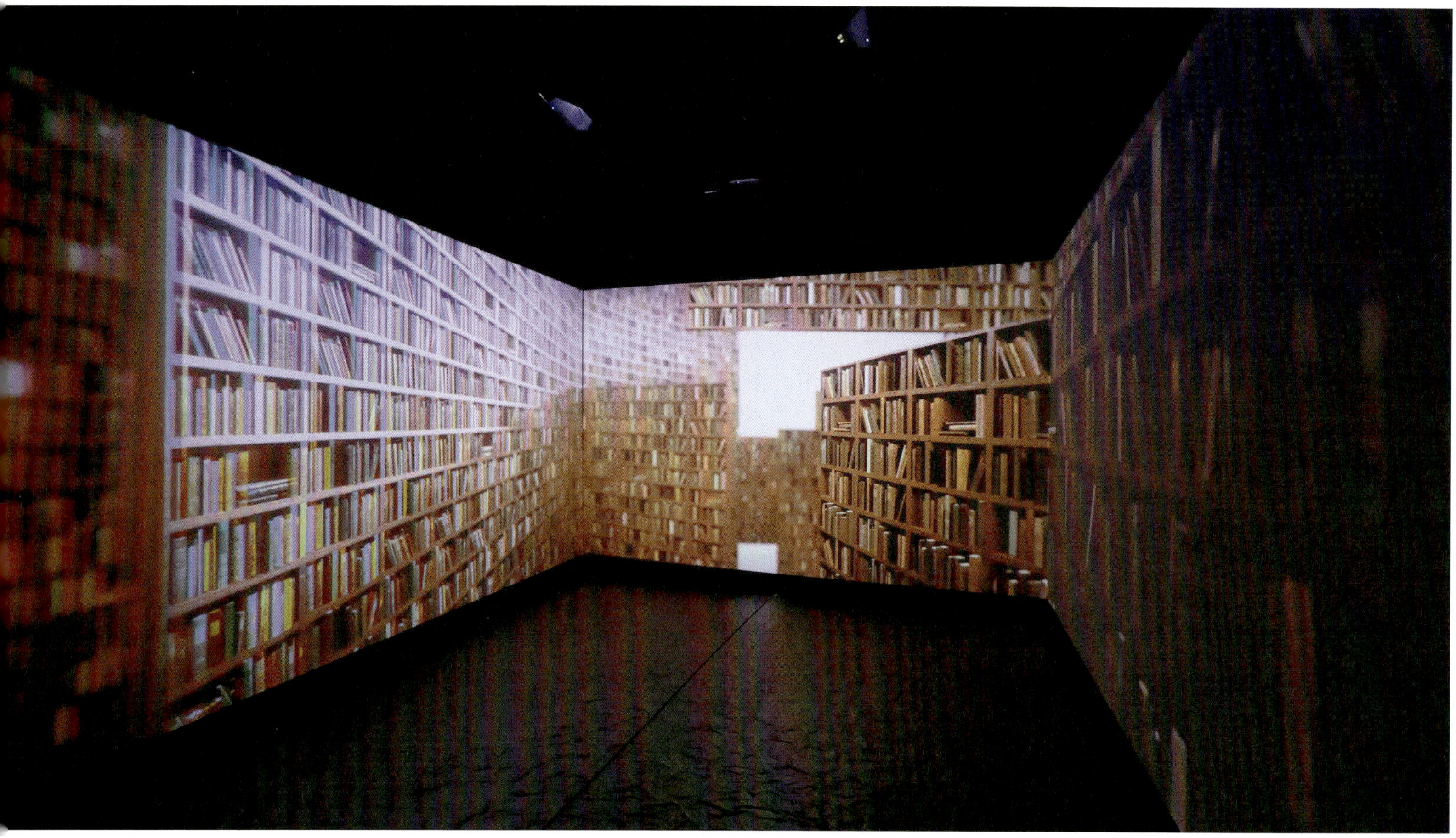

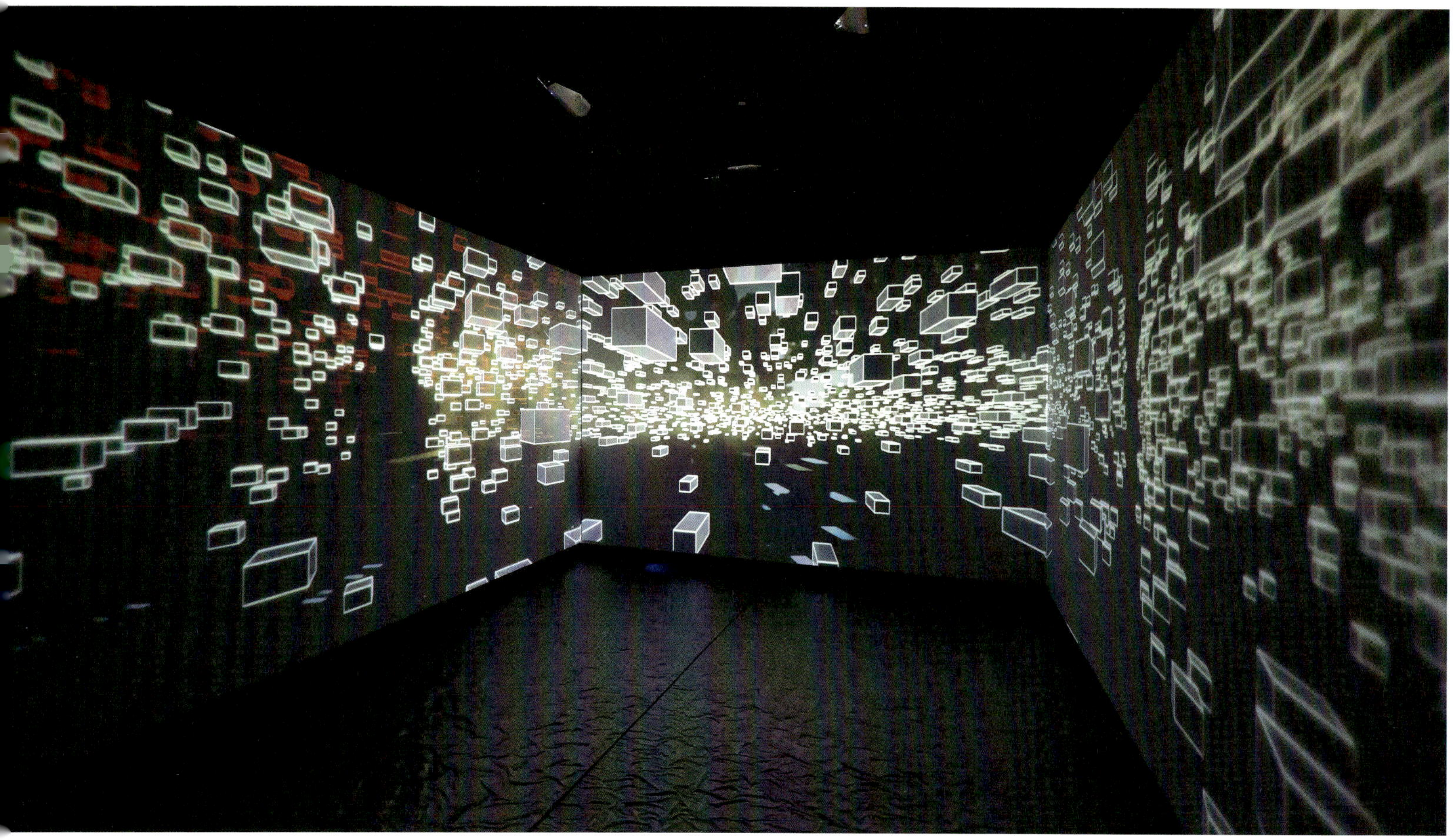

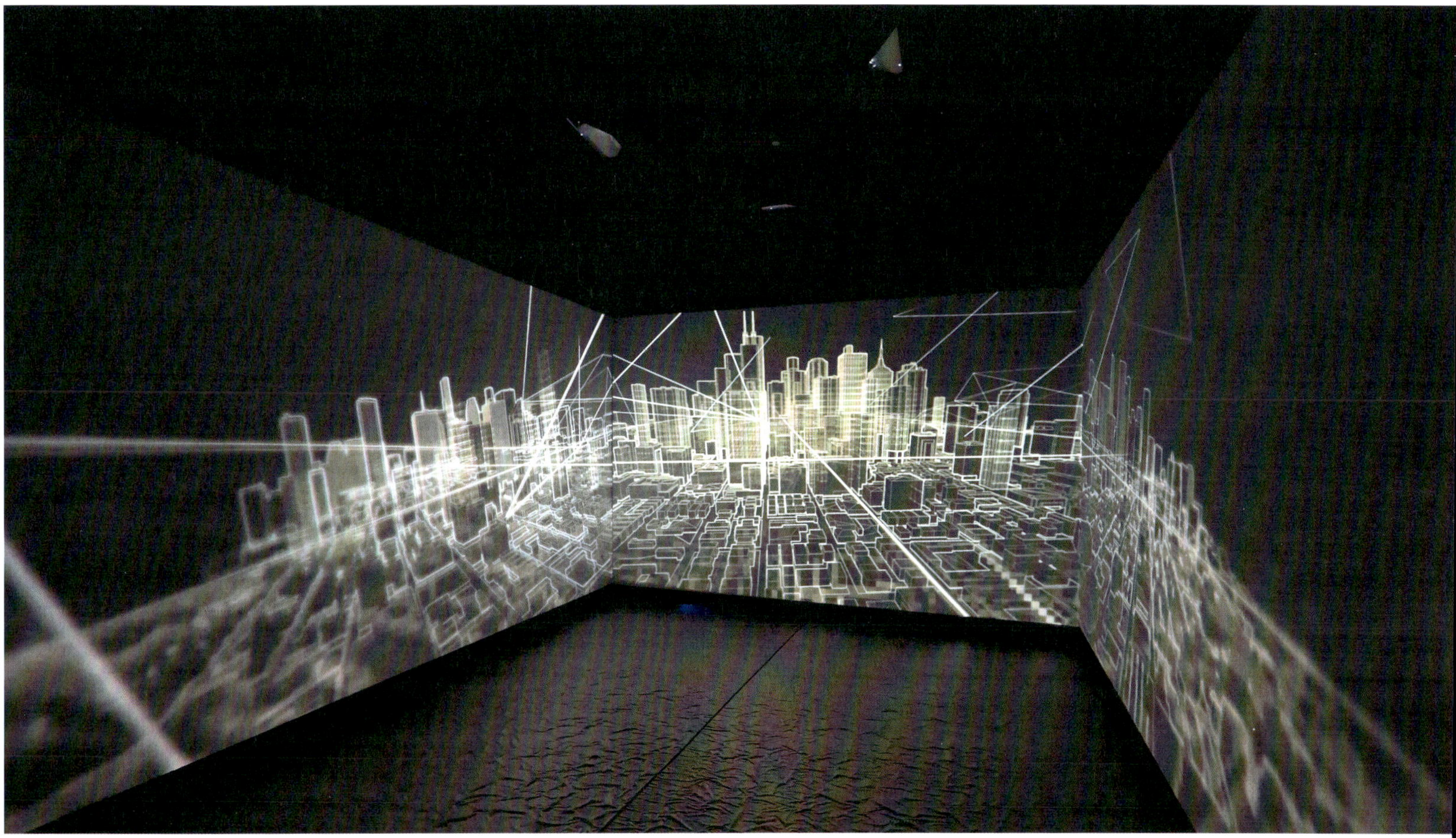

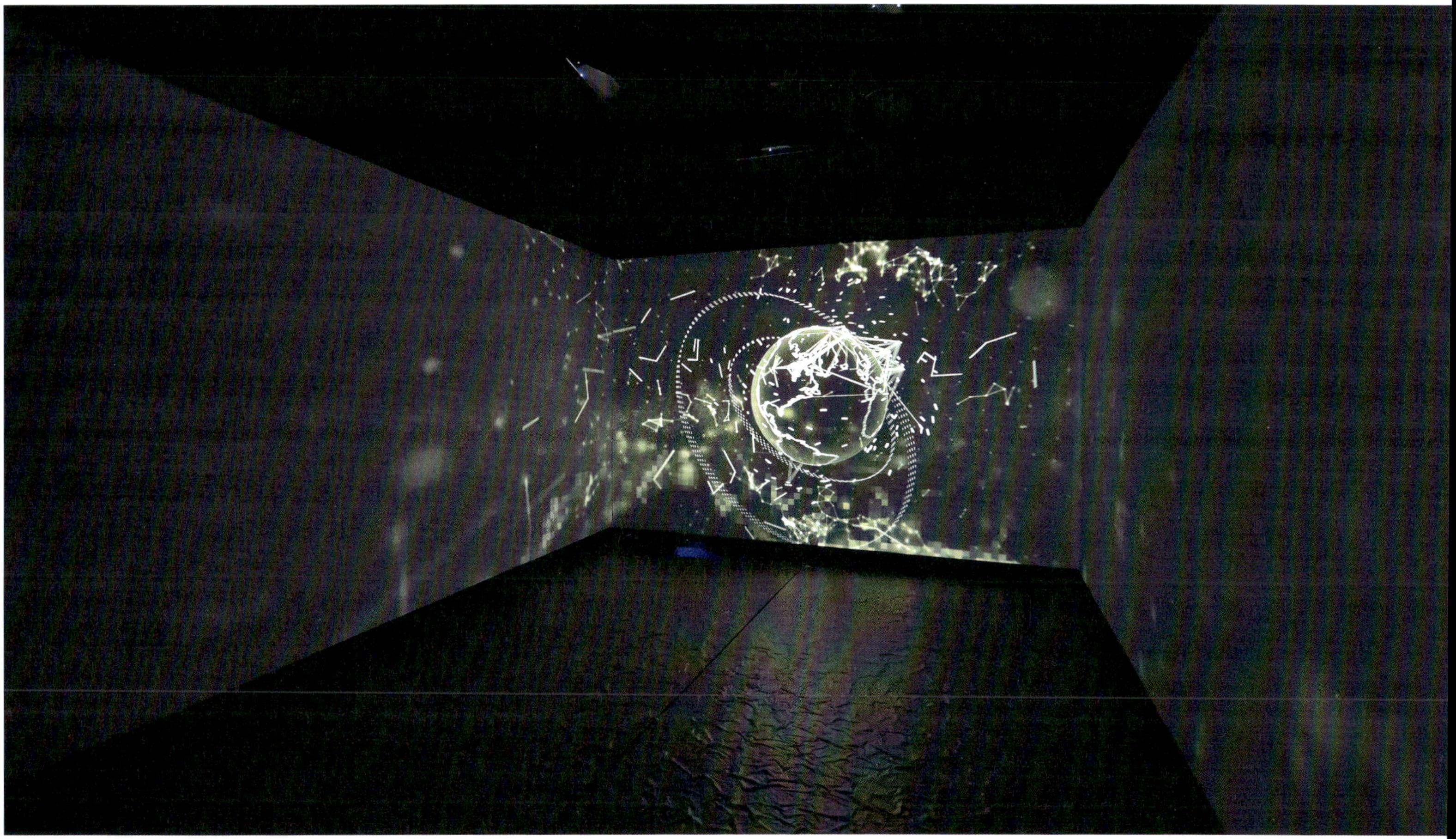

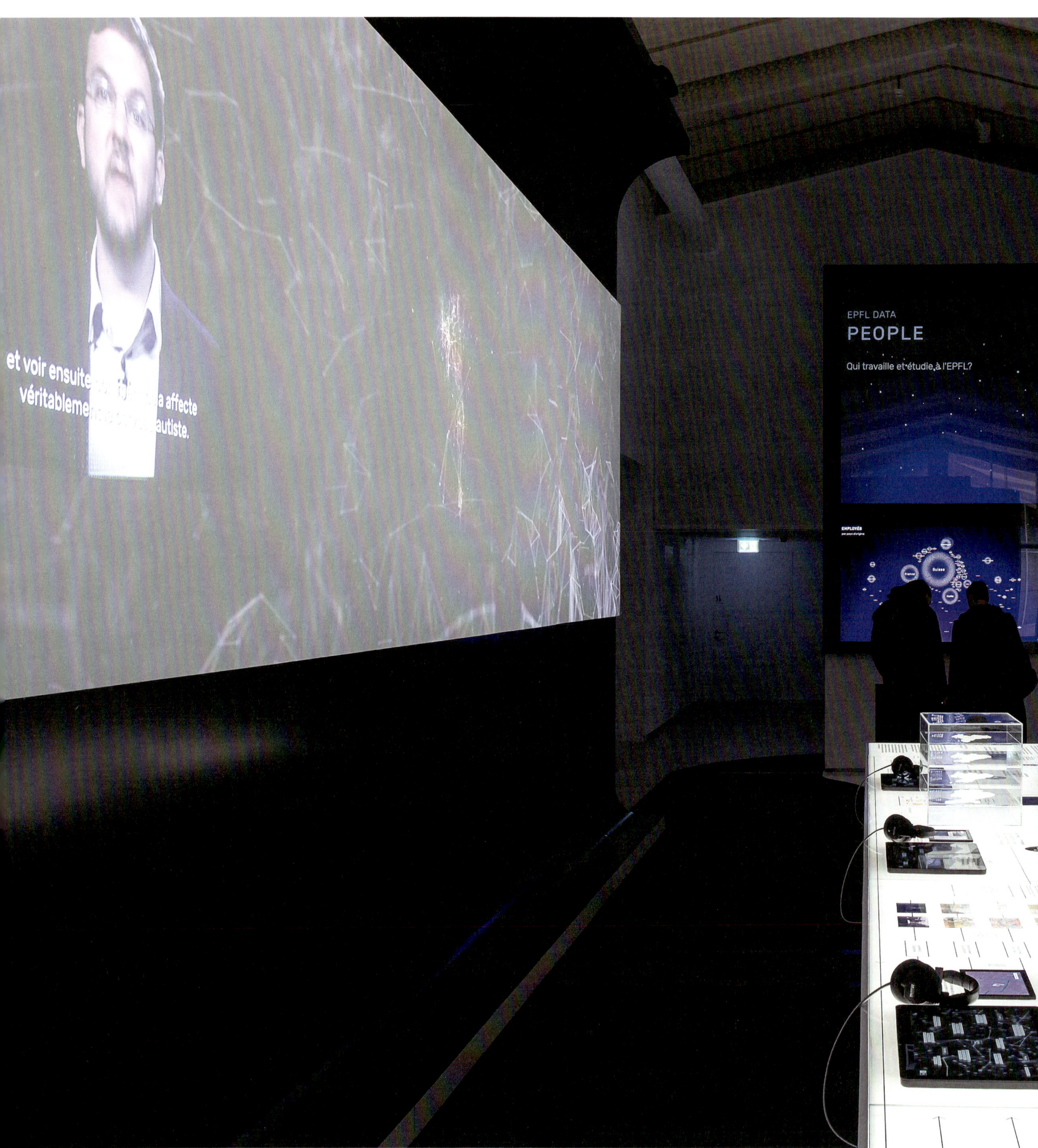
et voir ensuite
véritablement

affecte
autiste.

EPFL DATA
PEOPLE

Qui travaille et étudie à l'EPFL?

EMPLOYÉS

In essentially dark spaces, visitors discover large and small images and information about EPFL programs, including the Blue Brain Project.

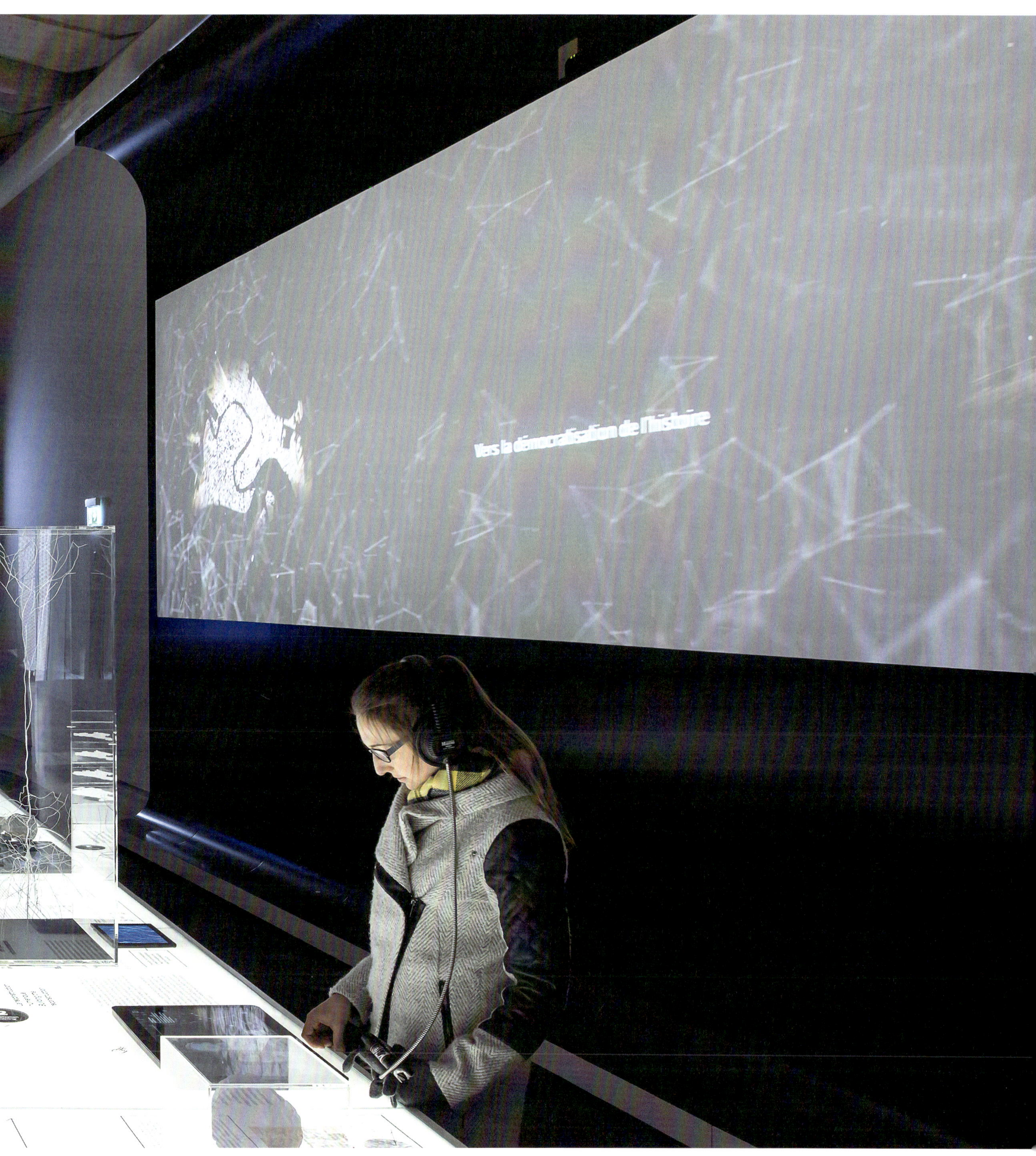

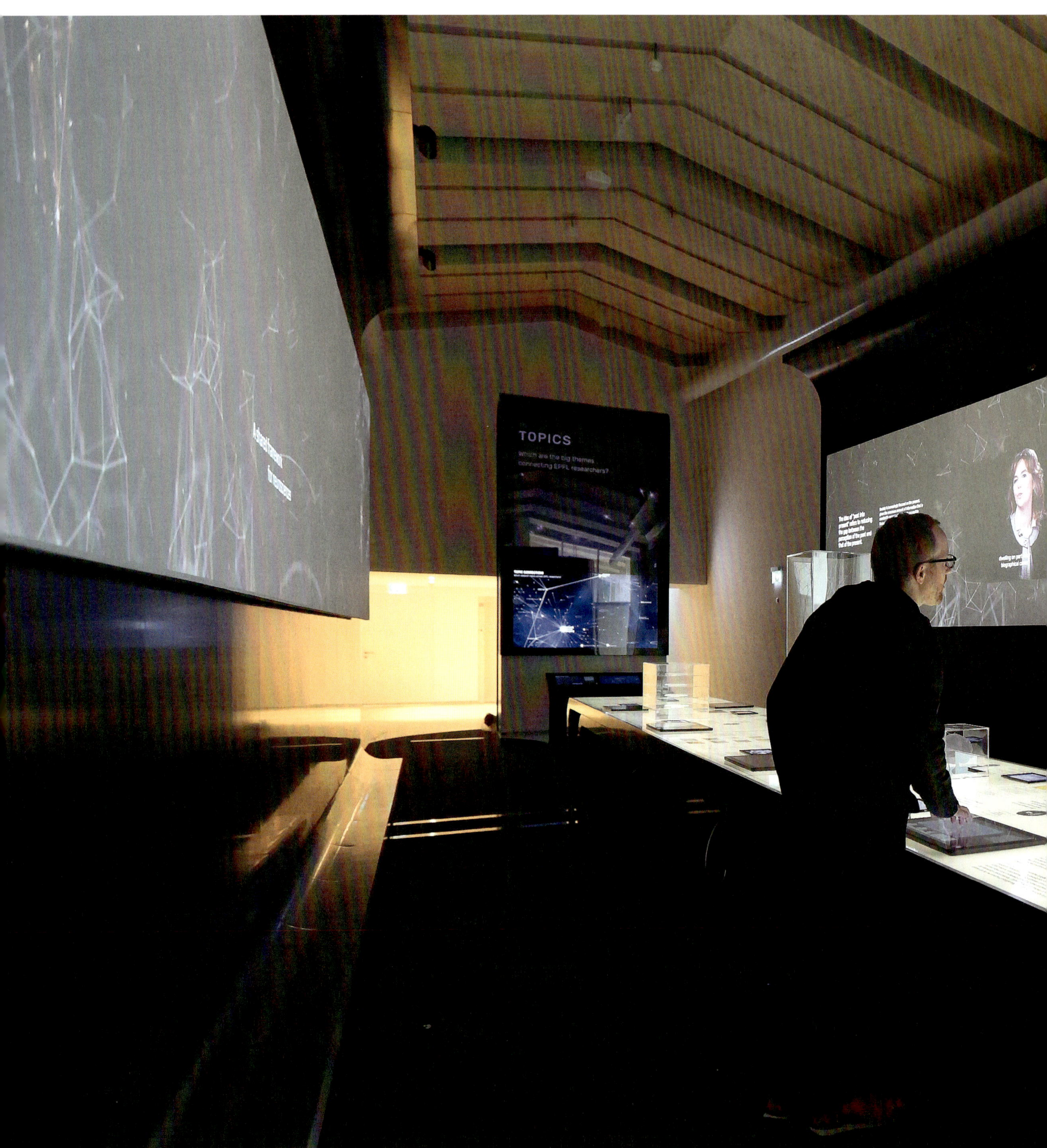

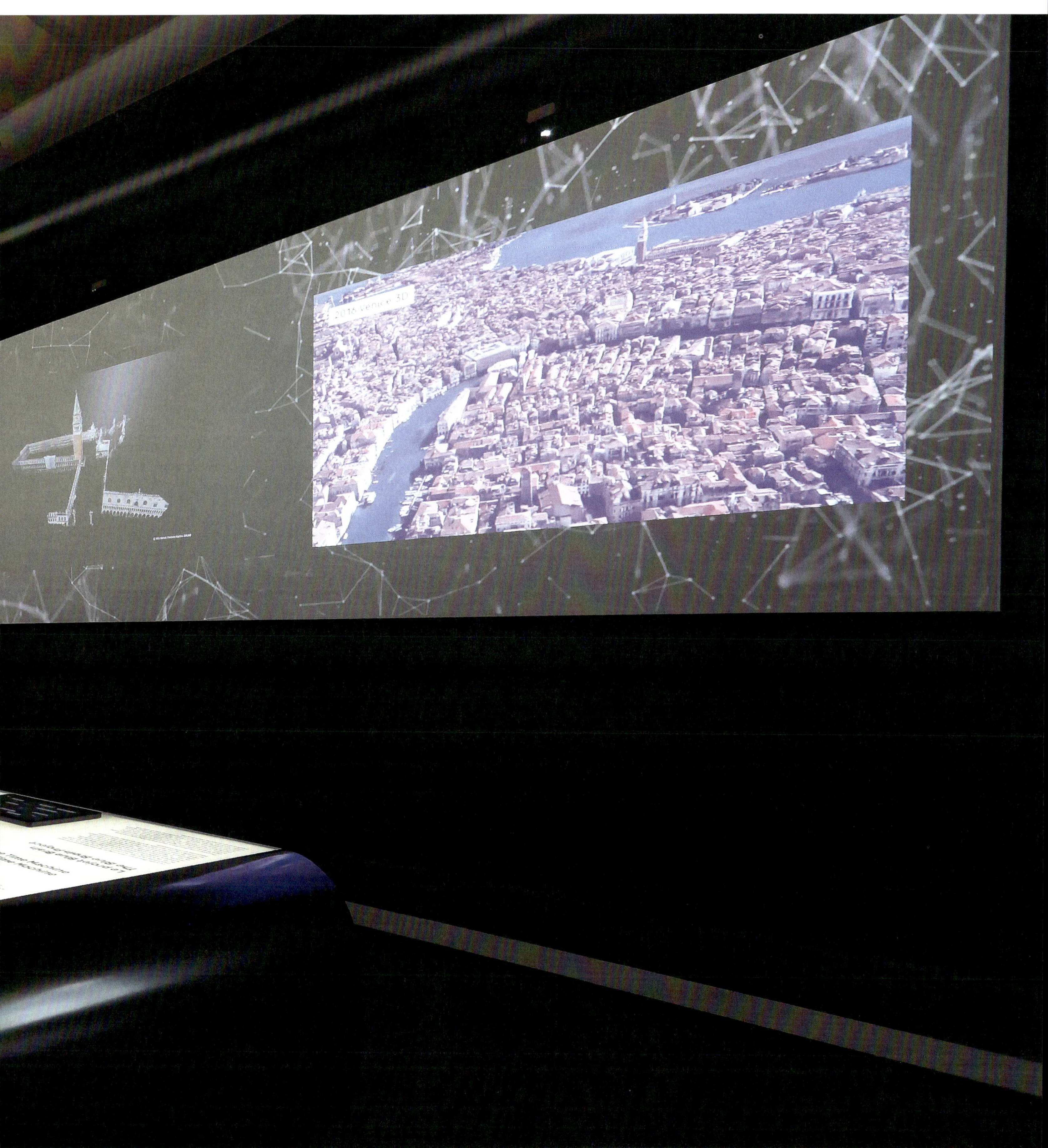

The Venice Time Machine aims to create a virtual model
of the Italian city through the centuries.

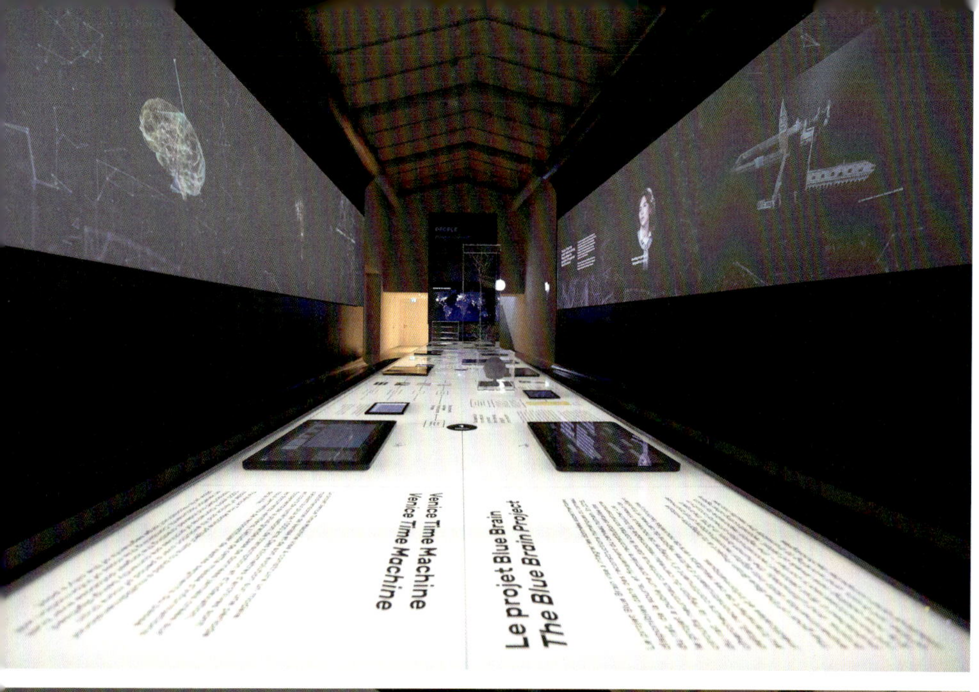

Venice Time Machine
Venice Time Machine
Le projet Blue Brain
The Blue Brain Project

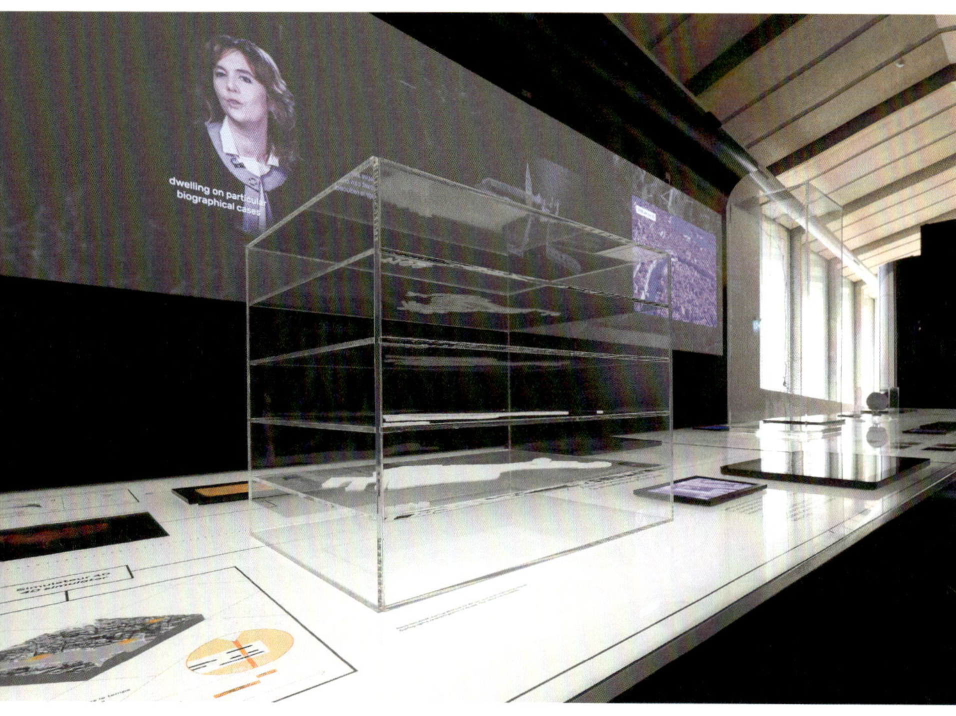

dwelling on particular
biographical cases

The Blue Brain Project presented in DataSquare involves supercomputer-based simulations that offer a new approach to understanding the structure and functions of the brain.

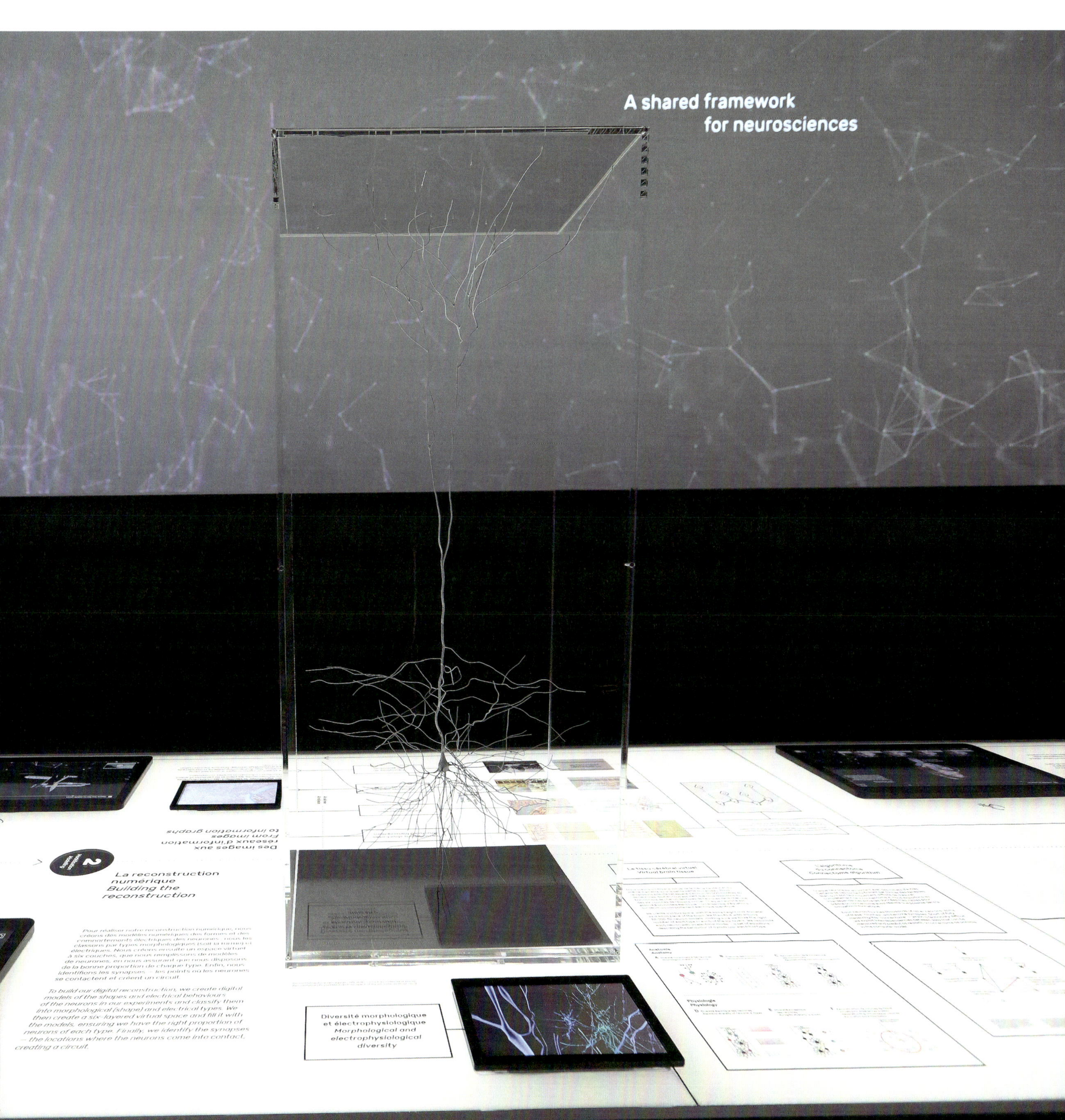

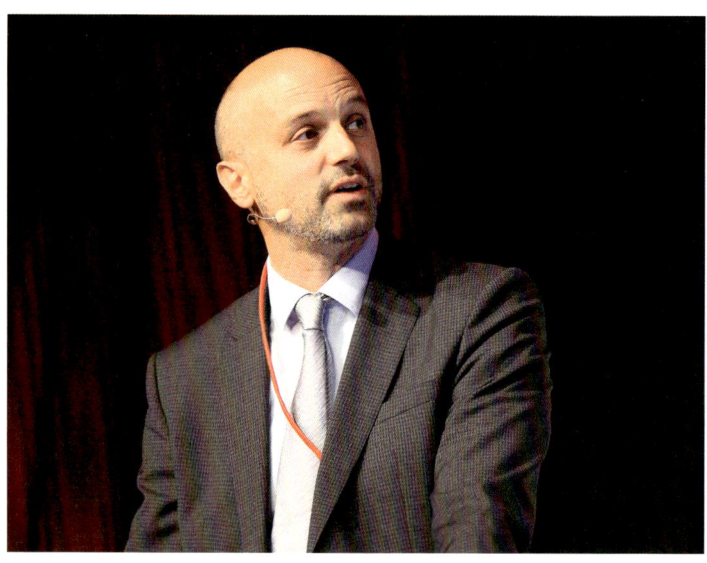

TO TRAVEL THROUGH TIME

There is no difference between time and any of the three dimensions of space except that our consciousness moves along it.

H.G. Wells, *The Time Machine*, 1895

The dream of travel through time has preoccupied men forever, or so it might seem. The English writer H.G. Wells famously explored this idea in his fairly dark novella *The Time Machine*. Even if looking into the future remains a task of more less informed speculation, the past may well be about to deliver many of its secrets. Advances in technology and computing power are at the point of being able to peer deep into archives whose meaning has faded with time. Imagine being able to walk through a virtual representation of Venice at any time in its storied history. This is the prospect offered by an EPFL project exhibited at ArtLab.

The Venice Time Machine project is an international digital humanities scientific program launched by EPFL and the University Ca'Foscari of Venice in 2012. It also involves the State Archive in Venice, the Marciana Library, the Instituto Veneto, and the Giorgio Cini Foundation. The international board of the project includes scholars from Princeton, Stanford, Columbia, and London universities. Three hundred researchers and students from different disciplines (basic sciences, engineering, computer science, architecture, history, and art history) have already participated in the program. The Venice Time Machine seeks to build "a multidimensional model of Venice and its evolution covering a period of more than 1000 years." The vast archives of the city are currently being digitized, transcribed, and indexed, creating the largest database on Venice. The information extracted from diverse sources "is organized in a semantic graph of linked data and unfolded in space and time as part of a historical geographical information system, based on high-resolution scanning of the city itself."[1]

Patrick Aebischer explains the first steps that led to this project: "We were approached by the insurance company Generali, which owns half of Piazza San Marco. They were wondering what they could do with this real estate. We thought that Venice was the perfect place to put technology, history, and the arts together. In 2012, we went to the archives of Venice with Frédéric Kaplan."[2] When he first visited the archives, Kaplan said: "I felt completely overwhelmed. Seeing what a thousand-year archive looks like, knowing that most of it was not available— I knew we needed to do it."[3]

Frédéric Kaplan holds the Digital Humanities Chair at EPFL and directs the EPFL Digital Humanities Laboratory (DHLAB). He created the first Digital Humanities master's course in Switzerland and is taking an active role in shaping a complete new curriculum at EPFL in this area. He was the local co-organizer of the Digital Humanities 2014 conference in Lausanne, the largest scientific meeting ever conducted in this domain. He directs the Venice Time Machine project, and is a member of the steering committee of the broader European Community Time Machine FET Flagship initiative.[4]

The nature of the Venice Time Machine project is such that it inevitably requires the input of archivists and historians to annotate manuscripts, and to provide the necessary context for data processing. The technology used includes scanners with robotic arms to turn pages, and a rotary scanner that can simultaneously scan a number of documents. A high-speed "non-contact" scanner, developed in conjunction with Factum Arte, a team of artists, technicians and conservators based in Madrid, London, and Milan, can digitize both sides of a document in four seconds. The overall system is capable of producing several thousand high-definition images per hour "feeding terabytes of information to servers in Venice for long-term storage, and to Lausanne, where high-performance computers transform the images into digital text ready for annotation."[5] The European Union-funded organization Recognition and Enrichment of Archival Documents (READ), which has made progress on the automatic reading of whole words that appear in old manuscripts, is also involved in the project. The machine-learning processes used employ algorithms to recognize words or names and to see how many times they appear in the database, for example. The next step in this process will be the use of computed-tomography (CT) scanning developed for medical purposes, which could read entire documents that are too fragile to be opened. As of the end of 2017, 190,000 records from the Venice State Archive, 720,000 photographs from Fondazione Giorgio Cini, and 3000 books on Venice's history held in the city's main libraries had been digitized as part of the Venice Time Machine project.[6] "That's less than 1% of everything that's out there. It's enormous!" says Frédéric Kaplan.

The year 2018 marks the middle of the twelve-year period allotted to the Venice Time Machine project. Frédéric Kaplan takes an imperative approach to the work he is doing, stating: "Any records that were kept before 2000 basically don't exist, because we have no means of viewing them. We urgently need to bring our archives into the digital age. We mustn't lose contact with the past." Kaplan is also closely involved in the European Community's FET Flagship which involves 160 partners in thirty-two countries and seeks to use artificial intelligence and machine learning to "extend the realm of big data to the past" by extending the ideas of the Venice Time Machine project across Europe. This effort "has a large expected impact on the sector of tourism (600 million tourists per year), media industries (new forms of virtual reality), and for the development of start-ups exploiting long data series analysis for making prediction using artificial intelligence techniques. It is not unlikely that the next Google will emerge out of these technologies."[7] In fact, Amsterdam, Nuremberg, Paris, Jerusalem, Budapest, and Naples have already started similar initiatives. The ambitions of FET are substantial. The organization states: "The second Internet revolution begins now, with the predicted demise of the current search engines and the introduction of new means of indexing information. The challenge is to be able to move through time, as easily as we already do with space, and to use the volume of data from the past to look into the future. It is not simply a question of recording the state of our machine world for a few years, but of building a bridge across the great gulf that separates the era of globalized information from previous, pre-computer eras."[8]

The Venice Time Machine project itself involves not only the exhibit at ArtLab but also seeks to give access to the public, both specialized and general, to the vast amount of data being generated. The project is currently launching its own search engine called Canvas, which will allow visitors to view scanned records from the Venice State Archives and search the database using keywords. For the Fondazione Giorgio Cini photographic archives, a search engine called Replica will allow research on text and images, and actually make it possible to discover links between the composition of photographs in the archives. In and of itself, the Venice Time Machine is clearly generating valuable records that will be explored for many years to come by researchers and authors. Ultimately, the project should generate a digital model of Venice over time, allowing visitors to have a virtual tour of any part of the city at any selected point in time. This idea verges on what might have been considered science fiction just a few years ago.

Through the efforts of Frédéric Kaplan and others, the Venice Time Machine is clearly already on the way to encouraging the creation of a Europe-wide program of a similar nature. Patrick Aebischer's idea that transversal links between disciplines and the value of European heritage in the emerging digital world is already generating concrete results. The exhibition in ArtLab is, of course, a small part of this overall effort, but, nonetheless, with the Venice Time Machine exhibition in DataSquare, ArtLab is participating in the information offered about the fascinating new world of digital humanities, which may well change the world much more than can be currently understood. Ultimately, the arcane world of archives could yield information that anyone can use—an unbelievable possibility.

1   At https://vtm.epfl.ch/page-109836-en.html (accessed on March 28, 2018).
2   Patrick Aebischer in conversation with the author, EPFL, March 13, 2018.
3   At https://www.vi-mm.eu/2017/07/26/the-time-machine-reconstructing-ancient-venices-social-networks/ (accessed on March 28, 2018).
4   At https://people.epfl.ch/frederic.kaplan/bio?lang=en&cvlang=en (accessed on March 28, 2018).
5   At https://www.nature.com/news/the-time-machine-reconstructing-ancient-venice-s-social-networks-1.22147 (accessed on March 28, 2018).
6   At https://www.researchitaly.it/en/news/venice-time-machine-two-million-images-of-the-large-venetian-archives-now-digitalized/ (accessed on March 28, 2017.
7   At http://timemachineproject.eu/#key-points (accessed on March 28, 2018).
8   At http://timemachineproject.eu/article.php (accessed on March 28, 2018).

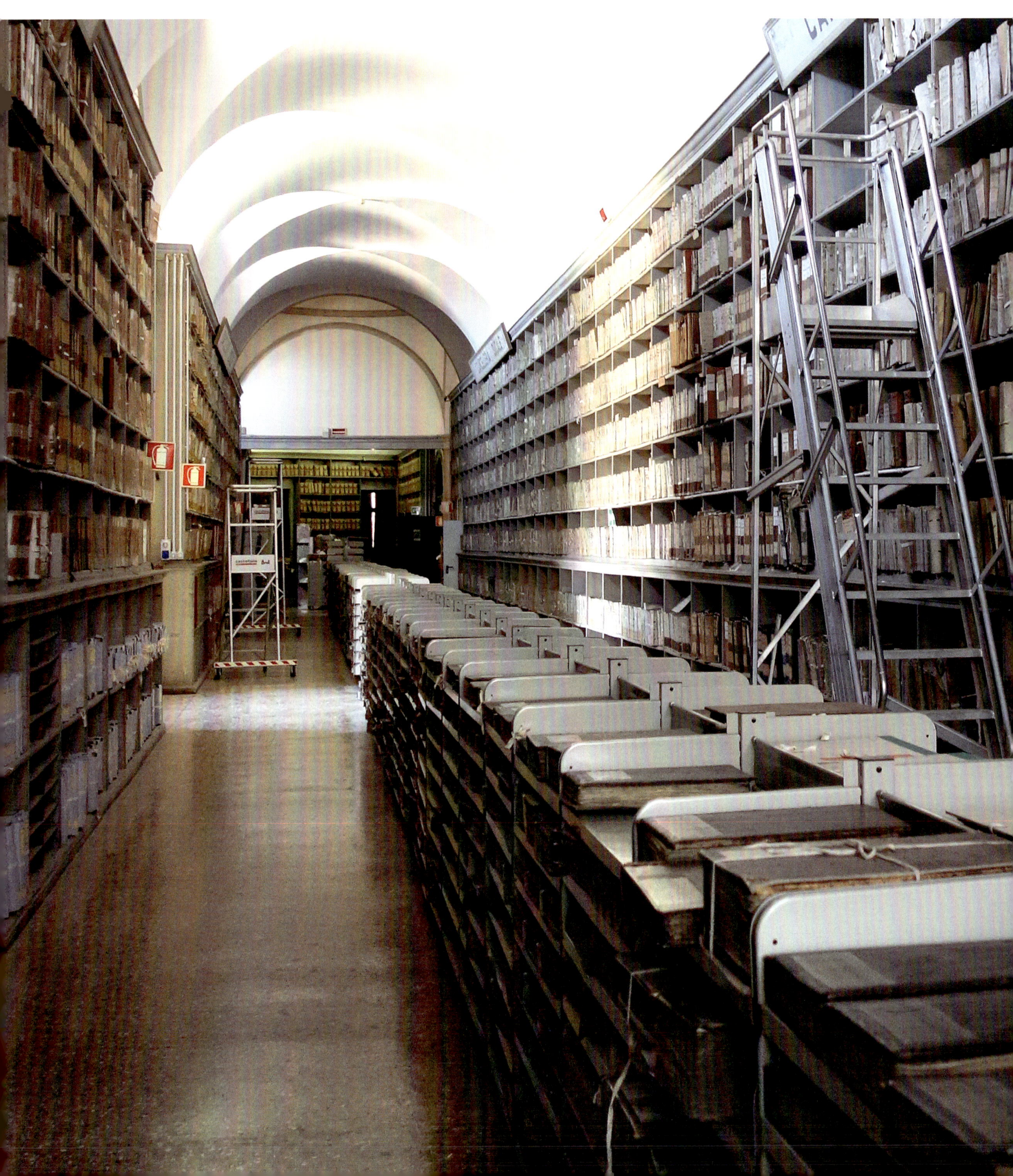

A corridor in the State Archive (Archivio di Stato) in Venice, one of the sources of information used for the Venice Time Machine project. Right, documents from the archive.

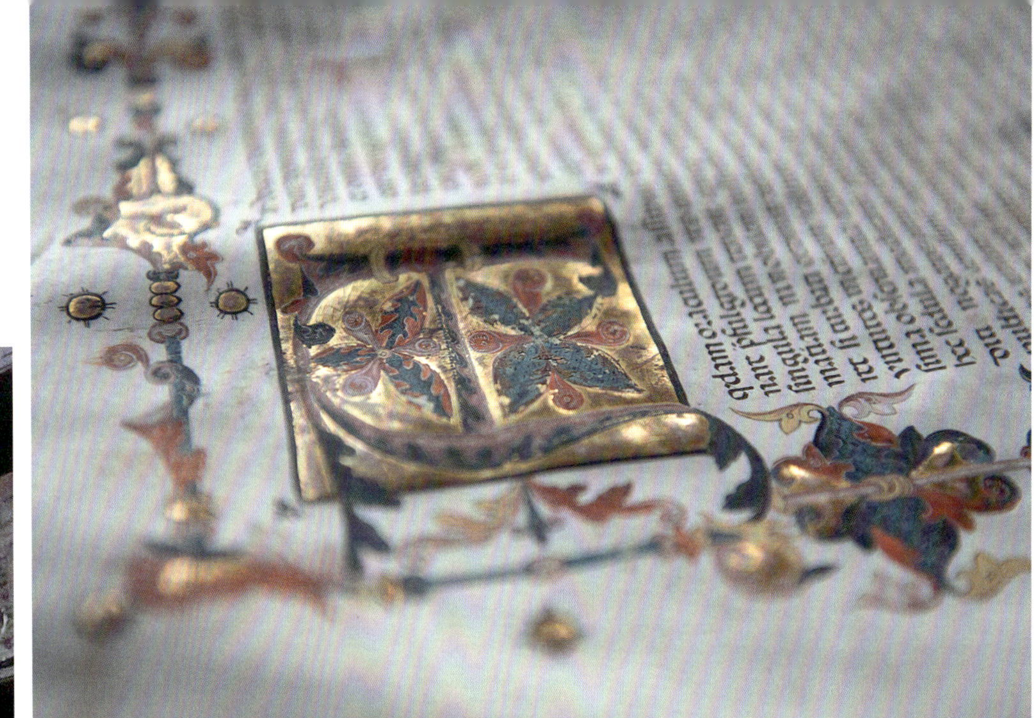

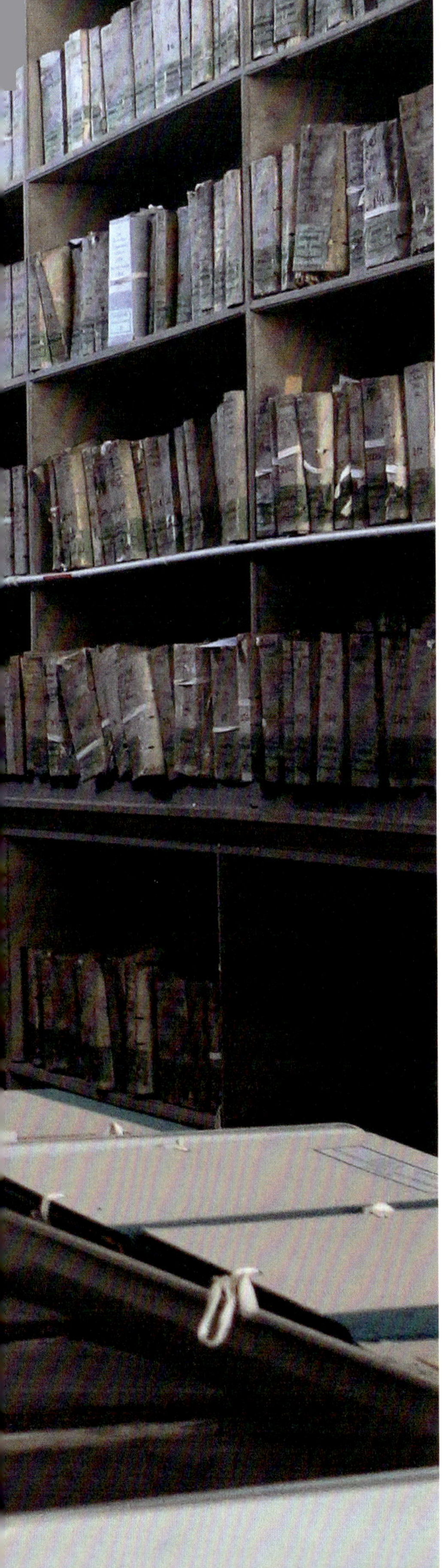

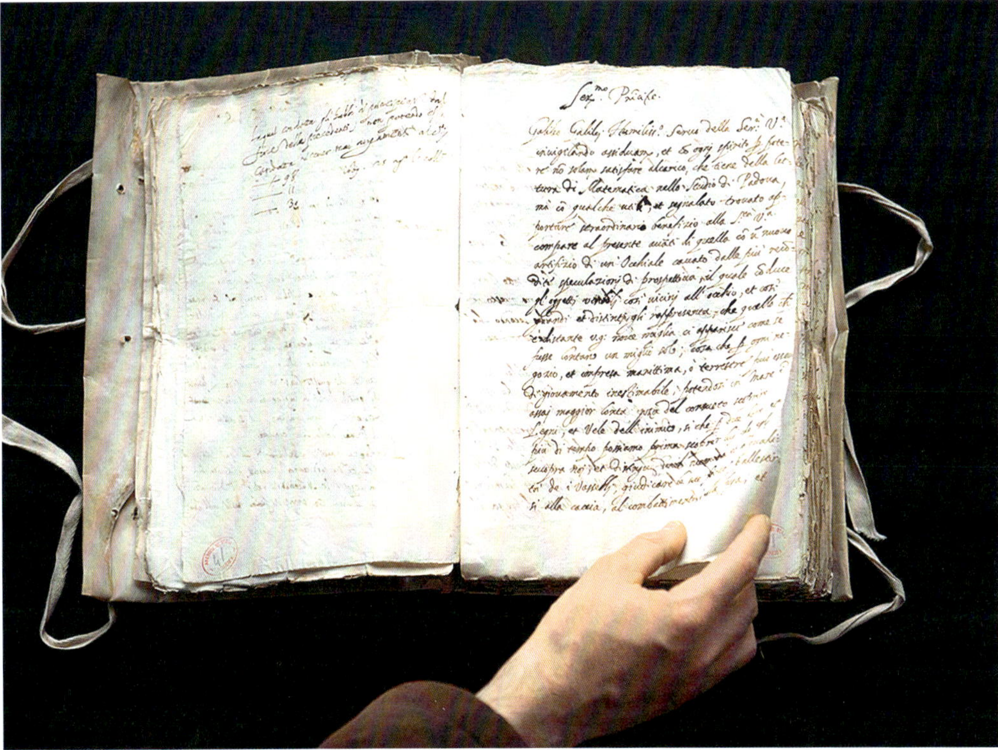

As vast amounts of archival material are analyzed and assimilated, the Venice
Time Machine will offer a more and more precise image of individual monuments.

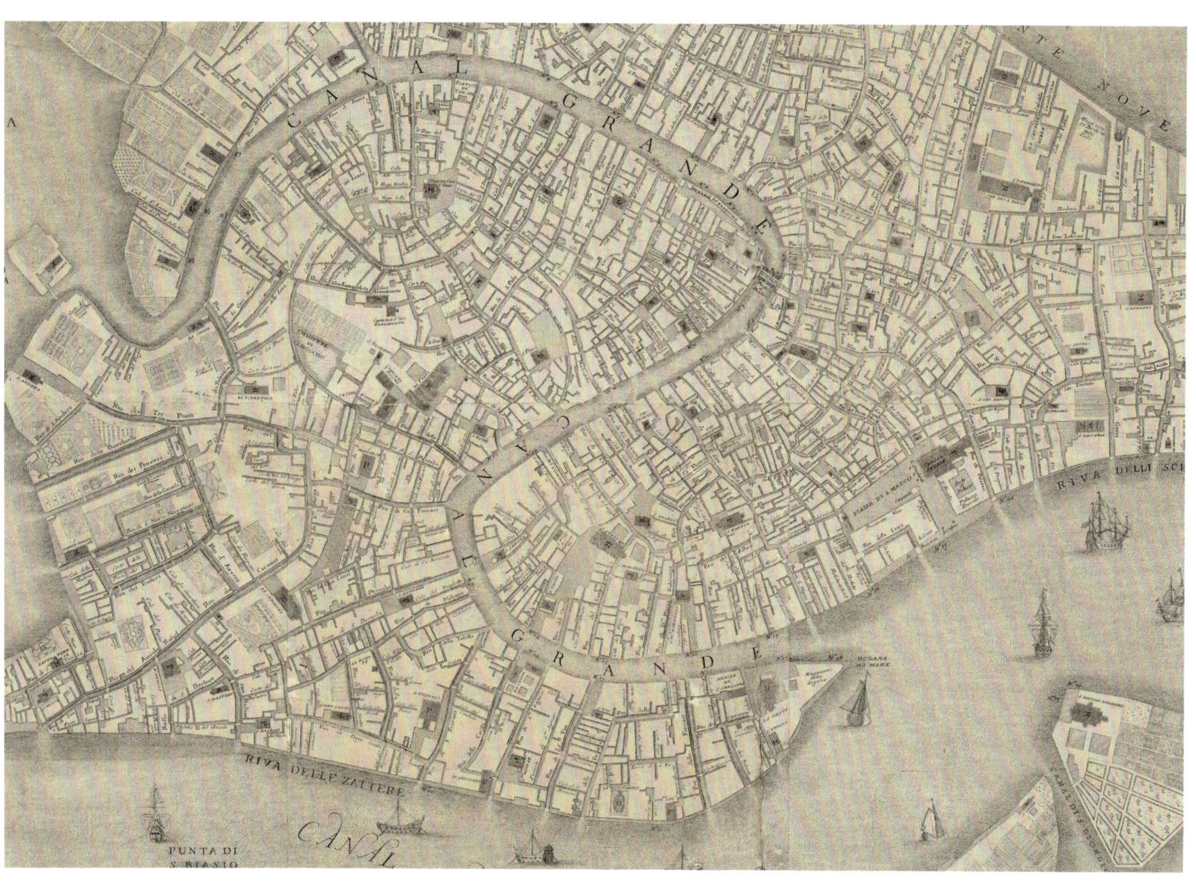

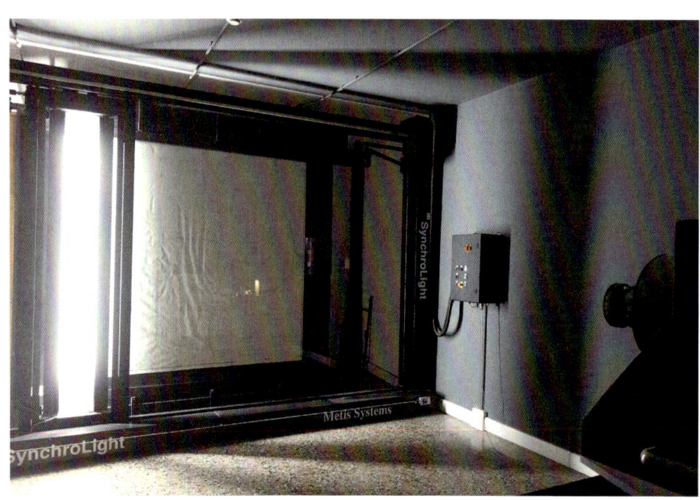

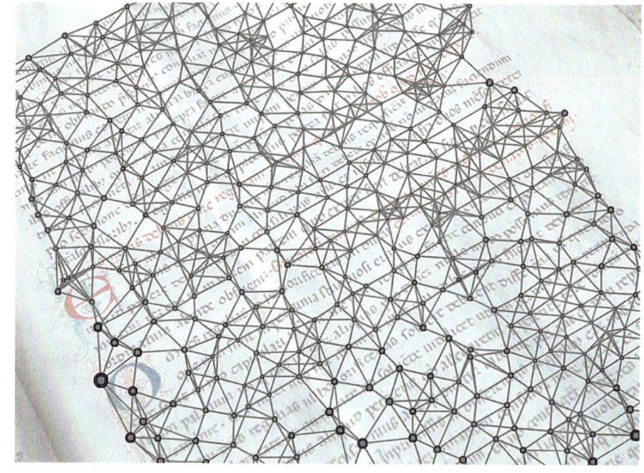

The Venice Time Machine will ultimately create a virtual model of the city
through the centuries, using archives, but also plans and works of art.

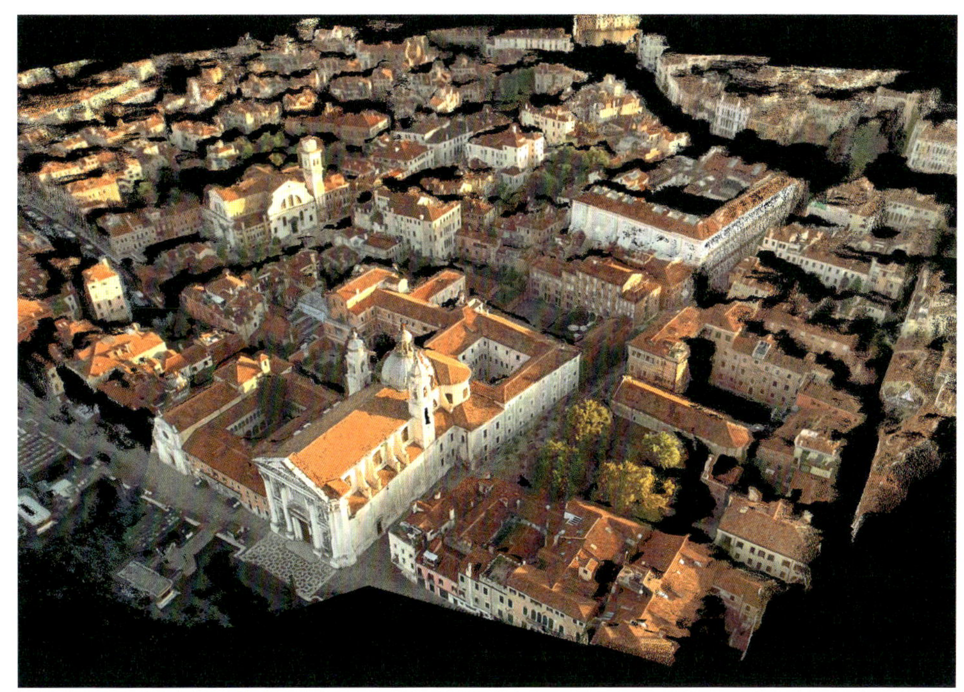

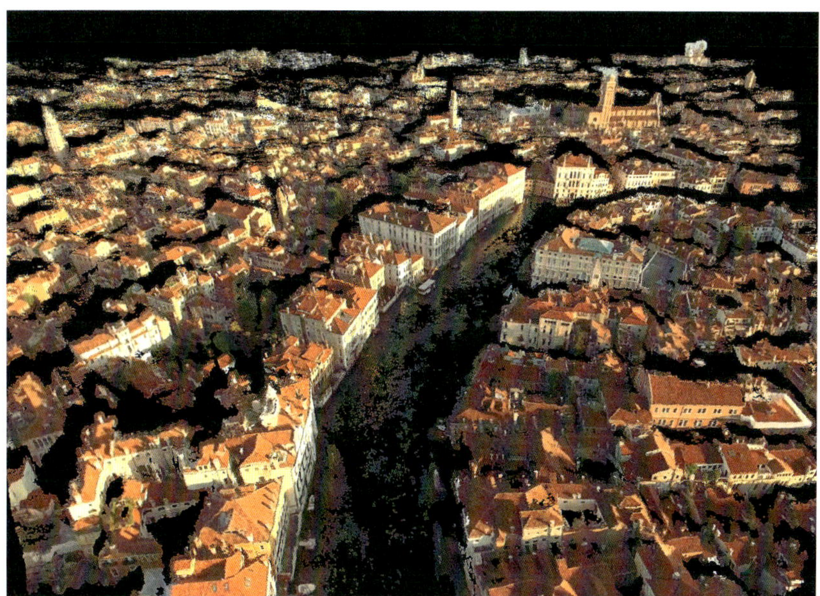

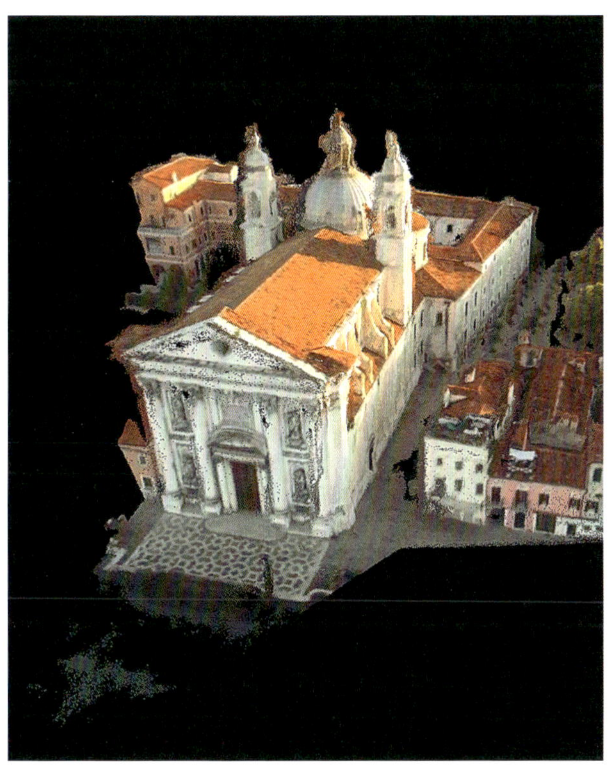

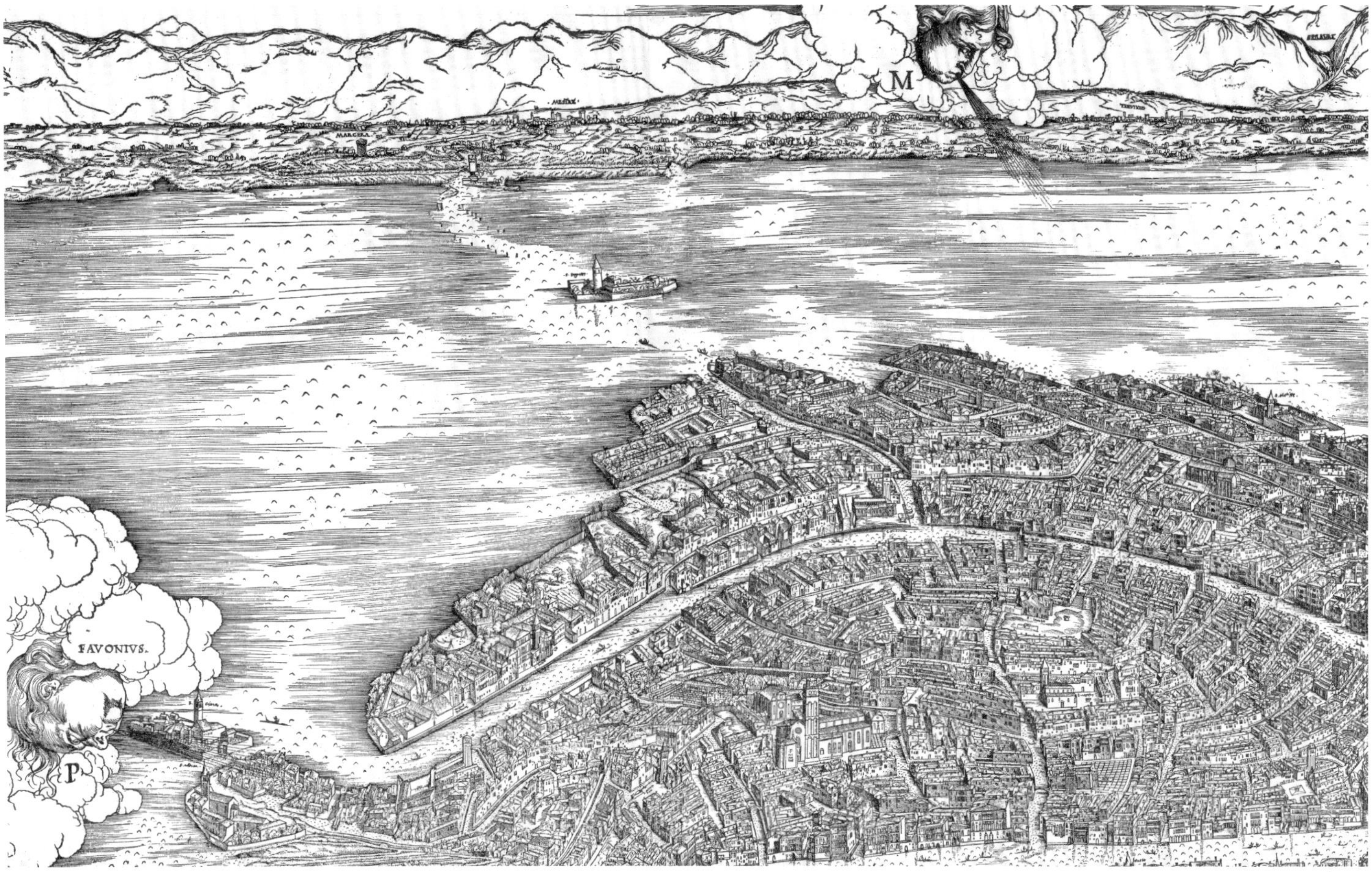

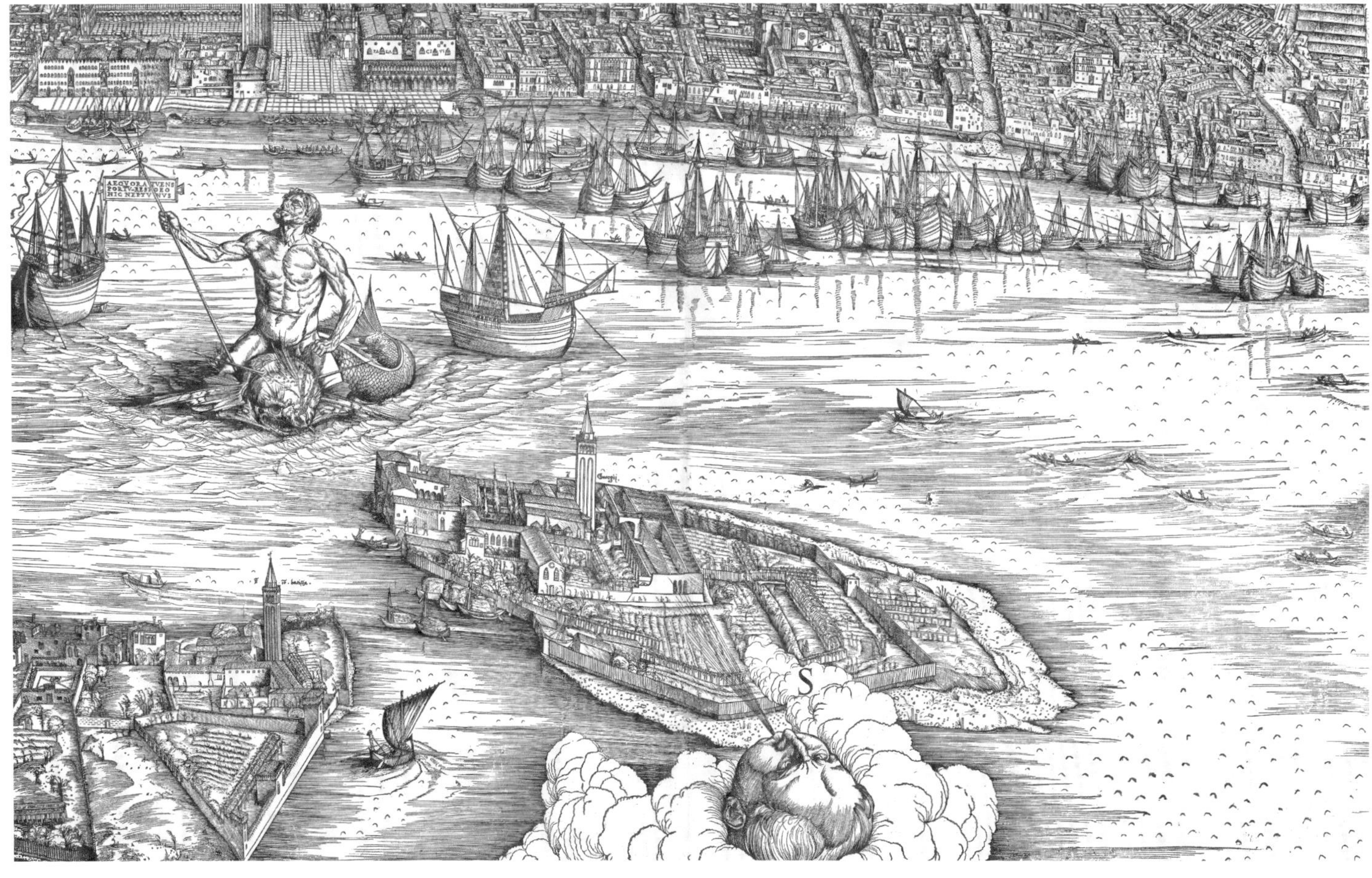
M
FAVONIVS.
P
S

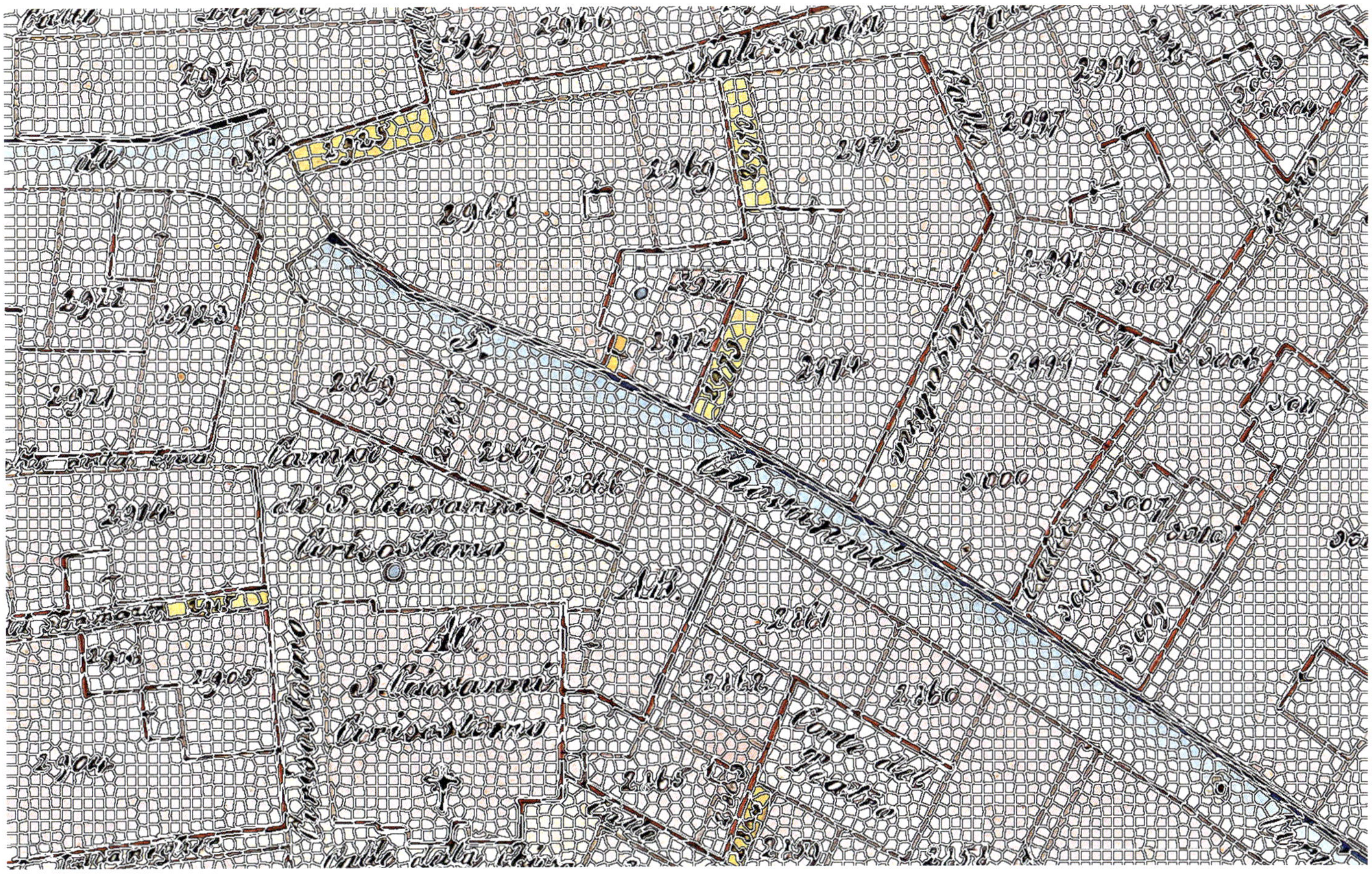

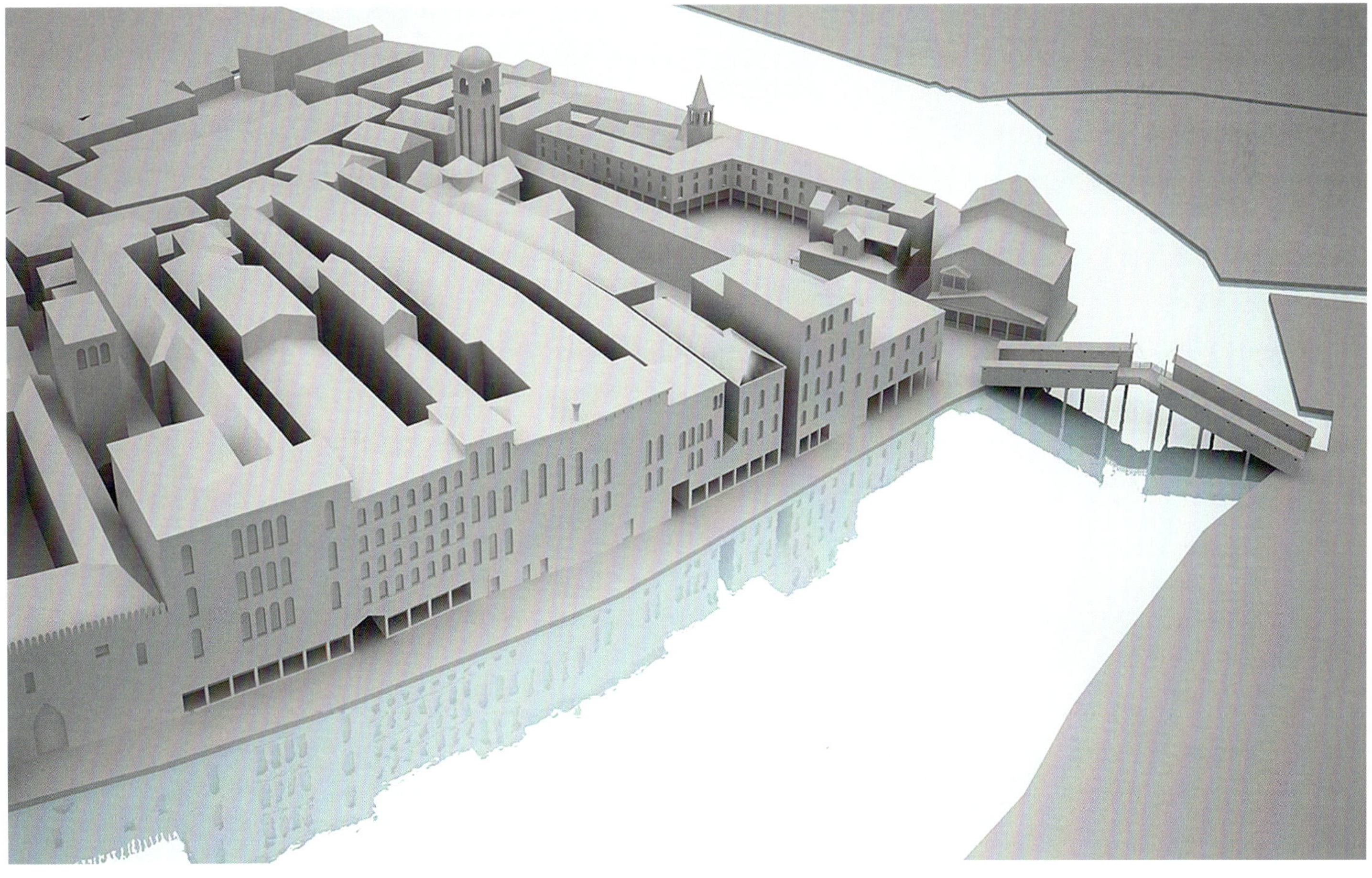

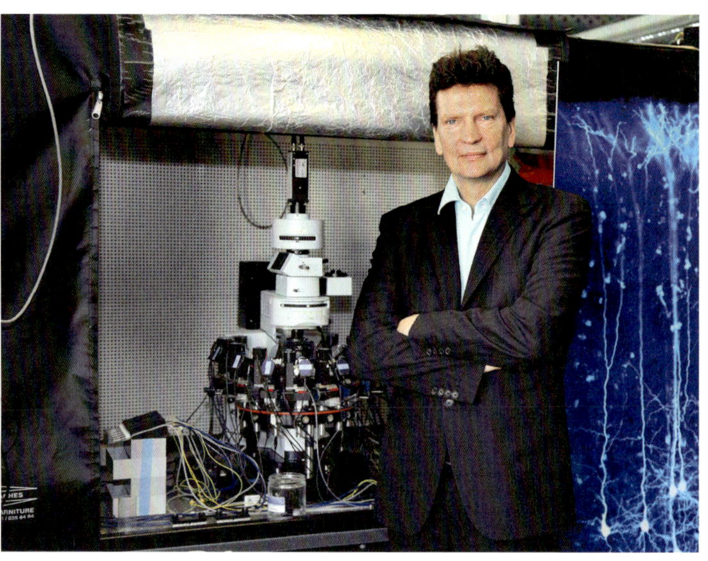

FROM HISTORY TO COGNITION

The Human Brain Project (HBP) is an FET Flagship. According to the EU: "Flagships are visionary, science-driven, large-scale research initiatives addressing grand Scientific and Technological (S&T) challenges. They are long-term initiatives bringing together excellent research teams across various disciplines, sharing a unifying goal and an ambitious research roadmap on how to achieve it."[1] Co-funded by the European Union, the Human Brain Project is coordinated by EPFL and based in Geneva and began operation in 2013. It makes use of exascale[2] supercomputers and a collaborative ICT (Information and Computing Technology) system that allows researchers all over Europe to participate. Combining computing, neuroscience, brain-based medicine, and even philosophy, the initiative aims ultimately to develop the fields of brain research, cognitive neuroscience, and brain-inspired computing, to be used by researchers worldwide. The

HBP ultimately envisages the creation of a digitized model of the brain, which can have vast implications for such areas as medicine, energy-efficient brain-inspired computing, data mining, telecommunications, and even intelligent appliances. Although perhaps not as ancient as the archives being used by the Venice Time Machine, existing studies of the brain have been varied both in terms of method and of the use of data. One problem for HBP is to bring existing information into a unified system that contributes to an overall understanding of the functioning of the brain. The complexity of detailed neuron representations means that their study and development into digital models requires vast amounts of computing power. HBP is divided into twelve sub-projects that deal with issues as different as Human Brain Organization, High-Performance Analytics and Computing, Neurorobotics, and Ethics and Society, which explores the ethical and societal impact of the overall project. The total cost of HBP is estimated at just over one billion euros, of which half is supplied by the European Commission and the rest by national, public, and private organizations.

The HBP emerged in part from the Blue Brain Project, created in 2005 as a collaboration between EPFL and IBM "aimed to build large-scale 'bottom up' numerical simulations of a rat's neocortical column, a set of about 100,000 neurons considered to be a functional unit within the brain."[3] The founder and director of this initiative is Henry Markram, a professor of neuroscience at EPFL, and director of the Laboratory of Neural Microcircuitry (LNMC). In 2014, Henry Markram announced an initiative to "reverse-engineer a fully functional supercomputer-powered simulation of the human brain in ten years."[4] Blue Brain is currently looking into "reconstructions and simulations on a larger scale than neural microcircuitry" and calling on the work of thirteen different labs at EPFL. Collaboration on such a wide scale within EPFL and with external partners is typical, like the Venice Time Machine, of the usefulness of a multidisciplinary approach. In fact, it has become apparent that any real study of subjects as complex as history and cognition requires reuniting the disparate domains of science and thought in order to combine enough energy and organization to resolve at least the basic issues. The evolution of technology, and in particular computational capacities, promises that future years will allow ever greater understanding based still on a transversal approach. The Blue Brain Project, now considered as EPFL's component of the Human Brain Project, "is already working with communities in the Human Brain Project and beyond to build digital reconstructions of whole brain regions (somatosensory cortex, hippocampus, cerebellum, basal ganglia) and eventually the whole mouse brain. This work will prepare the way for reconstructions of the human brain, on different scales and with different levels of detail."[5] Beginning in 2010, Henry Markram "created and coordinated the consortium of eighty European and international partners that developed the original HBP proposal."[6]

The Blue Brain Project presented in DataSquare involves supercomputer-based reconstructions and simulations built to offer a new approach to the understanding of the multilevel structure and functions of the brain. According to a description of Blue Brain: "The project's novel research strategy exploits interdependencies in the experimental data to obtain dense maps of the brain, without measuring every detail of its multiple levels of organization (molecules, cells, microcircuits, brain regions, the whole brain). This strategy allows the project to build digital reconstructions (computer models) of the brain at an unprecedented level of biological detail. Supercomputer-based simulation of their behavior turns understanding the brain into a tractable problem, providing a new tool to study the complex interactions within different levels of brain organization and to investigate the cross-level links leading from genes to cognition."[7]

The effort made to show the complex studies of the Blue Brain and Human Brain Projects to the public, in the same space as the Venice Time Machine, is a clear statement that EPFL has accepted that the very bases of academic study and knowledge are shifting and that new horizons are being opened. Presenting these two projects, ArtLab positions itself at the forefront of the tectonic change occurring at the interface between science, culture, and technology.

1   At http://ec.europa.eu/programmes/horizon2020/en/
  h2020-section/fet-flagships (accessed on March 28, 2018).
2   An exascale computing system is capable of
  performing one exaFLOP, or a billion billion calculations
  per second.
3   At https://www.nature.com/news/neuroscience-
  where-is-the-brain-in-the-human-brain-project-1.15803
  (accessed on March 28, 2018).
4   At http://thisisartlab.com/tag/human-brain-project/
  (accessed on March 28, 2018).
5   At https://bluebrain.epfl.ch/page-58067-en.html
  (accessed on March 28, 2018).
6   At https://bluebrain.epfl.ch/page-52741-en.html
  (accessed on March 28, 2018).
7   At https://bluebrain.epfl.ch/page-56882-en.html
  (accessed on March 28, 2018).

The Blue Brain Project employs an IBM BlueGene/Q supercomputer with 65,536 cores, hosted by the Swiss National Supercomputing Center (CSCS) in Lugano.

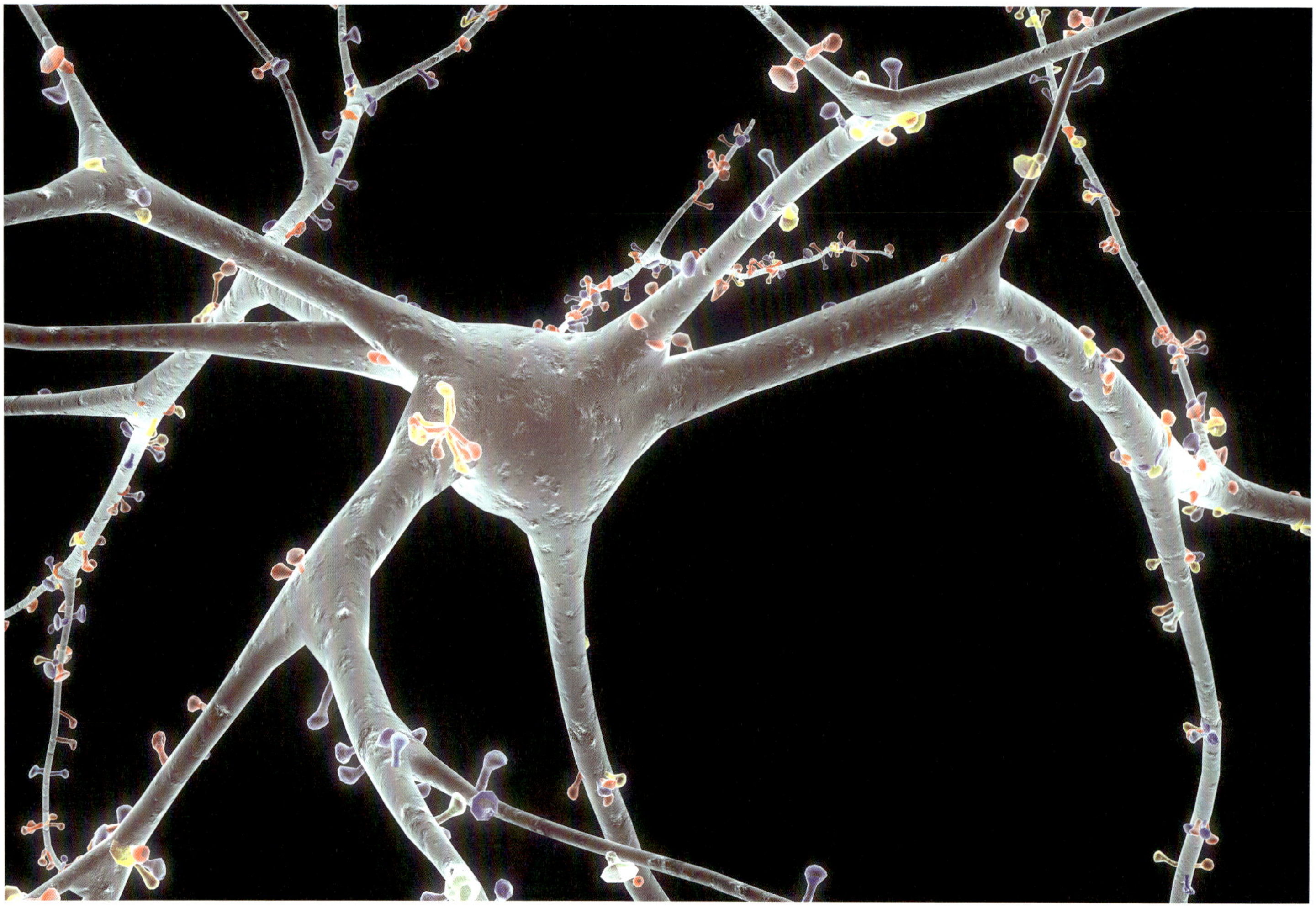

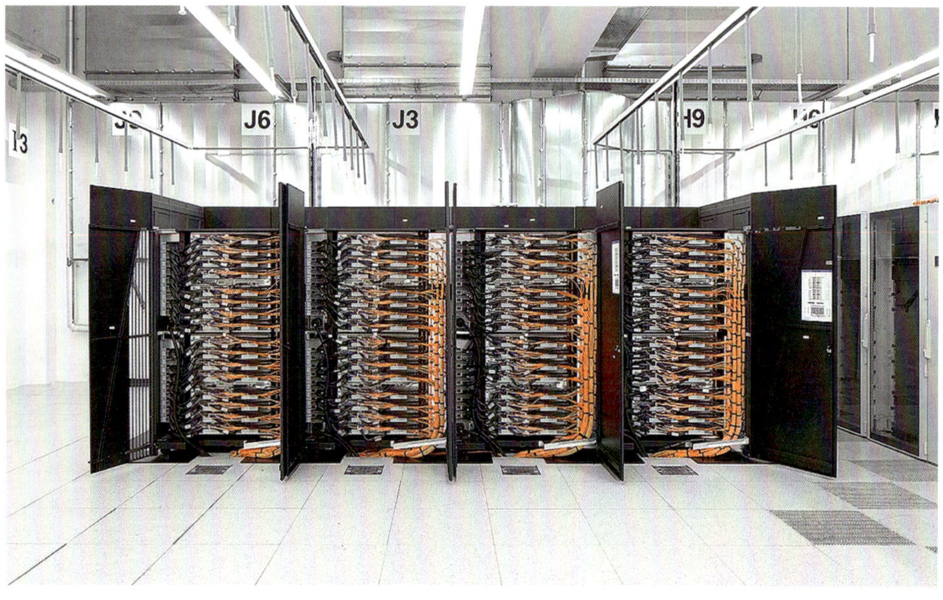

The Blue Brain seeks to use technological means to analyze the structure and functions of the human brain.

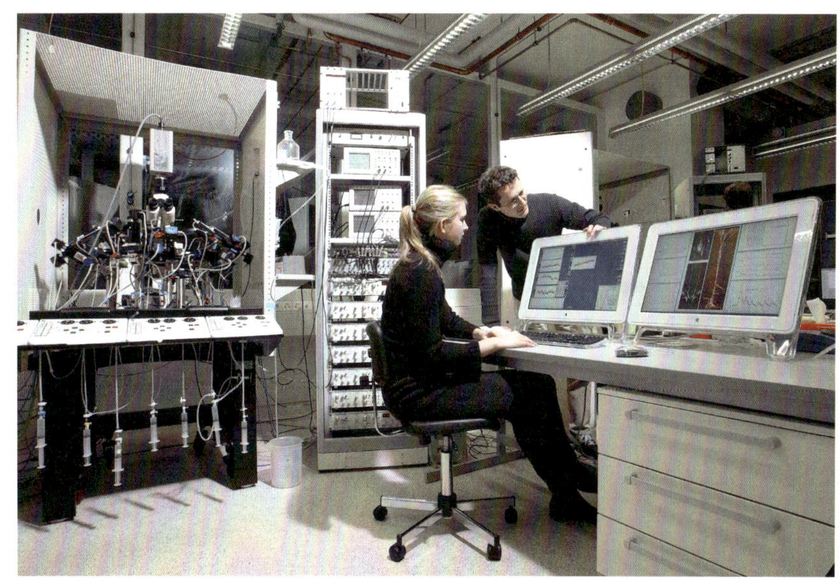

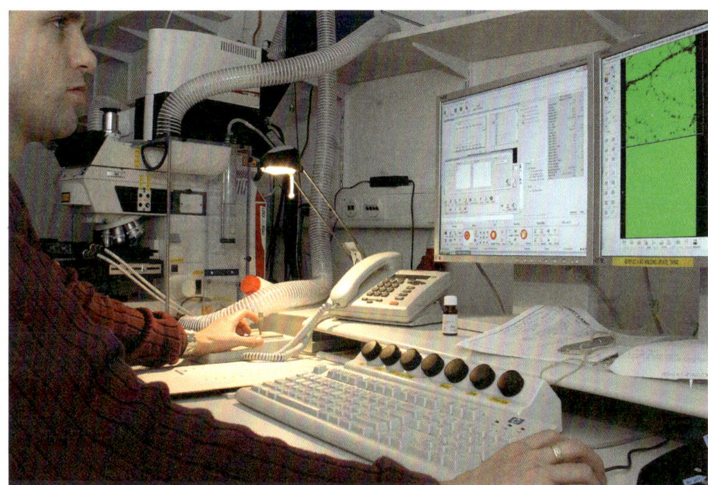

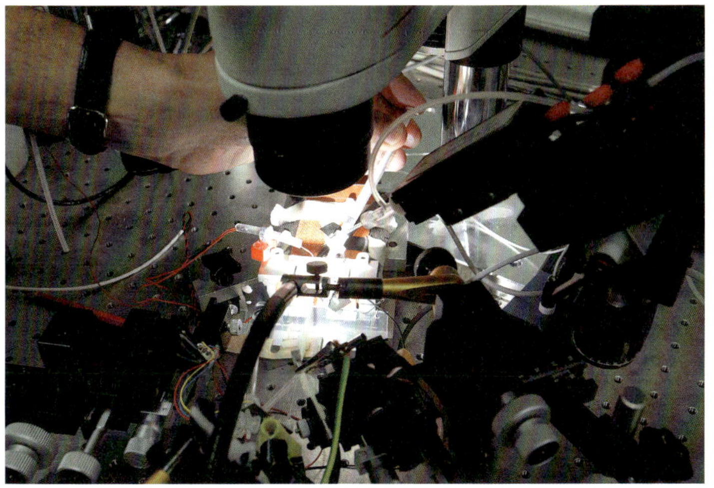

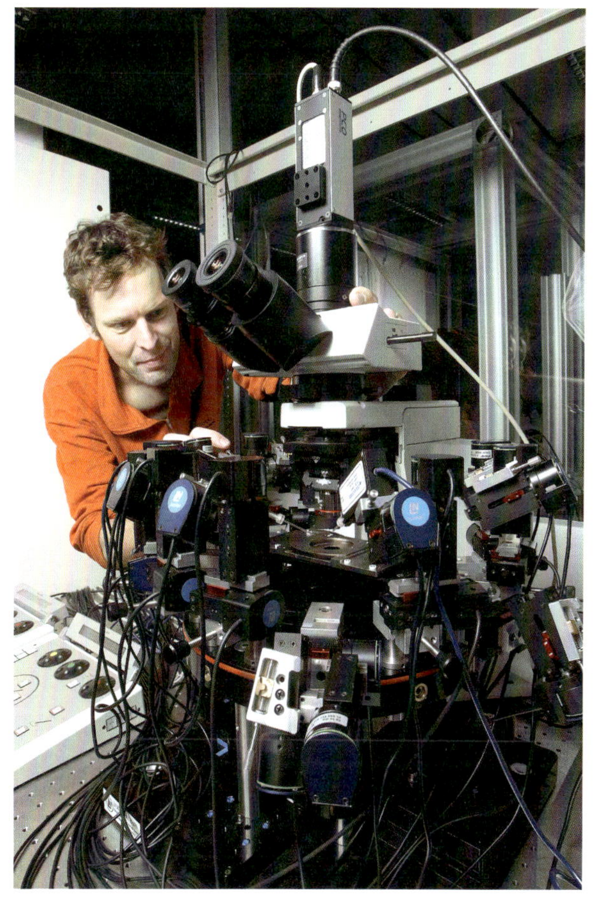

LOOKING TO THE FUTURE

Sarah Kenderdine was appointed Professor of Digital Museology at the Digital Humanities Institute of EPFL in July 2017. She has long worked on interactive and immersive experiences for galleries, libraries, and museums. She was the founding director of the Expanded Perception and Interaction Centre (EPICentre) at UNSW Australia. She was president of the Australasian Association for Digital Humanities (2015–17) prior to moving to EPFL. Sarah Kenderdine was recently named director of ArtLab and is creating a laboratory in Experimental Museology for EPFL in neighboring Saint-Sulpice. She is a member of the advisory board of ArtTech.

Sarah Kenderdine, who had recently arrived as director of ArtLab when this interview took place, lays out her ideas for the building and makes it clear that she imagines frequent evolution of the exhibitions in the future, beginning with a first show on *Kung Fu Motion* held from April 28 to August 12, 2018.

How do you imagine the future use of each part of ArtLab?[1]

There has been a shift in the management's interest in the building, and it is now under the control of the College of Humanities, which I am part of. They proposed that I became the director of ArtLab. I find that the old name "Under One Roof," which was the concept of Kengo Kuma, is absolutely a valid one. In any case, that name does correspond to the way I perceive the future use of the building. The way I see the three pavilions within the constraints of what we have and what has been done is that DataSquare is about the identity of EPFL. It is the place where visitors come to learn about the cutting-edge science at the university. I would like to turn it into an interactive data visualization framework where any great scientist here can upload their stuff and it can be displayed. There would be many projects and a visitor could come in and say: "I want to see project number 23." It is about building that entire pipeline, which is certainly feasible, and putting in a visual framework of the highest possible quality. I know how to do that, that's my business. This method would also allow us to create an archive of the work done here through time. This would allow the new science to come in as well.

What of the Experimental Exhibition Space?
The middle pavilion is really a place of exchange for projects that have to do with the relation between art and science, as it merges into the public domain. It is also a staging post. It is our mission to create exhibitions here that are of superior quality and can travel in the world. They should be that unique and that interesting. I would call this pavilion The Exchange.

The *Kung Fu Motion* exhibition held there in 2018 has to do with what we like to call body knowledge systems. It is not art as such, but the display is hugely informed by media art practice. These exhibitions will be filled with big interactive systems. It is a combination of art and science, in this case applied to intangible heritage. It is a classic merger of technologies based around living culture. Kung fu is difficult to deal with in terms of redisplay. It is about giving people an embodied understanding. Can you use a very high-fidelity set of motion-capture data and a 3D model to teach kung fu? The response to that question is not obvious. We are looking at a process where we teach novices with a digital master with 3D on the wall and on the floor to do these moves. Does it work, or doesn't it? This is a fundamental challenge. Otherwise, it is just an archive.

The second exhibition in 2018 is about Ramon Llull (*c.* 1232–1315), medieval thinker, inventor of computational thinking. The exhibition is called *Dia-Logos: Ramon Llull and the ars combinatoria* and is based on the ZKM Center for Art and Media Karlsruhe exhibition of the same name. He was a polymath, one of the inventors of the recombinations of ideas. The display will consist in medieval manuscripts through to contemporary arts. There will be a lot of digital content, it will be very dense. The whole EPFL campus is relaunching under the rubric of computational thinking.

Next year we are planning a show on machines that make art, and digital replication—everything to do with ultra-high resolution or 3D imaging. This is about the contest between real and digital objects in the art world, or where algorithms make paintings that look like the real thing—all issues that are subject to some debate.

The Montreux Jazz Café presents different challenges, does it not?
The Montreux Jazz Café is an archive and is about what you can do with an archive. It can be developed in different ways, there can be different iterations than what is presently visible. Given the investment by EPFL in that project and its huge potential, it could be fun to keep reconceiving that space around the same data. Keeping that space dynamic is important, there should be more change.

What I am doing now is a stop-gap measure and what we hope for is that a group of professors of the university actively debate and bring ideas to ArtLab. I have not been able to sufficiently consult them because exhibitions take a long time to plan and I came in with a much shorter period to set up a show. The movement of ArtLab from the office of the president to the College of Humanities has made the situation slightly different. I would like to significantly raise the number of visitors and to diversify the public. The way to do that is to invest in communications, which has not really been done. We are trying it for *Kung Fu* even though the budget for the exhibition is tiny. We can attract money, but we are not here to make money.

1   Sarah Kenderdine in conversation with the author, EPFL,
     March 6, 2018.

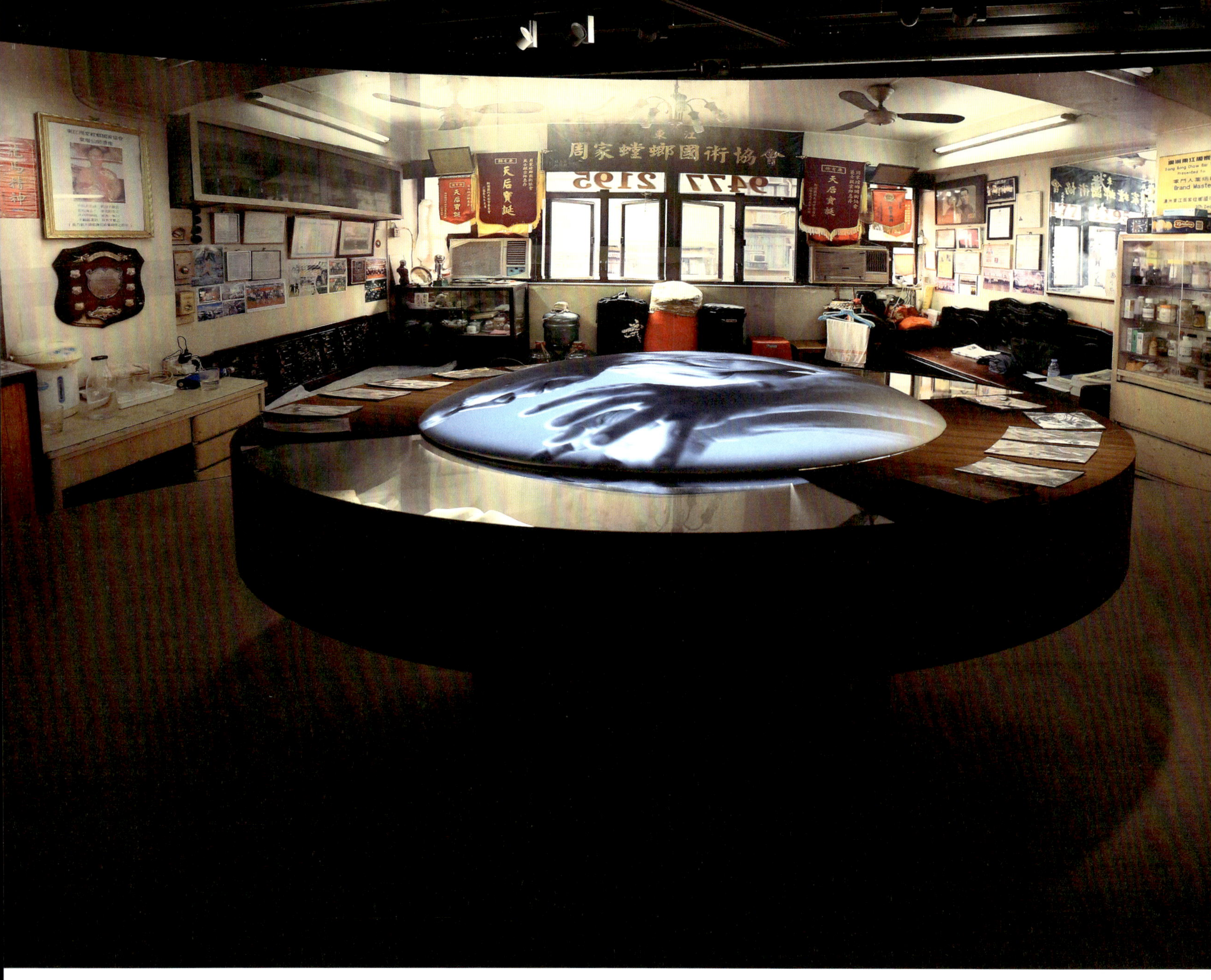

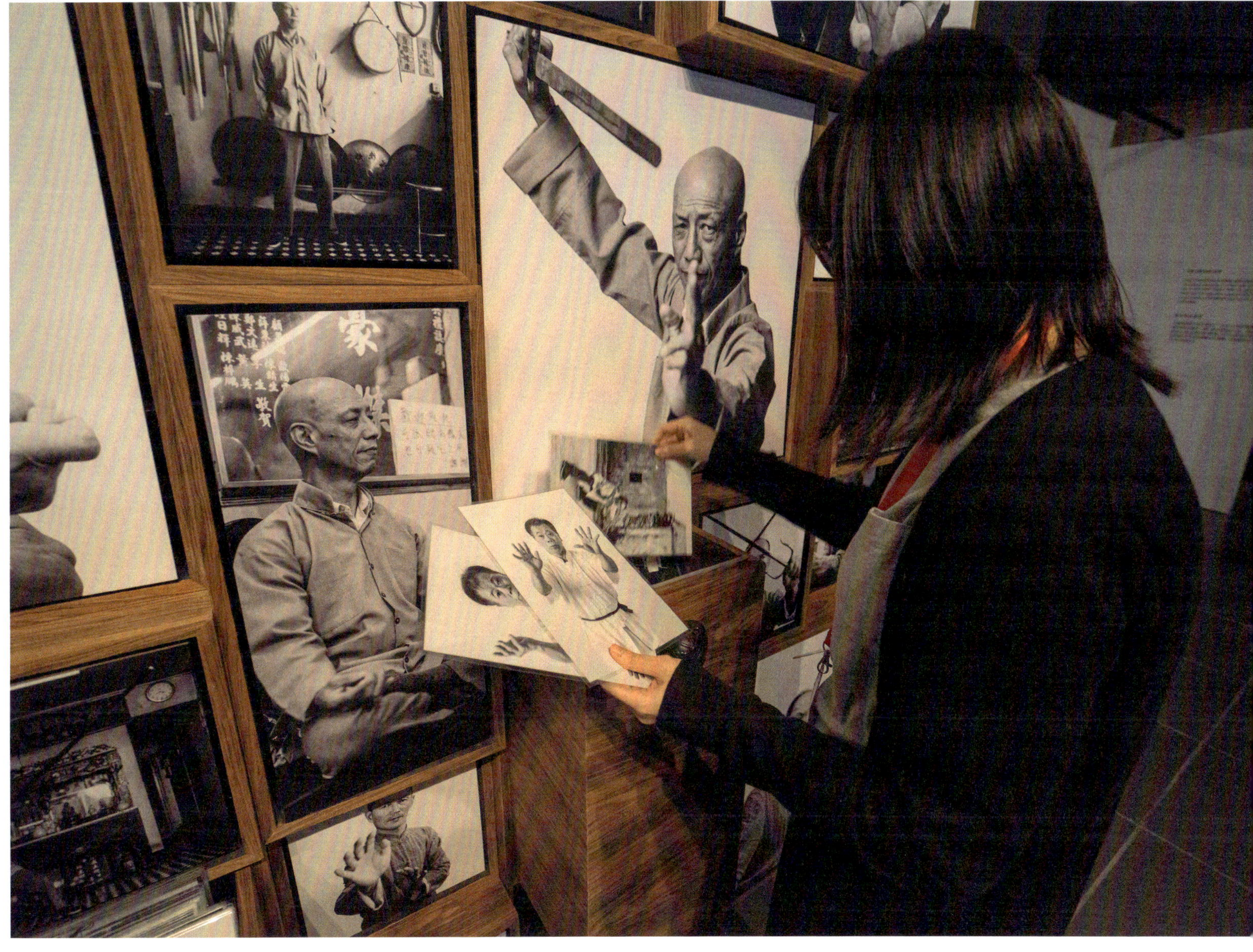

Views of the *Kung Fu Motion* exhibition. This ongoing research project is a collaboration between the International Guoshu Association, City University of Hong Kong, and the Laboratory for Experimental Museology (eM+), Digital Humanities Institute, EPFL.

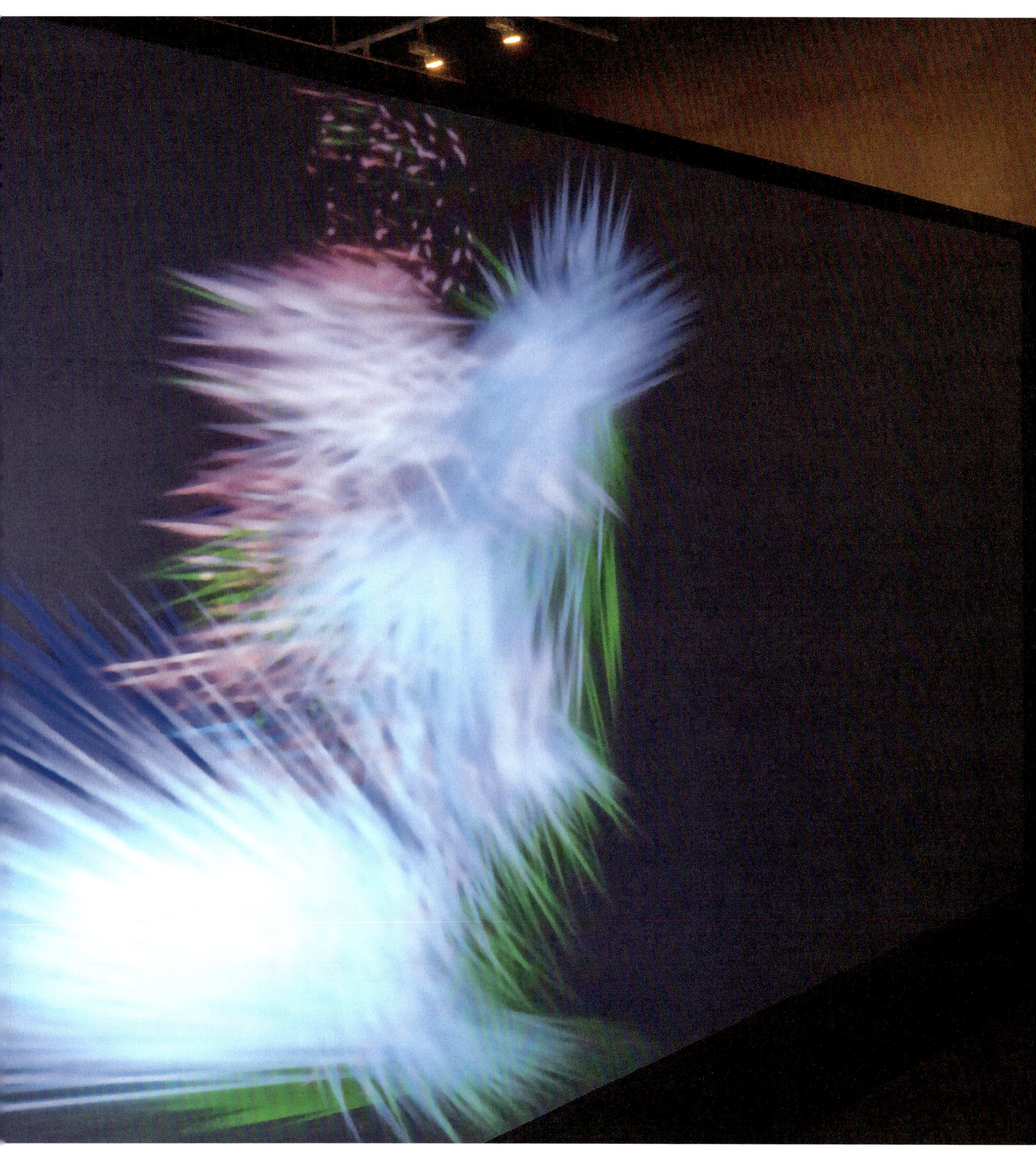

The *Kung Fu Motion* exhibition told the story of the dynamic traditions of Hong Kong's martial arts, seen through the lens of advanced archival technologies.

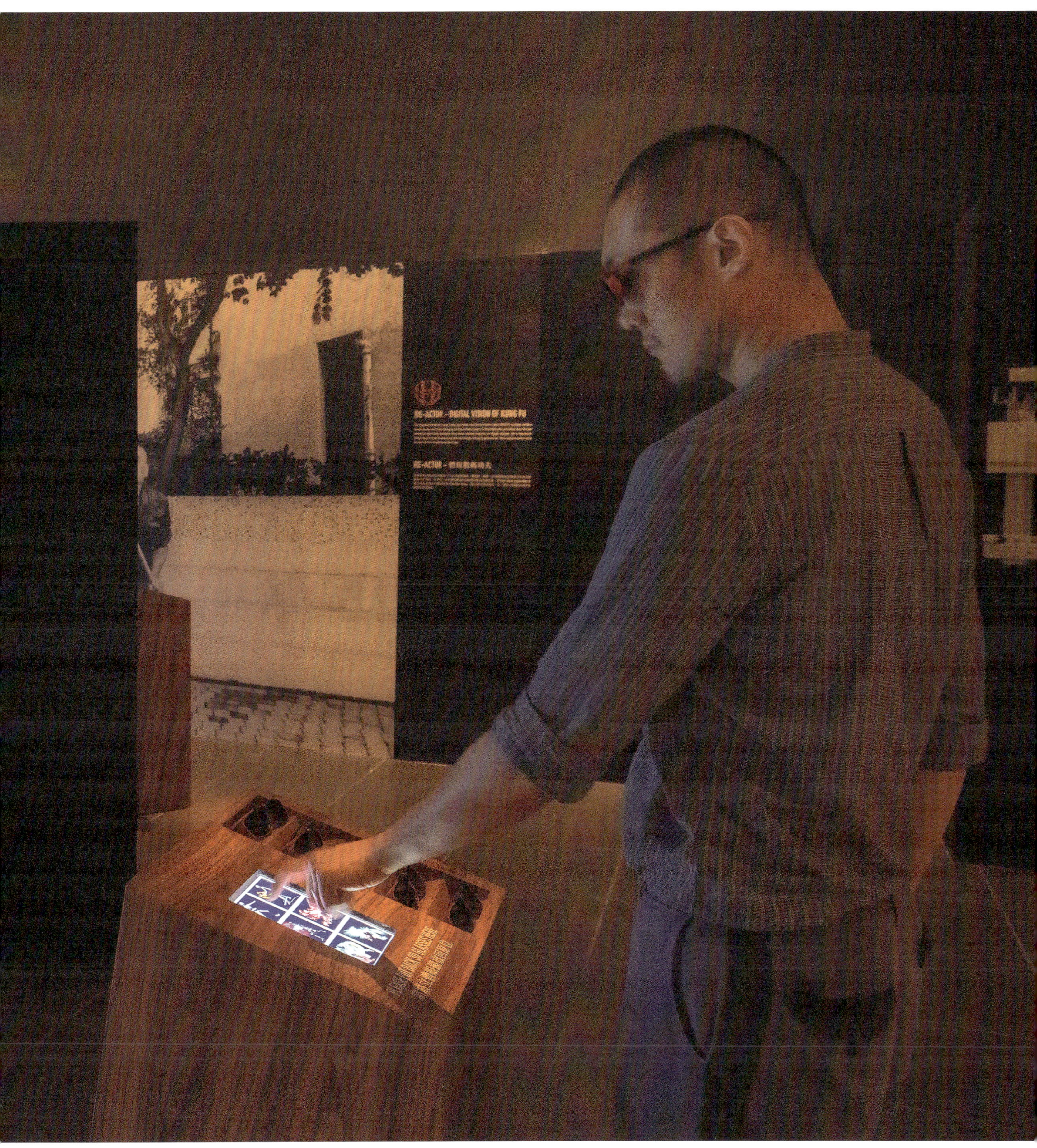

"Kung Fu Motion examines strategies for encoding, retrieving, and re-enacting intangible heritage in ways that allow these archives to be 'alive' in the present," says Professor Sarah Kenderdine.

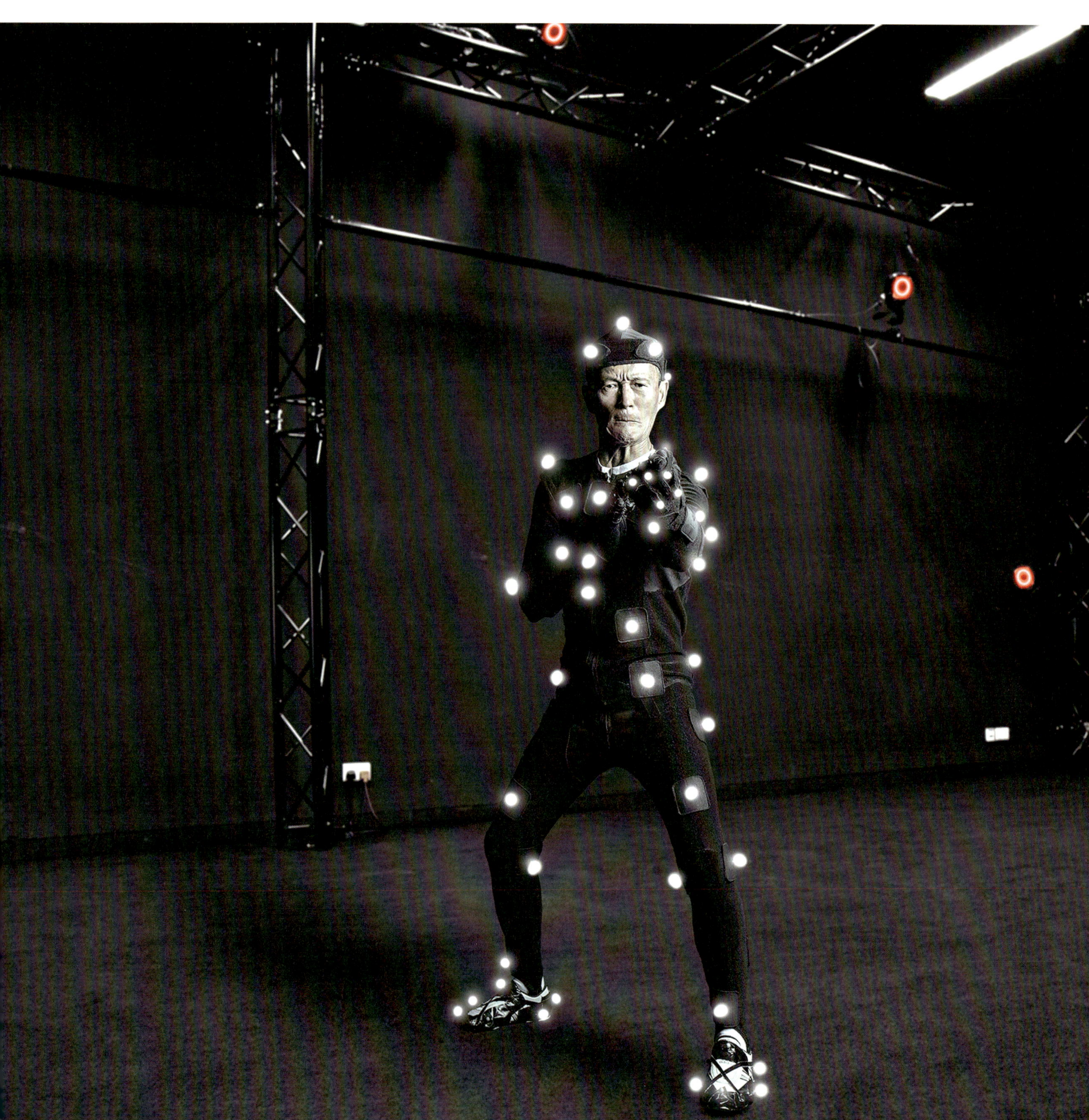

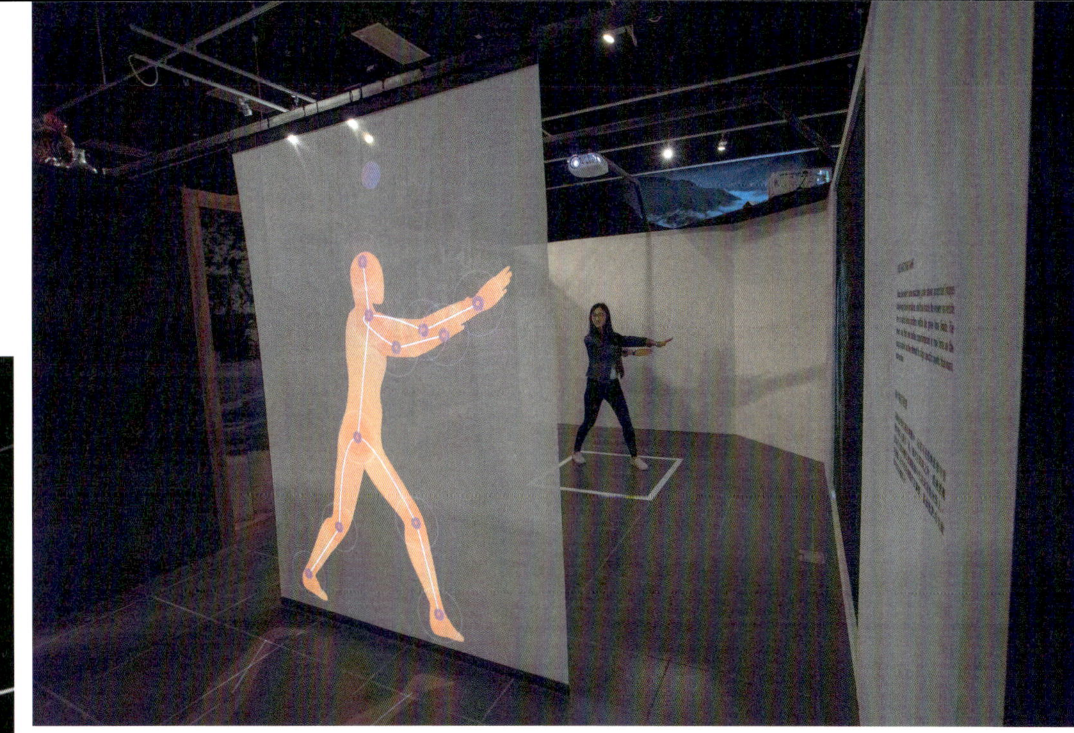

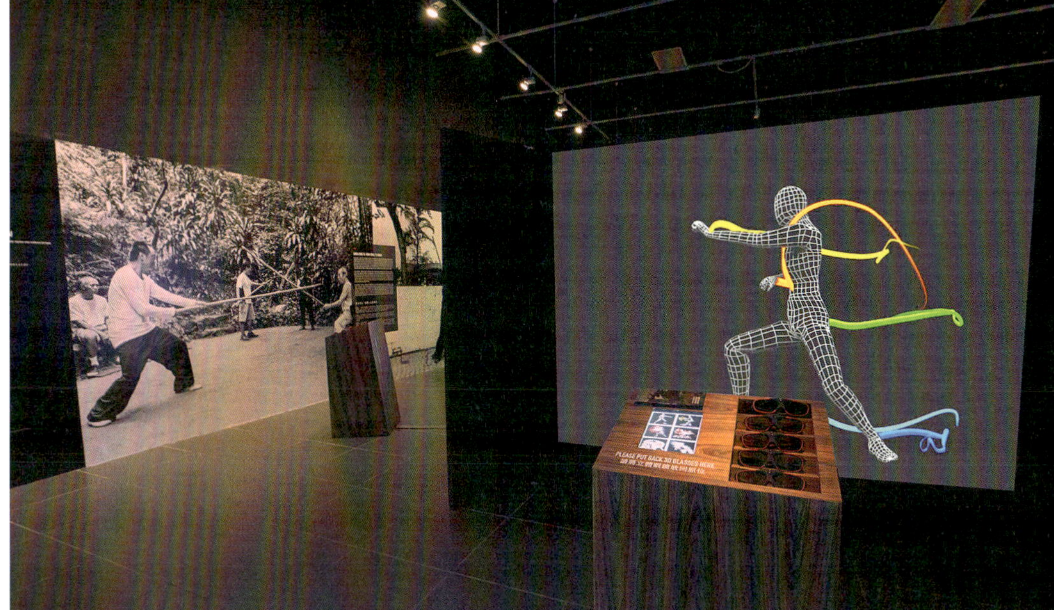

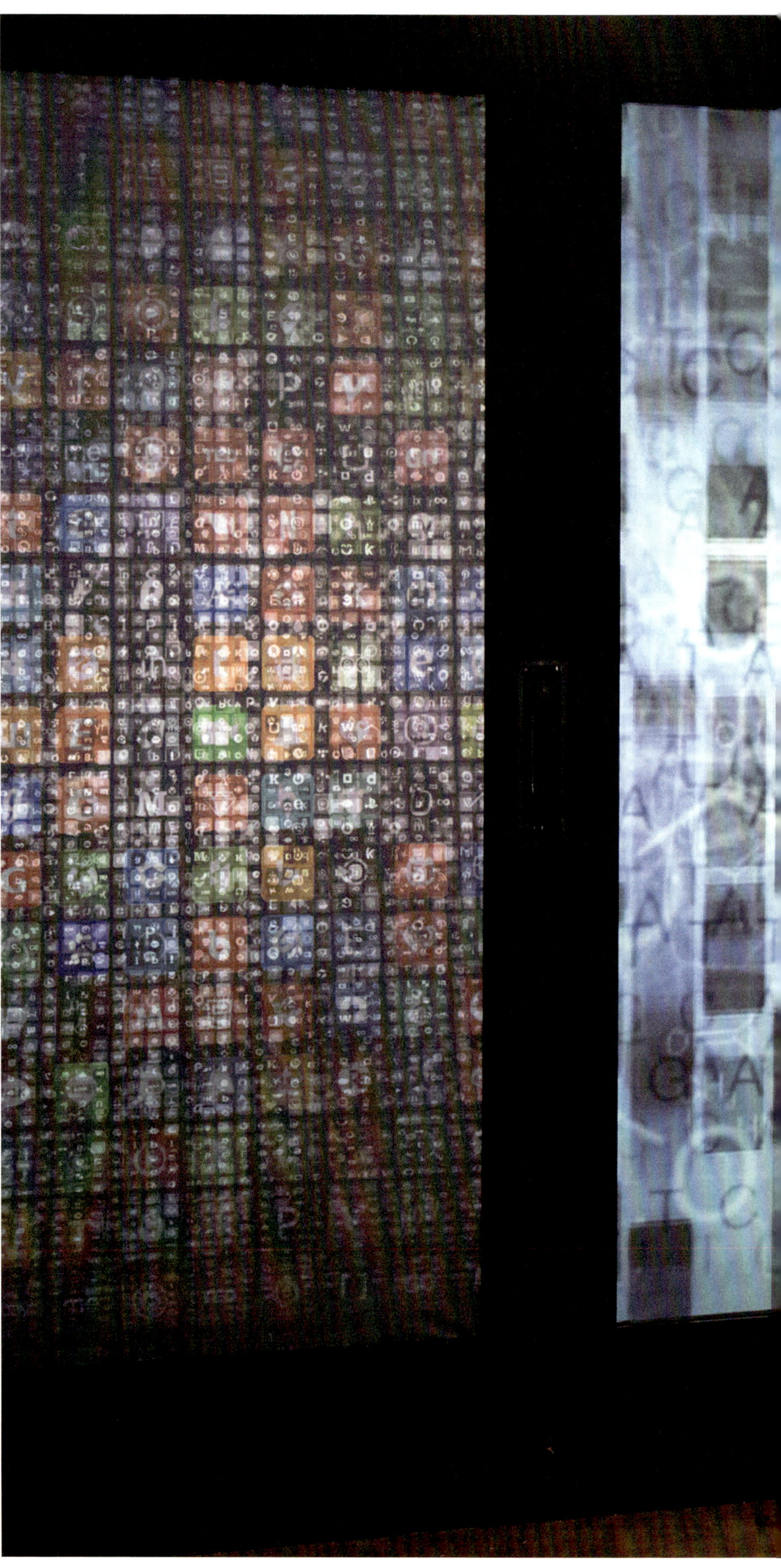

Bernd Lintermann, *YOU:R:CODE*, 2017. This is a work presented in the 2018 ArtLab exhibition *Thinking Machines*; it embodies the idea that the visitor can be "reduced to an industrially readable code."

164

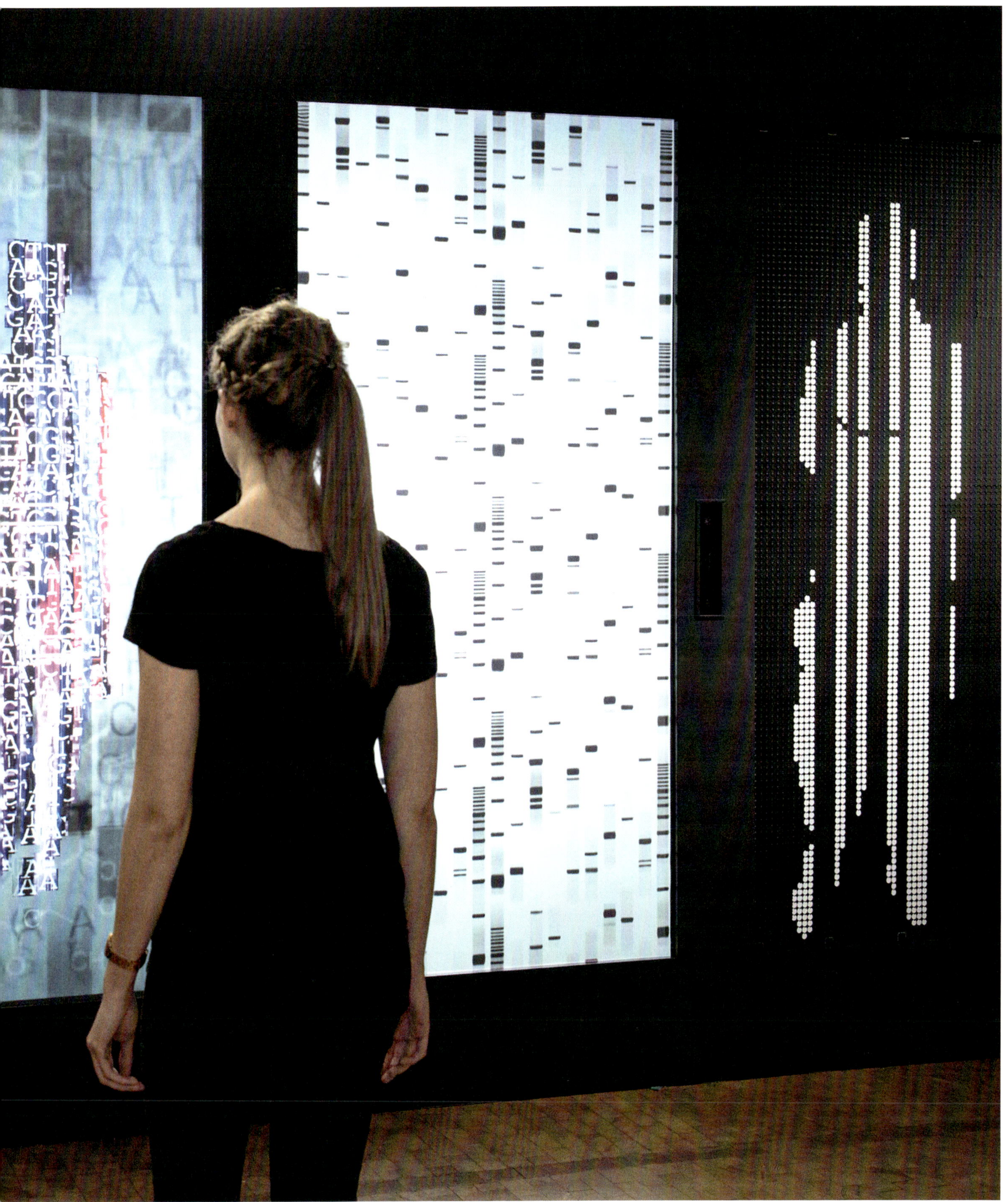

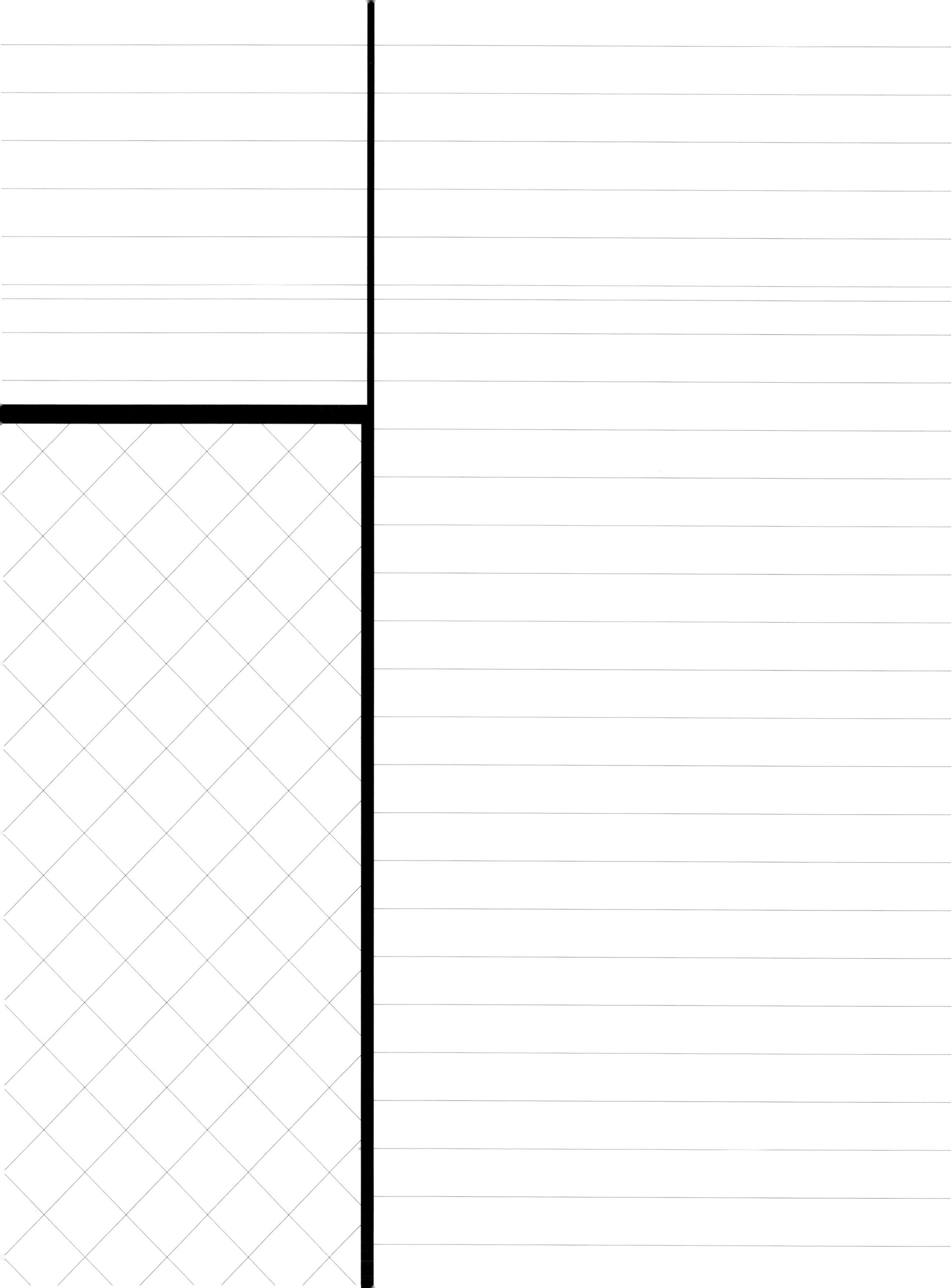

Front cover: Alain Herzog EPFL
Back cover (clockwise from top left): Alain Herzog EPFL, Adrien Barakat (5 images)

Above Summit / Christopher Harting: p. 46
Adrien Barakat: pp. 12 (bottom left), 54, 55, 66 (bottom), 67 (bottom), 76–77, 78, 79, 93, 102–103, 112–113, 114–115, 121, 122–123, 124–125, 128 (top), 130, 131, 138–139
Blue Brain Project EPFL: pp. 154, 155
Georges Braunschweig: pp. 15 Dexter Gordon © 1973 Georges Braunschweig (top right); Ella Fitzgerald, Count Basie © 1979 Georges Braunschweig (top left); Lenny Kravitz, Todd Harold © 2008 Georges Braunschweig (top middle); 118 Lenny Kravitz © 2008 Georges Braunschweig (top left), Marcus Miller © 2008 Georges Braunschweig (middle left), Miles Davis © Georges Braunschweig (top right); 119 Miles Davis © Georges Braunschweig (middle right); Ray Charles © 1997 Georges Braunschweig (bottom left)
Yves Dana: p. 95
Michel Denancé: pp. 12 (top), 60, 61, 62 (top), 64–65, 88, 89, 98–99
EPFL Laboratory for Experimental Museology, International Guoshu Association and City University of Hong Kong: pp. 12 (bottom right), 158, 159, 160–161, 162, 163
Felix Grünschloß: 164–165
Alain Herzog EPFL: pp. 2–3, 4–5, 6–7, 15 (bottom), 26, 27, 28–29, 32, 33, 34, 35, 37, 38, 39, 40–41, 42, 43, 52–53, 56, 57, 58–59, 62 (bottom), 63, 66 (top), 67 (top), 68–69, 80–81, 82, 83, 96–97, 108, 109, 132, 134–135, 136, 137, 140–141, 142, 143, 144, 152, 168–169, 170–171, 172–173, 174–175, 176

Hongkong University of Science and Technology (HKUST): p. 48 (bottom)
Courtesy of King Abdullah University of Science and Technology (KAUST): p. 49
Kengo Kuma & Associates: pp. 70–75; details pp. 8, 10, 16, 22, 44, 50,84, 110, 166 and endpapers
Poster designed by Monokini.ch (Biel/Bienne & Lausanne) for EPFL and Fondation Gandur pour l'Art: p. 126
Mathieu Rudaz, Philippe Forney – 24 Heures: pp. 20–21
Joël Tettamanti: pp. 106, 107, 118 (bottom), 119 (top), 128 (middle and bottom)
University of California, Santa Barbara (UCSB): p. 47
University of Cape Town: p. 48 (top and middle)
Venice Time Machine EPFL: pp. 146, 147, 148, 149, 150, 151

The author wishes to thank Patrick Aebischer, Kengo Kuma, Jean-François Ricci, Luc Meier, and Sarah Kenderdine for their help in the preparation of this book.

Artists' Rights
© Courtesy of the artist for reproduction of works by Etienne Krähenbühl.
© Bernd Lintermann, Foto © ZKM | Center for Arts and Media Karlsruhe
© VG Bild-Kunst, Bonn 2018, for reproductions of works by Yves Dana, Antoine Poncet and Pierre Soulages.

The works of art from the EPFL collection published in this book were given to the University by generous donors:
Yves Dana, *Pierre au firmament* (Stone in the Firmament, 2016), Gift to EPFL of Patrick Aebischer, 2016.
Antoine Poncet, *Aileiotrope* (1992). This work was purchased by the Federal Fine Arts Commission (Commission fédérale des Beaux-Arts) at the suggestion of EPFL (President Bernard Vittroz) in 1992.
Etienne Krähenbühl, *Bing Bang* (2016), purchased for EPFL by a Donor Committee represented by Mrs. Catherine Labouchère

Prestel Publishing Ltd.
14–17 Wells Street
London W1T 3PD

Prestel Publishing
900 Broadway, Suite 603
New York, NY 10003

A CIP catalogue record for this book is available from the British Library.

Editorial direction Prestel: Constanze Holler and Andrea Bartelt-Gering
Copyediting: Harriet Graham, Turin
Design and layout: Torsten Köchlin, Berlin
Production management: Corinna Pickart
Separations: LUDWIG:media gmbh, Zell am See
Printing and binding: aprinta druck GmbH, Wemding
Typeface: Agipo by Radim Peško
Paper: Profimatt

Printed in Germany

ISBN 978-3-7913-5805-5

www.prestel.com

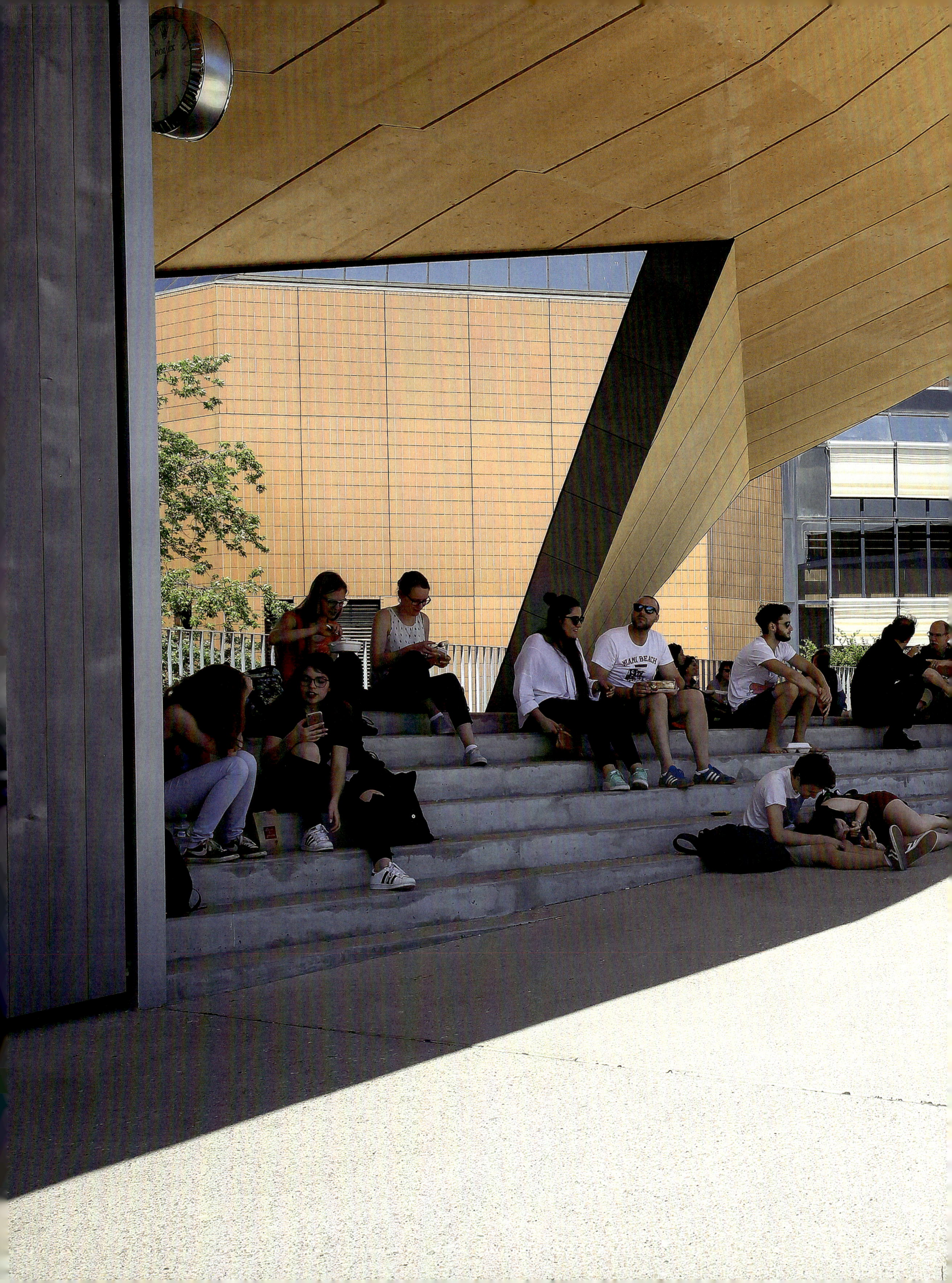

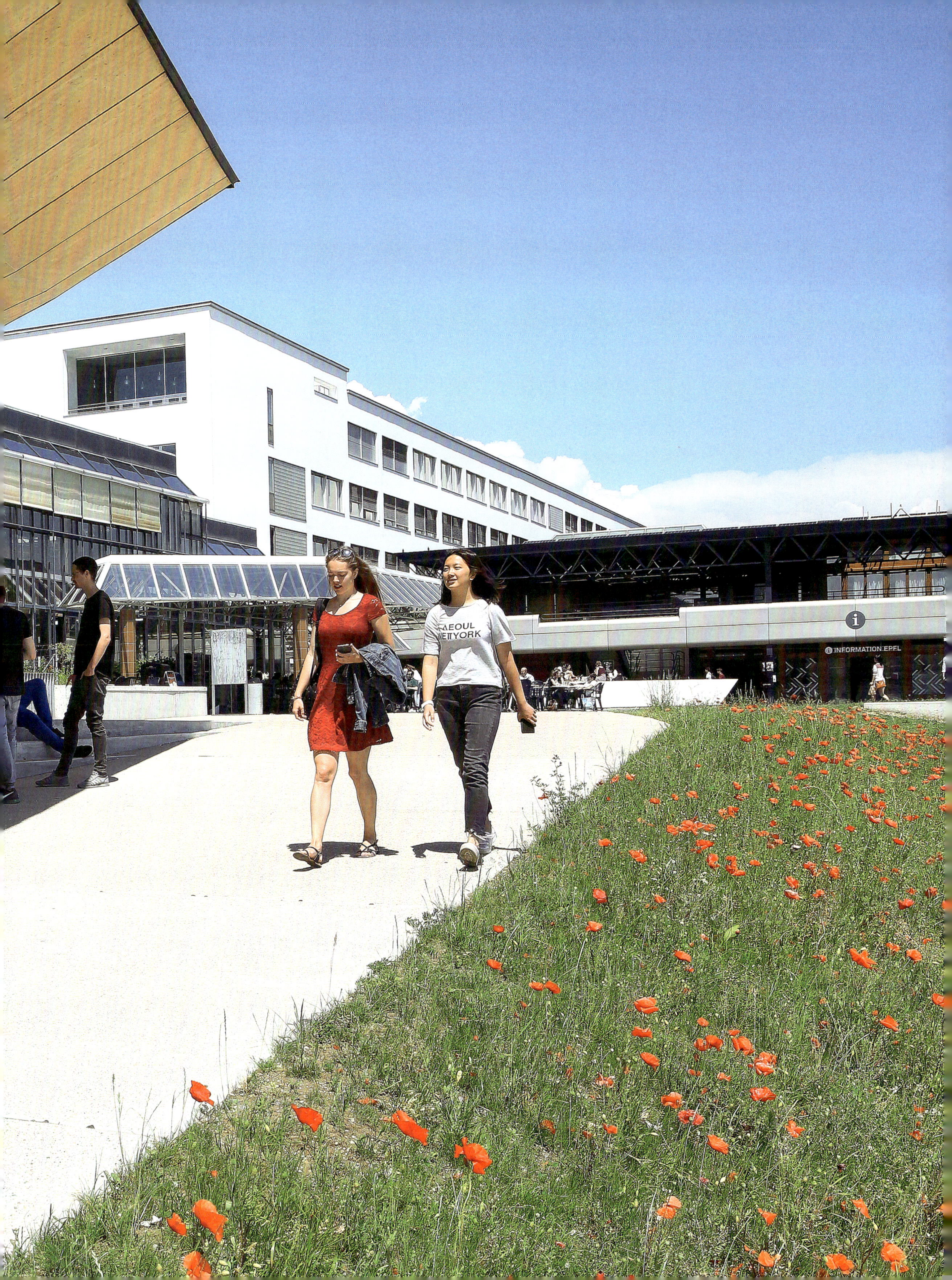
AEOUL
NEW YORK
INFORMATION EPFL

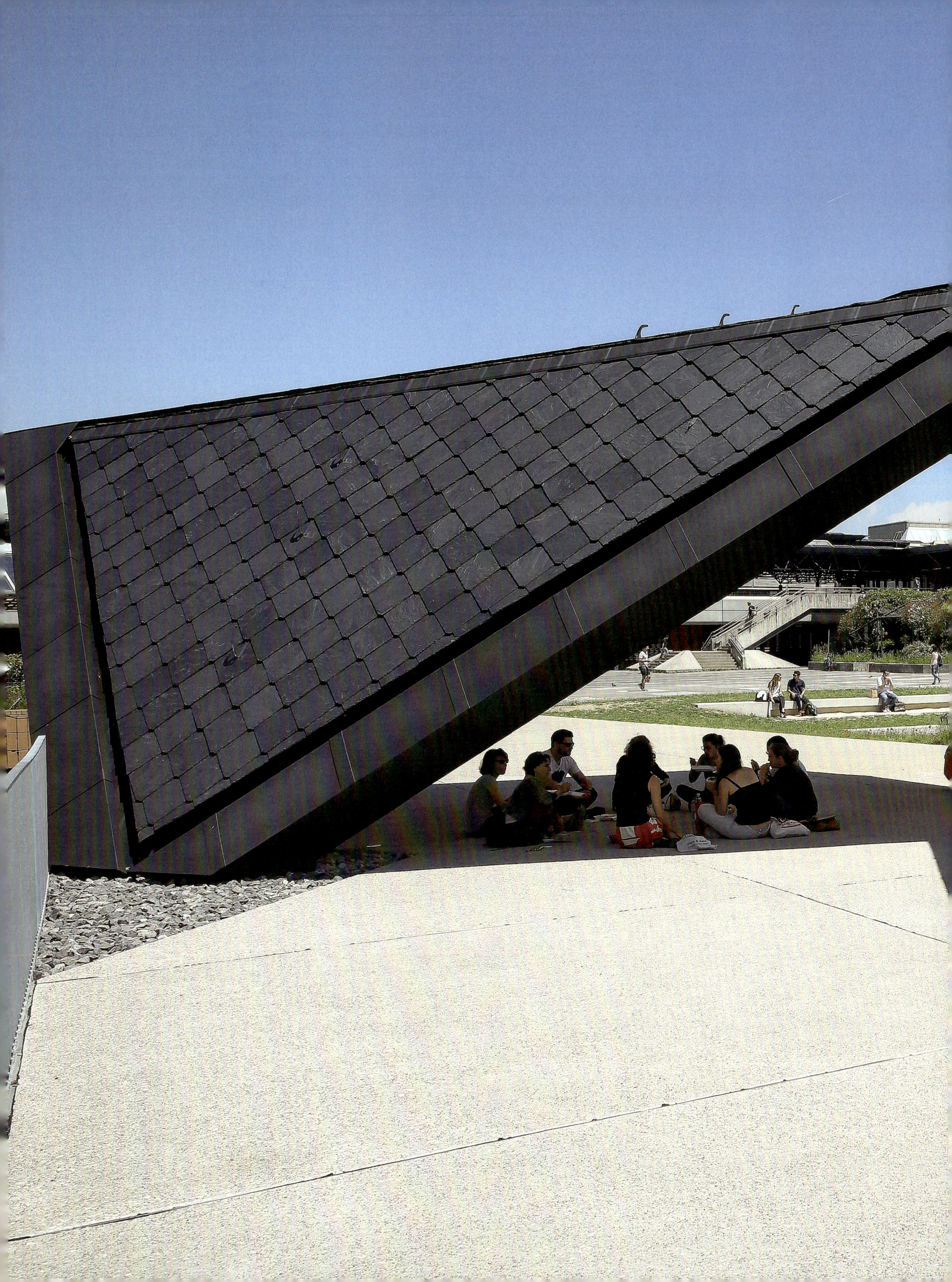

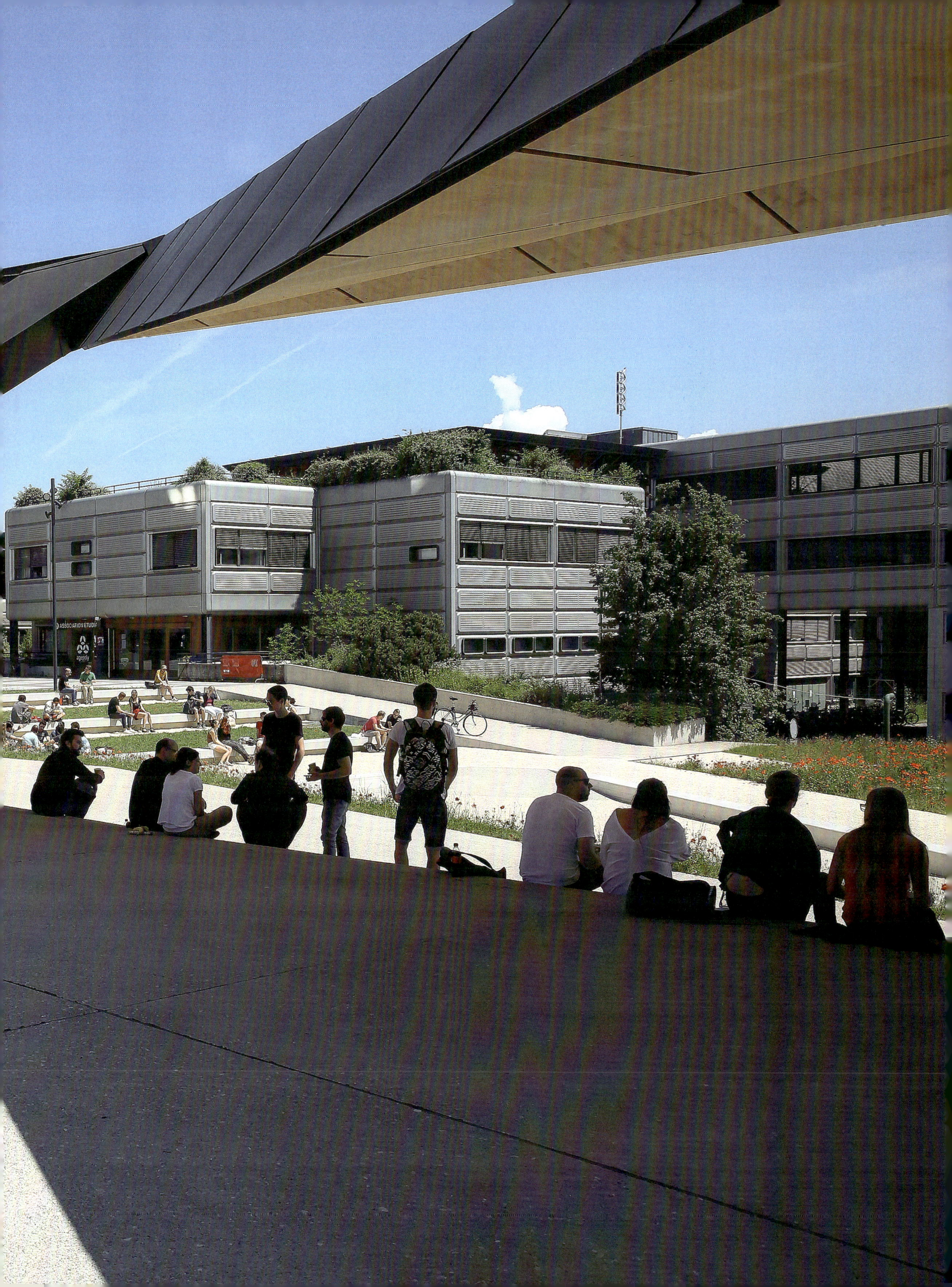

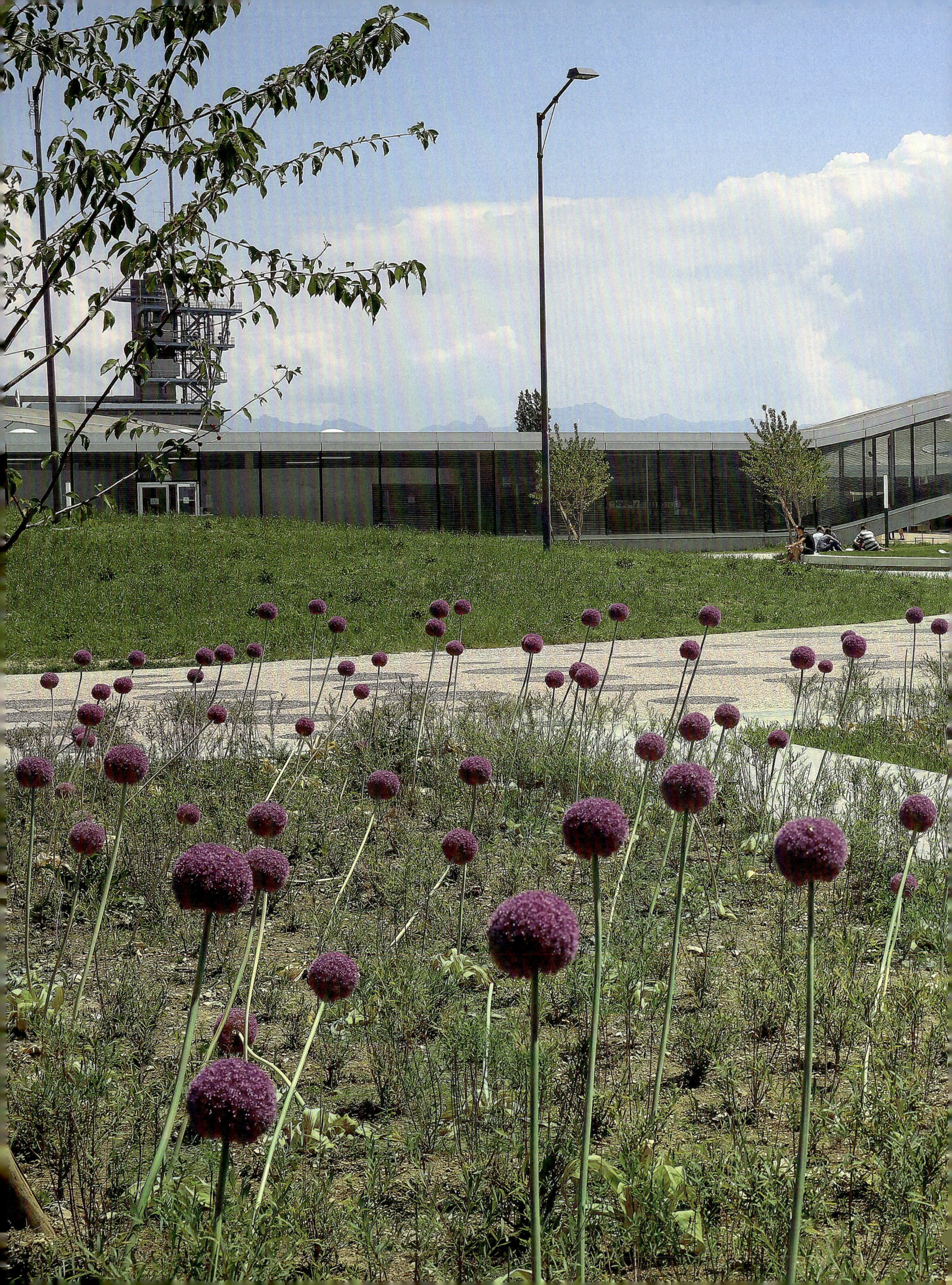

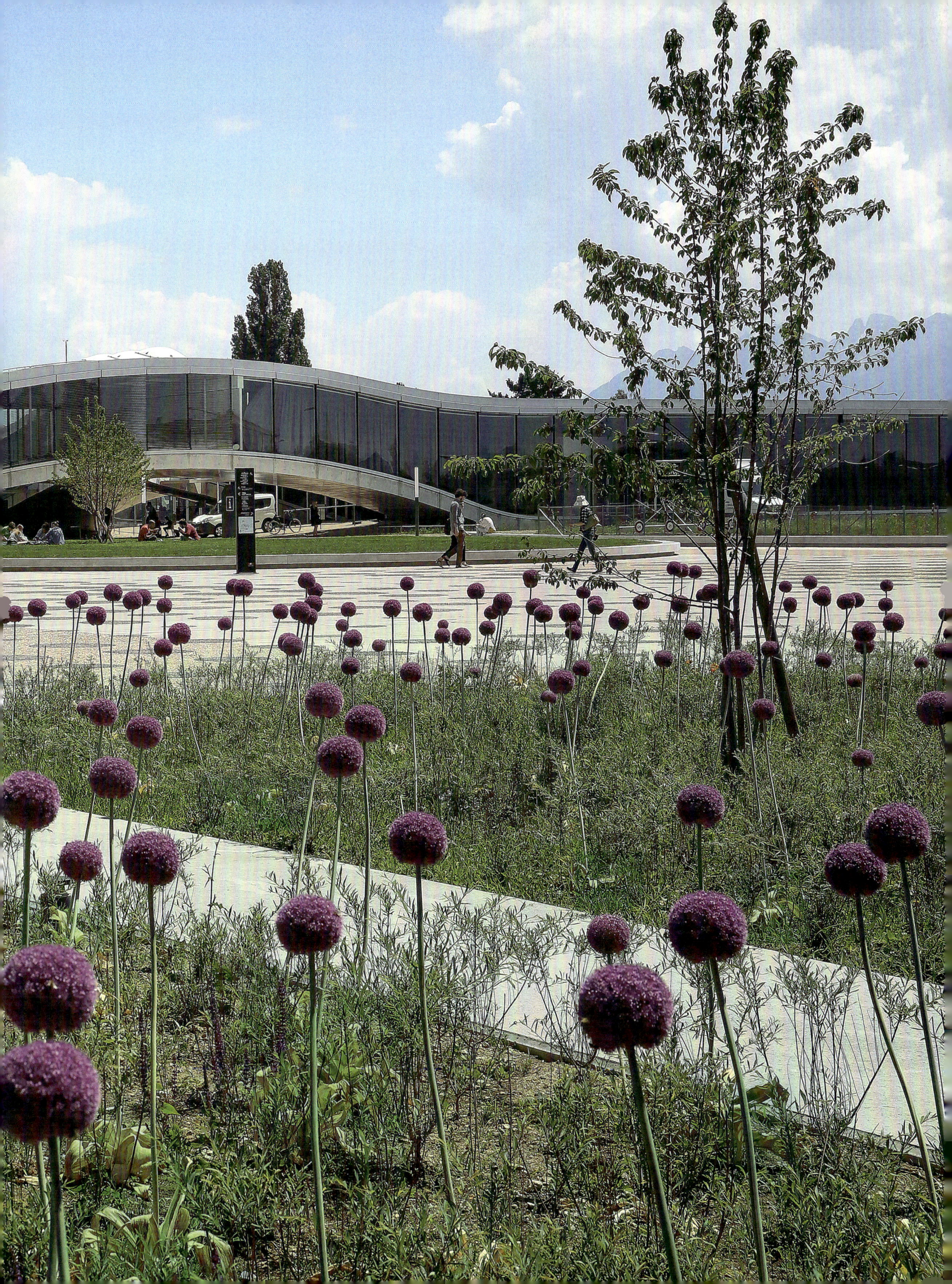

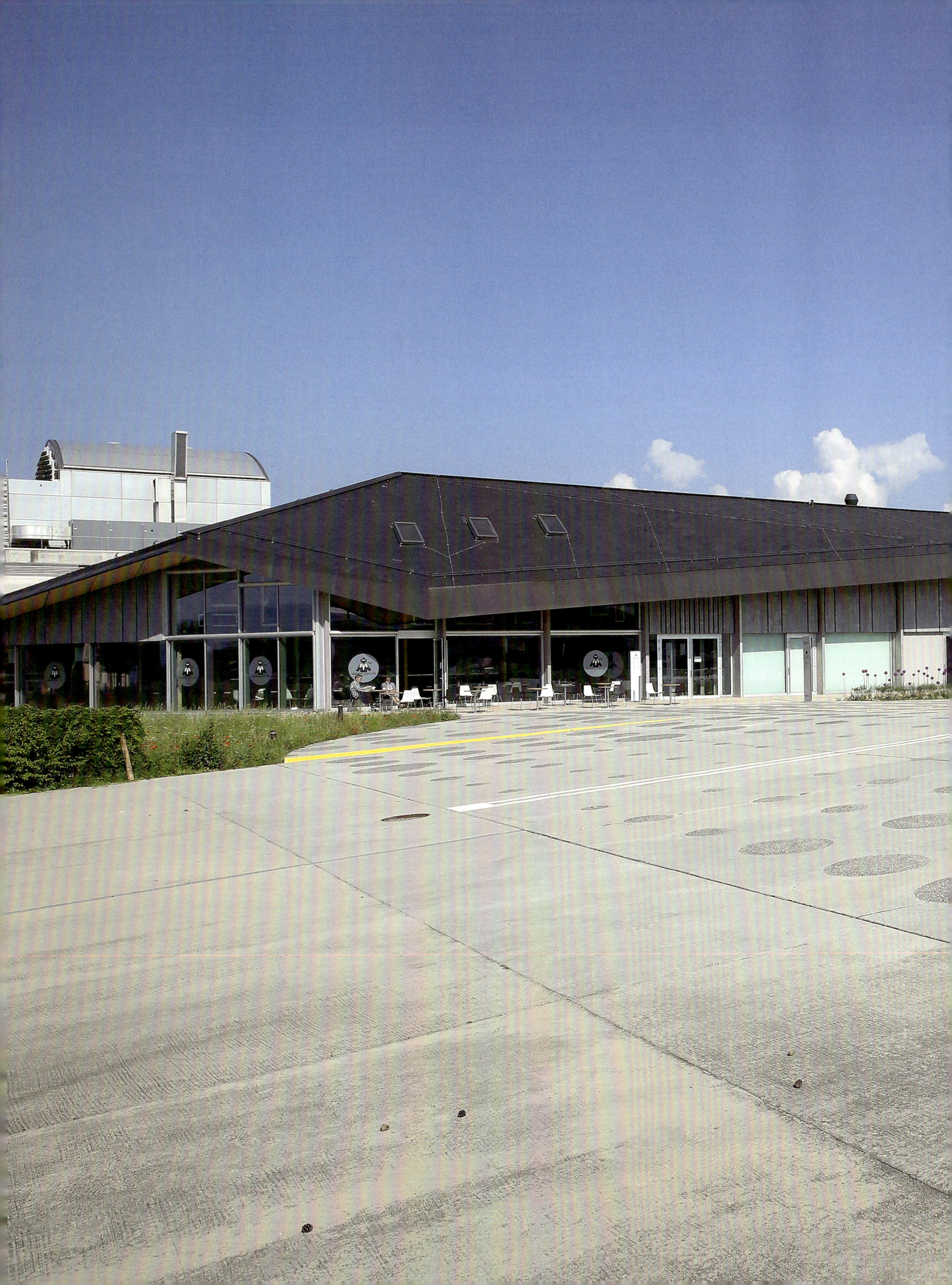

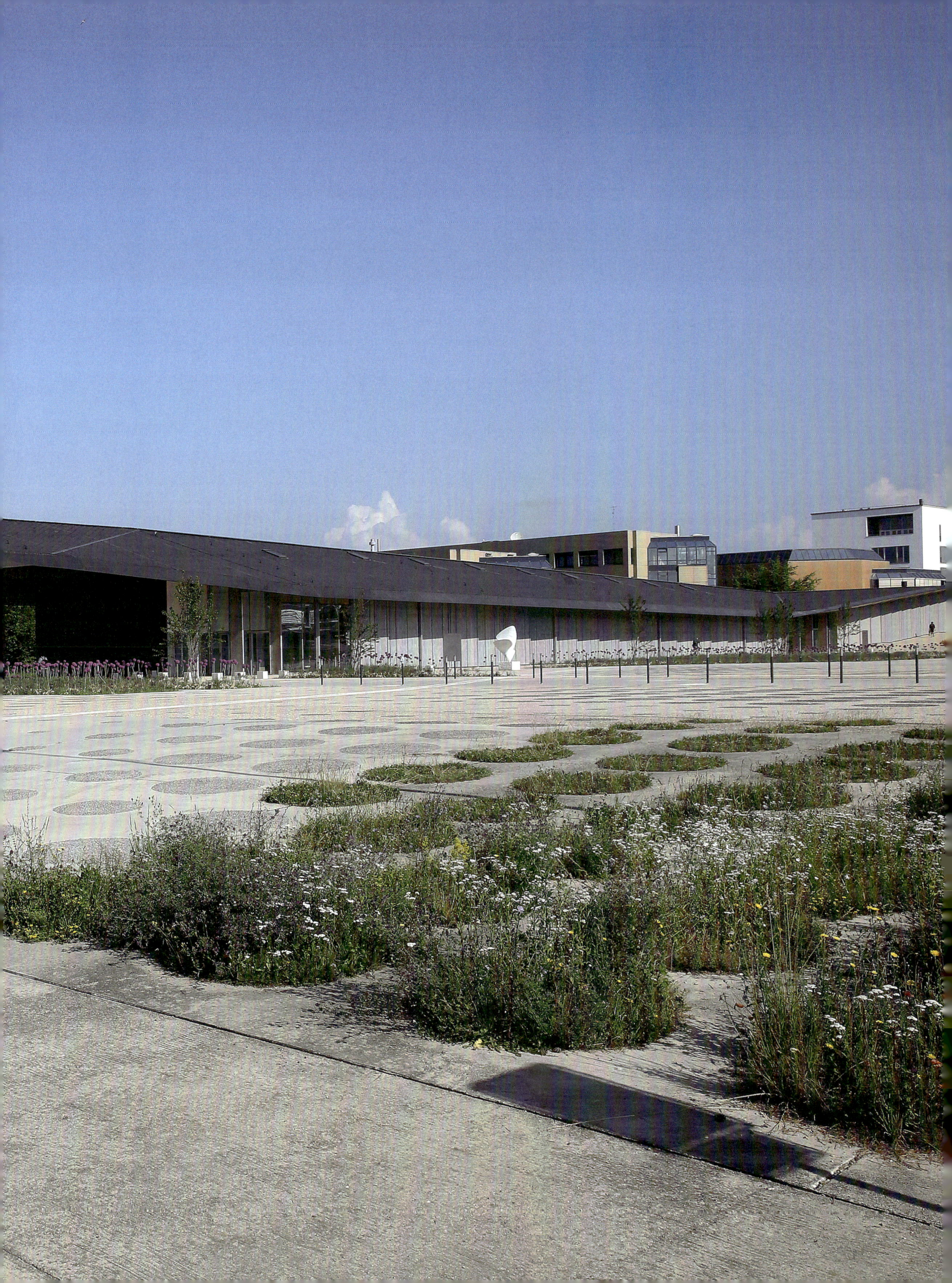

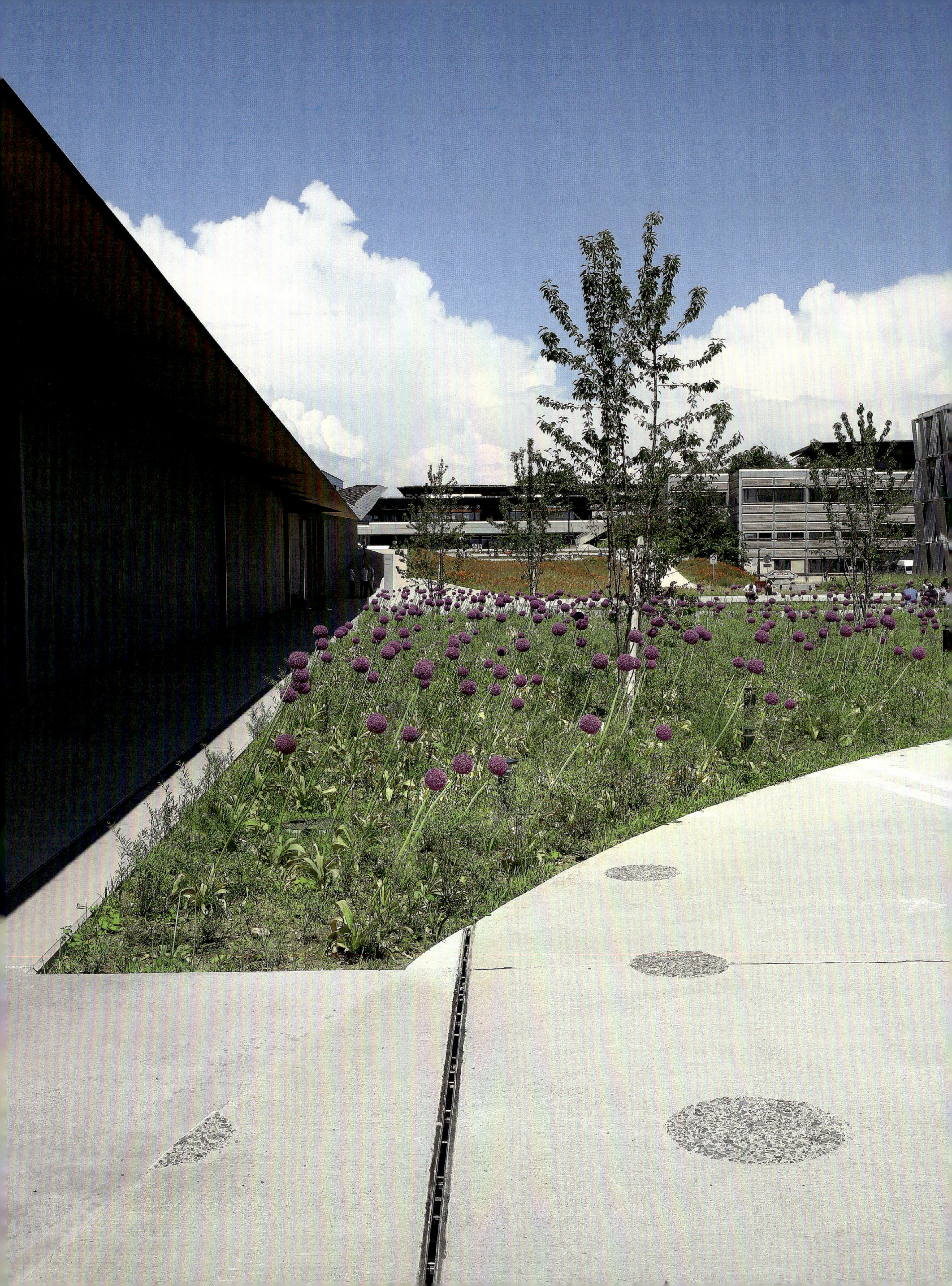

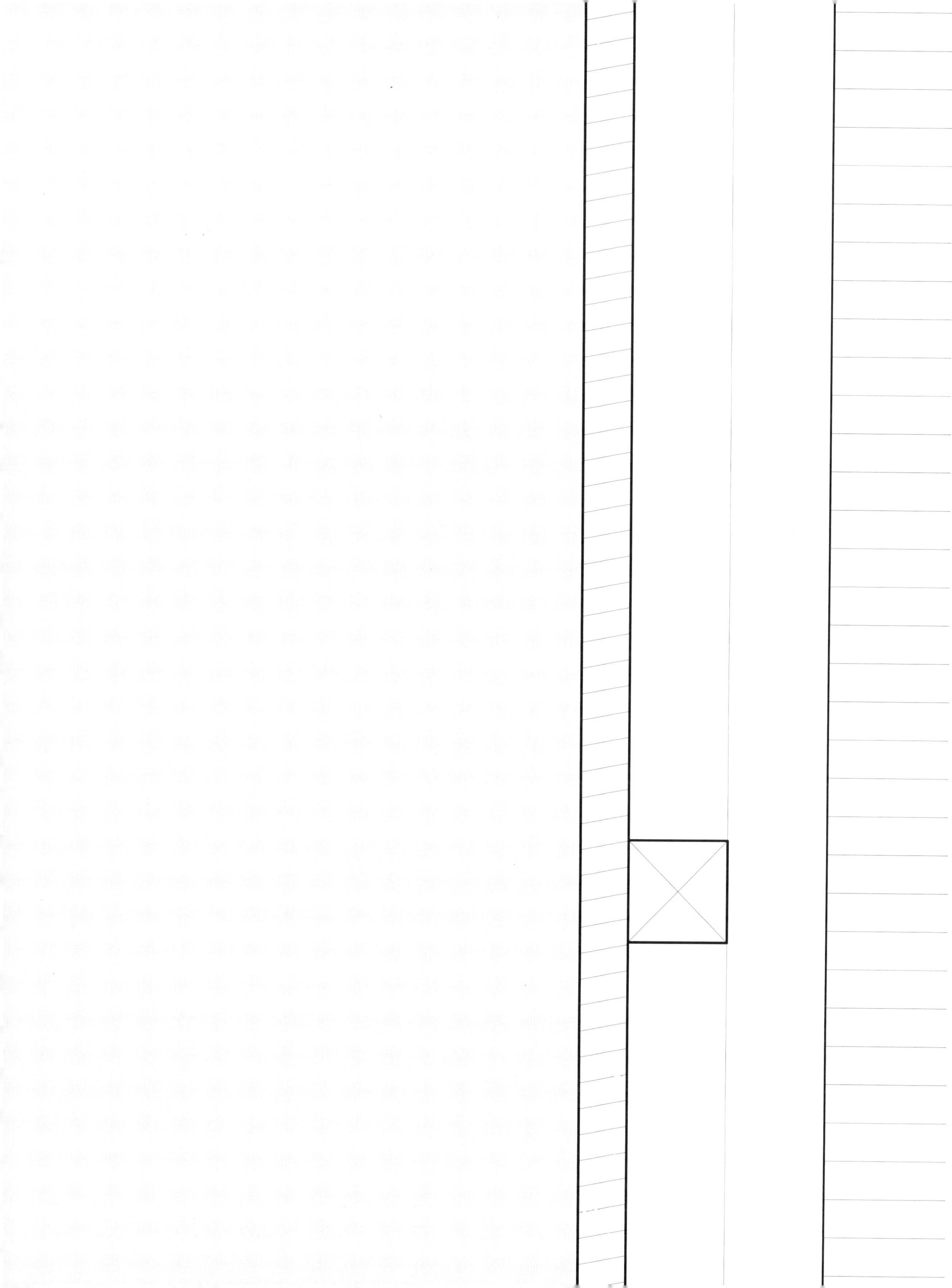

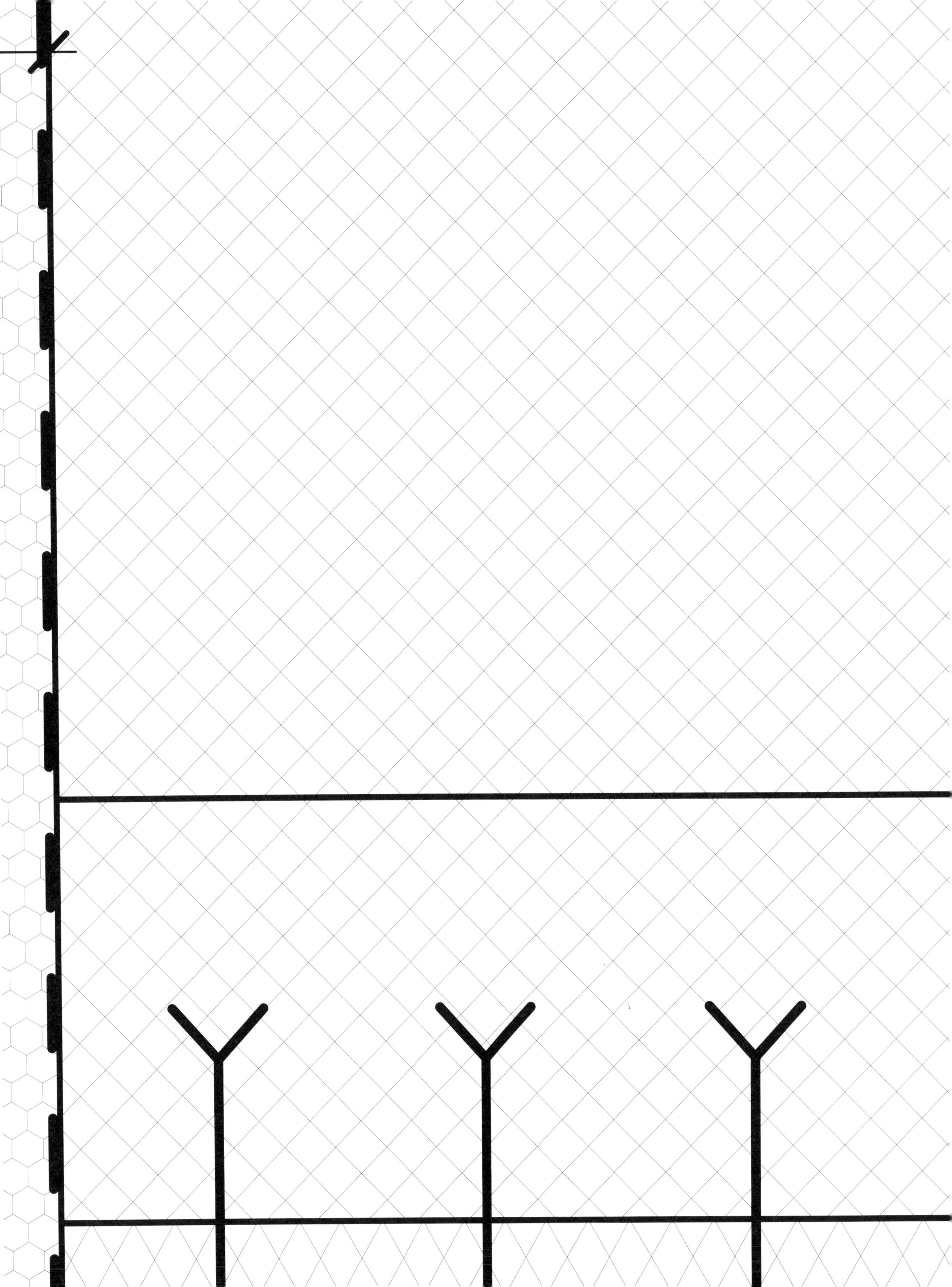